ENGAGING ANTHROPOLOGICAL THEORY

A Social and Political History

Mark Moberg

 Routledge
Taylor & Francis Group

LONDON AND NEW YORK

First published 2013
by Routledge
2 Park Square, Milton Park, Abingdon, Oxon OX14 4RN

Simultaneously published in the USA and Canada
by Routledge
711 Third Avenue, New York, NY 10017

Routledge is an imprint of the Taylor & Francis Group, an informa business

British Library Cataloguing in Publication Data
A catalogue record for this book is available from the British Library

Library of Congress Cataloging in Publication Data
Moberg, Mark, 1959-
  Engaging anthropological theory : a social and political history /
  Mark Moberg.
    p. cm.
  Includes bibliographical references and index.
  1. Anthropology—Philosophy. 2. Anthropology—History.
  3. Anthropology—Methodology. I. Title.
  GN33.M575 2012
  301.01—dc23   2012008708

ISBN: 978-0-415-69999-0 (hbk)
ISBN: 978-0-415-80916-0 (pbk)
ISBN: 978-0-203-09799-1 (ebk)

Typeset in Bembo
by HWA Text and Data Management, London

MIX
Paper from
responsible sources
FSC® C004839
www.fsc.org

Printed and bound in Great Britain by
CPI Group (UK) Ltd, Croydon, CR0 4YY

ENGAGING ANTHROPOLOGICAL THEORY

This lively book offers a fresh look at the history of anthropological theory. Covering key concepts and theorists, Mark Moberg examines the historical context of anthropological ideas and the contested nature of anthropology itself. Anthropological ideas about human diversity have always been rooted in the socio-political conditions in which they arose, and exploring them in context helps students understand how and why they evolved, and how theory relates to life and society. Illustrated throughout, this engaging text moves away from the dry recitation of past viewpoints in anthropology and brings the subject matter to life.

Mark Moberg is Professor of Anthropology at the University of South Alabama, USA, and has many years' experience of teaching anthropological theory. His books include *Slipping Away: Banana Politics and Fair Trade in the Eastern Caribbean* (Berghahn 2008).

CONTENTS

FIGURES

TABLES

BOXES

ACKNOWLEDGMENTS

As readers will soon learn, this text adopts a decidedly unconventional approach to the history of anthropological theory. Its orientation is rooted in a gradual evolution in the way that I have taught the subject to senior-level undergraduates over more than two decades. Having come of age professionally during the years that postmodern critiques redefined anthropology, I have sought ever since to reconcile the best of what is offered by the newer critiques and my own grounding in anthropology's traditional empirical conventions. I have also tried to convey to my students how anthropological ideas are rooted in broader social forces, including (among many others) the administration of colonial societies, movements for national independence, and domestic politics affecting the expression of academic thought. Finally, this book reflects my own idiosyncratic approach to teaching, recognizing that even ideas with serious import are often best conveyed with a dash of humor. Indeed, I have found occasional irreverence to be the most effective means of overcoming student fears of anthropological theory as a daunting and dry subject. To some extent, my approach to this book was inspired by a wonderful little volume by Thomas Cathcart and Daniel Klein, *Plato and Platypus Walk into a Bar: Understanding Philosophy through Jokes* (2006). Indeed, where their insights are relevant to the philosophical issues raised in anthropology over recent decades, I have cited a number of their witticisms in the pages that follow.

I would like to thank the Senior Publisher at Routledge, Lesley Riddle, for her steadfast support of this project through each of the steps of writing, review, revision, and publication. Given my difficulty in persuading other publishers of the merits of approaching anthropological theory in a less-than-somber fashion, I deeply appreciate her faith in this project. Throughout, her counsel and encouragement have greatly strengthened the final manuscript. Routledge's Senior Editorial Assistant, Katherine Ong, provided reassuring guidance throughout the formidable process of procuring permissions and illustrations for the volume. Thanks go as well to April Hopkins for her skilful renderings of three of the drawings featured in the book. And I owe my heartfelt gratitude to the five anonymous reviewers whose insightful critiques helped me to sharpen my arguments and rein in my occasional excesses. Any defects or lapses that remain are, of course, entirely my own.

Finally, I would like to thank the hundreds of students that I have taught over the years in my anthropological theory classes. Many have found themselves in the course not by choice but by their academic requirements. Nonetheless, they have been patient and always supportive audiences as I have tried to figure out what works in the classroom and what doesn't. Their responses, questions, and critiques have immeasurably improved my effectiveness as a teacher and loom large in the way I planned and executed this volume. I hope they will recognize something of themselves in the chapters that follow. Special thanks go to E.M.L., who encouraged this project from the outset, reviewed draft chapters, and assisted in the correction of galleys.

Every effort has been made to trace copyright holders and obtain permission to reproduce material. Any omissions brought to the attention of the publisher will be remedied in future editions.

1

OF POLITICS AND PARADIGMS

Slaying the anthropological undead: a note to students

If you have this text in hand, chances are that you are embarking upon a course in the history of Anthropological Theory, which is likely a required course if you are majoring in anthropology. If my experience in over 20 years of teaching this course is representative, there is a chance that you are anxious about the semester that awaits you. I'd like to begin with a word of reassurance: the large majority of students who enroll in such courses manage to complete them and from there go on to graduate with anthropology degrees. Some go on, despite their initial ambivalence about anthropological theory, to careers in anthropology. And not a few even emerge with a real love of the ideas and debates that have shaped anthropology over the history of our discipline.

Lest you think that you could have spared yourself this experience by majoring in anthropology at another university, let me quickly disabuse you of this assumption. Courses in the history of theory are required in virtually all anthropology programs; so, if nothing else, you are not alone. Think of it positively, as you are sharing a rite of passage completed by all previous anthropology students, and even your professors in their time! For those of you whose interests are physical anthropology or archaeology, this book may seem inexplicably far from your concerns, as we will focus here on the theory and history of cultural anthropology. Why do you have to take this course? Credit "the father of American anthropology," Franz Boas, who was responsible for the uniquely North American "four field" emphasis in our discipline. Boas viewed cultural anthropology, linguistics, archaeology, and physical anthropology as related fields examining distinct aspects of the human condition, a viewpoint that accounts for the fact that anthropology departments are usually comprised of a more disparate group of scholars than other programs. For this reason, the completion of your undergraduate education in anthropology requires some familiarity even with subfields far from your particular interests. If it is any consolation, I not only had to complete my share of archaeology and physical anthropology classes, but found myself teaching these subjects as a graduate student and newly-minted PhD.

I have devoted more energy and preoccupation to teaching anthropological theory than to any other course. Early in my career, after a few years of dissatisfaction in my offerings of the class, I participated in a session at the 1995 American Anthropological Association meetings devoted to "Teaching the History of Anthropology." It was packed with over 100 participants, all of them wondering how to make their theory courses more interesting and relevant, assuming, of course, that they couldn't pawn them off on some less fortunate, untenured colleague. I got a kick from a professor on the panel who admitted that she once found herself falling asleep when teaching her own course. She described it as "one dead white guy a week," and said her students wondered aloud why they were compelled to discuss ideas about human behavior that had been assumed to be safely dead and buried for generations. Yet, she described how each semester, the pale, rotting specters of Tylor, Durkheim, Malinowski, and Benedict rose from the grave in the form of anthropological zombies who strike not terror but torpor into the hearts of their victims. That the dead white guys (and gals) of the past were joined by less musty contemporaries, such as Geertz, Foucault, and Bourdieu, did not translate into greater student interest.

At that conference I learned from the experiences of colleagues who have taught this course in other places. From them I learned to avoid the rote memorization of minutiae, little of which would stick with students for more than ten minutes after a midterm exam anyway. Now, personally, I find it interesting to know that Karl Marx's hemorrhoids were inflamed by the hard benches at the British Library, where he compiled his research (leading some scholars to speculate that acute posterior discomfort fueled his indignation at the capitalist system). I was fascinated to learn that Emile Durkheim's parents were disappointed by his decision to become an agnostic sociologist and not a rabbi, breaking a seven-generation tradition in his family. In contrast, E.E. Evans-Pritchard's research into nonwestern belief systems led him to become an intensely religious man himself. Rather than offering up such tidbits, I hope that this volume will have some appeal beyond the few of you who will go on to my favorite TV game show, *Anthropological Jeopardy*. To do this, there will be two areas of emphasis in the chapters that follow.

First, we will examine the historical context of anthropological ideas. The theories of culture that anthropologists have developed must not be seen as simply novel ideas that randomly popped into the heads of those seeking to understand human behavior and thought. If you regard them this way, it becomes not only more difficult to understand them, but much less interesting as well. In a fascinating and encyclopedic volume, Moore (2009) describes how the biographical details of many anthropologists' lives influenced their ideas; what I want to show in addition is that anthropological theories have a situated social and historical context that cannot be understood apart from the broader economic, cultural, and political currents of their time. Why was it, for example, that in England in the seventeenth and eighteenth centuries scholars advanced the then-revolutionary idea that human behavior is learned from a social environment, replacing the longstanding belief that behaviors are somehow innate? Why did evolutionary perspectives on culture gain such widespread acceptance in Britain and the United States in the latter half of the nineteenth century? Why did the functionalists of the twentieth century who worked in the colonized parts of the world adopt a perspective that emphasized social solidarity and equilibrium, rather than conflict and change? Why did Marxism, after decades of banishment from the social sciences, suddenly reappear in the late 1960s and 70s? As we'll see, the answers to these questions lie in the nature of the societies in which anthropologists (and others who reflect on human behavior) were doing their work, the dominant political forces at work in those societies, and the political forces impinging on anthropology itself.

The feminist historian of science Donna Haraway expresses the relationship between ideas and culture in this way: knowledge, she writes, "is *always* an engaged material practice and *never* a disembodied set of ideas. Knowledge is embedded in projects; knowledge is always *for*, in many senses, some things and not others, and knowers are always formed by their projects, just as they shape what they can know" (2004: 199–200). As much as we like to believe that our thoughts spring with absolute originality from our minds, anthropological ideas are very much the product of the broader culture in which they occur. Indeed, that is likely one of the reasons why similar "novel" ideas often occur to different people at about the same time. When social, political, and economic circumstances are appropriate, certain ideas will take hold and diffuse into the broader culture when they might have perished without mention at another time.[1] Looking at the historical context of anthropological ideas involves some excursion into the philosophy of knowledge, particularly with regard to the *paradigmatic nature* of scientific knowledge (don't worry about this term now…there's plenty of time to panic about this later on!).

Second, we will examine the contested nature of anthropology itself. Students are often perplexed when they see that different anthropologists analyze culture differently, often leading to acrimonious debates about the "real causes" of cultural practices. For more than four decades now, a debate has raged about the reasons that India's Hindus do not eat beef. As you probably know, devout Hindus regard cattle as sacred animals, never to be eaten or slaughtered, notwithstanding how many people in India face malnutrition or systemic hunger. Hindus say this is because each cow is home to literally millions of gods and goddesses (I believe the actual number is around 334 million, give or take a few million). Traditionally, anthropologists accepted the reasons for this at face value, arguing that the Hindu beef taboo cannot be seen apart from a powerful sacred motivation, known as *ahimsa*. Indeed, in the past the taboo was often seen as an illustration of how religion could lead people to act in ways contrary to their material interests or physical well-being (imagine a scene of cattle wandering around unmolested—indeed, pampered—even as people go hungry in their midst. What could be more irrational?).

In 1966, Columbia University anthropologist Marvin Harris published a modest article in the journal *Current Anthropology* claiming that the taboo should be explained not in terms of Hindu beliefs but the ecological and economic role that cattle occupy in rural India. Far from being a case in which religion causes people to act irrationally, the Hindu taboo on eating cattle, Harris claimed, actually enhances the well-being of most rural Indians. His assumption was that human behavior is fundamentally practical (in terms of solving the problems of survival in a particular place) even if, at face value, it doesn't appear to make sense or even seems to compromise human welfare. Since he published his article, the debate has outlived its original participants (Harris died in 2001, but some of his former students have taken up the argument, against the continuing vociferous opposition of other anthropologists). If the original debate is not surprising, many students are discouraged that it is no closer to resolution today than it was almost a half century ago. Why can't anthropologists agree among themselves when they study culture? If we're all reasonable people, shouldn't we approach a common understanding after such a protracted period of data collection and debate? Yet it rarely works that way. Debates in anthropology seem to go on forever, neither side conceding to the other.

These disagreements are not just conflicts of personality; they reflect a deep disagreement about what anthropology should be and how it should obtain knowledge. Since the early 1980s there has been a widening rift within anthropology about the essential nature of the field (is it a science? Or something else? And if something else, what?). The result has been growing distrust and antagonism between anthropologists on either side of this divide. Some academic departments have even fractured over this question. In such places faculty on the two sides of the debate scarcely talk to each other, a pattern that often repeats itself in departments that have remained nominally intact. To understand where these tensions come from, before we begin to examine anthropological ideas we will consider anthropology's traditional claims to be a science, the critiques that have been offered of such claims in recent decades, and the implications of those critiques for how we understand society. While this rift has grown within the last 30 years, the debates that have occurred during this time reference the entire history of anthropological research and ideas.

Explanation vs. interpretation

At the risk of some oversimplification, let me summarily identify these divisions before we go on to examine their assumptions. On the one hand, there are those who contend that the goals of cultural anthropologists are basically no different from those of natural and physical scientists (for want of a better term, we will call the members of this anthropological camp the "scientists"). From their point of view, the goal of anthropology is to produce generalizations that explain the causes of human behavior and thought. The method of inquiry to be employed is explicitly scientific (more about this later). While this orientation predominated in anthropology from the end of World War II until the 1980s, there has always been a multiplicity of co-existing scientific and humanistic approaches to knowledge within the discipline. In 1964, Eric Wolf observed that scientific and humanistic approaches in anthropology were then regarded as complementary.² What makes today's divisions distinctive is that the former co-existence and accommodation has all but disappeared, with practitioners on each side of the divide emphatically convinced that their rivals are misguided and destructive. Within the discipline there are many (perhaps a majority) who now reject the validity of scientific approaches in cultural anthropology (quite unlike the more humanistically-oriented anthropologists of the past). They claim that the assumptions of scientific knowledge are not attainable when we seek to describe human action and thought; indeed, even if the scientific method could be applied in a fashion identical to the laboratory or physical sciences, it would still be undesirable in understanding human culture. Generalizations about the causes of human behavior are either misleading or so general as to be meaningless. Rather, individual cultures can only be interpreted (not explained) as unique systems of meanings, symbols, and power. Further, these meanings are understood in very different ways depending on the social position of both the cultural participant and anthropological observer, leading them to reject traditional conceptions of culture as being uniformly shared by a given human society. This camp we will call the "postmodernists." I employ this term very advisedly, as it embraces many contemporary, even contradictory trends in the social sciences and philosophy. Indeed, some anthropologists who I include in this camp may reject this designation or prefer another, but what most have in common is a profound distrust of the claims and capabilities of scientific inquiry, especially as applied to human thought and action.

At this point, you might be asking, what is the difference between "explaining" and "interpreting"? Writing at a time that these divisions were becoming increasingly pronounced, James Lett (1987) discussed the notion of scientific explanation at some length. A scientific explanation identifies some kind of relationship between separate phenomenon; in its purest form, "x causes y" or at least "x and y are interrelated." A good example would be Boyle's Law: "A rise in the temperature of a gas causes a proportionate increase in its pressure within a closed container." In science, explanations are provisionally accepted among most scientific observers after many repeated observations of this relationship. Interpretation, on the other hand, involves the projection of an observer's meanings and emotions onto a phenomenon. It is what we do when we study a piece of art or literature and attribute a meaning to it. When I read a symbolically-laden book like Melville's *Moby Dick* and I interpret it not at its surface level as a "fish story" but as an allegory of humanity's ultimately tragic efforts to overcome evil, I am engaged in interpretation. Interpretation, by its very nature, is highly personal, not subject to the consensus of observers, and therefore not subject to refutation or proof. My interpretation of *Moby Dick* may be entirely different from yours, but there is no way that I can "prove" mine to be correct. Nor would it be sensible to try, as interpretation is necessarily rooted in the values, experience, and emotional needs of the person doing the interpreting. Maybe now you're starting to see why the notion of "interpreting" culture—as if it were a text full of symbolic meanings, as Clifford Geertz argued—proves troubling to those who adopt an explanatory model of anthropology based on the scientific method. If our attempts to understand culture amount to no more than an interpretation, how can we claim that any one description of a culture is more truthful than another? This poses a huge concern for "scientists," but the ambiguity posed by interpretation is embraced by postmodernists.

In this volume, I want to examine these claims to knowledge, and how they lead to a contested status for anthropology as either an interpretive endeavor or as a science. We're going to see that there are very different assumptions about how we understand the social world around us that underlie most of the conflicts among anthropologists. To know why there are conflicting perspectives in anthropology, we have to understand these assumptions about knowledge. This requires us to make an excursion into the philosophy of knowledge as we examine theory in anthropology.

Empiricism and its discontents

Before we can discuss to what extent anthropology is (or should be) a science, we want to look at how scientific knowledge is produced. It may not seem initially that there is any direct relationship between philosophy and anthropology. The fundamental goal of many areas of philosophy is to develop methods of reasoning that help us discern truth. Since debates within anthropology concern what is a "truthful" account of a culture—what are the causes of cultural practices, or indeed whether those practices can be explained in terms of causes—you can see that anthropology's objectives and those of philosophy actually converge. The area of philosophy most relevant for us as anthropologists is the field of *epistemology*, which is the study of the nature and source of knowledge. Any statement of what we believe to be true is a claim to knowledge; epistemology is concerned with how we evaluate these claims and the basis on which we accept or reject them.

Before the 1980s, probably a majority of anthropologists considered theirs to be a scientific discipline, one that generates a type of knowledge different from fields such as literary or art criticism. The notion of a distinct category of knowledge that is "scientific" is unique to western civilization and is also of relatively recent development in our history. More than any specific technique of making observations (whether electron microscopy, radiocarbon dating, or participant observation), science is a method of reasoning. The epistemological foundations of science were established around 1600, when the English philosopher Francis Bacon advanced the then-novel idea that the truth of a proposition should be determined by the type of evidence used to support it. To us, it seems self-evident that a claim to knowledge based on observation (by which I mean not just sight, but any kind of sensory stimulus, such as taste, hearing, or touch) is more likely to be valid than one based on intuition, revelation, or scriptural interpretation. Such was not always the case during the Middle Ages (or even thereafter), where someone might be convicted of witchcraft or heresy based on revelation or an interpretation of scripture. We have Bacon (in part) to thank for the fact that that doesn't happen anymore because those forms of knowledge arising from observation are privileged (i.e. considered more truthful) and therefore superior to those gained from dreaming, hallucination, scriptural study, etc.

The philosophical principle founded by Bacon is known as empiricism: the doctrine that all valid (i.e. truthful) scientific knowledge must originate in experience and observation. In its original form, the doctrine of empiricism (which formed the basis of science as Bacon and his contemporaries such as Isaac Newton and Robert Boyle understood it) entailed five assumptions about the scientist and process of observation:

a) *objectivity:* the scientist is an unbiased observer whose perception of reality is unaffected by personal characteristics, such as his or her identity, beliefs, and desires. My description of a given phenomenon should be the same whether I am a Democrat, a Socialist, a Jew, an Atheist, a White, a Woman, a Person of Color…you get the picture.

b) *observational consensus:* reality exists independently of any one observer. There exists a "real world" out there independent of the language by which we describe it or our presence in the world. While as scientists, our knowledge of the world is derived from observation, the existence and essential nature of the world are not contingent on any one observer. (Remember the philosophical cliché of "if a tree falls in a forest, and no one is there to hear it, does it still make a sound?" Bacon would answer resoundingly "yes.")[3]

c) *replicability:* (this is a corollary of a) and b) above, but important enough to merit explicit identification). An objective observer who uses the same techniques as previous observers to describe a given phenomenon should achieve similar conclusions. In laboratory sciences, we know that the same procedures followed again and again under identical conditions by different investigators should yield the same results.

d) the method of reasoning is *induction:* the investigator sets out to make all possible observations of a phenomenon, and only after these observations are completed, s/he derives generalizations about how that phenomenon works. For example, Isaac Newton, after observing falling apples, acorns, and raindrops, derived via induction his laws of gravity. Inductive reasoning means that explanations of a given phenomenon are developed without preconceived notions of how it works.

e) *scientific progress* involves the steady accumulation of objective observations and inductively-derived generalizations, leading to a more reliable and accurate knowledge of the world. Progress in science is cumulative according to this view, leading ever closer to a singular Truth (always spelled with a capital letter, like Science and the American Way).

Hume's challenge and Popper's "solution"

Although these empiricist notions of the unbiased scientific observer, induction, and progress still make up most lay peoples' perception of how science operates, these assumptions were actually abandoned long ago by philosophers of science and scientists themselves. In his 1739 *Treatise on Human Nature,* the Scottish philosopher

David Hume pointed out two logical fallacies with empiricist claims to knowledge. The first of these is the Fallacy of Selectivity. Empiricists claim that science involves inductive reasoning from observations to general conclusions, not vice versa. Yet Hume pointed out that scientists never collect evidence in a conceptual vacuum, nor can they observe everything. Let me give you a thought experiment to illustrate his argument.

Let's say you wanted to explain the difference in burglary rates between New York City and Lake Wobegon, Minnesota, a small (admittedly fictional) Midwestern farming town (site of one of my favorite National Public Radio programs). When you approach this question, there are certain kinds of evidence that you might look for and other kinds that you overlook. You would probably want to collect information on unemployment, poverty rates, and age distributions (we might reasonably suspect that poorer, younger, and unemployed people commit more burglary than more affluent, employed, older people). You might be interested as well in educational levels, substance abuse, and family stability, with the idea that these also affect the incidence of criminal behavior. But these are not the only possible observations that you could make about Lake Wobegon and New York City. What about differences in rainfall, elevation, or average temperature? What about the number of visiting migratory bird species or the subsoil profiles of each place? What about per capita lime jello consumption in each place?[4] Sound ridiculous? Of course it is! But Hume would argue that if you were truly inductive in reasoning, you would gather each and every possible observation there is to be made about each place, including all of those I mention above and no doubt millions of others. In actuality, of course, scientists never do this. Instead, we find that their very selection of a problem for investigation means that they select some evidence as more relevant than others.

The process of selecting some things for observation while ignoring others means that the scientist does indeed operate with some preliminary expectations (let's call them what they are: biases) about the phenomena s/he attempts to explain. But to uphold the notion of an unbiased observer, strict Baconian empiricists would have to deny this fact. They argue that order and understanding are imposed on an unbiased investigator by objective facts. Hume pointed out, in contrast, that as soon as scientists collect certain kinds of evidence and disregard others, they are imposing their pre-existing sense of order on that phenomenon. Hume was not criticizing scientists for the fact that they do not practice inductive reasoning. Imagine what would happen if in order to explain the differences in burglary rates we did choose to gather all possible observations about New York and Lake Wobegon. We would never conclude our research! Even if we had teams of thousands of researchers, we could spend many lifetimes gathering data before reaching any kind of conclusion, if then. As the nineteenth-century philosopher William James said, "by itself, reality is a great, big blooming buzzing confusion." What he meant was that it is impossible to understand the world inductively because there is simply too much sensory input for us to make sense of it. Rather, it is our pre-existing beliefs (if you will, theories) that help us make sense of the world by imposing orderly perceptual categories on everything that we see.

Hume's second critique of empiricism might be considered the Fallacy of Objectivity. Empiricists claimed that science rests on a realm of given facts about reality, each of which can be understood in just one way. The assumption of observational consensus—that there is a reality independent of any one person's observation of it—implies that all reasonable people will agree on the form and content of an observation. The assumption of objectivity holds that our personal beliefs or identities play no part in our descriptions of reality. But does observational consensus apply to the complex behavioral observations that social scientists collect?

In the field of psychology, projective tests are used to elicit a response from a subject (or a patient) that is intended to reveal their dominant drives, emotions, and personality conflicts. Projective tests are invariably ambiguous, admitting many possible interpretations; in that sense, the informant projects his or her personality onto the image. The classic (and oldest) form of a projective test is a Rorschach, or "inkblot" test, in which an amorphous black blob on a white background is shown to someone, who then is asked to describe what it reminds them of. Given their ambiguity and associated difficulties of interpretation, Rorschach tests are less often used today in psychological testing than another projective test called a TAT, or Thematic Apperception Test. This is a drawing that shows some kind of interaction between people about which the subject is asked to compose a brief story. What is happening in this picture? What is being said? What is the relationship between these people? Figure 1.1 shows an example from a widely-administered TAT battery, one that has been in use since the 1940s. How would you interpret it?

Now, many people (but not all, as we will see below) would say that this picture is of some sexually charged scene. But what is the nature of this sexual interaction,

FIGURE 1.1   Adapted from a Thematic Apperception Test illustration. Courtesy of the artist, April Hopkins.

if there was one? Was it rape? Was it an extramarital encounter that the man now regrets? What about the woman, who appears inert? Is she resting? Drugged? Dead? Let me share with you two distinct responses to this picture, which reflect how we project our experience and values into our descriptions of reality.

The first description is by "Ginger" (not her real name), a former student who after completing her anthropology degree went on to a successful career as a fashion model. She always came to class dressed to the nines. In my Anthropological Theory class, she carefully studied the TAT picture for a few moments, and then pronounced her response (about the woman in the picture), "I'm almost *certain* that she had a boob job." (Her response…not mine!)

The other response was generated by an elderly man of the Dogrib tribe, which is a subarctic Athabaskan-speaking Native American group in northern Canada. My undergraduate professor, the late Dr. June Helm, did some TAT testing during the 1950s to identify the "group personality profile" of this tribe (more about this concept in a few chapters). After studying this same picture, the Dogrib man composed his description of the scene: "This man is very sad. His woman has died. Who will cook for him now?" Such is the importance of our preconceived notions about reality in generating two widely differing interpretations of the same scene.

Hume's critiques of empiricism point to the vital role that theory plays in science. It is theory that leads scientists to construe what they see in one way as opposed to another. Theories dictate the selection of relevant data for a problem and how those data are perceived (yes, the word "data" is plural). It even leads to the selection of different topics for research. Not only will Marvin Harris and Clifford Geertz understand behavior in different ways; their theories of human action will lead them to research completely different problems. Yet, for all its importance, the term "theory" is rarely used very precisely by anthropologists. Those without a background in the philosophy of knowledge often use theory synonymously with "model," although the terms have distinct meanings in the sciences. A model is an abstract aid to understanding, but does not offer an explanation itself. It is rather an analogy thought to be similar in some ways to the phenomenon being studied. For example, Emile Durkheim offered the "organismic analogy" (be careful when saying this term) of human society, suggesting that social institutions (e.g. politics, economics, kinship, religion, etc.) are analogous to the various organs of the body in that all are essential for the survival of society. Durkheim's model didn't suggest exactly how the economic, political, and religious institutions of society were causally interrelated, but merely that they were. Later on, we'll also consider what I have come to call Karl Marx's "birthday cake" model of society, in which he arranged social institutions in hierarchical layers. As we'll see, Marx's model was also accompanied by a powerful theory of how those layers were interrelated.

In his influential volume *Aspects of the Theory of Syntax* (1965), linguist Noam Chomsky distinguished a hierarchy of levels of adequacy for evaluating grammars (what we might consider "theories" of specific languages) that could apply equally well to all scientific theories. Chomsky noted that a grammar is *observationally adequate* if it tells you whether any given string of words comprises a recognizable sentence in a particular language. Applied more broadly to scientific inquiry, a theory might be said to have observational adequacy if it achieves an accurate description of empirical data. A *descriptively adequate* grammar for a particular language defines the potentially infinite set of grammatical sentences in a given language; that is, it describes the language in its entirety. More broadly within the sciences, a descriptively adequate theory formally specifies rules that account for all observed arrangements of the data. Finally, Chomsky observes that a grammar achieves the highest level of adequacy (that of explanation) if it provides insight into the underlying linguistic structures in the human mind; it not only describes the grammar of a language, but also makes predictions about how linguistic knowledge is produced. Similarly, an explanatorily adequate theory in science is one that has predictive power for events that have not yet occurred.

Chomsky's formulation parallels that of James Lett (1987), who distinguishes between nomological/deductive theories and statistical/probabilistic theories. Nomological theories are quantitative statements of relationship that occur universally between two or more types of phenomena. Examples might be Newton's $f = ma$ (the force of an object is equal to its mass times acceleration) or Einstein's famous $e = mc^2$ (energy = mass times the velocity of light squared). In both cases there is some quantitative relationship between phenomena: if you know the values of two of the variables, you can calculate the third. Nomological deductive theories are common in the laboratory and physical sciences, but largely absent from the social sciences; hence, we may disregard them for purposes of our discussion (don't you wish I had told you that a paragraph ago?). Statistical–probabilistic theories are much more common in disciplines such as anthropology, psychology, and sociology. These identify a probable association between two or more phenomena, whose actual frequency of association can be determined statistically. For example, in societies that practice some form of unilineal descent, we find that "patrilineal descent is usually associated with patrilocal postmarital residence" (if you identified this as observationally adequate in the Chomskian sense, you'd be correct). Now, there are occasional exceptions to this "theory" (fairly lame as it is), but in a statistical sense, when we look at a broad range of societies studied by anthropologists, we see that these practices are very commonly related to one another; i.e. we can generally predict that a society with patrilineal descent will have patrilocal postmarital residence. How often statistically? This is actually to be determined by the researcher, but most commonly in the social sciences, we say that if there is a greater than 95 percent incidence that such things co-occur, they may be considered related in some sense and not just randomly (that is, accidentally) co-occurring.

A popular philosophy text offers this humorous illustration of how science operates on the basis of probability rather than a complete knowledge of all possible "facts":[5]

> A scientist and his wife are out for a drive in the country when they pass a flock of sheep on a hillside.
>
> "Oh look!" the wife says. "All those sheep have been shorn."
>
> "Yes," says the scientist. "On this side."
>
> (Cathcart and Klein 2006: 57)

Now, in this joke we might think that the wife is expressing a commonsense view, while her husband is taking a more cautious "scientific" view in that he refuses to go beyond his direct observation. But it is actually his wife whose thinking is more aligned with the scientific method. The "experience" of scientists is not limited to what they observe at a given moment, because scientists also draw on their prior observations to calculate the probability of a given event. What she is in effect saying is, "I see sheep that are shorn of their wool on the side that is visible to me. From prior experience I know that farmers do not usually shear sheep only on one side and that, even if this particular farmer did so, the probability of the sheep lining up so that only their shorn sides face the road is infinitesimally small—certainly less than the 5 percent probability that we might consider this a random event. Therefore, I feel confident is saying that those sheep have been completely shorn." In contrast, the husband/scientist is acting more like a Baconian inductivist, who will never reach a conclusion because he believes that one must gather every possible observation of something before generalizing.

Theories are generalizations that suggest a relationship between classes of phenomena. They should tell us why certain observable regularities occur. For example, in the 1960s some anthropologists postulated that population growth causes societies to follow a sequence of evolutionary stages, from "band" to "tribe" to "chiefdom" to "state". This theory relates one factor present in human groups (population size and density) to social and political change. Theories are developed to explain observable phenomena, but they are not just descriptions of data. Instead, they employ abstractions that cannot be directly observed. For example, we can measure population growth and density quite directly in some numerical sense, but when we talk about the "tribe" level of political organization, we're referring to an abstraction. Theories are distinguished from hypotheses. While a theory is an explanatory statement employing abstractions, a hypothesis is a statement deduced from a theory that can be tested with observable evidence. This means it must operationalize (or define) the abstractions contained in the theory; for example, it must provide some way of defining a tribe as opposed to a band.

Finally, a scientific theory must be based on statements that can potentially be proven false by observation. This is the criterion of falsifiability, devised by the Austrian-born British philosopher of science Sir Karl Popper in the 1930s. Certain "non-falsifiable" statements lie beyond the realm of scientific inquiry, because they involve propositions that can neither be shown to be true or false given our sensory perception of the world around us. Hence, "everything that happens reflects God's will," or "after death, people rejoin their loved ones in heaven" are statements that can only be accepted on the basis of faith because there is no observational evidence that can be gathered to test them. That does not mean that they are "wrong" because such articles of faith—like an interpretation or revelation—are not subject to testing and proof. To the extent that a given religion is based on non-testable articles of faith it is no more "false" than is my interpretation of *Moby Dick*. I realize that some religious believers may object to this equation of faith and interpretation, but from the perspective of the philosophy of science both are similar in that they cannot be falsified. On the other hand, when articles of faith do inform hypotheses (for example, the Book of Genesis reinforced in the minds of some past scholars an earth-centered conception of the solar system, or the notion that the earth is young in geological terms), they may indeed be subject to falsification.

However, Popper recognized that falsifiability does not simply mean that science can deal only with testable propositions. Rather, it implies that a theory can never be proven true, but can only be proven false. The statement "all ducks have webbed feet" can never be proven true because it is impossible to collect observations on all ducks that exist today, ever have existed, or ever will exist. Does this mean that we know nothing reliable at all about duck feet? Not at all. We say that the statement is "provisionally accepted" unless and until we encounter a duck without webbed feet. You may still retain the mistaken notion (widely if erroneously disseminated in high school science classes) that a "fact" is a "theory that has been proven true through repeated observation." Despite the ubiquity of this idea, it is not how philosophers understand science, or how scientists view their own work. All we can say is that until observations disprove a theory that it is "provisionally accepted."

This notion of falsifiability may sound like something of a letdown. But according to the model of the scientific method that has emerged since Popper's work, it is key to how science operates in practice and to his assertion that, over time, more accurate explanations of the world replace less accurate ones. His model of scientific procedure, known as *logical positivism*, involves some revisions to empiricism. In an upcoming chapter you will note that the term positivism was originally coined by Auguste Comte, an eccentric French social theorist in the early 1800s. Comte's use of the term, as well as that of all later social scientists, simply refers to any approach in the social sciences that seeks generalizations about human behavior. Popper borrowed the term from the social sciences to refer to the actual method that scientists employ to test theories with empirical evidence. There's no contradiction between the two uses of the term, but they do remain distinct in meaning. (I thought I would provide this note as a form of helpful "pre-confusion.")

The steps involved in Popper's logical positivism are as follows, and are (ostensibly) those adopted by scientists today as they conduct their investigations. Popper's notion of the scientific method doesn't begin with an open-minded inductive collection of "objective" evidence. Instead, the scientist makes observations with a certain problem in mind (this method of reasoning, as you might have guessed, is deduction, which starts with some assumptions about reality and then leads to the collection of relevant observations). These observations are selected by the scientist according to tentative solutions (that is, theory) that he or she has formulated for that problem.

Such tentative solutions are formalized for a particular set of observations as hypotheses, which state what is to be expected empirically in a certain place or time. Our theory might be "population growth causes social inequality." This remains too abstract for testing in a particular place and time, so our hypothesis operationalizes (i.e. refines) the theory as a testable proposition for a given society. This might be our hypothesis: "population growth leads to inherited (ascribed) political leadership among the Oingo Boingo" (my favorite fictional culture for purposes of illustrating a hypothetical point). Now we have our propositions framed in such a way that we can actually gather observations to evaluate them. The hypothesis is then tested with empirical data from that society. If the hypothesis is contradicted by available evidence, it is rejected (e.g. we find population growth, but it is accompanied by an egalitarian political system or one based on achievement, not ascription or inheritance). The theory is then revised in a way that might accommodate our findings (and re-tested accordingly). If, on the other hand, the hypothesis is not rejected, it is said to provide tentative (provisional) support for the theory from which it comes. The theory then may be re-tested under different circumstances or conditions.

Popper claimed to have solved the Fallacy of Objectivity that Hume had noted in the eighteenth century. If there are multiple conflicting theories of a phenomenon, which is correct? Popper argued that out of many conflicting statements about reality, scientists following the procedure above would weed out the incorrect ones, leaving one standing as "provisionally accepted" while all others are falsified and rejected. Science in this sense is akin to natural selection, eliminating the "less fit" variants of a species. Popper's model of logical positivism describes how scientists actually view their activities, not the naïve and impractical notion of Baconian empiricism. Yet, some philosophers have noted that the problem of interpretation has not always, in fact, been solved by logical positivism. For example, a scientist encountering a black water bird will not say "this falsifies my hypothesis that all swans are white" but may rather conclude that "this black bird is not a swan." In other words, our favored theories are often not overturned by contrary evidence; rather the evidence is interpreted to provide support for the theory! This "confirmatory bias" in science arises because, as the historian Thomas Kuhn noted, our views of reality are structured by paradigms, which arise not just for their explanatory power but for their congruence with the scientist's world view, identity, and even politics.

Kuhn's problem with Popper

Since Popper claimed to have solved the Fallacy of Objectivity in the mid-twentieth century, some philosophers of science have noted that the rigorous testing of rival theories via logical positivism has often not resulted in the emergence of a single "provisionally true" theory as Popper had anticipated. The 45+ years of contention between Marvin Harris and his rivals with regard to the Hindu sacred cow have been accompanied by very systematic ethnographic, ecological, and economic data collection from India (not to mention more information on Indian bovine demography and sex ratios than most people would really want to know). All of these data were collected to test Harris' hypothesis, yet this testing has not led either side to "throw in the towel." Neither Harris nor his opponents conceded, "ok; you've proven your point; I was wrong and you were right after all." If anything, they became more entrenched in their original positions; indeed, often the evidence accumulated by scholars on one side to support their position is interpreted by those on the other side as support of their position (this may sound familiar to those of you who have been in a long-term relationship).

How do we account for the fact that observations frequently do not overturn the theories they are designed to test, but are instead interpreted as support for them? The tenacity with which scientists cling to their theories, attempting to confirm rather than disconfirm them in Popper's model of logical positivism, suggests that they are not dispassionate about the ideas they are evaluating. Instead, many philosophers of science now recognize that the theories we use in our research are explicit formulations of our pre-existing beliefs about the world. To argue that science in principle can be entirely objective in the way it goes about selecting a problem for investigation, advancing a tentative solution, and testing that solution through observation, is to say that a person doing the investigation in principle can be without beliefs, values, or emotions. Ironically, the founder of empiricism, Sir Francis Bacon, recognized that one's beliefs would get in the way of making objective observations (that is, he anticipated the Fallacy of Objectivity that Hume was to advance over a century later). But he thought he had found a novel, indeed, foolproof way around that dilemma. Bacon argued that scientists should employ uneducated, illiterate assistants to make observations for them (!). This, he thought, would insure that the scientist, with his pre-existing biases, would not select certain "favorable" observations and overlook others that are not so "convenient." While Bacon wasn't as naïve as some philosophers think, it is also the case that later investigators have not taken seriously his proposed "solution" to Hume's problem.

In a related vein, historians of science have also called into question longstanding notions of scientific progress; that as time passes, scientists are pushing forward the horizons of understanding, leading to a closer approximation of the Truth. To do this, they build upon the data gathered by past scientists and refine the theories developed in previous research. While this conforms nicely to our cherished ideal of the progressive role of science, it is no longer accepted by many philosophers of science. If we look at the history of science, we see a very different way in which our understanding of reality changes over time. Scientific progress is not always incremental. Modern astronomy, which originated with Copernicus and Galileo during the sixteenth and seventeenth centuries, is based on a rejection, not a refinement of ancient Ptolemaic astronomy (named after Roman astronomer Claudius Ptolemy [c. 90–168 AD], who placed the earth at the center of the solar system). Modern physics is based upon Einstein's theory of relativity, which rejected and did not refine the physics of Newton. We can't argue that Newton and Ptolemy were less "scientific" in their observations than Einstein and Copernicus: they were in fact rigorous even by modern standards.

The history of science is one of such repeated revolutions, in which previous systems of knowledge were overturned, rather than augmented through gradual change. According to physicist and historian of science Thomas Kuhn (1922–1996), this is because scientific research is organized by paradigms. Kuhn notes that, at any one time, members of a specific scientific community (e.g. all physicists or geologists) will have essentially the same training, share the same goals, and refer to the same literature, all the result of what we academics call a common "professional socialization," which begins with our university educations. They generally agree among themselves in matters of professional judgment and appropriate areas of research. Areas outside of these "appropriate" fields will be considered at best "marginal" and at worst "unprofessional" or even "crackpot." Because of this shared background and consensus, scientists within a certain discipline at any one time will tend to share a single paradigm.

A *paradigm* is a set of dominant beliefs within a field that establishes standards of scientific investigation. It does this in three ways: a) it defines the problems considered relevant for research—what is considered worthy of explanation; b) it sets forth a tentative explanation of those problems; and c) it establishes rules and standards for scientific procedure. In short, a paradigm determines at any one time within a field what are relevant data, what is considered an acceptable method of investigation, and how observations are interpreted. In a very general sense, philosophers have identified paradigms as the often unstated and implicit world views of scientists that govern their understandings of the world and their research into how it works.

Paradigms, according to Kuhn, supply the broader, often unstated assumptions about reality from which specific theories are derived. In anthropology, for example, "cultural evolution" is a paradigm, but there are many different theories that arise from this view that cultures change in systematic, broadly similar ways over time. There is the "unlinear evolution" of the nineteenth-century anthropologists Tylor and Morgan, the "historical materialism" of Karl Marx, the "multilinear evolution" of cultural ecologist Julian Steward, the "energetic evolution" of Leslie White, the "general vs. specific" evolution of Marshall Sahlins, not to mention the many differing models (if you will, the ways in which the stages of evolution were labeled), as advanced by Elman Service, Morton Fried, Allen Johnson, and Timothy Earle.

Now for the controversial bits. According to Kuhn, the transition from one paradigm to another (to use an anthropological example, from the evolutionism of the late nineteenth century to diffusion at the beginning of the twentieth) does not involve the progressive accumulation of knowledge. Rather, one system of scientific knowledge overthrows another. Changes in science involve radical, revolutionary breaks with the explanations of previous scientists. Boas did not build upon the assumptions of previous anthropologists such as Tylor and Morgan regarding human behavior; rather, by and large, he rejected them. Only when a paradigm is dominant within a certain field does science progress in a cumulative fashion. That's because the specific theories derived from that paradigm are being tested, leading to refinement, reformulation, and the gathering of new knowledge. While it is possible to test and improve upon specific hypotheses, the fundamental assumptions of paradigms are rarely questioned. These assumptions are what define the boundaries of acceptable debate within the field. Within archaeology, for example, there may be legitimate arguments among two rival investigators as to whether pottery found at a field site was independently invented or borrowed from another culture. However, should a third investigator advance the idea that the pottery was brought to earth in spaceships by extraterrestrial beings or deposited by one of the biblical tribes of Israel, they are likely to find themselves marginalized as crackpots or at best marginal thinkers by the other two "legitimate," if still feuding, archaeologists.

Here's an example of how research proceeds within a given paradigm. In economics, there are two major rival paradigms: those of *neo-classical economics*, which originated in the work of Adam Smith (1776, *The Wealth of Nations*), and those of *political economy*, which originated in the work of Karl Marx (1867, *Capital*). If you're a scholar committed to neo-classical economics, as are the majority of US economists, your world view is based on the assumption that capitalism is a stable, smoothly functioning system that is sustainable in the long term. On the other hand, if you're a political economist, you assume that capitalism is prone to instability, such as periodic recessions, depressions, and accompanying unemployment and general misery. From Marx's original perspective, these will eventually culminate in revolutionary upheaval among working people that brings an end to capitalism itself, ushering in a system of socially-owned property. If you are a neo-classical economist, no amount of empirical evidence, such as business closures, unemployment, or ensuing political instability, is likely to cause you to change your commitment to the rival Marxist paradigm that views capitalism as inherently unstable.

Initially, as a neo-classical economist, you might ignore evidence of economic instability, preferring to sweep it under the proverbial paradigmatic rug. But when evidence of crisis accumulates to the point that you cannot ignore it, you try to interpret that evidence in ways that correspond to your broader paradigm. You might redefine "stability" to accommodate such things as unemployment within your existing beliefs. That's exactly what neo-classical economists have done. They now argue that economic downturns are self-correcting. During a recession, large numbers of people are laid off when businesses can't sell their goods. But as goods stockpile and inventories remain unsold, retail prices start to plummet because of weak demand. The fall of prices stimulates consumption (the consumer thinks: "OK, so maybe I'm a little worried about my job, but I still have some money coming in, and who can pass up that great deal on a brand new car!"). These trends eventually use up the unsold stockpile of goods. When this happens, factories reopen, workers are rehired, and the economic system supposedly recovers. Thus you can make use of the very same evidence that Marxists use to illustrate the instability of capitalism, but analyze it instead to mean that capitalism is stable, at least over the long term. Conversely, the general failure of the proletarian masses to rise up in a social revolution has not, to Marxists anyway, invalidated their paradigm. Rather, they have modified it to try to account for the frequent absence of revolutionary consciousness among people whom they still believe to be oppressed by capitalism; in other words, each paradigm has been driven to try to account for the things that it was originally unable to explain.

Kuhn's broader argument is that contrary evidence by itself does not cause a shift in paradigmatic thinking among researchers. It takes more than that to overturn our cherished worldview. Now, we all know of at least a few scholars who have made radical shifts in their thinking during their lifetimes, although most researchers that I know have clung tenaciously to some variation of a single cherished notion throughout their careers. As an old, outspoken friend in graduate school often observed, "everybody in academia has their favorite pinhead point. And they defend it to their dying breath." But if you think about it, those people who do undergo radical change don't change their commitments in response to the weight of evidence. Unless the entire academic field undergoes a "revolution," it's often a personal experience or even crisis that causes them to change their world view.

Take the case of a mainstream economist at an Ivy League university who is a highly published scholar and an excellent classroom teacher, but who nonetheless is denied tenure after her probationary six years as an assistant professor. The denial of tenure stems not from any lack of merit or performance on her part: perhaps it resulted from gender bias in her department (economics is an overwhelmingly male-dominated discipline), a poisonous working environment, or for want of good political connections with her Dean or Provost. Now unemployed, she takes a job teaching economics to slacker business students at Podunk State College in some provincial backwater. From teaching one seminar a semester to brilliant grad students, she is now delivering four or more sections of Intro Economics each semester to hundreds of half-awake freshmen. Having seen her professional and personal aspirations dashed by this drastic change in circumstances, she becomes indignant at the "system" and those who control it. She may find a Marxist paradigm with its advocacy of social justice and revolutionary change to be politically and personally congenial under the circumstances where she feels that she, too, has been treated unjustly. Over the course of a few months, she has made her own personal paradigmatic revolution. Soon a whole crop of indoctrinated Marxist revolutionaries (but still slackers) will be emerging from her classes at Podunk State.

Kuhn's point is that contrary evidence is a necessary (but not sufficient) condition for a paradigm to be overturned. This is because we subscribe to our paradigms as much for political, social, and emotional reasons as for their explanatory potential. So it is only when broader political or social changes take place, or when the investigator's own emotional status or values shift, that a paradigm yields to contrary evidence and gives way to a new framework; that is, a new way of looking at things. Kuhn doesn't make these points to suggest that scientists are engaged in some kind of charade. In fact, he argues that our belief in the "rightness" of a paradigm and the inability of empirical evidence by itself to refute it is what makes productive science possible. If people didn't have strong commitments to the underlying assumptions of their research, it would be almost impossible to conduct meaningful research. Most of the problem solving that takes place within a scientific paradigm is directed to those things that the paradigm isn't able to account for. The need to explain that "gap" between the paradigm and reality motivates scientists to conduct their research and makes progress possible within a reigning paradigm. If you were to abandon your paradigm for another at the first sign of conflicting evidence, your research would never get off the ground. Furthermore, when you switch to a rival paradigm, you will find that there are problems that it won't explain. Unlike Baconian empiricists, who would deny that bias exists, or Popper's logical positivists, who supposedly weed out inaccuracies through scientific testing, our personal, emotional, and political commitment to what we believe is important, according to Kuhn, because it drives us to explain discrepancies between our paradigm and reality.

From his reading of the history of science, Kuhn notes that usually a single paradigm will dominate any given field for fairly long periods of time (one difference that he mentions between the physical sciences and social sciences is that in the latter there may be several paradigms fighting it out at the same time, although probably one of these will still be dominant). This period of paradigmatic consensus is known as "normal science," in which scientists test hypotheses within a reigning paradigm in order to refine it. They may perceive inconsistencies between the paradigm and empirical reality, but these inconsistencies are initially ignored or viewed as "experimental error." When it is no longer possible to ignore them, they are reinterpreted in terms of the paradigm's assumptions. During normal science, some "marginal" thinkers within the field may advance rival views. But since their views don't accord with the dominant perspective, they are dismissed as "out of the mainstream," or at worst, crackpots and wingnuts.

At certain points in the history of a discipline, its reigning paradigm is called into question, beginning a period of "revolutionary science." Discrepancies between observations and the paradigm accumulate to the point that they can no longer be ignored; nor can they be re-interpreted any longer to conform to the broader paradigm. In the ensuing explanatory "crisis," a view advanced from the margins may have an opportunity to eclipse the previous view if it better accounts for unexplained anomalies. Einstein was an obscure clerk in the Swiss patent office when he advanced his revolutionary theory of relativity, and was virtually unknown to academic physicists at the time. He was, safe to say, completely outside the reigning Newtonian framework in which academic physicists then operated. Eventually, scientific consensus shifts to the new paradigm, signaling a break with the past. The scientific revolution is complete, with the older views being overturned. The (old) paradigm is dead! Long live the (new) paradigm!

It is obvious that this view of the history of science differs sharply from the empiricist view that science progresses with increasing precision and accuracy of knowledge. The notion of paradigmatic science is also troubling for some philosophers of science. As some (but not all) have interpreted Kuhn's ideas, they suggest that different paradigms simply involve different ways of interpreting the world, none of which can necessarily be compared for their "truthfulness." Each paradigm involves a different conceptual vocabulary which defines reality differently. There is a close resemblance between the notion of paradigmatic science and the way some anthropologists have viewed the relationship between language and cultural perception. Linguists Edward Sapir and Benjamin Lee Whorf put forth the *linguistic relativity* hypothesis in the 1930s–40s, suggesting that different languages—because of their differing conceptual vocabularies and grammatical rules—predispose their speakers to view the world in fundamentally different ways. As Sapir expressed it, "Human beings...are very much at the mercy of the particular language which has become the medium of expression for their society" (1949: 69). From Sapir and Whorf's point of view, the world literally looks different to people who speak "substantially" different languages (they would say that given their shared ancestry, most European languages are similar in world view, but not so if they are compared with Native American or African languages).

This is comparable to the way people operating within different paradigms view the world. In the first volume of his work, Kuhn argued that different paradigms are incommensurable: they cannot be compared with one another for their validity because they employ different terms, operationalize terms differently, and seek different kinds of data. Just as some linguists might claim that Navajo can express some concepts that can never be faithfully translated into English, and vice versa, Kuhn would say that two paradigms cannot be compared with one another for their accuracy. From his point of view, it makes no more sense to ask whether cultural evolution is "more truthful" than diffusion than to ask whether English is "more truthful" than Navajo. As Kuhn originally outlined this idea in the *Structure of Scientific Revolutions*, this is a highly relativistic stance toward epistemology. By this, we would mean that "truth" is seen as relative to the person who is describing the world, and that there is no reality apart from our descriptions of it. Hence, the pursuit of some absolute truth independent of our perceptions is impossible. (To return to our hackneyed example: does that tree make a sound if it falls and there's no one there to hear it? Some "strong" relativists would say, "nope!" Others, who may concede that there is some reality out there [but one that we still could not understand apart from our perceptions] would say, "we just don't know!") In subsequent editions of his book, Kuhn softened his earlier relativism. After all, we now know from astronomical observations since the advent of the telescope in the seventeenth century, not to mention the advent of space travel since the 1950s, that the Copernican model of the solar system is indeed much more accurate than the Ptolemaic one! If we accept Kuhn in his more recent, "softer" version, I think we can find much that is useful in the notion that our knowledge is organized paradigmatically.

Having laid bare some of the assumptions and challenges to logical positivism, let's turn in our next chapter to how these arguments have played out in the debate over what anthropology is and what it should be. For readers who find this discussion a little too mind-bending, don't worry: soon enough we'll arrive at "one dead white guy a week!" But as we cover the history of anthropological theory in the chapters that follow, keep in mind the notions of paradigmatic science that we have covered in this chapter.

Through the upcoming chapters, I invite you to consider the following things:

- For a given paradigm, what assumptions does it make about human thought and action?
- How do these assumptions differ from what came before?
- What do anthropologists in this paradigm consider relevant topics for research? What kind of data would they collect in that research?
- Finally, I'm going to relate these paradigmatic assumptions to what was taking place in society at that time, so that we will see that a particular set of assumptions seems to correspond to appropriate social, political, and economic conditions. What broader societal circumstances might help us understand the shift from one paradigm to another?

BOX 1.1   Feyerabend: Science as dogma?

The late UC-Berkeley philosopher Paul Feyerabend (1924–1994) carried relativism to a position that anticipates postmodern philosophy.[6] Feyerabend argued that scientists hold essentially untestable assumptions about the world, just as do theologians or others in a non-scientific tradition. Provocatively asking, "what's so great about science?" Feyerabend claims that scientific understandings of the world are not inherently superior to nonscientific traditions: "what makes modern science preferable to the science of the Aristotelians or the cosmology of the Hopi?" (1978: 73). In contrast to those who regard science as liberating, he argued that as currently practiced it is incompatible with democracy and freedom of conscience. Now that social consensus favors science as a privileged way of understanding, he says it has become a dogmatic, constraining force. Until the nineteenth century, when science was merely a competitor with other "belief systems," the individual had more freedom of thought. Now other systems of knowledge are denigrated as "superstition" or "myth," while their followers are ridiculed as ignorant. This is an argument that we will encounter in more detail later, as its implications have been developed by one of the most influential postmodern historians of the late twentieth century, Michel Foucault (1926–1984).

Feyerabend attempted to show that scientists make claims that cannot be considered logical, at least when compared with the data used to support those claims. He looked at the birth of modern astronomy in this fashion. The ancient Ptolemean model of the solar system, in which the planets and sun were thought to circle a stationary earth, was supported throughout the Middle Ages by the Catholic Church, which claimed that God had placed man and the earth at the center of His creation. Copernicus of course challenged this notion in the sixteenth century, with the more or less modern view of the solar system as one that was helio-centered (sun-centered). From studying Copernicus' original measurements, Feyerabend argued that his model was less able to explain the observed motion of the planets than refinements of the Ptolemaic system that had been worked out by the 1400s. It was initially the modern heliocentric view that was held by dogmatic faith, rather than the ancient view, which was well substantiated by the many measurements of stellar and planetary motion that had occurred over 1,500 years of Ptolemaic thinking.

Feyerabend argued that Copernicus won out not because of the empirical superiority of his work, but because he was supported by powerful political patrons who had a stake in his conflict with the Church. Copernicus' work, he said, was supported by a wealthy merchant class that had arisen everywhere from Holland to northern Italy and which was looking for ways to break with Catholicism. They had chafed at the Church's severe strictures over commerce, which labeled almost all lending as usury and therefore morally unacceptable.

continued...

Box 1.1 continued

In Feyerabend's view, Copernicus (and later Galileo) became political pawns to be used by merchants in their conflict with Church teaching, a conflict reflected in the Protestant Reformation that eventually stripped the nascent capitalist societies of England and northern Europe from the Catholic orbit (don't you like that astronomical metaphor?). So science, according to Feyerabend, cannot be considered a logical undertaking involving the dispassionate collection of data and testing of hypotheses. Scientists hold their beliefs as doggedly as theologians, Feyerabend argued, and often promote their views whether or not they are supported by the observations they make.

Feyerabend didn't discuss, but would no doubt offer as evidence for his claims, recent controversies over the testing of pharmaceuticals. Since much of the research assessing the efficacy of pharmaceutical drugs is underwritten by the drug companies themselves, how much of that research can be considered to be truly "objective" (i.e. not motivated by drug companies' concerns to generate profits)? After investing millions in developing a drug, how likely is it that the company would tolerate experimental results showing that the drug was ineffective or even harmful? Knowing that his employer could easily terminate his career, how likely is it that a drug company researcher would insist on publishing such results in the spirit of "open" and "objective" scientific inquiry?

Quiz yourself

Answer True or False to each statement

1   As a form of knowledge, interpretation is highly personal, not subject to the consensus of observers, and therefore not subject to refutation or proof.
2   As originally formulated by Bacon, empiricism allowed that scientific observers would be guided in the collection of data by their theories about a given phenomenon.
3   Replicability refers to the assumption that an objective observer who uses the same techniques as previous objective observers to describe a given phenomenon should achieve similar conclusions.
4   Nomological/deductive theories are as common in the social sciences as in the physical sciences.
5   The criterion of falsifiability holds that a scientific theory must be based on statements that can potentially be proven false by observation.
6   Scientists refer to a "fact" as a theory that has been proven true by repeated observation.
7   In studying the history of scientific discovery, Thomas Kuhn observed that scientists frequently rejected the findings and assumptions of their predecessors rather than building upon them.

8   Hume's "Fallacy of Selectivity" points out that scientists do not reason inductively, but allow their pre-existing beliefs to guide their observations.
9   According to Kuhn, scientists adopt a given paradigm because it has been shown as more accurate and superior in its explanatory power than its rivals.
10 Kuhn originally argued that scientific paradigms are incommensurable, in that they could not be evaluated against one another in terms of their validity.

2

CLAIMS AND CRITIQUES OF ANTHROPOLOGICAL KNOWLEDGE

A history of controversy

Since the early 1980s, an intense debate has grown over the claims of anthropologists to apply the scientific method (in the modern sense of logical positivism) to explanations of culture. By the end of that decade, many—even most—cultural anthropologists claimed that the field was in the midst of a crisis. This crisis has been phrased as one of identity ("is anthropology a science, or something else?") as well as one of "representation" ("how do we represent other cultures in our published work, who has the right to produce such representations, and can different anthropologists agree on these accounts of other cultures?"). The crisis is one from which the field has yet to emerge, although the initial acrimony of the debate has lessened somewhat as the rival camps have simply gone in their separate directions, content in their belief that their opponents are profoundly misguided, if not entirely in league with Satan. While traditionalists continue to insist on the appropriateness of the scientific method as a means of gathering data and explanation as a goal of cultural anthropology, a growing and vocal segment of the discipline has rejected these goals and methods.

In explaining their opposition to a scientific anthropology, postmodernists often invoke past inconsistencies in ethnographic accounts. These, they argue, illustrate the breakdown of scientific assumptions when one set of human beings (anthropologists) makes another set of human beings ("their" culture or informants) a subject of study. At times in the history of anthropology, inconsistencies in the ethnographic record posed intense controversy, even long before the postmodern wave of discontent. Two famous controversies are regularly cited in the debate of whether anthropology could or should model itself after the other sciences.

In 1926–7, University of Chicago anthropology doctoral student Robert Redfield studied the village of Tepoztlán in the state of Michoacan, Mexico, resulting in the 1930 volume *Tepoztlán, a Mexican Village: A Study in Folk Life*. In it, Redfield anticipated his later concept of "the folk–urban continuum," a way in which he contrasted the types of social relationships found in rural peasant communities with those of large urban areas. While he characterized social relations in cities as impersonal, contractual, and bureaucratic, Redfield viewed "folk" societies as involving more face-to-face interaction, trust, and interdependence (some have noted that Redfield romanticized rural communities as more cohesive and socially integrated than cities; as we'll see, this is merely one expression of a longstanding "Rousseauian" tendency in anthropology). Not surprisingly, Redfield depicted Tepoztlán in this light and emphasized the cooperative and reciprocal nature of village life. Seventeen years later, University of Illinois anthropologist Oscar Lewis returned to Tepoztlán to conduct the first community "restudy" ever done in anthropology.[1] In his volume published in 1951 as *Life in a Mexican Village: Tepoztlán Restudied*, Lewis portrayed the community as one of brittle and distrustful relationships, with extensive abuse within families and virtually no cooperation between them. In a later volume based on his 1940s fieldwork, Lewis portrayed interpersonal relations in this way:

> In Tepoztlán the motives of everyone are suspect, from the highest public officials of the nation to the local priest and even close relatives. It is assumed that anyone who has power will use it to his own advantage. Honest government or leadership is considered an impossibility; altruism is not understood. Friendships are few. To have friendships outside the extended family is not a Tepoztecan ideal, nor is there a long tradition of a "best friend." Adults consider friends a source of trouble and a waste of time.
>
> (Lewis 1960: 90)

The portrayals were so starkly different that other anthropologists immediately questioned who got it "right," with many criticizing the younger Lewis for raising doubts about Redfield's work (Redfield was by that time a prominent senior faculty member at Chicago). Lewis' methods were more systematic than Redfield's; he led a team of researchers armed with various psychological test protocols, including the TAT tests mentioned in the last chapter. After having been asked about the contradictions between his and Lewis' work, Redfield said that the differences were attributable to the initial questions that informed their research; while he had sought to identify the source of meaning and fulfillment for people in Tepoztlán, Lewis had inquired about their greatest sources of concern and anxiety. Redfield's diplomatic explanation was accepted by some observers of the very public debate between the men, although Lewis himself rejected it, finding fault with Redfield's data and his "folk–urban" continuum. Redfield nonetheless raised a valid point; when ethnographers enter the field with different objectives, these in turn shape their observations and the questions they ask. If you assume that people are cooperative and trusting, would that not lead you to interact with and perceive people differently from someone who starts with a differing set of assumptions, e.g. that they are nasty, rancorous, and suspicious? Such contrasting assumptions about human nature ultimately arise from the theories favored by ethnographers. As Thomas Patterson points out in *A Social History of Anthropology in the United States*, "the functionalist theoretical perspectives of Redfield and [fellow Chicago anthropologist Sol] Tax led them to emphasize the relative cultural homogeneity of the communities, the harmony of social and interpersonal relations and the value orientations shared by the majority of their members" (2001: 86).

Many anthropologists since have sided more with Lewis' characterization of Tepoztlán than with Redfield's. Lewis worked in many places beside rural Mexico over the course of his long career: Puerto Rico, Mexico City, New York, India, and even revolutionary Cuba at the time of his death (1970). Interestingly, he found evidence of social disorganization, conflict, and family breakdown in each of these places! Perhaps Lewis' most famous (and controversial) contribution to anthropology was his notion of the "culture of poverty," an idea suggesting that the cultural practices in which poor people grow up perpetuates poverty across generations. In the hands of some policymakers, this has suggested that the poor are themselves responsible for their poverty, rather than structural economic problems or institutional racism. Interestingly, Lewis grew up in extreme poverty and as a graduate student a shortage of funds forced him to skip fieldwork in favor of a library-based dissertation.[2]

A more recent, and still-unresolved controversy in anthropology concerns Margaret Mead's (1901–1978; Figure 2.1) best-selling 1928 study *Coming of Age in Samoa* and Derek Freeman's much later (1983) critique of Mead's work. As Mead herself described the goal of her research, "Are the disturbances which vex our adolescents due to the nature of adolescence itself or to civilization? Under different conditions does adolescence present a different picture?" To answer this question,

FIGURE 2.1 Margaret Mead. Courtesy of the Library of Congress.

she conducted her study in a Samoan village of 600 people, where she interviewed (through an interpreter) 68 young women between the ages of 9 and 20. She concluded that the passage from childhood to maturity in Samoa was a smooth transition and not marked by the emotional distress or anxiety often seen among teens in the United States. Mead shocked many at the time with her claim that Samoan teens and young women deferred marriage for many years while enjoying casual sex; only after many such relationships do Samoan women eventually settle down, marry, and rear children. Of course many readers immediately saw this as an attack on the western notion that monogamy and premarital chastity were preferred norms for all people, and that any deviation from these norms must, at a minimum, cause emotional and social disruption.

In 1983, five years after Mead's death, New Zealand anthropologist Derek Freeman (1916–2001) published the volume *Margaret Mead and Samoa: The Making and Unmaking of an Anthropological Myth*, in which he disputed Mead's findings about sexuality on Samoa. Freeman claimed that Mead had been naively misled by her informants, who essentially "fed" her the information that they politely thought she wanted during her inquiries about premarital sex (as we'll see below, there is some evidence that informants often do in fact respond in this "helpful" fashion). She was not only gullible in taking their responses seriously, but, according to Freeman, she was inclined by her own personal biases and behavior to overemphasize the extent of casual sex in Samoan society. Freeman claimed that Mead had written an ethnographic account designed to justify her negative attitudes about prevailing norms of sexuality and marriage in western society. (Between the 1920s and 40s, Mead was married three times and had several well-known affairs—including with her professor Ruth Benedict—all, of course, during an era when such things would have been widely considered scandalous. Mead's unconventional love life is acknowledged among her biographers, but throughout his book Freeman wastes no opportunity to remind us of it!)[3]

Freeman's own research on Samoa was concluded many years later, in 1967. His decision to wait before publishing his attack on Mead until she could no longer respond troubled many observers. Nonetheless there seems to be no shortage of partisans on both sides of the "debate" (if you can call a one-sided "exchange" a "debate," as it was mostly up to Mead's surviving friends and students to take up for her). Following Freeman's criticism, some have noted that Mead seemed to greatly overstate her command of the difficult Samoan language. She peppers her book with Samoan words and phrases, as if to convince the reader of her fluency, but in fact her work was either conducted through translators or in pidgin English. This fact may well be significant in considering the accuracy of her claims, for who is likely to disclose intimate sexual behavior through a translator or to someone with little command of their language? And it is almost inconceivable that pidgin, whose restricted vocabulary confines its use to trade or communication with foreigners, would be a useful idiom for discussing intimacy. On the other hand, in evaluating Freeman's work, we must keep in mind the 40 some years that elapsed between Mead's research and his own, a time that corresponded to intensive Christian missionary activity on the islands. Could it be that both researchers were "correct" for their own time periods, or that they both projected their own values on Samoan society? Anthropologists will probably never know, but it seems likely that some of both are true.

These and other disparities in anthropological reporting have contributed to much of the recent skepticism about the scientific status of anthropology, raising questions about whether the methods of science can be applied to studying culture. Critics claim that the very nature of the anthropologist as an observer, and the nature of what s/he observes, differ from the subject/object distinction in the rest of the sciences. When an anthropologist participates in another culture, s/he changes it (specifically the behavior of those being observed) in ways that can't be predicted, controlled for, or even necessarily identified. This makes social science fundamentally unlike the natural or laboratory sciences. Yet, the problematic nature of the subject/object distinction in anthropology was largely dismissed until recent decades, the assumption being that the anthropologist is an all-seeing yet non-intrusive observer whose presence in another society will not affect the data he or she records.

Why anthropological observation is problematic

The identity and goals of the anthropologist affect how people behave in his or her presence and the responses that they provide to the anthropologist's questions. Social scientists have long recognized the impact of *interviewer effects* on informant responses. By this, we mean that the identity (nationality, race, gender, age, etc.) of the researcher will often skew how people answer the questions he or she poses during the study. The results of public opinion polling confirm that the identity of an interviewer often influences how people respond to a particular survey question. When an informant is interviewed by a member of the opposite gender or another race, a response that the informant fears will be seen as gender-biased or racist, for example, is usually self-censored. How might interviewer effects apply to anthropology? There are usually huge differences of education, wealth, and perceived social status between anthropologists and the people they study. As a result, researchers may be perceived as being far more similar in their values and expectations to local elites than to the relatively poor villagers who often make up the subjects of anthropology. Imagine, for example, how you, as a middle class (but by local standards, unimaginably wealthy), white male graduate student with many years of education might be perceived by illiterate, lower-caste members of a South Asian village where you are conducting your research. If your subjects place you socially in the same category as wealthy landlords, bureaucrats, and other powerful people, how likely would they be to volunteer information about the injustices or day-to-day reality of the caste system in which they occupy the lowest rungs? Fearing social or economic retaliation for airing complaints about the social system in which they live, would they voice such concerns or describe their landlords in anything less than flattering terms? As we will see in a later chapter, one of the classic studies of political anthropology, Fredrik Barth's *Political Leadership among Swat Pathans* (1959), was conducted in Pakistan under precisely such circumstances. A later anthropologist, Talal Asad, who is of Pakistani origin, noted that Barth implausibly portrayed the extremely unequal relations between landless tenants and their powerful landlords as being governed by reciprocity and mutual respect. Could such findings reflect the inherent status differential between the anthropologist and his informants?

Closely related to this point about bias is the *Hawthorne effect*, where people modify some aspect of their behavior simply in response to the fact that they are being studied. The term was coined after an analysis of time–motion studies done among workers at the Hawthorne Works factory near Chicago during the 1920s. The factory had commissioned a study to see if workers would become more productive in higher or lower levels of light. The workers' productivity seemed to improve when they believed that the changes had been made and slumped when the study ended. It was suggested that the productivity gain was due to workers being more motivated by the interest shown in them by researchers. In social science research, the Hawthorne effect occurs when people modify their responses or behavior in ways that they believe conform to observers' expectations. Sometimes this occurs as people provide what they believe to be a socially acceptable response to a particular question. Asked, "how many alcoholic beverages, if any, did you consume last night?" a respondent will tend to answer in terms of what they believe to be a societal norm, such as "two beers" and not "half a bottle of vodka," even when the latter is the case. (I was reminded of this recently when I encountered anti-drinking ads on campus presenting survey data that "70 percent of all university students have three or fewer drinks per week." Most of my students regard these ads as laughably inaccurate.) The Hawthorne effect has often been noted in pre-election polling in which one candidate is an ethnic minority. In 1990, Douglas Wilder was elected the first African American governor of Virginia, an election that he won by less than one-half of one percent. The narrowness of the outcome surprised observers, as the pre-election polls predicted that Wilder would win by about 7–8 percent. The discrepancy was explained by the fact that before the election many white voters, afraid of being perceived as racist when answering public opinion polls, had falsely stated their intention to vote for Wilder (this is also sometimes called "the Bradley effect" after a previous black candidate for California governor, who was predicted to win based on surveys done before the election, but went on to lose by about 5 percent). Another illustration of this occurred in 1992, when former Klansman David Duke ran for governor of Louisiana. Telephone polling had suggested that Duke would lose in a landslide, but in fact he came within a few uncomfortable percentage points of winning the election. Presumably, white voters who supported Duke were reluctant to admit this to pre-election pollsters. In anthropology, the Hawthorne effect might have been at work when Margaret Mead interviewed young women on Samoa, who politely (again, remember the difference in nationality, race, and status between researcher and informants) provided the answers that they thought Mead was looking for.

Notwithstanding the demonstrated impact of the interviewer and Hawthorne effects on social science data, traditional ethnographic publications made virtually no reference to the identity of the anthropologist who compiled them. The first person pronoun "I" almost never appeared in ethnographic writings in the past, which as a result essentially "wrote the author out of the picture." Instead, they employed a third-person narrative style that reinforced the view of an anthropologist as an unbiased, objective but omniscient (all-seeing) observer. Because of such conventions, casual readers could easily overlook the question of the anthropologist's identity, how it might have affected the information he or she gathered, and indeed, whether another observer so situated would have reached the same conclusions.

By means of illustration, a traditional (if fictitious) ethnographic passage might take this form: "upon marrying on the island of Kiriwina, men receive from their brothers-in-law conspicuous gifts of yams, whose obvious phallic connotations are meant to symbolize the fertility of the newly united couple. Sexual banter is especially overt in ribald exchanges between husband and wife at the time of consummation." Today's critical reader might pose the question, how conspicuous are these gifts? How do we know that yams "obviously" have phallic connotations? "Obvious" for whom: the anthropologist or Kiriwina natives? What is the basis of his description of "ribald" exchanges during a sexual act; did he observe this (most unlikely), and if not, who told him of it? In sum, how much of this statement contains the anthropologist's direct observations, how many are based on his interpretations of what he saw, and how much of it is based on the observations, interpretations, and claims of his informants? Finally, of informants' reports, how much is direct reporting ("my husband and I engage in ribald exchanges during sex") and how much is a third-person description provided by a knowledgeable "key" informant? We'll never know the answers to these questions, because our traditional anthropologist doesn't provide us with the information that we need to understand his position in this society, except as an omniscient, objective observer of not only all that goes on before him, but even, presumably, behind closed doors. Hence, the narrative style is designed to enhance our trust in his objectivity, knowledge, and authority, rather than raising fundamental epistemological questions such as "how does the anthropologist claim to know this, and what are the limits to his claims to knowledge?"

My use of the male pronoun here is intentional. Although American anthropology has always enjoyed greater representation of women scholars than most disciplines (largely due to the willingness of Franz Boas to promote the careers of his female students), the sciences as a whole remain heavily dominated by men, as feminist historians of science have pointed out (Latour and Woolgar 1979; Martin 1992). Moreover, it has only been in relatively recent decades that many scientific fields have opened their doors to any women at all. Historian Elizabeth Potter (2001) relates how the Duchess of Newcastle, an erudite natural philosopher in her own right, triggered a dilemma for the British Royal Society in 1667 when she requested a demonstration by the experimental chemist Robert Boyle. Reluctant to offend an important patron, Boyle arranged for the experiment in private, but it was the last time for nearly 300 years that any woman was allowed into the exclusive confines of the Society! For most of that time the Royal Society governed most scholarly activity and experimental science in Great Britain. As much as we concede in our popular culture that women and men often approach the world socially, perceptually, and linguistically in very different ways, philosophers of science (with the exception of those mentioned above, among others) have largely ignored the myriad ways in which gender can influence scientific investigation and the analysis of data. Historian Donna Haraway (1989) has revealed how male and female primatologists reached significantly differing conclusions regarding chimpanzee social organization, gender relations, and reproductive strategies, even when studying the same community of chimps over time.

The personalities, representativeness, and goals of informants influence both the sources and quality of information provided to the anthropologist and his or her social position within the community. What sort of local person would want to collaborate with a visiting anthropologist in the first place? As noted above, foreign researchers are often wealthy (by local standards), and socially and culturally far removed from those they study. While this power, economic, and cultural differential certainly affects many residents' responses and behavior toward the anthropologist, perhaps the most common response, at least initially, is profound caution and avoidance. Most local people have utterly no idea why you arrived in their village, and the only precedent in their minds for having been "studied" in the past was likely some kind of government-sponsored effort which they probably resented or opposed. Even a community-wide meeting to "introduce" you and your goals to the village *en masse* does little to dispel these concerns; indeed, if the person or persons who call such a meeting are not widely held in good repute (as local leaders often are not), your attempted introduction may only raise the level of speculation and rumor concerning your "real" (and naturally, insidious) purposes. When beginning my dissertation research in Hopkins, Belize during 1986–7, I asked the village council to hold a community-wide meeting at which I would be introduced and would describe to everyone present the purposes of my residence there. Those attending the meeting nodded politely, a few shook my hand afterwards, and then they dispersed. I thought I had done a good job. I did not realize then the village council was dominated by one political faction viewed by its opponents as "communist," a label which they naturally extended to me after they saw me talking and laughing with the council chairman. To compound matters, the subject of my study—agricultural change—led me to associate closely with members of the local farmers' cooperative, almost all of whom belonged to the same political party as the one dominating the village council. I was blissfully unaware of the negative way that about half of the village's politically active residents viewed me until I had become the subject of a police investigation into the "espionage" activities of a "possible East German spy"—me! A pair of policemen arrived unannounced to my house to "interview" me about my background and the purpose of my residence in Belize, all apparently after someone had reported my "suspicious" activities. I came that close to being escorted from the village and maybe even deported, and was only saved by a letter of introduction that I had earlier obtained from a Belizean scholar who by sheer good luck happened to be a cousin of one of the policemen who interrogated me at length.

Put yourself in your hosts' position. They didn't ask you to reside in their community or study their way of life, and the mere fact that you are doing so strikes most people as completely implausible. After all, since many residents of the developing world want to come to the United States or another developed country and leave their poverty behind, why would a wealthy, educated (probably white) person choose to live in such a backwater and "learn its way of life?" That is, unless they had some ulterior motive, probably involving the exploitation of the villagers and the theft of their resources. From such generally-held suspicions, anthropologists almost always find themselves treated initially, at best, as non-persons. Despite the fact that most of us pass through this curiously liminal and lonely state, only a few works, such as Clifford Geertz' famous and entertaining essay, "Deep Play: Notes on the Balinese Cockfight" (1973a), ever acknowledge this difficult transition. So who steps forward in this vacuum of human contact to provide the anthropologist's initial understandings of a society? In my experience and those of most ethnographers that I know, those who make themselves known to the anthropologist most readily are fairly marginal members of their communities, who perceive the visitor as a source of material reward otherwise unavailable to them. My "key informant" for the first month or so of my research was one of the most notorious alcoholics in the village. "Charles," as I'll call him, was a well-educated but chronically unemployed man (he had been a school principal until his drinking interfered), and he quickly turned to me when he figured out that I might be a ready source of cash. While highly intelligent and insightful (when sober), Charles was also socially isolated and hardly well-integrated with the mainstream of village life. This could not help but affect, for some time, my own reputation in the village ("there goes that communist again! Considering who he's hanging with, he's probably a drunk as well!") and my understandings of the behavior and attitudes of its residents.

Indeterminate and unanticipated factors of local history affect the anthropologist's reception in his or her host community. Arriving in a community, you will probably never know that village's prior experience with outsiders similar to yourself, but those experiences will color the way its residents react to you and the information they provide. I once met "Betsy," a female cultural anthropologist living in San José Poaquil, a Maya village in highland Guatemala. She had gone there because it was the site of a successful weaving cooperative, and she was interested in the village's involvement in the broader world economy, especially given a handicraft textile market in the US and Europe that was then taking off. Of particular interest was how this process was affecting gender relations, as weaving was a task in which men and women had complementary roles in the production and marketing of rugs. Unlike all of her previous experiences in the same region, where men readily cooperated with her requests for interviews and information, Betsy found herself the constant target of sexual harassment from men in San José. She was able to gather data in the village only from female informants, or from males only if other women were present. This affected the representativeness of her data in ways that couldn't be controlled for. Later, Betsy learned that the only previous North American woman to have lived in the village—someone associated with a Canadian development agency that had come to assist in earthquake relief—had had several casual sexual liaisons with village men (now, whether or not Mead's conclusions about Samoan sexuality were accurate, this kind of behavior was completely unprecedented and scandalous in the Maya highlands!). Given their limited (but no doubt highly memorable) experiences with a previous female *gringa* visitor, San José men assumed that all North American women were similarly disposed to casual sex. Indeed, they couldn't understand why the anthropologist turned down their propositions.

The postmodern critique

Pointing out the occasionally embarrassing discrepancies about particular cultures that have been studied by different anthropologists (e.g. Redfield/Lewis and Mead/ Freeman), and these uniquely anthropological problems with data collection, postmodernists have mounted two major attacks on the applicability and desirability of scientific approaches in anthropology.

Many have argued that the criterion of objectivity in social science is impossible to attain in practice. When anthropologists claim to be objective observers in the pursuit of scientific explanation, postmodernists claim, they are being either naïve or outright deceptive. From this point of view, one should not be surprised that Redfield and Lewis, and Mead and Freeman, came to disparate conclusions. Postmodernists claim that in the process of conducting their observations, anthropologists can't help but project their values and emotions on the people they study. The argument is that, however "scientific" they claimed to be, anthropologists in practice engage in an activity closer to interpretation than explanation.

Bronislaw Malinowski (1884–1942; Figure 2.2) was among the first anthropologists to describe himself as avowedly scientific in his approach to ethnographic research. Spanning more than 500 pages and compiled over nearly three years of fieldwork on the Trobriand Islands, his mammoth ethnography, *Argonauts of the Western Pacific* (1984, orig. 1922), is considered to be a milestone for in-depth anthropological description. In his introduction to the volume, Malinowski ridiculed earlier, anecdotal, travelogue-like descriptions of indigenous cultures, claiming that his study set a new, higher standard for objectivity: "The time when we could tolerate accounts of the native as a distorted, childish caricature of a human being are gone. This picture is false, and like many other falsehoods, it has been killed by Science." (The capital "S" was Malinowski's own usage!) So far, so good. If anyone could claim ethnographic authority (i.e. the Truth), it should be Malinowski, right?

Then there occurred another anthropological embarrassment: 25 years after his death, Malinowski's private diaries from the field were translated from their original Polish and released by his widow. Published under the title, *A Diary in the Strict Sense of the Term* (1989, orig. 1967), the 800-page manuscript was highly personal, detailing, among other things, the author's sexual fantasies, his frustration with native Trobrianders, and his severe homesickness. He mentions his intense dislike of certain individuals and occasionally refers to the Trobrianders with breathtaking vitriol (see Box 2.1). Many anthropologists were deeply dismayed and embarrassed at the

FIGURE 2.2 Bronislaw Malinowski. Courtesy of the London School of Economics and Political Science Archives.

damage that the *Diary* did to Malinowski's reputation as an empathetic observer of native life. To be fair, as his defenders noted, Malinowski did not write the entries with the intent for anyone else to see them; most anthropologists have also maintained occasionally soul-searching field diaries as a kind of psychological outlet during a time of isolation and loneliness. Yet, how reasonable is it to conclude that Malinowski was able to compartmentalize these intense inner emotions, and even express hatred for his hosts, while elsewhere faithfully recording unbiased observations for publication in a way demanded by "Science"? Is the claim of objectivity under such circumstances realistic, or is it a ruse to take in the reader? In a scathing review of Malinowski's diaries, in which he referred to the diarist as "a disagreeable man," the late Clifford Geertz (1926–2006) wrote, "[Malinowski's] achievement was to compile a faithful, lifelike, and indeed moving record of a primitive way of life, against psychological odds that would have crushed almost anyone else. For if the Trobrianders are 'bloody niggers'[4] in his private diary, in his ethnographic works they are, through a mysterious transformation wrought by science, among the most intelligent, dignified, and conscientious natives in the whole of anthropological literature: men, Malinowski is forever insisting, even as you and I" (Geertz 1967).

More generally, the disparity between Malinowski's personal journals and his official, published accounts has raised questions about why published ethnographic accounts are written in the manner they are. In his book *Works and Lives: the Anthropologist as Author* (1989), Geertz, a predecessor of later postmodernist approaches in anthropology, analyzed the textual construction of four classic ethnographic accounts in light of other, more personal writings left behind by the

BOX 2.1 Excerpts from Malinowski's A Diary in the Strict Sense of the Term (1989, orig. 1967)

12.19 [1917]. Got up at 7. Yesterday, under the mosquito net, dirty thoughts: Mrs. [H.P.]; Mrs. C., and even Mrs. W...I even thought of seducing M. Shook all this off...Today got up at 7—sluggish; I lay under the mosquito net and wanted to read a book instead of working. I got up and made the rounds of the village. Studied barter trade. I resolved absolutely to avoid all lecherous thoughts, and in my work to finish off the census, if possible, today. At about 9 I went to Kaytabu where I took the census with a bearded old man. Monotonous, stupid work, but indispensable.

12.27 [1917]. As for ethnology: I see the life of the natives as utterly devoid of interest or importance, something as remote from me as the life of a dog. During the walk, I made it a point of honor to think about what I am here to do. About the need to collect many documents. I have a general idea about their life and some acquaintance with their language, and if I can only somehow "document" all this, I'll have valuable material. Must concentrate on my ambitions and work to some purpose. Must organize the linguistic material and collect documents, find better ways of studying the life of women [domestic implements], and system of "social representations." Strong spiritual impulse.

Tuesday, 4.24 [1918]. Last night and this morning looked in vain for fellows for my boat. This drives me to a state of white rage and hatred for bronze-colored skin, combined with depression, a desire to "sit down and cry," and a furious longing to "get out of this." For all that, I decide to resist and work today—"business as usual"—despite everything. In the morning, after writing the diary and a letter, I went to the village to interview the policeman, then went to Okina'i and met Ginger and Co. [Hiai] offered to take me to Sinaketa. Still shaking with anger. After lunch went to Kaulaka to take pictures. Then to the beach; clear afternoon with one enormous white cumulous cloud casting strong reflections on the seas, the thickets of bushes grown together with the rock on the crests of the pandanus. I did not think of the niggers or the work, I was still depressed by everything that had happened. I thought a little about tomorrow's mail, which as I supposed, was waiting for me at Sinaketa. Turned in early.

same anthropologists (Malinowski, Mead, Ruth Benedict, and E.E. Evans-Prichard). Geertz finds that all of their published ethnographic work tends to correspond to certain conventions: it is written in a dispassionate, third-person narrative style; it is liberally peppered with terms transcribed from the native language of the cultures they describe (with these terms then helpfully translated into English within adjacent parentheses), and there is little or no indication of how anthropologists found out about the particular claims to knowledge represented in those accounts. Geertz argues that the avoidance of the first person "I" in their written work has allowed anthropologists to deny their own existence as living, sentient, human beings with their own emotions and beliefs. By doing so, they avert questions about their reputation as objective observers; indeed, the very reputation of scientific anthropology, Geertz says, depends on a denial of the anthropologist's identity, beliefs, and state of mind.

Like other authors, Geertz argues, anthropologists construct their texts using certain literary styles that advance their arguments, which in this case depend on establishing their credentials for objective observation and their ethnographic authority. The all-knowing, dispassionate third-person narrative style is coupled with enough of a smattering of native terms to convey the impression that the anthropologist really "was there" and knows what he or she is talking about. Without siding with Freeman (whom he accuses of his own biases cloaked in the language of science), Geertz notes that Margaret Mead's *Coming of Age in Samoa* is not only interspersed with Samoan words, but even contains on its front page an untranslated dedication in Samoan (of course nowhere in Mead's book or other writings does she confess her lack of fluency in the language). With her dedicatory opening page, Geertz argues, Mead seems to be laying claim to a particularly exalted form of ethnographic authority; i.e. that she is at least as Samoan as American.

A second, major criticism is that scientific approaches in anthropology promote the views of anthropologists over those of the people they study. It "privileges" one form of outside ("scientific") knowledge over the local knowledge of native people themselves, and thus disregards people's own reasons for their actions and attitudes. This "privileging," in turn, is related to a broader claim that scientific knowledge has had repressive, disempowering consequences for those unable by circumstances or societal positioning to claim it. This is a rather complex critique, but gets to the heart of a central tenet of postmodern philosophy: a profound skepticism and distrust toward all claims to scientific knowledge. According to the late but endlessly influential French postmodern historian and philosopher Michel Foucault (1926–1984; Figure 2.3), scientific knowledge is primarily a discourse of power, a way in which formidable bureaucracies, states, corporations, and other institutions exert control over others: "There are no power relations without the correlative construction of a field of knowledge, nor any knowledge that does not presuppose and constitute at the same time power relations" (1984: 175). Consider the assertion that scientific knowledge is superior to other ways of knowing about the world and presents a unique avenue to Truth, a claim traceable back to Francis Bacon. Foucault claims that, in practice, those institutions claiming a command of scientific knowledge in turn employ that discourse to justify their control over other members of society. Science becomes simply another weapon in the arsenal of the powerful. While the view of science originating in the Enlightenment was one of its liberating potential (for freeing people from "ignorance" and want), twentieth-century history has shown that it was not only harnessed to oppress and kill people

FIGURE 2.3   Michel Foucault. © Bettmann/CORBIS.

in unprecedented numbers, but that it has also operated as a means of legitimating the states and other institutions that engage in such action.

Consider this as an illustration of Foucault's argument: a government entity, in conjunction with a powerful corporation specializing in waste disposal, wants to establish a hazardous waste landfill. They have determined (or so they say) that the ideal "objective" conditions for siting such a facility with regard to groundwater, geology, and soil profile happens to be next to your neighborhood. As we live in a "democratic" society, in which presumably all entities—corporate and citizen—are entitled to have a voice in such policy decisions, your state's environmental protection authorities schedule a public hearing about the proposed landfill. Most hearings are held during the day so that government officials can attend them during their working hours. Who, of course, shows up to protest about the proposed siting of a landfill? Mostly "housewives," full- or part-time homemakers who have some time free to attend such a meeting during the day. Indeed, considering that their young children might be playing in proximity to a landfill, it will come as no surprise that some of the most vociferous opponents are mothers residing in the adjacent neighborhood.

At the public hearing, various scientific experts (mostly engineers and geologists in white lab coats well-equipped with pocket protectors) run through a series of PowerPoint presentations designed to "prove" to the public (via *Science!*) that this is, indeed, the optimal place in which to dispose of hazardous waste. After they have completed their presentations, the public is invited to comment. One after another, the audience members approach the microphone set up in the auditorium for public comment. Their concerns, expressed in unquantifiable but nonetheless real anxieties about their children and families, are answered in an obfuscating manner with data that even a PhD geologist would have difficulty understanding. Scientists and bureaucrats roll their eyes at the "stubborn," indeed "hysterical" refusal of the members of the public to accept their patiently delivered "scientific consensus." All of the audience members' stated opposition is futile, in any case, since the state agency is legally mandated to approve the permit in the absence of any "scientific" evidence to the contrary. Public comments and mothers' fears about the well-being of their children do not rise to this lofty scientific criterion. Unlike the evidence presented by geologists, their fears and comments are "hearsay," "anecdote," or "intuition." The facility is constructed over their objections, and soon their children are playing in proximity to the landfill.

By the way, what about that claim that your neighborhood represents the most geologically ideal site for a landfill? Read any of the studies completed by Robert Bullard (e.g. *Dumping in Dixie: Race, Class and Environmental Quality*, 2000) and other sociologists who have pioneered in the study of "environmental racism." What they have demonstrated is that communities of color and working class communities are more likely by several orders of magnitude (we're talking four to five times more likely) to become the sites of undesirable land uses such as waste dumps (even after public hearings) than are white and middle or upper-class communities. So was your community selected because it was geologically ideal? Or because it was politically powerless? Your objections as a resident of the community, in any case, were disregarded because you lack the command of "scientific" knowledge presented by the waste disposal corporation and its allies in white coats. But how does the argument that claims to scientific knowledge bolster the powerful over all others relate to anthropology?

While postmodernists such as Foucault emphasize the power deployed by bureaucracies and institutions when they invoke claims to "privileged" scientific knowledge, others assert that all knowledge—including Science—is socially constructed in that it is the product of the individual's social position and identity. A leading proponent of this view, Jacques Derrida (1930–2004), argues that the world does not exist except in the language by which we habitually describe it. Each culture, in turn, constructs a largely self-contained world of meaning based on its particular language and significant symbols. By definition, Derrida argues that these language-based systems of meaning cannot be fully translated or understood through other languages (many linguists would, however, disagree with this claim). When ethnographers employ their conceptual language and categories of analysis to describe other cultural worlds, they distort native understandings by forcing them into western systems of meaning. Consider, for example, the conventional construction of a written ethnography, which divides any given society into the same conceptual categories, with separate chapters devoted to economics, kinship, politics, religion, and so on. Is this conceptual grid meaningful for the people comprising that society? Or does it impose a preconceived western understanding upon a culture for which it has little or no relevance? In doing so, postmodernists claim that scientific approaches in anthropology recreate a colonial hierarchy of authoritative western observer and exotic nonwestern "Other," the very same colonial relationships from which anthropology itself was born during the nineteenth century.

The question of interpretation thus lies at the forefront of many postmodern critiques of anthropology. If scientific ethnographers offer their views as the authoritative account of a culture, many postmodernists argue, they in effect "silence" or de-legitimate all other accounts. Historically, most published ethnographic accounts were produced by white males from western industrialized countries. Although ethnography is usually about nonwesterners and non-whites, the voices of the people who were the subjects of such studies were absent, or were represented *through* the lens of white, western observers. Indeed, this privileging of the social scientists' views over the perspectives of those they study is intrinsic to the major tradition in the sociology and anthropology, one known as positivism.

A brief history of arrogance

The formal disciplines of anthropology and sociology trace their origins to the work of the French scholar Auguste Comte (1798–1857), who coined the term *positivism* as the attempt to explain the workings of the society according to general laws that could be identified through scientific observation. Comte's notion was that the fields of physics and astronomy, which were then developing general laws to account for the workings of the universe, could provide models for understanding human behavior. In fact, his early writings referred to "social physics," the idea that human actions could be reduced to the operation of several principles such as the laws of gravitation and motion. Comte, whose sanity was occasionally questioned by his contemporaries, only changed the term *social physics* to *sociology* when a rival of his also began using the former term to describe his work. It was a fundamental tenet of Comte's positivism that "there are laws as well defined for the development of the human species as for the fall of a stone." Today, positivism in the social sciences involves the search for general principles that account for social behavior. Anthropological theory as defined by the discipline's scientific proponents is strongly positivist in orientation; this is certainly the case for all varieties that substitute the scientist's categories and concepts for those of the people being studied.

The search for these laws takes positivists beyond the realm of people's own explanations of their behavior. Native explanations of behavior are often treated as normative justifications of action, rather than the "real" causes of that action, which is only discernible to an outside, scientific observer. This is certainly the case for all varieties of anthropology and sociology influenced by functionalism, a viewpoint that dominated both fields for a good deal of the twentieth century. Hence, while a member of a particular society might account for their participation in ritual in terms of their need to address a spiritual concern or to worship a supernatural entity, functionalists would usually substitute their own category of analysis. Most commonly, functionalists would explain engagement with the supernatural in this sense: "the social function of religious life is to enhance a sense of shared identity through common participation in ritual, thereby promoting social solidarity." Note that this explanation has little to do with the informants' stated reasons for their action or belief. Modern anthropologists of a scientific orientation, such as Marvin Harris, have devoted themselves to developing explanations of behavior that often have nothing to do with people's own explanations of their behavior. Further, Harris insists that his explanations, which are based on what he calls an *etic* point of view— that of an objective scientific observer—are more systematic, coherent, and logical than explanations based on an *emic* point of view, or how native people explain their own behavior. This is despite the fact that members of the cultures that Harris describes often do not understand or even dispute his explanations for why they act the way they do. To return to the example with which I started this course, Harris argues that a scientific observer would identify a rationality and purpose to the Hindu cattle taboo that most Hindus themselves would not perceive, because they explain their actions through the limited conceptual vocabulary of their emic point of view.

What, then, do postmodernists propose in place of anthropology's traditional use of the scientific method to produce generalizing explanations of culture? We will examine this question in more depth at the very end of this volume, but allow me to quote at some length one of the pioneers of this critique, the anthropologist Stephen Tyler. In one of the first postmodern manifestos in anthropology, *Writing Culture: The Poetics and Politics of Ethnography* (ed. by James Clifford and George Marcus, 1986), Tyler identified the central problem of ethnography as:

> the inappropriate mode of scientific rhetoric that entails "objects," "facts," "descriptions," "inductions," "generalizations," "verification," "experiment," "truth," and like concepts that, except as empty invocations, have no parallels either in the experience of ethnographic fieldwork or in the writing of ethnographies. The urge to conform to the canons of scientific rhetoric has made the easy realism of natural history the dominant mode of ethnographic prose, but it has been an illusory realism, promoting, on the one hand, the absurdity of "describing" nonentities such as "culture" or "society" as if they were fully observable, though somewhat ungainly bugs, and, on the other, the equally ridiculous behaviorist pretense of "describing" repetitive patterns in isolation from the discourse that actors use in constituting and situating their action, and all in simpleminded surety that the observers' grounding discourse is itself an objective form sufficient to the task of describing acts.
>
> (1986: 130)

Although many anthropologists since then have been influenced by postmodern arguments, no single school of "postmodern" anthropology has emerged. But three separate tendencies seem to mark those works influenced by these trends.

The first of these is that anthropologists should seek to "evoke"[5] culture rather than to explain it and should acknowledge their own subjective state in their writing. Traditional anthropologists often generalized about an entire realm of behavior and thought of which they obviously could not claim complete knowledge (think back to our fictional ethnographer's reference to Kiriwina sexual encounters). Instead, some postmodern anthropologists claim that they should seek to "tell stories" about those limited realms with which they have some familiarity. Because these are based on the firsthand experiences of the anthropologist during fieldwork, such accounts are necessarily highly subjective and "partial" accounts rooted in the particular experiences of a given fieldworker. Thus, in addition to the fact that the anthropologist produces an idiosyncratic interpretation that cannot be compared to some absolute notion of Truth, ethnographic accounts must be "reflexive." By this, postmodernists say that an honest ethnographer should abandon the omniscient third-person narrative style and "write themselves into the story," first of all by using the first person pronoun ("I") in their accounts. Anthropologists' accounts should foreground their own experiences, subjectivity, emotional state, and values. This embraces the "poetics" of ethnography mentioned in the subtitle of Clifford and Marcus' book, above. An early, highly influential illustration of this approach was Renato Rosaldo's 1989 essay "Grief and a Headhunter's Rage." In it, Rosaldo described the sudden, accidental death of his wife, Michelle, while they were doing fieldwork in the Philippines. Besides conveying his own grief as a result of her death, he employed the incident to describe how it enhanced his own anthropological understanding of Ilongot emotional life, specifically how unspeakable grief compels Ilongot men to avenge killings of their kinsmen. Similarly, Lila Abu-Lughod's 1995 "A Tale of Two Pregnancies" describes her own pregnancy within the context of her anthropological work in Egypt. This kind of foregrounding of the anthropologist's experience is a significant break from the third-person, omniscient narrative style employed in traditional ethnography.

A second approach argues that anthropology should acknowledge the ways in which past ethnographers (and other writers) have recreated colonial hierarchies in their writing that "silenced" the voice of the "Other." The latter encompasses those groups traditionally not represented among scientific practitioners; colonized people, people of color, sexual minorities, etc. Geertz' *Works and Lives* (1989) represents one such approach to the ethnographic canon, entailing a re-interpretation of older work based on postmodern sensitivities to "voice" and representation. This approach entails "deconstructing" the ways in which literary devices and conventions are employed in anthropological texts to reveal the kinds of meanings that are promoted by them and those that are delegitimated by them. In the final chapter of this volume, we will consider recent applications of this approach to visual images presented of cultural Others in print advertising and popular magazines such as *National Geographic*. The goal of such work is to demonstrate how popular culture has represented issues of race, gender, privilege, and modernity, often in ways that validate western stereotypes of nonwestern people and ethnic minorities.

Finally, some postmodernists argue that, having freed themselves from the artifice of "objectivity," anthropologists should be politically engaged. Their work should attempt to give voice to the "silenced" Other, particularly by identifying sources of oppression (racial, colonial, gender, sexual…any others I left out?)

and championing the liberation of the oppressed. Why (such scholars ask) have anthropologists who have worked in some of the world's most impoverished and oppressive societies been so reluctant in the past to openly adopt a stance favoring social justice and liberation? They claim that traditional anthropologists' refusal to advocate on behalf of the oppressed was simply another pretense of their claim to "objectivity" (that is, if ethnographers had disclosed any political sentiments or advocacy they would have compromised their reputation as authoritative scientific observers). This politically-engaged anthropology, of course, embraces the "politics of ethnography" mentioned in the subtitle of *Writing Culture*. In a famous exchange with anthropologist Nancy Scheper-Hughes,[6] the science-oriented anthropologist Roy D'Andrade disparagingly calls this a "moral model" in anthropology that forsakes description for moral indignation and posturing. Among the dangers inherent in this, D'Andrade says, is that a moral model is not subject to refutation by evidence, while the account produced by an "objective" model can always be disproven or refined by the weight of evidence. He does not believe that scientists who employ an objective model are unbiased, but that the accounts produced by them stand or fall on the weight of evidence, not whether their authors want them to be true.

Scientists push back

Postmodern critics have raised some important concerns about the way in which science and ethnographic research have operated in practice. Indeed, they have altered in a fundamental way the manner in which most anthropologists write about and relate to the people they study. Absolute objectivity in the sense that Bacon described it is obviously impossible. As Kuhn noted, our conceptual commitments are indeed critically important in creating that stimulus to scientific research and creative activity. However, when postmodern criticisms are taken to an extreme, as in Derrida's claim that the world is nothing more than the language by which we describe it, there are certain inherent dangers that result. What appears to be very liberating in terms of our newfound sensitivity to "many voices" and "multiple ways of knowing" has oppressive implications of their own. At its most extreme, postmodern philosophy embraces a kind of epistemological relativism, in which it is impossible to evaluate rival claims to knowledge because they involve differing assumptions about the world that are incommensurable. This, in turn, implies that all claims to knowledge are equally valid when seen in their own terms. I would note that there is a serious problem with this assertion, arising from the fact that it is self-refuting (that is, it contradicts itself). Tyler's argument, in which he denounces the search for "facts," "descriptions," "verification," and "truth," actually negates itself. If all claims to knowledge (that is, truth) are equally valid, then why should I accept his particular claim as truthful? This might sound like simply a clever rhetorical argument, but it has serious real-world consequences. In his volume *Cultural Materialism*, Marvin Harris notes the sinister implications of this celebration of all claims to knowledge, in particular by taking on Paul Feyerabend:

there are domains of knowledge in which epistemological relativism poses a grave threat to our survival. Medicine is one such domain, and there are many others in the social sciences. One cannot remain indifferent to whether cancer is caused by witchcraft or some defect in cellular chemistry. Nor can one let unbridled imaginations determine the causes of poverty, or the existence or nonexistence of a ruling class in the United States. It cannot be a matter of taste whether you believe or do not believe that pollution is a menace, that the underdeveloped countries are getting poorer, that the multinationals are promoting a nuclear arms race, that war is instinctual, or that women and blacks are inferior. *Let Feyerabend stand before the ovens of Dachau and say that a scientific understanding of sociocultural systems is ultimately nothing but an "aesthetic judgment."*

(1980: 23, emphasis added)

If you are a literary critic, it doesn't matter that your interpretation of a work of fiction or poetry is at odds with someone else's. But there is more at stake when we study human society: we're not seeking knowledge about texts, but about people's lives. Anthropologists work in places where there is racial injustice, class oppression, genocide, and exploitation. I concur with Scheper-Hughes (1995) that it is vitally important that we document these things; indeed, anthropologists are uniquely situated through participant observation to do so. But if, as others claim, we hold that our description of these ethnographic realities is merely one interpretation among many plausible views, why should anyone take our concerns seriously? Why should anyone even acknowledge that such injustices exist? More to the point, if we admit the validity of all claims to knowledge, does that not compel us to accept arguments that the Holocaust never existed, that whites are genetically superior to nonwhites, and other Nazi-inspired claims?

In recent years, it has not been only academics but those with the ability to make life and death decisions (for example, concerning war) who have embraced the same assumptions about knowledge; i.e. that "the only reality is the one that we consider worth knowing." *New York Times* journalist Frank Rich has shown how the George W. Bush administration remained impervious to evidence contradicting its stated reason for invading Iraq: "the same conservatives who once deplored postmodernism and relativism were now eagerly promoting a brave new world in which it was a given that there could be no empirical reality in news, only the reality you wanted to hear (or that they wanted you to hear)" (2006: 163). When he challenged the administration's claims that Saddam Hussein's Iraq constituted a threat to the United States, Ron Suskind, another reporter from the *Times*, described the following response of a presidential aide:

The aide said that guys like me were "in what we call the reality-based community," which he defined as people who "believe that solutions emerge from your judicious study of discernible reality." I nodded and murmured something about Enlightenment principles and empiricism. He cut me off.

"That's not the way the world really works anymore," he continued. "We're an empire now, and when we act, we create our own reality. And while you're studying that reality...we'll act again, creating other new realities, which you can study too, and that's how things will sort out."

(quoted in Rich 2006: 3–4)

The attempt to construct an alternate reality based on ideological claims is the *modus operandi* of a leading cable news channel that often disseminates false assertions in the guise of news reporting. The result is that a sizable segment of US citizenry is actively deceived about the state of the nation and world. I am not simply expressing an opinion here; a Fairleigh Dickinson University poll of public knowledge on topics ranging from foreign relations to US wealth distribution to climate change reveals that viewers who rely on Fox for information are more likely to subscribe to demonstrably false beliefs than those who rely on Comedy Central's *Daily Show*, which admits to being "fake news" (Vorhees 2011)! Most Fox viewers, for example, still believe that Saddam Hussein was involved in the terror attacks of 9/11, a claim repeatedly advanced by the Bush administration to justify the invasion of Iraq in 2003. When the news media and powerful officeholders represent nonfactual ideological assertions as "facts," is it possible to have an informed citizenry? Of course not. And in the absence of that, a functioning democracy is impossible.

In sum, this is your author's position (you are welcome to yours, of course): over time I have come to accept the postmodern critique that absolute objectivity of the type claimed by past ethnographers such as Malinowski is impossible, if not openly deceptive. The postmodern sensitivity to voice, representation, and power is also a welcome corrective to traditional approaches that relied upon the authority of an omniscient narrator. Carried to the logical extreme of epistemological relativism, however, a refusal to privilege some forms of evidence over others has darker consequences that can lead to very unliberating consequences. Indeed, empowering all claims to knowledge must necessarily include those with noxious or oppressive implications, as we will explore in greater detail in the final chapter of this book. Having dismissed evidence as unnecessary or inevitably biased, anthropologists such as Stephen Tyler have disarmed themselves from challenging ideas that differ from their own. An illustration of this was the largely ineffectual scholarly response to one of the most controversial social science publications in recent years. In their 1994 book *The Bell Curve*, Richard Herrnstein and Charles Murray argued that IQ was genetically inherited and that racial differences in test scores and socioeconomic achievement reflected these inherent differences in intelligence. The book could have been challenged on many fronts in the flawed nature of the data (almost all of it very old, much of it inaccurate and based on archaic and culturally-biased IQ measures) and its faulty statistical assumptions. Many cultural anthropologists chose instead to challenge its politics, alleging that it contained racist implications. While this point could and should have been made, that was about as far as most anthropologists' critique went. Had anthropologists not simply debated the book's implications but critically examined its use of evidence, they could have demolished the authors' arguments on scientific grounds. Instead the debate was framed in political and moral terms that probably failed to convince any sympathetic readers of Herrnstein and Murray's book. Once you claim that all science is socially constructed and contains oppressive consequences, you surrender your ability to challenge flawed science, such as that involved in *The Bell Curve*.

Quiz yourself

Answer True or False to each statement

1   Postmodernists often point to inconsistencies in different ethnographic studies of the same societies (for example, Tepoztlán, Mexico, and Samoa) as evidence that "objective" accounts of culture are impossible to attain.

2   In *Coming of Age in Samoa*, Margaret Mead admitted that she had little knowledge of the Polynesian language and that most of her information had been gathered through translators.

3   Bronislaw Malinowski specified that his *Diary in the Strict Sense of the Term* was not to be published until after his death so that it would not diminish the attention given his academic publications.

4   The interviewer effect refers to the fact that the identity (nationality, race, gender, age, sexual orientation, etc.) of the researcher will often skew how people answer the questions he or she poses during the study.

5   Traditional ethnographic accounts by past anthropologists such as Mead, Lewis, and Malinowski made extensive use of the first person pronoun "I," emphasizing the anthropologist's personal experiences in the field.

6   According to postmodern philosopher Michel Foucault, when government and corporate bureaucracies claim to have scientific expertise they often use that claim to extend control over other, less powerful members of society.

7   Nineteenth-century social theorist Auguste Comte argued that human behavior simply did not permit the kind of scientific generalization then developing in the fields of physics and chemistry.

8   In advocating a "reflexive" anthropology, some postmodern ethnographers view themselves as story-tellers whose accounts foreground their own experiences, subjective and emotional state, and values.

9   According to Roy D'Andrade, a politically-engaged "moral model" of anthropology is not subject to refutation by contrary evidence.

10   Opponents of epistemological relativism, such as Marvin Harris, contend that it empowers all claims to knowledge, even those with noxious or oppressive implications.

3

THE PREHISTORY OF ANTHROPOLOGY

Classical foundations and fallacies

In this chapter, we examine perspectives on human differences that originated well before the formal origins of anthropology. While some of these ideas can be readily dismissed today, others (mostly dating from the Enlightenment) have been so influential as to form the basis of all of today's social sciences. As a formal academic discipline devoted to the study of cultural differences, anthropology had emerged in Great Britain and the United States by the 1870s. In recent decades, as anthropologists have looked more critically at the discipline's history, they have often noted how the field arose in conjunction with colonialism. The consolidation of European empires in Africa and Asia during the nineteenth century, and consignment of North American Indians to reservations during the same time, provided the first opportunities for anthropologists to conduct field research among colonized peoples. As we will see, in some instances, anthropologists worked hand in hand with colonial authorities in providing information to better administer and control native populations. But while anthropology as a formal discipline owes its origins to colonialism, the questions that have motivated anthropologists extend far back into classical antiquity, if not before. Probably as long as people have been aware of others unlike themselves there have been efforts to account for those differences.

As early as 500 BC Greek historians produced accounts of cultural traditions among the different peoples of Greece that anticipate modern ethnographies. The most well-traveled of these historians was Herodotus, whose *Histories* recorded the local cultural traditions of the lands of eastern Asia, Egypt, and the Aegean Islands. In some significant ways, writers of antiquity anticipated the work of modern ethnographers. For example, they contrasted local differences in politics, economics, religion, sex roles, and philosophical notions, dividing their observations into categories that resemble the institutions described by modern anthropologists when describing other cultures. In addition, they recognized that local traditions significantly constrain the choices of individuals. Classical scholars recognized that individuals are not completely free in their selection of values and behaviors; they're at the mercy of the traditions in which they are brought up. For example, the historian Xenophon described how the militaristic values of the city state of Sparta influenced the family life and education of young males. Virtually everything in Spartan culture contributed to producing vigorous, obedient citizens considered necessary in such a militaristic society.

Yet at the same time there was no agreement among classical writers as to what accounted for human differences. What today we would call cultural traditions were regarded as biologically innate, so that all people were thought to be born with certain predispositions of values and behavior. And early historians exhibited virtually no tolerance for the differences that they described. A term that has come down to us as an ethnocentric reference to people unlike ourselves—*barbarian*— originated in the Greek language of this time. It was a derogatory reference to anyone who was not of Greek origin and did not speak Greek (the actual etymology of the word derives from the word for "shepherd," as the sounds produced by the Germanic tribes encountered by travelers reminded them of the bleating of sheep). Then, too, the early Greek and Roman historians were guilty of a problem that plagued anthropology well until the end of the nineteenth century; the problem of unbridled speculation. Where Herodotus, Thucydides, and Xenophon did not have first-hand access to information on other cultures that were known to exist, they simply speculated on what these cultures were like. These speculations were then recorded as facts, side by side with much better documented societies.

Perhaps the most bizarre if influential account provided by a writer of classical antiquity were the speculations of the Roman naturalist Pliny the Elder, who lived in the first century AD (a resident of Pompeii, he died in the eruption of Mt. Vesuvius in 79 AD). Pliny is often regarded as one of the first natural scientists as he observed the natural world and tried to explain it in its own terms, without supernatural intervention. His voracious interests ranged from geology to the animal kingdom to the differences in behaviors among human populations of the time. Pliny is also notable for one of the first attempts to categorize human groups based on their physical characteristics, or what we would today consider a racial classification. In addition to providing fanciful accounts of people who had been encountered by Roman soldiers and administrators in Europe, the Middle East, and North Africa, Pliny postulated the existence of people who had never been seen by Europeans, beyond the limits of the known world. He then attempted to characterize what these unknown races of humans were like and even compiled drawings of their physical forms. The result was a conception of non-Europeans that has become known as the *Plinian races* (note that this is a modern designation; the term "race" did not enter the English language until the 1580s). The Plinian races exhibited often grotesque, part-human, part-animal characteristics and were responsible for a lasting belief that non-Europeans were in some physical and behavioral sense less than fully human. These ideas persisted for centuries after Pliny had devised them; the fact that they lasted into the period of European colonization of the Americas and Africa suggests that such beliefs may have served as convenient rationales for colonial endeavors that deprived native people of their labor and resources. After all, if the natives of the colonized world are not fully human, what inherent rights do they enjoy more than, say, livestock or any other useful species?

> First described by Pliny the Elder in his masterpiece, *Historia Naturalis*, the Sciopod's name is Latin for 'shade-foot' (Figure 3.1). Their native region is often stated as Ethiopia, and they're known for their habit of reclining at midday and using their single huge foot as a parasol against the blazing sun. As they keep cool in the shade, the sun bakes their soles into hard, black leather. Tough soles aren't a drawback, though, as the Sciopods' feet are subject to a lot of punishment as they hop around the countryside. Being one-footed doesn't slow them down, either. A Sciopod's leg is enormously powerful, and the long hops it makes can propel it faster than a horse and rider, and almost as fast as a gazelle.
>
> (Zenko 2006)

During the European Middle Ages, Pliny's speculations were supplanted with scriptural interpretations of human differences. Between the fourth and thirteenth centuries AD, knowledge was increasingly sought through revelation and scriptural study. The Old Testament Book of Genesis accounted for the linguistic diversity of

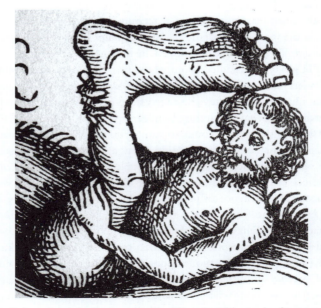

FIGURE 3.1   Sciopod, originally described by Pliny the Elder in the first century AD, but here depicted in a woodcut from the Nuremburg Chronicle of 1493.

humans with the story of the Tower of Babel. After the biblical flood, the descendants of Noah were said to be one people with a single language. Under the direction of their king, Nimrod, they began building a massive tower to glorify his name and legacy. "Then the Lord came down to see the city and the tower which they had built…and [he] mixed up the language of all the people and from there he scattered them all over the earth" (Genesis 11.6–9). Hence, the profusion of tongues was attributable to divine retribution for human sinfulness, as reflected in the efforts of people to arrogantly elevate themselves over God. Similarly, the differing achievements or standards of living of human groups were seen as reflections of God's favor or disapproval. Medieval models of physical difference mixed Pliny's ideas with the biblical notion that all humans were descended from Shem, Ham, and Japheth, the three sons of Noah, producing distinct Semitic (Asiatic), Hamitic (African), and Japhetic (Indo-European) peoples. The Jewish scripture, the Talmud, identified the dark-skinned descendants of Ham as cursed, and depicted Ham and his descendants as sinful. Yet, as a whole, Europeans of the Middle Ages were *far less* likely to distinguish between groups of people on the basis of their physical appearance than on the basis of belief (i.e. Christian vs. non-Christian). What we consider to be a racial hierarchy placing whites of European ancestry over blacks of African ancestry only arose in conjunction with (and as a rationale for) the Atlantic slave trade in the sixteenth and seventeenth centuries.

Biblical notions of human difference were surprisingly long-lived in some quarters. During their colonization of North America, some English settlers regarded American Indians as descendants of one of the "lost tribes" of Israel, a claim that first arose among officers on Columbus' initial voyages. In a research project for a professor of mine during my graduate school years, I came across the diary of a US cavalry officer who fought Indians on the frontier during the 1870s. In one portion, he enumerated the supposedly "Jewish" characteristics (all of them negative) of the Indians he had encountered. He managed thereby to slander two ethnic groups based on his short-lived and violent encounters with just one. No small accomplishment!

Scriptural accounts played much less of a role in the work of Ibn Khaldun (1332–1406), a Muslim scholar whose interests centered on differences among the societies of North Africa. His major contribution was a multi-volume history published in Arabic in 1377. The *Muqaddimah* (meaning "Introduction") is the portion most commonly read by non-Arab speakers. Khaldun's history has been considered the first major work in cultural anthropology; its significance can be judged from the fact that it anticipated many of the conclusions that European scholars were to reach only 400–500 years later. Khaldun lived and worked in Spain during the Moorish occupation of that country, and was familiar with both contemporary European beliefs as well as the classical writings of Aristotle, Plato, and Socrates. He rejected prevailing European ideas of the time about human skin color differences, claiming that black skin was due to the hot climate of sub-Saharan Africa and not due to the descendants of Ham being cursed. (Khaldun was off the mark here. Heat by itself has nothing to do with pigmentation, but long-term exposure to ultraviolet radiation in the form of sunlight does.)

Khaldun begins his work with a comparison of human and animal behavior which distills the distinct capabilities of humans. He observes that both humans and some animal species, ranging from bees to lions, form social groups. Yet whereas a given species of social animals consistently forms the same kind of group to survive, human groups are infinitely variable in their size and characteristics. This leads him to conclude that *reason* is the distinguishing feature of humans. Unlike animals, which form social groups from natural "instinct," people think through solutions to the problems of existence. This capacity for reason is why so many different solutions have been reached to common problems. Much of Khaldun's work deals with the contrast between the pastoral Bedouin of the Middle East and sedentary agriculturalists. Because the Bedouin must remain highly mobile, they are restricted to the bare material necessities of food, clothing, and shelter. The fact that there is little occupational diversity, and also that the Bedouin are warlike in raiding agricultural settlements to survive, creates a strong sense of shared identity. In terms of their values, Bedouin are distinguished by this sense of solidarity, a strong defense of their independence, and tremendous courage.

Sedentary societies, on the other hand, subsist through agriculture. Their larger size provides a greater degree of specialization, resulting in more affluence and comfort. Here solidarity doesn't depend on the homogeneity that exists with the Bedouin. Rather, it grows out of the division of labor, because specialization creates mutual dependence. At the same time, the ease and comfort of urban life breed a kind of decadence that prevents a growth of the strong moral values characterizing Bedouin culture. Interestingly, while describing the Bedouin way of life as one of hardship, Khaldun suggests that strong moral values thrive under such conditions.

Khaldun's work may be the first ethnographic description of a culture that attempts to explain why members of that culture act in the way they do without invoking the idea of innate behavior. His explanations focus on environmental features and how they shape each culture's way of making a living. Pastoralism creates small undifferentiated social groups that hold values of intense independence and solidarity. Agriculture creates stable, large urban communities with much specialization but a greater emphasis on commerce rather than autonomy and independence. This is a *materialist* mode of analysis that anticipates a good deal of modern anthropology (we'll say more about this later, but the essential idea here is that a culture derives its general characteristics from its *material* foundation, i.e. how people make a living and satisfy their basic needs). Khaldun's observations on social solidarity closely parallel those of Emile Durkheim in the late nineteenth century. That is, Khaldun recognized that solidarity, or social cohesion, can be created when there is little or no specialization (a characteristic that Durkheim identified as "mechanical" solidarity). But it can also be created through mutual dependence, which occurs when there is a complex division of labor and people following different occupations come to rely on one another (what Durkheim identified as "organic" solidarity). Khaldun's work would compare favorably with—indeed, it is more accurate and much less judgmental than—much anthropological writing in the late 1800s. Yet it was to have little influence outside the Arab world until portions of it were translated into French and English in the 1870s. By then, some of Khaldun's concepts had been independently discovered in Europe.

Colonial encounters and conversions

Ibn Khaldun's work found a counterpart in the writings of the legendary Venetian explorer and merchant Marco Polo (1254–1324), who compiled a detailed account of his voyage overland through the Middle East and his prolonged residence in China. Writing at the beginning of the European Renaissance, Polo described the people he encountered with a degree of curiosity and objectivity notably absent from most Medieval European speculations on human difference. From his account readers learned of then-novel Chinese practices, such as the use of paper money and eye glasses. The broad dissemination of his account, however, was restricted by the need to copy manuscripts by hand, and the fact that most copyists focused their attention on religious texts.[1] Without doubt, the greatest impetus to proto-anthropological thinking in Europe was the growth of colonialism three centuries later, by which time news of human difference could be widely disseminated via the printing press. Yet Polo's influence on later colonialism is reflected in the fact that Columbus brought with him on his 1492 voyage a much-annotated copy of Polo's account.

Trans-oceanic voyages vastly increased Europeans' awareness of human diversity, without in most instances increasing their toleration of such differences. Having arrived on the island of Hispaniola (present-day site of the neighboring countries of Haiti and the Dominican Republic), Columbus encountered the Taino people, whom he insisted on calling Indians from the belief that he had reached the East Indies. He noted at the time that such "beings" would serve admirably as slaves. Both he and later European explorers continued to express a faith in the existence of Plinian races and provided tantalizing descriptions of their fleeting observations of mermaids and other fantastic humanoids in the Americas. These longstanding beliefs eventually died out during the 1500s, as explorers captured Native Americans and returned them to Europe as curiosities. Yet, the question of the essential nature of Native Americans remained unresolved for some decades; notably, whether they were human, albeit in some exotic and inferior form, or were so different from Europeans as to be considered fundamentally non-human.

To some extent, this question was answered by means of a religious doctrine. Although historians have often portrayed the Spanish conquest of the Americas as a monolithic undertaking by soldiers (*conquistadores*), the Spanish Crown, and the Catholic Church, in fact there were widely diverging interests between these forces that became apparent as soon as the fighting had ended (Wolf 1959: 159–164). The date 1519 was notable for two reasons: it marked the beginning of the Conquest of Mexico (the most populous land of the Americas) and the excommunication of the German priest Martin Luther, a process that would end with almost all of northern Europe becoming Protestant, stripping the allegiance of millions of people from the Catholic Church. In this context, the hierarchy of the Church saw the newly conquered people of the Americas as a pool of converts that would offset its

FIGURE 3.2 Bartolomé de las Casas. As Archbishop of Chiapas, Mexico, Las Casas outraged Spanish settlers by denying communion to those who kept Indian slaves. © Hilary Morgan/Alamy.

losses of membership and prestige in Europe. The Conquerors, echoing Columbus, regarded Indians as an apparently inexhaustible source of labor, one which could be worked to exhaustion and death in the pursuit of precious metals. They had little interest in seeing the conversion of Indians to Christianity. Indeed, in most instances they opposed it as it would secure for Indians some basic guarantee of their status as human beings (keep in mind that these men came from a fundamentally Medieval Europe in which the essential status distinction between people was defined in terms of faith, rather than race).

As Wolf (ibid.) notes, the friars and priests who oversaw the process of conversion were in many instances utopians who recognized in the New World the opportunity to recreate a form of Christianity untainted by the hypocrisy and corruption of Europe. Those who presided over the conversion of Indians were often appalled by the way in which their new charges were treated by Spanish settlers. The most well known of these was the crusading Dominican monk Bartolomé de las Casas (1484–1566; Figure 3.2). As a young man, Las Casas had sailed for Hispaniola as a soldier, but he was disillusioned by what he experienced of the Conquest. He returned to Spain in 1506, was ordained a Deacon, and then returned to Hispaniola determined to seek the conversion of native people. In 1512, he became the first Catholic priest ordained in the New World. Horrified by their treatment at the hands of the Spanish, Las Casas returned from the Americas in 1520 to seek an audience with the King of Spain. To him he described in graphic detail the brutality to which Indians were exposed by the *conquistadores*, culminating in his book *The Devastation of the Indies*, published in 1542. In that account Las Casas wrote of the first decades of Spanish settlement:

> [F]orty-nine years have passed since the first settlers penetrated the land, the first so claimed being the large and most happy isle called Hispaniola, which is six hundred leagues in circumference. Around it in all directions are many other islands, some very big, others very small, and all of them were, as we saw with our own eyes, densely populated with native peoples called Indians… And of all the infinite universe of humanity, these people are the most guileless, the most devoid of wickedness and duplicity, the most obedient and faithful to their native masters and to the Spanish Christians whom they serve. They are by nature the most humble, patient, and peaceable, holding no grudges, free from embroilments, neither excitable nor quarrelsome. These people are the most devoid of rancors, hatreds, or desire for vengeance of any people in the world… They are very clean in their persons, with alert, intelligent minds, docile and open to doctrine, very apt to receive our holy Catholic faith, to be endowed with virtuous customs, and to behave in a godly fashion. And once they begin to hear the tidings of the Faith, they are so insistent on knowing more and on taking the sacraments of the Church and on observing the divine cult that, truly, the missionaries who are here need to be endowed by God with great patience in order to cope with such eagerness… Yet into this sheepfold, into this land of meek outcasts there came some Spaniards who immediately behaved like ravening wild beasts, wolves, tigers, or lions that had been starved for many days. And Spaniards have behaved in no other way during these past forty years, down to the present time, for they are still acting like ravening beasts, killing, terrorizing, afflicting, torturing, and destroying the native peoples, doing all this with the strangest and most varied new methods of cruelty, never seen or heard of before, and to such a degree that this Island of Hispaniola once so populous (having a population that I estimated to be more than three million), has now a population of barely two hundred persons.
>
> (las Casas 1992: 27–29)

Las Casas' graphic and indignant account of the Conquest—and his probably exaggerated depiction of Indian receptiveness to Christianity—had its desired effect. As far as the Catholic Church was concerned, the "Indian question" was resolved by Pope Paul III shortly after meeting Las Casas in 1537, when he declared in the Bull *Sublimis Dei* ("The Sublime God") that American Indians were "truly men" possessed of rationality and a human soul and therefore deserving of the sacraments (Wolf 1959: 175). In the same document, he declared the slavery of American Indians to be sinful in the eyes of the Church. This declaration was ratified in the Spanish Crown's policy toward the Americas, which outlawed Indian slavery throughout its New World holdings in 1542, although the Crown's ability to enforce this policy in the distant Americas, so far removed from direct Spanish oversight, remained highly ineffectual in most areas.

BOX 3.1   Behind the "Black Legend"

When Bartolomé de las Casas' *The Devastation of the Indies* was translated into English in the late sixteenth century, it inspired the so-called "Black Legend" of Spanish cruelty toward native peoples. This long-lasting belief in Spanish perfidy served English interests well by implying that their settlement of the Americas was a benevolent force in comparison. Ironically, in such claims, the Church figures prominently as a perpetrator of genocide in Spanish America, overlooking the fact that English settlement was almost never accompanied by advocates, such as Las Casas, who opposed abusive treatment of native people. The differing attitudes toward native peoples in North America versus areas settled by the Spanish correspond in large part to the differing goals of these respective empires (Harris 1964: 82). Nearly four times as many people from the British Isles settled in the North American colonies as the number of Spaniards emigrating to Central and South America. This comparatively small cohort of settlers viewed Indians as a necessary labor force for Spanish mines and plantations, and therefore Spanish and Indian settlements co-existed. Further, since the Spanish Crown severely restricted the emigration of women (in order to prevent a decline in an already sparsely populated nation), the men who settled in New Spain frequently took Indian women as wives and concubines. In order to maintain the native population as a labor force, Indians in Spain's colonies were resettled into centrally-planned villages (known as *reducciones*), each of which was provided with communal parcels of farmland for the support of residents when they were not laboring in Spanish mines and plantations.

Unlike Spain, which discouraged scarce labor from migrating to the New World, the English Crown sought to displace much of the British Isle's burgeoning population by exporting landless tenants and the unemployed to the Americas. This was accomplished in large part by prescribing "transportation" (exile) as one of the most common punishments for even petty crime. Transportation acted as a "safety valve," sending into exile a politically explosive class of poor people with no visible means of support. Many had been displaced by Parliament's Acts of Enclosure, which allocated the common lands of peasant communities to wool-producers for the English textile industry. Exiled from their homeland, the poor of Britain flooded into North America seeking land that they themselves could farm. In this process, the native inhabitants of North America were seen as a nuisance, impeding the creation of a new class of English yeoman farmers. The North American colonies obtained land for white settlers by banishing Indians to a steadily westward moving frontier through rarely-honored treaties and fighting them when they resisted displacement. The ideological groundwork for England's policy of displacement in North America was laid out by English political philosopher John Locke in his 1669 work *The Fundamental Constitutions of Carolina*. Among his arguments was the idea that "unenclosed" property (by which he meant land that was occupied traditionally by a group of people rather than privately owned) should be replaced by individual private ownership. This was not an abstract economic argument but justified the displacement of American Indians from land that they had communally held by tradition; in other words, it provided the ideological basis of the English colonial policies designed to separate Indians from their lands for the benefit of white settlers. English (and, by extension, later US) policies seeking the displacement of Indians account for the fact that the remaining native population in North America today is but a fraction of that in Mexico, Central America, or the Andes.

The significance of *Sublimis Dei* for the later development of anthropology was considerable, if indirect. It unleashed several orders of missionary priests in the areas of the Americas that had been colonized by Catholic powers (mostly Dominicans and Franciscans in Spanish America and Jesuits in French Canada). These priests lived among the people they sought to convert, learned their languages, and studied their customs to find out which native practices might be used (or co-opted) to promote their conversion. (The 1991 feature film *Black Robe* draws upon the encounter of one such French Jesuit with various Canadian tribes, and offers an exacting recreation of Indian society at the time of European contact.) The "Jesuit ethnographers" sent back to France very detailed (if ethnocentric) descriptions of Canada's Indians during the 1500s and 1600s, which fascinated European readers of the time. This growing evidence of cultural diversity also prompted some serious efforts among social philosophers to address the question of human behavioral differences.

French essayist Michel de Montaigne (1533–1592) attempted to place this new-found cultural diversity in perspective in a series of books in the late 1500s. Montaigne never visited the New World; his sole contact with it was in the writings of French priests working there and a Brazilian Indian who had been brought to France, whom he had been able to interview. Montaigne claimed that the cultural diversity of the world argued for a relativistic viewpoint on morals. In his essay "Of Cannibals," Montaigne doubted whether absolute standards could be applied to local traditions, insisting instead that such traditions, rather than universal standards, determine what is moral. Hence, to a Brazilian Indian the practice of eating one's dead father is considered honorable, even if Europeans regard it as repugnant. For Montaigne, the newly discovered peoples of America were "savages," but significantly he employs that term in a manner distinct from the way it is usually interpreted in English. The American Indians were *au sauvage* in that they were "natural" and uncontaminated by the pretensions of "civilized" society (a later French philosopher, Jean Jacques Rousseau, was to elaborate on this theme in his influential notion of the "noble savage"). Montaigne's cultural relativism was, however, atypical of the time, as most

Europeans believed Indians to be incapable of the kind of rational thought found among "civilized" people.

Despite the greatly increased awareness of cultural diversity in Europe following colonization of the Americas, until the late 1600s there remained little agreement about how cultural traits developed (in fact, the first use of the term "culture" in anthropology is usually credited to Edward Burnett Tylor in the 1870s, and as we'll see it differs somewhat from how modern anthropologists use the term). The closest approximation to a modern anthropological conception of culture and its origins was in Ibn Khaldun's work, but that would remain inaccessible to Europeans for several more centuries. Later developments in European intellectual history were to provide this culture concept (even if it was not identified as such), together with the origins of modern anthropology.

Locke's "empty cabinet" and the challenge to monarchy

From the standpoint of explaining (rather than simply describing) human differences, the most significant phase in European thought is associated with the *Enlightenment*. This period of intellectual inquiry is conventionally defined as lasting from about 1600 to the end of the Napoleonic wars in 1815. Its signature trend was an increasing secularization of knowledge, a tendency to explain the workings of the world in terms of observable, natural processes rather than scriptural interpretation. During this time the doctrine of empiricism was advanced and the modern natural sciences of astronomy, physics, and chemistry began to develop (in some instances, as in the case of Galileo, over the opposition of religious authorities to the new scientific findings). Where human differences are concerned, perhaps the most important development was the publication of John Locke's *An Essay Concerning Human Understanding* in 1690. Locke laid out many of the basic assumptions shared by Enlightenment social and political philosophers. He also set forth the premises of modern behavioral sciences, such as psychology, sociology, and anthropology, which emphasize the relationship between a conditioning environment and human behavior.

Recall that prior to this time there existed no clear notion of the origins of behavioral and thought differences in different human groups. It was recognized that some types of behavior, such as language, could be learned even as an adult, but one's essential personality was established at birth and was relatively fixed. Therefore, there was a close association in many people's minds between the notions of biology and behavior (or, if you will, race and culture); people of a certain physical origin were believed to act and think in a similar fashion. These behavioral traits were common to the entire group because both physical make up and personality were inherent.

Locke's revolutionary contribution to the social sciences was his vehement rejection of this doctrine. Locke begins by posing the question of the origins of human knowledge. What gives any particular individual his thoughts, appetites, and predispositions? He answers this question in a way that refutes the then-prevalent notion of innate ideas. The mind at birth, Locke argues, is an "empty cabinet," which contains no pre-existing thoughts or values (later commentators would substitute the

Latin expression *tabula rasa*, or "blank slate"). This void is filled over the individual's lifetime, as he acquires knowledge. Where does knowledge come from? In a word, experience. That is, the individual acquires the sum of his knowledge, values, and predispositions from those individuals and practices that he is exposed to over his lifetime.

No doubt you will recognize that Locke was anticipating what is popularly known as the "nature–nurture" debate; i.e. how much of our behavior is learned ("nurture") and how much is under some form of genetic control, even if indirectly ("nature"). Although most modern social scientists have strongly supported the Lockian (or "nurture") side of the argument, some psychologists now argue that some individual behavior is attributable to a complex mix of heredity and environment. We know that certain forms of mental illness appear to "run in families," as does addiction. Yet even here, our genes are not our destiny. If someone does not come in contact with an addicting substance, they are unlikely to exhibit that behavior; similarly, millions of people have learned to overcome or control their destructive addictions to heroin, alcohol, cell phones, Facebook, etc. through various means. *Hence, even for those behaviors for which we know there is a genetic component, there is always also a learned, or environmental, component.*

For anthropologists, who are much more interested in group behavioral differences between populations than in differences between individuals, the "nature" argument simply cannot account for such differences. We know from abundant evidence that a male infant born to a peasant family in rural China but raised in, say, suburban Chicago, is going to grow up speaking English, eating McDonald's hamburgers and dressing much like all those around him (i.e. wearing a baseball cap backwards and enormous, baggy clothes). He or she is not going to exhibit some compulsive, uncontrollable appetite for fermented eggs, an inherent dexterity with chopsticks, or an innate fluency in Mandarin. Far from it; his compulsive, uncontrollable impulse will be for texting his buddy who is two rows away from him in class and addressing every other male of his age, and even his professors, as "dude." Group-level differences of this sort can only be explained by the social environment to which he is exposed.

Locke's argument is that different kinds of experience (or to use the modern equivalent, different conditioning environments) will produce differences in behavior. This seems commonsensical to us today, but let's consider some of the then-radical implications of this characterization of human nature. For one, Locke's view is fundamentally optimistic in its rejection of innate behavior. It stands in notable contrast to the political philosophy of his predecessor Thomas Hobbes (1588–1679), who argued that war and suffering were inevitable among humans living "in a state of nature" because of our purportedly selfish dispositions. In his volume *Leviathan* (1651), Hobbes claimed that such propensities require the existence of a strong state and sovereign, whose role it is to secure a measure of peace and security otherwise absent from human society.

Writing a generation after Hobbes, Locke reached diametrically opposite opinions in the political realm, conclusions stemming from his view of human behavior. *If all minds are fundamentally the same at birth, then all people are equal in their potential.* It is only the *circumstances* in which people grow up (and nothing about their inherent nature) that account for the inequality between them as adults, their differences in morality, reason, or knowledge. This doctrine of human equality (in potential) became one of the core values of the American and French revolutions in the late eighteenth century. In both cases, revolutionaries cited Locke in refuting the notion that certain kinds of social orders were inevitable because they reflect innate differences between people. The monarchies challenged by both revolutions were predicated on the assumption that monarchs enjoy the right to rule because they are *inherently* superior, wiser, and more capable than their subjects. When Jefferson wrote in the American Declaration of Independence, "We hold these truths to be self-evident, that all men are created equal…" he was implicitly invoking the legacy of Locke in refuting the ideological premises of monarchy. Like all liberal and democratic thinkers of the time, Jefferson was well-steeped in Locke's arguments.[2]

Why did Locke's ideas appear when they did, and why did they take root among political and other philosophers of the time? I argued in Chapter 1 that ideas that become a prevalent part of the culture (as opposed to simply withering away for lack of support) are those that serve a useful purpose for a significant segment of society. During the late seventeenth century an increasingly wealthy and influential class of merchants and industrialists (Karl Marx would later call them the bourgeoisie) sought to challenge the economic prerogatives of the English king. Among these was the doctrine of *mercantilism*, the notion that foreign trade should be conducted in ways that benefit the Crown. Hence, the Crown stipulated that sugar should be imported into Britain only from Britain's colonies in the West Indies, tea should be imported from Britain's colonies in South Asia, and tobacco from its North American colonies, even though such items may be more profitably obtained elsewhere. Merchants wanted to trade with whoever could provide raw materials and commodities more cheaply, even if they came from French, Spanish, or Dutch colonies. In 1688, two years before Locke's *Essay* was published, King James II was removed from the throne and exiled. In part, this event, known as the "Glorious Revolution," stemmed from the fear that James II would reinstate Catholicism in England, which had been violently suppressed since Henry VIII. But the major effect of exiling the King and replacing him with one supported by Parliament was a significant strengthening of the powers of the House of Commons. This marked England's emergence as a constitutional monarchy and fundamentally shifted power away from the King to the elected representatives of the people (keep in mind that at the time, "the people" constituted only those with sizable amounts of property that granted them the right to vote—in other words, the very bourgeoisie mentioned above!). And of course, similar demands for free trade played a major role in the American war of independence against England 90 years later. A shift toward greater (if still very limited) democracy and greater restrictions over the prerogatives of the king would obviously be well-served by an assertion of the basic equality of people that was at the heart of Locke's work.

Locke's *Essay*, then, provided an intellectual foundation for a capitalist social order based on free trade and (limited) representative democracy. Indeed, at the time of the Glorious Revolution, Locke had published a pamphlet advocating a limited monarchy and the exiling of James II.

During the Enlightenment, then, we see a recognition that traditions are learned and passed on between generations through the medium of language; in other words, that human behavior is the result of what we would today call culture. As early as 1750, the French historian and statesman Robert Turgot called for the development of a discipline of "universal history" that examines how traditions are developed and passed on. Turgot also developed a concept of culture virtually identical to the definitions employed by modern anthropologists: *"Possessor of a treasure of signs which he can multiply to infinity, man is able to assure the retention of acquired ideas, to communicate them to other men, and to transmit them to his successors as a constantly expanding heritage"* (quoted in Langness 2005: 1). There is everything in Turgot's definition that modern anthropologists would recognize as a definition of culture, including an emphasis on use of symbols (i.e. language) to communicate and pass on knowledge and an emphasis on a shared heritage of learning.

Enlightenment social theory

For the Enlightenment philosophers, the notion that the social environment (or, in our terms, culture) determines behavior was axiomatic. But this still left the question of where culture came from. How did Enlightenment thinkers try to explain the cultural differences between groups? There are *two answers* to this question, both rooted in Locke's notion of the all-important role of the social environment in shaping behavior. While some Enlightenment thinkers embraced the notion of historical progression, others emphasized the direct impact of environmental and climatic factors on human behavior.

As noted earlier, Locke's arguments entailed an optimistic view of human potential, suggesting that human behavior can be improved given improved social conditions. Changes in the environments to which people were exposed could eradicate ignorance and vice and help to perfect human character. Significantly, this period witnesses the rise of movements for the abolition of slavery and universal education. One consequence of the Enlightenment belief in perfectibility was the notion of progress, a sense of satisfaction with present trends and a faith that even better is yet to come. Progress became as much a tenet of Enlightenment thought as did the era's faith in the potential of science and democracy. (You could argue that the roots of modernity were established in the seventeenth and eighteenth centuries, and what gives "postmodernity" much of its defining quality is that it breaks from these Enlightenment beliefs.)

Embracing the assumption of social progress over time, some eighteenth-century social philosophers simply attributed cultural differences to differing degrees in the mastery of rational thought. This idea is particularly noticeable in the "universal histories" or evolutionary schemes of culture that arose at this time. These schemes all suggested that societies move through a consistent sequence of stages. Such evolutionary notions are often attributed to nineteenth-century anthropologists, but they were actually developed well over a century earlier. For example, in his "universal society," Turgot contrasted the features of hunting, pastoral, and agricultural stages of society. In his 1767 *Essay on the History of Civil Society* the Scottish historian Adam Ferguson (1723–1816) also drew upon the eighteenth-century belief in progress to develop a model of cultural evolution. It was Ferguson who first attempted to place all known human societies on a three-stage scale of savagery, barbarism, and civilization. Ferguson's model was specifically developed with respect to the North American Indian cultures then being documented by French Jesuits in Canada. Ferguson assumed that all human societies passed through the same three stages of development, and that all could be assigned a particular place on that sequence depending upon their livelihoods, cultural practices, political systems, and technology. Ferguson's was the first known use of the *comparative method*, the assumption that contemporary "primitive" societies represent the early stages of cultural evolution. In other words, members of a civilized society can understand their own distant past by studying existing primitive societies. This notion persisted through the work of the late-nineteenth-century evolutionists; it was rejected by Franz Boas, and resurrected in the mid-twentieth century by contemporary anthropologists.

Ferguson's model was actually well informed ethnographically, and not that distinct from the work of later cultural evolutionists in anthropology. In some respects, in fact, it is more accurate than the ideas of Morgan, who is often erroneously credited with devising the savagery–barbarism–civilization evolutionary model. In the state of savagery, according to Ferguson, people lived from hunting and gathering, held little private property, possessed no formal government, and maintained a strong sense of equality. Improvements in food production associated with agriculture ushered in the state of barbarism. Here there was life in settled villages, greater disparities in wealth, and greater conflict. Finally, civilization arose from the growth of trade and government, which came into existence to control warfare and social disorder (this is reminiscent of Hobbes, who regarded government as essential to combat the unending "war of all against all" that arose from humanity's selfish nature). The growth of trade and the growing specialization of labor result in large, differentiated urban populations removed from direct involvement in food production. Among the specialists who arise in this stage are political leaders who make up the state.

This all has a modern sound to it, but there remain major differences between schemes such as Ferguson's and those of twentieth-century evolutionary anthropologists. Reflecting the Enlightenment notions of progress through reason, Ferguson suggested that rationality was the prime mover of history. In the process of cultural evolution people literally thought themselves out of a primitive state. Rational thought would lead to more and more reasonable institutions, customs, and subsistence practices. Hence, the civilizations of Europe were believed to have left behind "superstitions" in favor of a world view based on science. Although Ferguson believed, like Locke, that all people had the same intellectual *potential*, "savages" had not mastered that potential to the extent of Europeans. Despite its relatively complete documentation, then, Ferguson's model remained highly ethnocentric, reflecting the widespread view of German Enlightenment philosopher Gottfried von Leibniz that "this is the best of all possible worlds."

Not all Enlightenment thinkers shared Ferguson's and Leibniz' position. Jean Jacques Rousseau was bitterly critical of the pretensions of eighteenth-century aristocratic society, arguing that "everywhere man is in civilization and everywhere he is in chains." Rousseau compared Europeans unfavorably with those of the "simpler" but more forthright Native Americans, about whom he actually knew very little. Rousseau's reference to such societies was that they represented "the noble savage," a kind of honest humanity lost amidst the pretensions and hypocrisy of civilized Europeans. Rousseau tended to romanticize the "savage" and decry the "civilized," a tendency that has often been attributed to twentieth-century anthropologists as well. For Rousseau, clearly life in a state of "nature" (or savagery, as others referred to it) was preferable to the artifice of civilized existence. Yet, his remained very much of a dissenting opinion among Enlightenment social philosophers.

Also in France, Charles de Montesquieu (1689–1755) rejected the assumption of social evolution (i.e. progress) in favor of a theory directly relating human behavior to the effects of the physical environment. This was a somewhat literal reading of Locke about the influence of the environment on behavior. In the *Spirit of Laws* (1748), Montesquieu proposed a "climatic theory of government"; i.e. that geography and climate directly influence human temperament, leading to different legal systems. He argued that the heat of southern lands (such as Italy or Spain) induces both indolence and strong passions. Authoritarian governments were needed in such places to exert restraint on people. These ideas, still occasionally invoked as journalistic clichés to "explain" violence in some regions, were ridiculed in their day by some serious thinkers. One asked, "how the sun which once shone on the freedom loving Greeks is today shedding different rays on their degenerate descendants?" (D'Holbach quoted in Harris 1968: 42). It is obvious that societies go through phases of development independent of their geographical and climatic conditions, and that people living under similar geographical conditions often exhibit different cultural practices. To be fair to Montesquieu, however, this was a problem that cultural anthropologists were not able to resolve until Julian Steward and the development of cultural ecology in the mid-twentieth century. Similarly imaginative arguments were advanced by John Arbuthnot, a Scottish philosopher who argued that languages as well as national character were determined by climate. For example, northern peoples have languages with many consonants because they are afraid to open their mouths and let in cold air. On the other hand, southern peoples, who need extra ventilation, specialize in vowels!

Absurd as they might appear, there was something of merit in these climatic/ geographical explanations of behavior: the notion that customs are adaptations to local conditions. Prior to Montesquieu, philosophers had argued that laws could be evaluated with respect to universal principles, true in all times and places. Montesquieu looked at law in a more relativistic fashion, saying that a country's laws reflected the "spirit" of the community, its general sense of moral values. The appropriateness of laws could be judged only in terms of their relationship to those values, not standards that ought to apply in all places. For example, Montesquieu compared a single eighteenth-century statute in England and France concerning false testimony. In France, it was a capital offense to level a false accusation of a crime against someone, while in England, a false accusation was a minor offense. Montesquieu said that the difference could not be understood in isolation; instead, laws had to be viewed in terms of their relationship to other practices in each legal system. In France, when someone was accused they could be summoned and tortured to obtain a confession. An accusation alone could do great harm to a person, and for that reason the law against false accusations imposed a severe penalty. In England, the accused could not be tortured and was allowed to call his own witnesses. A single false accusation could do little harm, and someone could only be prosecuted for a crime from the evidence of many accusations. So the law was designed to encourage witnesses to come forward without fear. Montesquieu's point, without passing judgment on either system, was that each law was equally appropriate when looked at in conjunction with the other aspects of the legal system where it occurred. Montesquieu's *Spirit of Laws* recognized, in the terminology of modern anthropology, that culture was integrated in that cultural practices are interrelated and mutually reinforcing. Aspects of culture could not be understood in isolation, but only in context. For this reason, Emile Durkheim once wrote of Montesquieu that he was the first to understand the nature of "social facts." In a sense, he anticipated Franz Boas' doctrine of *cultural relativism*: cultural practices should be understood within the broader context of the society in which they occur.

Toward the end of the Enlightenment, the Prussian-born folklorist and philosopher Johann Gottfried von Herder (1744–1803) also anticipated one of Boas' doctrines in his recognition of the fundamental unity of all people: "notwithstanding the varieties of the human form, there is but one and the same species of man throughout the whole earth" (1968: 3). In some ways a paradoxical figure, Herder was one of the first to propose the relationship between language and world view later formalized as the Sapir–Whorf hypothesis, a recognition that led him to closely study German folklore and literature. His claim that the residents of the many then-fragmented German states constituted a distinct *Volk* (people) based on their common language and culture was to inspire more sinister advocates of German nationalism during the twentieth century (Curran 2000: 401). Yet, contrary to his latter-day interpreters who gravitated toward Nazism, Herder himself flatly rejected the ethnocentric belief that any one nation or people could claim superiority over others: "No nationality has been solely designated by God as the chosen people of the earth; above all we must seek the truth and cultivate the garden of the common good. Hence no nationality of Europe may separate itself sharply, and foolishly say, 'With us alone, with us dwells all wisdom'" (in Butler 1985: 28). As will be seen, such beliefs in human equality, commonplace among Enlightenment thinkers, were to fare poorly in the decades that followed.

Censors and fundamentalists

The year 1815 marked the end of the Napoleonic wars, an event formalized by the Congress of Vienna. The Congress brought together representatives of the victorious powers who redrew the boundaries of Europe and restored monarchies to power in France and other nations that had been allied with Napoleon. The newly (re)empowered Bourbons in France, Hapsburgs in Austria-Hungary, and Romanovs in Russia proceeded to install the machinery of nascent police states to ensure that the earlier wave of revolutionary upheaval never returned. There ensued a suppression of the ideas of the Enlightenment that had proven so powerful during the American and French revolutions. These revolutions had terrified the aristocrats and ruling classes of Europe, who (correctly) recognized the subversive potential of Enlightenment beliefs in freedom, equality, and progress. In 1824 the Hapsburgs imposed a set of repressive laws, known as the Carlsbad Decrees, that banned "subversive" publications and expelled university students and faculty who expressed political dissent. Spies and informants flourished in markets, taverns, and other settings of daily life, and answered to police eager to demonstrate their loyalty to imperial governments. Writers and composers responded by withdrawing into the inward emotional expression of romanticism, as even those who innocently associated with known dissidents came under suspicion.[3] Artists such as Stendhal, Delacroix, Pushkin, Byron, and Beethoven "were not apolitical; they internalized and sublimated revolution in an age of political repression and transformed it into what we call Romanticism" (Sachs 2010: 104).

The physical sciences and engineering, essential to industrial economies increasingly dependent on steam power, continued to make great strides during this time. Unlike technology, social thought and political expression were constrained by the twin forces of harsh political censorship in France, Austria-Hungary, and the German states (Germany was not a unified country until 1871) as well as a theological resurgence that sought to restore biblical interpretations of history and the natural world. In Britain and the United States there were intensely fundamentalist Protestant revival movements (the "Great Awakening" in the US, and the "Christian Evidences" movement in England), while in the Catholic countries of Europe the Church regained a degree of direct political power that it had not seen in centuries.

The fate of evolutionary theories during this time illustrates the extent of the conservative backlash. While social philosophers such as Adam Ferguson did not address theological issues directly, their ideas implicitly challenged biblical notions of history. Christian fundamentalists held that modern-day "primitive" societies were descended from the people who had been scattered by God after the construction of the Tower of Babel. Because all people were assumed to have been "civilized" before that event, fundamentalists argued for the doctrine of *degenerationism*, i.e. that contemporary primitives had degenerated to their present state from an earlier condition of civilization. Obviously, this belief was not compatible with an evolutionary view of historical progress. During the early nineteenth century, following the more egalitarian and democratic sentiments of the Enlightenment, there developed increasingly strenuous arguments for racial determinism, which claimed that whites enjoyed inherent advantages over blacks with regard to intelligence and potential. It should come as little surprise that such arguments were advanced at the same time that slavery was strengthened by the rapid expansion of plantation-based cotton farming in the American South. Indeed, slavery had been limited primarily to tobacco farms until the invention of the cotton gin in the 1790s made large-scale cotton production profitable.

While we conventionally attribute the theory of evolution to Charles Darwin, it is important to bear in mind that the first such theories arose many decades before the publication of *Origin of Species* in 1859. In the late eighteenth century, Jean Baptiste Lamarck (1744–1829) had proposed a theory of evolution based on the (mistaken) notion of the inheritance of acquired characteristics, as had Erasmus Darwin (1731–1802), Charles' grandfather.[4] Lamarckian evolutionary theory, as it is known, involved the idea that the traits acquired by organisms during their lifetimes would be passed on to their offspring, resulting in long-term change over generations. As we'll see, these ideas were refuted by the time of Charles Darwin, but had a powerful (and destructive) resurgence in the Soviet Union under the agronomist Trofim Lysenko.

When evolutionary ideas were first advanced in the eighteenth century, they prompted little controversy and were accepted as plausible by most educated people of the day. By the 1820s and 30s, however, these arguments were denounced by fundamentalist writers seeking to restore biblical interpretations of history and the natural world. The French royalist propagandist Joseph De Maistre labeled Ferguson's social evolutionary arguments "the mother-error of our century" while his contemporary Louis De Bonald described Lamarck's evolutionary theories to be a "monstrous hypothesis" (Harris 1968: 56–57). New monarchist governments established offices of state censors, whose job was to review all written works prior to publication and to suppress those that offended the sensibilities of rulers and the Church. One of the difficulties in reading works by philosophical commentators of the time is that they often had to be written in convoluted or coded ways in order to avert direct censorship. This was especially true for the early works of Marx, written while he still lived in Prussia, one of the most repressive of the German states. By the time Charles Darwin completed his work in the 1850s, attitudes toward evolution had so changed that he hesitated for years to publish the *Origin of Species* from a fear that he would receive a torrent of abuse from theologians and the general public.

It was from this hostile and oppressive atmosphere that modern social theory developed. The two most prominent social thinkers in the 1820s–30s, Henri Saint-Simon (1760–1825) and Auguste Comte (1798–1857), did not try to attack the fundamentalist backlash directly. Their major concern was to avoid being considered subversive. Both were highly eccentric men; some argue that they adopted this eccentricity intentionally to prove themselves politically inoffensive. For both, however, there seems to have been a genuine question of sanity: Comte was hospitalized for a period of time in an asylum, while Saint-Simon was left partially blind by a suicide attempt. Both had a series of disastrous marriages and were incapable of managing money. A student present at Comte's first and only university lecture noted that he dismissed the class after "a severe attack of cerebral derangement." His odd behavior and stream of consciousness manner of speaking prevented him from ever holding a secure academic position.

Comte's major work was a gargantuan six-volume, occasionally incoherent tome known as the *System of Positive Polity*. Comte believed that humanity had progressed through Theological and Metaphysical stages and was now entering a Positivistic stage, all of which were defined with reference to French history. (Comte appears to have been dismissive of our ability to learn anything from the study of contemporary "primitive" societies. As we'll see, later social theorists who were influenced by him, such as Durkheim, made far more references to "primitive" societies, although the quality of their evidence was often dubious.) The Theological phase was seen as preceding the Enlightenment, in which society's restrictions upon humanity were referenced to God. People blindly believed in what they were taught by traditional authority figures such as priests, kings, and parents and ancestors. By the Metaphysical phase, he referred to the problems of French society subsequent to the revolution of 1789. The Metaphysical phase is known as the "stage of investigation," because people started questioning traditional sources of authority, although little systematic scientific evidence had yet been assembled to openly challenge religious explanations of the world. In the Positivistic phase, which came into being after the failure of the revolution and fall of Napoleon, people could find solutions to social problems through scientific investigation. At this point scholars would replace supernatural explanations of the world with scientific ones based on universal laws.

Comte called for the development of a positivist science of society that would apply the same principles as those of the natural sciences to understanding social phenomena. Comte labeled this scientific discipline as "social physics," but when his rival Adolphe Quetelet began to use the same term to describe his theories of society, Comte quickly changed the name of his discipline to "sociology." This impulsive decision earned Comte the reputation of being "the father of sociology," despite the fact that his ideas were not entirely original. There was nothing new, for example, in Comte's evolutionary scheme or his suggestion that society could be understood in terms of universal laws. Saint-Simon, his former teacher, had made the same points earlier. But Comte denied all evidence of Saint-Simon's influence on him, denouncing him in the last year of Saint-Simon's life as a "depraved charlatan" while crowning himself the "pope of positivism." The selection of the term "pope" was intentional. Both Comte and Saint-Simon recognized that religion had a major influence over people's behavior. They also thought that they could gain converts to their view by promoting "Positive Religion", which was to be a religion based on science. To prevent the contamination of people's minds by non-scientific ideas, Comte proposed the contradictory idea that a dictatorship be established to preserve freedom of speech. He also compiled a list of 150 books that provided general scientific knowledge and argued that all other titles should be burned.

Notwithstanding his more bizarre claims, Comte made some lasting observations that influenced subsequent social theorists, especially Emile Durkheim. One of these was his distinction between *statics* and *dynamics* in the study of social phenomena. The study of society in its static aspects deals with "laws of coexistence," demonstrating how social institutions (e.g. religion, politics, kinship, economics) are related to one another. Comte's assumption here is that they form an integrated, harmonious whole so that change in one of these institutions would provoke corresponding adjustments in others. The study of social phenomena in their dynamic aspect provides "laws of succession," which explain how social institutions develop over time, in an evolutionary fashion. Comte's distinction is one that many succeeding sociologists and anthropologists have made. British social anthropologists in the twentieth century substituted the terms synchronic for the study of the relationship between institutions, and diachronic for the study of the evolution of institutions. Despite this change in terminology, the meanings are the same as Comte's usage.

Comte was also the first to use an *organismic* analogy, which was later adopted by Durkheim. He referred to the subject of his study as a "social organism." By this, Comte suggested that a society has diverse, interrelated structures, comparable to the structures of a body. In studying the physiology of organisms, description of the whole must precede analysis of the parts. This suggests that each structure of society plays a role in maintaining the whole entity. This also became a cornerstone of Durkheim's theory and the anthropologists influenced by him.

Finally, Comte represented a strongly *idealist* tendency in accounting for "social dynamics," or the evolution of society. By idealism, we mean a philosophical orientation holding that a society derives its basic character from its belief system, and that ideas are what drive historical change. Each of Comte's evolutionary stages of society is characterized by its dominant mode of thought. In accounting for the shift from theological, metaphysical to positivist stages of society, Comte argues that advances in reasoning bring about this change. This is little different from the ideas of Ferguson, who argued that society evolved as people increased their command of rational thought. While late-nineteenth-century anthropologists such as Morgan and Tylor largely shared this idealist perspective, as well as Comte's German contemporary Georg Hegel, a few decades later Marx was to offer a very different view of the motive forces of history.

Comte represents one tradition in the social sciences of the nineteenth century, a relatively conservative tradition that, as we'll see, continues through Durkheim and the twentieth-century functionalists. The slogan of his positivist religion was to be *Order and Progress*. This motto implied that the science of society was to be used to bring about greater stability as well as gradual but beneficial change. Comte's work actually received considerable support from the rising European bourgeoisie (unlike Saint-Simon, whose advocacy of socialism early in his life left him suspect in the eyes of potential patrons). Political and economic elites of the time saw this fledgling field of sociology as the means to perfect a society that had already made them quite prosperous. In fact, it had considerable international appeal; many Latin Americans studying in Paris during the early nineteenth century returned to their countries determined to enact Comte's ideas to "modernize" their societies, which in practice meant favoring light-skinned persons of European descent over people of native and

African descent. We even see the legacy of this on the flag of Brazil, which contains the motto "Order and Progress" (in Portuguese, *Ordem e Progresso*). If Comte was to be the founder of a conservative tradition in the social sciences, Marx was to found a radical and much more critical perspective on modern society. It is to that tradition that we turn next.

Quiz yourself

Answer True or False to each statement

1   Although prevalent in the ancient world, the notion of Plinian races died out long before the beginning of European colonization of the New World.
2   A Papal declaration of the 1500s (Sublimus Dei) declared that American Indians lacked human souls, and therefore could be freely enslaved by Europeans.
3   At birth, according to John Locke, the mind is an "empty cabinet," and is devoid of any inherent values, beliefs, or predispositions.
4   Locke's ideas acquired political significance as the ideological basis of democracy and the American and French revolutions.
5   Charles de Montesquieu advanced the idea that societies evolved from savagery to barbarism to civilization as their members increased their command of rational thought.
6   Although both Jean Baptiste Lamarck and Erasmus Darwin had advanced evolutionary theories long before Charles Darwin, such ideas became increasingly controversial and unacceptable in the first decades of the 1800s.
7   After the Napoleonic wars, most of Europe witnessed a decline in censorship and greater freedom of speech.
8   The first decades of the nineteenth century witnessed a continued decline in the influence of institutionalized religion and religious belief in England and the United States.
9   Auguste Comte coined the term "sociology" to refer to the study of society, but only did so after a competitor adopted his term "social physics" to refer to this field.
10   Comte's ideas were generally ignored by political and industrial leaders of his time, largely because of his extremely odd behavior.

4

MARX

The social origins of Marxism

The considerable support that Auguste Comte gained from the elites of European society was largely due to what was occurring in Europe in the 1840s and 50s. To industrialists of the time, the immediate future seemed to suggest anything but "order and progress." The very survival of society as they knew it seemed at stake. In the factory towns of Britain, the first rumblings of discontent with the effects of capitalism were being felt by the 1810s. These took the form of the Luddite rebellion, a widespread, spontaneous effort by unemployed craft workers to break into factories after hours and destroy the machinery that had displaced them from their jobs. In 1811 alone, more than 1,000 factory looms were destroyed surreptitiously by disgruntled former workers around Nottingham in the English Midlands, and the rebellion soon spread throughout the country. Because these acts of sabotage appeared to be uncoordinated, individual actions, they were exceedingly difficult to detect and suppress. Parliament responded with severe penalties as a form of deterrence, specifying in 1812 that anyone who destroyed factory equipment would be punished with hanging.[1] The Luddites (Figure 4.1) drew their name from their supposed leader, a shadowy unemployed weaver by the name of Ned Ludd, who, not coincidentally, was believed to live in Sherwood Forest like his rebellious predecessor Robin Hood. Police and employers searched in vain to apprehend this "mastermind," but it was likely that the character of Ludd was a fiction designed to throw the authorities off track. By the way, the term "sabotage" originated around this time and was derived from the Dutch word "sabot," referring to a kind of wooden shoe worn in Holland. Dutch factory workers found that if they inserted their shoes into their machinery they could disable or damage the equipment, in effect gaining a break during their 16-hour work day.

FIGURE 4.1 Luddites breaking machinery. In posters widely distributed during 1811, authorities offered an award of 50 guineas (£52.50) for information leading to the arrest of "evil-minded" factory saboteurs. The size of the reward was extraordinary for the time, amounting to more than an average workingman's annual income! It also offered a reward and pardon for convicted Luddites who turned in their accomplices. Yet very few were apprehended in this fashion, suggesting that the rewards offered for betraying fellow workers did not offset the sense of solidarity among them. © Mary Evans Picture Library/Alamy.

Opposition to the emerging industrial order did not just take the form of scattered acts of sabotage, but soon entered the political realm. Workers' parties began to formally organize throughout Europe during the 1820s, at a time when the large majority of working people did not have the right to vote. These parties at first petitioned for reform, seeking higher wages and shifts less than the customary 16 hours. As these demands were ignored by employers and governments, many workers' organizations adopted openly *communist* platforms, demanding an abolition of private property and its redistribution to workers. In 1848, successive workers' rebellions swept continental Europe, and were suppressed at the cost of thousands of lives.[2] It was in the same year that Karl Marx published his *Communist Manifesto*, a work that began with the words, "a specter is haunting Europe, the specter of Communism," and that ended with the appeal "Workers Unite! You have nothing to lose but your chains!" Unlike Comte, his concern was not order and progress. It was first to understand the social basis of workers' grievances. And second, it was to provide a theory of capitalism that would provide guidance to these workers' movements.

Contrary to popular belief, history has not ended

As an advocate of revolutionary social change, Karl Marx (1818–1883; Figure 4.2) is best known as a political philosopher and "the father of communism." During the Cold War, to the extent that his work was read in classrooms in the west (something that instructors could only justify to wary high school and university administrators as "knowing your enemy"), the most commonly assigned book was his relatively brief political tract *The Communist Manifesto* (1848), co-authored with his life-long collaborator Frederick Engels. While this is a powerful and lucid statement of Marx's political beliefs, it is also somewhat atypical. Since the collapse of the Soviet Union and the Eastern Bloc planned economies, Marx is much less often assigned in the classroom. Some have claimed that the fall of the USSR "disproved" the assumptions of Marxism and revealed it to be an obsolete and irrelevant belief system. The conservative commentator Francis Fukuyama (1992) pronounced the demise of the Soviet Union as the "end of history," meaning that the future belonged exclusively to the global expansion of capitalism and the liberal democracies in which it is based.

These claims are dubious on a couple of counts. It is important to keep in mind that Marx died (1883) long before the USSR came into existence (1917), so he can no more be held responsible for how his ideas were interpreted by the USSR's Lenin and Stalin than, say, Jesus Christ could be blamed for such controversial modern-day interpreters such as Pat Robertson or Jerry Falwell. Marx actually had little to say about how a communist society would operate in practice (other than brief, very general allusions in the *Communist Manifesto*); instead, most of his work took the form of a systematic critique of industrial capitalism as it existed in the nineteenth

FIGURE 4.2 Karl Marx. Courtesy of the Library of Congress.

century. Although Marx's predicted revolutions in the industrialized countries failed to come to pass (mainly because of societal reforms enacted long after his death), his fundamental analysis of capitalism remains sound. Indeed, aspects of it have been incorporated into at least one branch of mainstream economic thinking, that developing from the work of John Maynard Keynes in the 1930s.

In his 1968 volume *The Rise of Anthropological Theory*, Marvin Harris credits Marx with devising a model of society and theory of social change that can be of great utility in examining the causes of cultural similarities and differences. Harris is also critical of Marx for wedding his social analysis to a strenuous political argument, with Harris suggesting that social science should instead be "value free," or essentially apolitical. This doctrine originated with the early-twentieth-century sociologist Max Weber, who asserted that the personal values of a social researcher should not influence the collection and interpretation of data. It's worthwhile to note that the idea that social science should be "value free" was unknown in social science's infancy. Both Comte and Marx took explicitly political positions on the issues of the time. Harris finds fault with Marx for his insistence on "the unity of theory and practice," the idea that social theory should be used to guide political change.

This misrepresents the Marxist position on "value free" social science. Marxists would argue that the very choice of a problem for investigation reflects the politics (if you will, values) of the investigator. A Marxist would, for example, be interested in class conflict, whereas a Durkheimian might look at sources of cooperation and solidarity in society. Rejecting value free science has nothing to do, as Harris seems to imply, with dishonesty in the gathering or representation of evidence. Rather, it means that our political and other preferences inevitably influence what it is that we study and the kind of data we collect. More critically, knowledge is not seen as an end in itself, but as a guide to action to transform society. Marx would have been appalled to see modern-day scholars attempting to confine his ideas to the classroom. As he once famously wrote, "Philosophers have only interpreted the world; *the point, however, is to change it!*" (1977c: 158).

Like many German intellectuals of his generation, Marx had been schooled as a young man in the philosophy of Georg W.F. Hegel (1770–1831). Many modern readers find Hegel impenetrable, although his influence in Continental philosophy of the early 1800s cannot be overstated. In schematic terms, Hegel viewed history as the continuous unfolding of ideas. The major contrast between his view of the evolution of ideas and that of Comte is that Hegel considered this evolution to be *dialectical*. Historical change for Hegel occurs through contradictions in that each historical epoch also contains "the seeds of its destruction." Hegel believed that the very assertion of any proposition (thesis) would lead to the expression of its opposite (antithesis). From the struggle between thesis and antithesis a new proposition (synthesis) would emerge. Each historical epoch, Hegel said, was characterized by a *Geist* ("spirit"), or prevailing attitude. During the late eighteenth century, intellectuals in Europe regarded theirs as an "age of reason," in which rational thought was believed to guide human behavior. That provoked the counter-reaction of *romanticism* in literature, music, and art of the early nineteenth century, which indulged emotional extremes and uninhibited expression. In historical terms, Hegel identified the French revolution as the "negation" of the monarchy of Louis XVI, resulting in the "synthesis" of Napoleon's Empire.[3] By the 1840s, Marx said that he "stood Hegel on his head," retaining the notion of dialectical change while denying Hegel's idealism as a motor of historical movement. For Marx, the driving force of history does not consist of a sequence and struggle of ideas but of the economic arrangements whereby people satisfy their material needs. Each of these "modes of production" contains within it fatal contradictions, generally involving class struggle, that would lead to the emergence of another, successive economic arrangement. Only with the eventual emergence of a truly classless society (communism) would the process of dialectical change finally come to an end; hence, communism represents the endpoint of historical change.

Why capitalism is doomed, or maybe not

The dialectical view of history became integral to Marx's view of capitalist society. Marx argued that like all economic arrangements that preceded it, capitalism contained *contradictions* that would result in its destruction. As outlined below, the fundamental contradiction in capitalism pointed out by Marx arises between production and consumption in that the productive capacity of society regularly exceeds the capacity of its members to consume the goods that they produced. Capitalism would experience, Marx predicted, ever greater "crises" that would yield ever greater misery and poverty for the large majority who worked for wages for a living. Eventually, workers would refuse to accept the conditions to which they had been subjected, rising up to demand social control over what had been private property.

What do we mean by capitalism? The specific economic arrangements associated with this mode of production originated in northern Europe in the late sixteenth century. Capitalism is based on the production of commodities not for use by those who produce them, but for sale at a profit. Under capitalism, those who provide the labor for the production of commodities own or control no productive resources ("the means of production": factories, mines, farms, stores) of their own, and therefore must sell their labor for wages to the owners of such resources. Hence, in capitalist society, there are two basic social classes: the owners of the "means of production" (employers or the bourgeoisie) and the large majority of society's members (wage workers or the *proletariat*). Finally, Marx points out that the relationship between bourgeoisie and proletariat is based on economic exploitation.

Marx doesn't use the term exploitation in an arbitrary or propagandistic sense; rather, he says that it is inherent in the payment of wages for labor. Marx's argument was developed in his three-volume opus *Capital*, first published in 1867. Capitalists derive profit from the production and sale of goods produced by wage laborers who own no property of their own (that is, property that will bring them income). On the surface, it appears that the paying of wages is an equivalent exchange of money for labor. We see this idea expressed in notions such as "an honest day's work for an honest day's wage." But Marx argues that capitalist profit is based on *surplus value*;

that is, value provided by the worker to the capitalist in excess of what he or she is paid. If the capitalist is to remain in business, he must pay each worker less than the value of his or her labor. The worker may produce $600 worth of furniture every day, but is only paid $80 for his work. Much of this difference is surplus value; in effect it is labor provided by the worker free of charge to the capitalist. This is what Marx means by *exploitation*; not that it involves injustice or bad treatment, but that the capitalist must necessarily pay the worker less than the value of his labor. Hence, even a "good" employer who appears to treat his workers with dignity and affords them benefits still exploits them in the sense of paying less than what their labor is fully worth. To be more precise, Marx talked about three components of the value (v) of what is produced by a worker in a single day. There is constant capital (cc), which are the non-wage costs of production (raw materials, the cost of production facilities, energy, depreciation); there is variable capital (vc, the wages paid for the labor involved in a given volume of production); and there is surplus value: $sv = v - (cc + vc)$.

How does this wage relationship create "contradictions" that will destroy capitalism? In order to compete with one another to sell their goods, capitalists constantly look for ways to lower the cost of production and therefore the price of their goods. This necessarily involves reducing one of the three components of the price of a good (cc, vc, or sv). Marx argues that invariably the component that comes under the greatest pressure for reduction is vc (wages), since the costs of cc (raw material and energy) are relatively inflexible and reducing sv (surplus value) means reducing the capitalist's own profit. Reducing vc can be done through employing machinery, which displaces labor; this incessant competition fueling technological innovation was what Marx admired about capitalism as its most "progressive aspect." Capitalists also reduce vc through directly lowering the wages of their workers. In fact, just to survive in the market capitalists are forced to employ as much machinery and lower wages to the same point as other manufacturers of the same kind of item. On the one hand the use of machinery increases the productivity of labor, causing more goods to be produced. On the other hand, the lowering of wages and displacement of workers by machines lowers the purchasing power of workers.

Let's say you are employed in a furniture factory; to compete with other factories producing similar goods the owner pays you the federal minimum wage, currently $7.25 per hour. (Bear in mind that at the time that Marx wrote, there was no legally mandated minimum wage. His argument was that competition among capitalists led them to reduce wages to the point of mere subsistence. I leave it up to you to decide whether you can survive on today's legal minimum.) After you buy your groceries and pay your rent, will you be able to purchase any of the furniture that you manufacture? Then imagine this happening throughout the economy as all capitalists seek to out-compete one another by lowering wage costs. The chief contradiction, as Marx summed it up was, "to each capitalist, the total mass of all workers, with the exception of his own workers, appear not as workers, but as consumers, possessors of exchange values (wages), money, which they exchange for his commodity" (1993: 419).

When wages throughout the economy are suppressed essentially to subsistence levels, workers are unable to purchase the goods that they produce. Because competition induces capitalists to employ more machinery, larger and larger volumes of goods are produced even as workers' purchasing power declines. The result is growing inventories of unsold goods, declining sales and profits, culminating in the lay off of still more workers and eventual closure of factories. The economy enters a crisis of declining consumption and widening unemployment. Capitalism's "seeds of destruction" are present in the deepening misery of the working class. Further, as the labor process is increasingly based on production using machinery, the need for skilled labor diminishes as all workers are reduced to the same minimal skill: that required to simply operate a machine. A working class once differentiated by differing levels of skill, status, and pay is increasingly homogenized by skill and uniformly impoverished. The increasingly complex division of labor in industrial capitalism, in which workers perform one menial task over and over again throughout the day (or even their entire working lifetime) causes *alienation*, as workers no longer identify with or feel pride in the products of their labor (as any of you who have ever worked in mass production—whether of automobiles or hamburgers—can identify). Misery among workers builds in tandem with their class consciousness, until it reaches the point where revolutionary upheaval occurs. Workers organize themselves and overthrow the political system based on capitalist private property.

Why didn't this happen, at least in most countries? Marx expected revolutionary change to take place in the most developed industrial economies rather than in the relatively undeveloped economy of Russia, where it did occur in 1917. The fact that the socialist revolution as Marx predicted it did not take place is by no means a repudiation of Marx's analysis of capitalism. Not even conservative economists can dispute the tendencies toward crisis inherent in capitalism, a tendency that was first noted by Marx (mainstream economists call this not a "crisis" but a "business cycle" of expansion and contraction). What Marx failed to see was that the workers' movements in which he participated would in the end be partly successful. That is, many of the reforms that they demanded, as in union representation leading to higher wages, social security, and welfare measures, would improve the living conditions of the working class.

In 1932, when Franklin Delano Roosevelt (Figure 4.3) was elected president, the US and other industrialized economies were experiencing the most severe economic crisis in recent history.[4] Unemployment was estimated at over 30 percent, the Gross Domestic Product had declined about 35 percent since the stock market crash in 1929, and millions of people eked by with no visible means of support other than occasional charity. To millions more, the huge disparities of wealth that had accrued in the 1920s and the simultaneous existence of poverty and hunger in the midst of the world's most productive economy only illustrated the irrationality of the capitalist system. Membership in the Communist Party USA, other leftist parties, or "communist front" organizations reached historic highs. Many leaders in industry and government feared that Marx's predictions of an impending revolution were likely to come true. Roosevelt, however, announced a series of reforms that he

FIGURE 4.3   Franklin Delano Roosevelt. Courtesy of the Library of Congress.

said would "save capitalism from the capitalists." Broadly defined as the New Deal, Roosevelt's reforms fundamentally altered the way capitalism operated. A man of privileged background who saved capitalists despite the best efforts of capitalists themselves, Roosevelt was hated by big business, which saw him as a traitor to his class. Indeed, some conspired with leaders of the armed forces to overthrow him in a military coup in 1934, an effort that was exposed and put down by Marine General Smedley Butler. Despite these threats, FDR was stalwart in defending the New Deal from its conservative critics: "They hate me, and I welcome their hatred."

Among the changes championed by the Roosevelt administration was federal protection of the right of workers to organize unions. Having unionized the largest manufacturing industries (most of the automobile manufacturers, with the exception of Ford) by the mid-1930s, organized labor was able to secure higher wages for workers, increased benefits, and shorter hours, all of which reduced the appeal of more radical responses to economic crisis. During this time, unions also came under pressure by government and employers to purge their leadership ranks of known Communists; in effect, many employers told their workers, "we'll let you have unions if you purge them of the Reds." The federal government introduced Social Security retirement and disability benefits, so that workers could both look forward to old age security and the possibility of income if they were injured or otherwise unable to work (the notion of "retirement" for most workers was largely unknown before this time; in most cases, people worked until they physically were no longer able to).

Unemployment insurance provided short-term support for those who lost their jobs. And the Works Project Administration and Civilian Conservation Corps absorbed about 3.5 million unemployed people in public sector projects ranging from constructing national park facilities and roads to recording folklore and painting post office murals. The Federal Housing Authority (FHA) guaranteed loans on 30-year mortgages with low down payments. This was a revolutionary development as prior to this time, mortgages were short-term and a prospective home buyer had to put down about *half* of the total purchase price of a home. In effect, the FHA created a nation of homeowners out of what had been a nation of renters. In addition, the government adopted policies adjusting the interest rates at which banks could make loans; during an economic downturn, interest rates are lowered to increase the availability of credit, in turn stimulating the purchase of consumer goods and housing. These were the policies that led many working people to redefine themselves from "workers" to "middle class"; indeed, the very notion that ours is a middle class society in which the large majority of people are neither very poor nor very rich owes itself to the New Deal.

Finally, following the lead of Henry Ford during the 1920s, some employers recognized their own long-term self-interest in policies that supported higher wages for their workers. Ford introduced the $5 per day wage for his workers at a time when most auto workers earned only about a third of that amount. Ford did this not because he was a nice guy; in fact, he hated unions, created a "Sociology Department" that intervened in the lives of his workers, and employed thugs who broke the legs (and worse) of labor organizers. Ford Motor Company was the last major US auto manufacturer to recognize unions. But Ford understood that his policy of raising wages rather than suppressing them greatly reduced turnover and created a ready market for his Model T. This process of *Fordism*—linking increases in wages to increased labor productivity—allowed workers to buy back a portion of the goods they consumed. It also gave them a stake in the system: however primitive, a Model T automobile (as Ford himself joked, it was available in any color as long as it was black) brought about a significant change in its owner's outlook. It signaled that a working man was now a member of the so-called "middle class" and enjoyed a level of prosperity undreamed of in, say, Stalin's Russia, the "worker's paradise" upheld by the CP USA. Fordism, combined with New Deal reforms, not only brought the Depression to an end, but probably saved capitalism from the fate that Marx had predicted for it in the previous century.[5]

All of these represent reforms that lessened the appeal of revolution to industrial workers in the US and elsewhere, and were developments that Marx could not have foreseen in the nineteenth century. Yet, Marx did recognize toward the end of his life that his predictions of an increasingly homogeneous and cohesive working class with a sense of class consciousness may have been unrealistic, given the divisions that exist among working people (we'll revisit this argument later). Because Marx is mostly known for his analysis of capitalism, many anthropologists in the past believed that his work was of limited relevance to anthropology, which has traditionally focused on small-scale, non-industrialized societies. In actuality, Marx's materialist perspective on society provides a powerful tool for understanding the origins of cultural practices. It is this theory, known as *dialectical materialism*, to which we turn next.

The dialectical materialist birthday cake

During much of the twentieth century, most anthropologists assumed that they had little to gain from studying Marx. Nearly all of his writing focused on industrial capitalist societies, while anthropologists typically studied non-capitalist societies. This neglect by anthropologists overlooks the fact that Marx developed a social theory that aspires to universal applicability, that of dialectical materialism. Like other social scientists, Marx delineated the basic institutions of society (economy, politics, kinship, religion, etc.). Unlike many others, he argued that *the material basis* of society stands in a determinant relationship to these other institutions. *Dialectical materialism holds that a society derives its basic character from its economic institutions.* In this sense, he inverted Hegel's formulation that characterized societies by their dominant ideas, or "spirit" (as Marx said, "it is not the consciousness of man that determines his social existence, but his social existence that determines his consciousness").

Marx distinguished three levels in any society:

* *Ideology:* Values, religion, philosophy, aesthetics, folklore (think of this as society's belief system)
* *Juridico-political arrangements:* Politics, social structure, kinship, gender (think of these as the social relationships between people)
* *Mode of production* consisting of two components:
  a) *Social relations of production:* patterns of property ownership, organization of work
  b) *Forces of production:* technology, resources, and knowledge of how to use them.

I have come to think of this as Marx's "birthday cake" model of society, with each set of institutions forming a "layer" that rests upon those institutions below it. The lowest layer (and for Marxists, the tastiest and most important) is the Mode of Production. In reality, Marxists don't talk about the "birthday cake" analogy, but they do sometimes distinguish between the "base" of society (its *mode of production*) and its "superstructure" (*ideology* and *juridico-political arrangements*). Marx states that every society derives its general character from its mode of production. A mode of production is the way that members of a society satisfy their material needs and socially distribute the products of their labor. It consists on the one hand of the *forces of production*, or the technology and knowledge that a society employs in production. It also consists of the *relations of production*, or the social relationships existing between people in the process of production. This is not just how people join together to produce something (for example, whether agriculturalists work individually on a family-run farm or many families work together cooperatively). The relations of production also include the relationship between people and the productive resources that they use. If one individual owns all of the resources that everyone else depends on, this will presuppose different relations of production than if all people owned equal shares of those resources.

The second aspect of Marx's work is how the mode of production is related to the rest of society. Marxist theory involves a distinction between the economic, social,

BOX 4.1 "First the grub, then comes culture"

Bertolt Brecht (Figure 4.4) memorably expressed the doctrine of philosophical materialism when he quipped, "Zuerst das Fressen, dann kommt die Kultur"; translated, this means "First the grub, then comes culture." Brecht's use of a vulgar term for food in this quote suggests that people must attend to their basic, crude biological needs before they can develop elaborate or refined cultural practices.

Brecht provided the words, and Kurt Weill the music, to the often-performed song "Mack the Knife" from the 1928 musical, *The Threepenny Opera* (originally *Die Dreigroschenoper*). The musical centers on the amoral exploits of a Victorian anti-hero Macheath ("What is the robbing of a bank compared to the founding of a bank?"), but Brecht's political commentary is based in the observation of Polly, Macheath's wife, that "the law was made for one thing alone, for the exploitation of those who don't understand it, or are prevented by naked misery from obeying it." Brecht's 1939 anti-war tragedy *Mother Courage and her Children* inspired the medical anthropologist Paul Farmer (2008) to tally the costs of the Iraq war as reflected in the experience of a Haitian refugee and her son who joined the US Marines. Brecht's life epitomized the repeated dislocations faced by artists and writers espousing Marxist politics in Europe and the United States during the mid-twentieth century.

Brecht had been closely associated with communist politics in 1920s Germany and so was forced to flee after the Nazis came to power in 1933,

FIGURE 4.4 German Marxist playwright Bertolt Brecht (1898–1956), author of *The Threepenny Opera, The Rise and Fall of the City of Mahagonny, Mother Courage and Her Children* and many other politically provocative plays. © Mary Evans Picture Library/Alamy.

when one of Hitler's first acts was to send known communists and socialists to concentration camps. The Nazis immediately banned the performance of Brecht's plays, which had enjoyed considerable popularity in Germany during the late 1920s and early 30s. By 1941 Brecht had arrived in Hollywood, where he worked as a screenwriter. After the onset of the Cold War in the late 1940s, however, he was blacklisted from working in the entertainment industry and eventually left the United States as a result of his inability to find work.

In 1947, Brecht and 41 other writers and directors were summoned to Washington DC by the congressional House Un-American Affairs Committee (HUAC) to testify about communists working in the movie industry. While ten of those subpoenaed refused to testify (the so-called "Hollywood Ten," who were prosecuted for contempt of Congress as a result), Brecht opted to appear before the Committee. Although those who refused to collaborate were critical of Brecht's willingness to testify, as a witness he proved distinctly, even intentionally, unhelpful. He arrived wearing his trademark overalls and delivered his testimony in broken English and German, which his translator rendered in a way that neither he nor the Committee members could understand. He also waved around a large stinky cigar that sickened a number of people in the room. Two years later, after fruitlessly seeking work in Hollywood, he left the US for the German Democratic Republic (East Germany), where he was received as a hero. There he founded a theater company under that country's pro-Soviet communist government. Brecht died in East Berlin in 1956.

and ideological levels of society. Each mode of production has corresponding social relationships (particularly political relations) and ideologies (in the form of aesthetic, religious, and ethical beliefs). These relationships and ideas correspond to the society's material basis in that they order and sanction the relationships involved in production. For example, a hunter–gatherer society in which people maintain equal access to communally–held resources is likely to have an egalitarian political structure without powerful chiefs or leaders. Dialectical materialism would also predict that it has a system of morals and folklore that stress cooperation and equality rather than competition and meritocratic rewards. A society whose mode of production involves payment of tribute to a powerful chief will exhibit political and ideological characteristics that sanction those economic relationships, that is, that support the chief's power. He may be seen as supernaturally powerful or even god–like, suggesting that he has a moral right to demand political loyalty and tribute. Marx noted, for example, that the religious doctrine of the "divine right of kings" corresponded to more general economic and political relationships in the European Middle Ages. This doctrine was the notion that kings received their right to rule directly from God, and that therefore the political economic relations order was supernaturally sanctioned; in Engels' words, "the Church gave a religious consecration to the secular feudal state" (Marx and Engels 1957: 267).[6] It is easy to see how this would support economic relations in which rulers claimed a portion of the production of peasants. According to dialectical materialism, then, the relationships and beliefs found in the juridico–political and ideological levels of society are determined by a society's mode of production.[7] Dialectical materialism in this sense is a powerful theoretical tool for helping to understand cultural similarities and differences.

Marx also proposed an evolutionary theory of society, one referred to as *historical materialism*. Unlike the idealist views of Enlightenment philosophers, Marx held that the cause of all historical movement is to be found in society's material base; as changes occur in the mode of production with regard to technology and social relations of production, corresponding changes occur at the socio-political and ideological levels. His scheme was that "primitive communism" (i.e. hunting-gathering societies, which even at the time of Marx were known to have little private property or social ranking) was replaced by "ancient" modes of production based on slavery (here he is thinking of the Greco-Roman world), then by *feudalism*, then *capitalism*. Each of these modes eventually collapses due to contradictions within it (the dialectical aspect of his thinking), to be replaced by a new, more complex mode of production. Capitalism, according to Marx, has its progressive elements, notably the technological innovation that stems from competition between capitalists, but it, too, would eventually succumb to internal contradictions.

Capitalism would give rise to proletarian class consciousness and organization, culminating in a revolutionary seizure of the state and a transition to *socialism*, in which the state ruled on behalf of workers' class interests. As we'll see below, Marx regarded the state as an instrument of power in the hands of society's dominant classes; indeed, from the Marxist perspective the state first comes into existence in order to bolster and defend the interests of a dominant class against those whom they exploit. Under capitalism, the state generally rules on behalf of the interests of the bourgeoisie. Under socialism, the state continues to exist, but is supposed, at least in theory, to be controlled by the working class.[8] "Building socialism" requires that the state exercise its power on behalf of workers and also guard against the possibility of a bourgeois counter-revolution. Eventually, the need for state intervention of this kind (mainly to repress latent capitalist interests) would fade as conflict between classes disappeared. The state would "wither away" as now unnecessary and be replaced by *communism*, a classless social order governed by the maxim "from each according to his abilities to each according to his needs." Note that none of the so-called "communist" societies around the globe actually described themselves as having attained this communist state. Societies as diverse as the USSR, the German Democratic Republic, Cuba, China, and North Korea have described themselves as being in the transitional socialist stage of development.[9] Orthodox Marxists still use Marx's original evolutionary scheme. Western neo-Marxists, such as the anthropologist Eric Wolf, have renamed these stages based on more current anthropological thinking. Wolf, in his modern classic *Europe and the People without History* (1982), distinguishes between *kin-ordered*, *tributary*, and *capitalist* modes of production.

What prevented revolution?

What keeps people from challenging a social order that oppresses them? In 1848 (the year of the Communist Manifesto) Marx predicted an impending workers' revolution that would seize capitalist-owned industries and would turn them to social uses. By the end of his life (1883), Marx recognized that numerous impediments stood in the way of a successful revolution. He devoted much effort to examining this failure of his earlier predictions.

Primary among the forces standing in the way of revolution is the capitalist state. In dialectical materialism, political arrangements and ideologies develop as means of reproducing the material relationships within the mode of production. Marx described the state in capitalist society as "a committee for arranging the needs of the bourgeoisie." The primary role of the state in capitalism was to impose the interests of capitalists over society at large: the state defended private property (both legally and by force) and typically took the side of the powerful in disputes between capitalists and workers. That meant that workers who challenged the status quo would face often brutal repression by forces of the state (e.g. police and military called in to break up strikes or disrupt meetings). To an extent, then, Marx argued that the repressive apparatus of the state was deployed to prevent uprisings by striking fear into would-be revolutionaries and by punishing those who actively challenged capitalist property. More recent neo-Marxist theorists have suggested that under capitalism, the state actually has some autonomy from direct capitalist control. Nicos Poulantzas (1978), for example, contends that capitalists are too diverse to act in a concerted fashion politically. They benefit, however, from a moderately autonomous state which intervenes in the economy (a là the New Deal, for example) to manage its periodic crises in order to maintain the general outlines of a capitalist economy.

Marx also devoted attention to the role of ideology in class-based societies as a prime means of how ruling classes maintain power. Marx wrote, "The class which has the means of material production at its disposal, has control at the same time over the means of intellectual production, so that thereby…the ideas of those who lack the means of intellectual production are subject to it" (1977b: 178). Hence, the newspapers and other media, educational institutions, organized religion, and all other institutions essentially promulgate the values of capitalist society, effectively preventing subordinate classes from clearly seeing the conditions of their existence. And of course this mystification inhibits people from doing anything to change those conditions. For example, the laborer thinks that she receives an honest day's pay for an honest day's work. She does not see that she is working free of charge for the capitalist for the majority of her workday. The idea that she is selling her labor at value prevents her questioning the conditions under which she works.

The Italian communist Antonio Gramsci (1891–1937) went further and argued that ideology was the primary means by which dominant classes maintained their control over capitalist society, and that in only extreme instances did capitalists have to resort to the brute force of the state. In his *Prison Notebooks* (1971), compiled while he was imprisoned by Mussolini's fascist government between 1929 and 1935,

Gramsci coined the term *hegemony* to refer to such ideological control. Hegemonic ideologies represent an existing social order as natural or desirable, thereby preventing people from challenging the political, economic, and social conditions of their lives. For example, the belief that US society is predominately middle class is hegemonic in that it suggests that most people have a stake in maintaining the political and economic status quo. But do all people really benefit from existing economic arrangements? Data on wealth distribution in the US suggest that the top 1 percent of the population controls nearly 50 percent of the country's wealth; the next 19 percent controls 46 percent of its wealth, and the bottom 80 percent controls just 6 percent. In contrast to our view of the US as a "middle class" society, our society's wealth distribution is more uneven than that of India.

How does this convergence between dominant class interests and dominant ideas of a certain epoch take place? Marx argues that dominant classes control the access of subordinate groups to ideas. They do this through control of wealth and the political process, which in turn allows them disproportionate control of educational institutions and the media. Religious, national, gender, and racial prejudices also ultimately benefit the dominant classes by keeping workers divided among themselves. In a letter written in 1870, Marx recognized that such divisions played a critical role in preventing English workingmen from seeing common cause with the Irish immigrants beside whom they labored (Figure 4.5):

> Every industrial and commercial center in England now possesses a working class divided into two hostile camps, English proletarians and Irish proletarians. The ordinary English worker hates the Irish worker as a competitor who lowers his standard of life. In relation to the Irish worker he feels himself a member of the ruling nation and so turns himself into a tool of the aristocrats and capitalists of his country against Ireland, thus strengthening their domination over himself. He cherishes religious, social and national prejudices against the Irish worker. His attitude towards him is much the same as that of the "poor whites" to the "niggers" [*sic*] in the former slave states of the U.S.A...
>
> This antagonism is artificially kept alive and intensified by the press, the pulpit, the comic papers, in short, by all the means at the disposal of the ruling classes. This antagonism is the secret of the impotence of the English working class, despite its organization. It is the secret by which the capitalist class maintains its power. And that class is fully aware of it.
>
> (1977d, original 1870: 591)

This argument is a powerful one, if we look beyond Marx's archaic and offensive language. Anthropologists and others have examined numerous contexts in which ethnic, racial, linguistic, and gender differences within the work force are manipulated in ways that heighten worker disunity and thereby prevent strikes, unionization or other challenges to employer prerogatives (see, for example, Bourgois 1989 and Moberg 1996 for ethnographic examinations of this process in industrial agriculture). Sociologists Gordon, Edwards, and Reich (1982) have used

THE USUAL IRISH WAY OF DOING THINGS.

FIGURE 4.5 "The Usual Irish Way of Doing Things" cartoon ca. 1871. During the nineteenth century the Irish were reviled in both Britain and America, and cartoon portrayals of them emphasized their supposed indolence, drunkenness, and violence. This US cartoon of the 1870s is typical of this genre, and illustrates Marx's contention that the newspapers and other media of the day fostered anti-Irish prejudice. Interestingly, they were usually portrayed as non-white in appearance, and in the antebellum Southern states were even considered "colored," a second-class legal category that included free blacks. © CORBIS.

this "class segmentation theory" to examine disparities within the contemporary US work force. Their data show that those industries exhibiting the greatest wage disparities by race also have lower average wages than more ethnically egalitarian industries. In a sense, to employ Gramsci's terminology, these data would suggest that racial superiority is a hegemonic ideology that operates to the detriment of all workers, regardless of race.

Marx and religion: understanding opium

When mentioning ideology in capitalist society, many commentators focus on a *famous* reference by Marx to religion as "the opium of the people." This expression is usually presented out of its broader context (indeed, you almost *never* see even the entire sentence from which it is extracted). This out-of-context reading is usually interpreted to suggest that Marx disparaged religion as a kind of "false consciousness" that prevents people from clearly understanding their social circumstances or working to change them. Commentators eager to assert the supposed incompatibility between Marxism and religion then support their misreading of Marx's position with the fact that socialist societies, ranging from the USSR to China, have persecuted individuals who profess some kind of religious affiliation. I would argue instead that these societies persecuted members of churches because the ruling Communist parties viewed churches or any other independent segment of civil society as a possible rival for peoples' loyalties, rather than because of anything that Marx had said about religious consciousness. Religious people were persecuted in these totalitarian societies for the same reason that members of independent trade unions, political parties or human rights groups were also persecuted. As evidence, I would point out that the government of China has long recognized official, state-sanctioned churches whose members may worship without interference. If, however, you attempt to engage in religious activity outside of these "acceptable" realms (for example, attending a Roman Catholic rather than state-sanctioned Catholic Church), you are almost certain to be prosecuted. Here, by the way, is the complete quote by Marx, which reveals a more nuanced attitude toward belief than a non-contextual reading would suggest: "Religious suffering is at the same time an expression of real suffering and a protest against real suffering. Religion is the sigh of the oppressed creature, the feeling of a heartless world, and the soul of soulless circumstances; it is the opium of the people" (1977e: 64).

Much of the misinterpretation of this passage, I think, actually resides in how our popular view of opium has changed since Marx wrote those words. While opium today is seen as a mind-altering substance because it is the source of heroin, in the pre-aspirin, pre-Tylenol, pre-Ibuprofen time of Marx, opium was virtually the only medication available to suppress pain. What Marx is saying, to my mind, is that religion is a source of *solace* in a society otherwise governed by capitalist values of efficiency, competition, and profit, a much less negative assessment of religious faith than what is usually attributed to him. Of course, the non-contextual view of this quote that dismisses religion as simply "false consciousness" served well the political purposes of the twentieth-century dictatorships established in Marx's name. To my mind, then, there is an interesting point of convergence between conservative thinkers who misinterpret Marx in order to caricature his views on religion, and the Leninist and Stalinist leaders who do the same in order to consolidate their political control over society.

The tens of millions of people who identify with the movement known as liberation theology, a variant of Christianity particularly prominent in the developing world, believe that there is no incompatibility between social justice (or socialism) and faith. Rather, liberation theology suggests that the central message of both the Old and New Testaments was one of a radical "preferential option for the poor," meaning that people of faith should act both in charity and to effect political change that alleviates the suffering of the oppressed. As the Vatican's Advisor for Economic Affairs recently stated, "Let's start by honestly recognizing that the spirit of capitalism doesn't agree with that of the Gospel. The heart of Christianity is love for others. The nucleus of capitalism, rather, is competition, which is the opposite of love" (Delaney 2009). I think you would search in vain throughout Marx's published work for references to love, but I also think this is a sentiment he probably would agree with. While organized religion has often been suppressed in "communist" countries, liberation theology is often deemed so threatening to the prevailing power and economic interests in developing countries that its advocates have also been persecuted or killed. This is precisely because its tenets call upon people of faith to struggle for greater social justice and equality.

Although ideology can impair the ability of people to understand the conditions of their existence, that doesn't mean that subordinate groups are doomed to continued exploitation. This is where the dialectic enters into Marx's analysis. People are the victims of social circumstances only as long as they fail to understand them. When ideology is plainly contradicted by the conditions that people experience in their day-to-day lives, that ideology may lose its grip over human action. It is at that point that the oppressed become agents of their own destiny. People are the products of their history in that they inherit traditions that constrain their vision and restrict their choices. But they also can make history to their benefit once they see through the mystifying ideologies that they inherit. Indeed, the spontaneous uprising that began on Wall Street in October, 2011, and then spread to local "Occupy" movements around the world is one such illustration of this process, reflecting a growing public indignation at neoliberal policies that have produced widening wealth disparities in most of the industrialized world in recent decades.

In the past, Marx was often ignored by many anthropologists who viewed his preoccupation with capitalism as irrelevant, given the kinds of societies that anthropologists traditionally studied. But quite a few others claimed that Marx's social theory was worthy of scholarly interest, although many paid a price for saying so. In the 1950s, even scholars who did not identify themselves as Marxists found themselves the subject of investigations if they taught Marx in their classrooms or believed that his theories of society merited attention. David Price's 2004 book *Threatening Anthropology: McCarthyism and the FBI's Surveillance of Activist Anthropologists* reveals that the FBI maintained extensive records throughout the 1950s and early 1960s on dozens of anthropologists who had either discussed Marx in the classroom or engaged in political activism considered to be "leftist" in nature. Under those circumstances, it is little surprise that many scholars retreated to the safe confines of "value free" social science. We'll examine the fate of such activist anthropologists during the Cold War in a later chapter.

Quiz yourself

Answer True or False to each statement

1   English industrialists and government leaders found it difficult to suppress the Luddite rebellion because rebels carried out uncoordinated, individual acts of sabotage against factory machinery.
2   In "standing Hegel on his head," Marx rejected the dialectical notion of change through contradiction while advancing the idea that historical change occurs at the level of ideas and beliefs.

3   Because Marx was an active participant in the Russian revolution of 1917, it can be said that the collapse of the Soviet Union effectively repudiates and refutes Marx's ideas.

4   For Marx, exploitation under capitalism meant that all employers treat their workers with abuse or injustice.

5   According to Marx, the central contradiction in capitalism exists between consumption and production. Workers produce more than they are able to consume, leading to factory closures, rising unemployment, and deepening poverty.

6   According to Marx, class consciousness among workers would occur as skill differences among them are reduced to the least common denominator (the ability to operate machinery), and as employers reduce wages in the pursuit of lowered production costs.

7   The New Deal reforms introduced by FDR were strongly supported by US business leaders as a means of preserving the basic outlines of a capitalist economy.

8   According to dialectical materialism, a society's belief systems (ideology) and social relations (juridico–political structure) derive their basic character from that society's mode of production, or material base.

9   According to Marx's evolutionary scheme, under communism conflicts between social classes would finally disappear, leading the state to "wither away" as unnecessary.

10 Hegemony refers to a condition in which the dominant beliefs in a society represent that social order as "right" or natural, and therefore prevent people from challenging the political, economic and social conditions of their lives.

5

DURKHEIM AND WEBER

Solidarity: Durkheim's answer to Marx

The Marxist tradition in social theory examined in Chapter 4 continues today in the so-called *conflict theory* of sociology, which examines how the divergent interests of social groups (mostly social classes) led to significant conflicts in society. In mid- to late-twentieth-century anthropology, as we'll see, Marxism inspired a variety of materialist perspectives that have sought to understand the origins of cultural practices in terms of the material conditions of life. The other tradition of nineteenth-century thought, a conservative tradition originating with Comte, developed in reaction to Marx by proposing an alternative conception of modern society. The major inheritor of Comte's sociology was his French compatriot Emile Durkheim (1858–1917; Figure 5.1).

Unlike Marx, Durkheim was concerned primarily with how societies could maintain their integrity and coherence in the modern era, when a shared religious and ethnic identity among all of society's members could no longer be assumed. Durkheim had read Comte and adopted from him his positivism and use of the organismic analogy, but he also set out to answer one of Comte's concerns about the nature of industrial society. While stating that the goal of social science should be to insure *order and progress*, Comte had also expressed worry about the possibly corrosive effects of the growing division of labor in industrial society. If people occupied many different roles it might be expected that society's moral consensus would fray. The effect would be similar to what Marx had predicted, with an industrializing society creating conflicts that would endanger that social order itself.

Whereas the concern of Marx was to identify what would cause modern society to fly apart, Durkheim attempted to show why it would hold together. In this respect, his response to Comte could also be considered a conservative rejoinder to the arguments put forth by Marx. Most importantly, Durkheim's assumption that

FIGURE 5.1   Emile Durkheim. The seven generations of eldest sons to precede him in his family had all become rabbis. © Bettmann/CORBIS.

societies will tend toward stability is one that was acquired by all anthropologists who were influenced by him. This is particularly true of the twentieth-century British *structural functionalists*, who applied Durkheim's theory to the analysis of small-scale societies in Britain's colonial holdings in Africa, Asia, and the Pacific.

In his first major work, Durkheim attempted to show why the dire predictions of social breakdown in industrial society would not come to pass. This work was *The Division of Labor in Society* (1933, orig. 1893), an outgrowth of his doctoral dissertation. In it he argued that the division of labor in industrial society actually created a superior form of "social solidarity" or cohesion. In "undifferentiated" (i.e. pre-industrial) societies, people experienced "mechanical solidarity." This is cohesion among individuals because of their overall similarity in activities and responsibilities. Group solidarity is intense because people are alike in most respects. Durkheim cited the Australian aborigines as an example of a society organized on the basis of mechanical solidarity, but it is clear that his scheme is fairly speculative as he offered very little ethnographic data to demonstrate the supposed homogeneity of such groups. (The notion that people in "primitive" societies are more homogeneous than people in industrialized societies is one that many sociologists—even modern day theorists—have accepted from Durkheim. This notion is rejected by most anthropologists today, however. As we'll see when looking at the twentieth-century psychological anthropologists, their efforts to identify a common personality type in specific tribal societies tended to ignore the psychological variation found in all cultures. We now recognize that a relatively undifferentiated division of labor does *not* imply any greater psychological homogeneity among society's members.)

In mechanically integrated societies, Durkheim claims, there is substantial social pressure favoring conformity. As a result, it is difficult for individuals to freely vary from group norms, and social change is extremely slow. Under mechanical integration, the individual's personality is almost totally absorbed by society, and consequently the individual is given little regard in collective life. He has few rights as a person and his suffering is not a source of pity among other members of society. Violations of norms are met with extreme punishment because such acts threaten patterns of social solidarity based on homogeneity. Durkheim even makes the claim that society's homogeneity is somehow physically "impressed" upon society's members, who tend to outwardly resemble one another more than do the members of modern European societies (!). (This curious claim probably arises from the fact that people are generally less able to distinguish physical differences among the members of other races than they are among their own. During my 2010 fieldwork in rural Dominica, whose residents have relatively little experience with white people, for some time I was confused with the only other white person living in my village—despite the fact that we look nothing alike and that he spoke English with a pronounced Dutch accent!) Notwithstanding this odd argument, Durkheim rejected any appeal to racial factors as the basis of behavior. This was quite unlike some anthropologists of his time, such as Lewis Henry Morgan. Durkheim wrote that race was clearly not a determinant of behavior since the "most diverse forms of organization are found in societies of the same race, while striking similarities are observed between societies of different races" (1933: 350). In this sense, he resembled his near-contemporary, Franz Boas, in separating the concepts of race and behavior, a position that was very liberal-minded among scholars of the late nineteenth century. Indeed, while the functionalist social theory associated with Durkheim has quite conservative implications, he himself was regarded as a progressive proponent of democracy and individual liberty for his time.

There was no doubt in Durkheim's mind that the individual enjoys greater rights in modern industrialized societies. In contrast to those who argued that the growing division of labor will lead to social disintegration, Durkheim suggested that increasing dissimilarity presents no threat to social cohesion. In fact, it leads to an "organic solidarity" of greater interdependence. Organic solidarity means that industrial society is held together through the interdependence of people occupying many different, but complementary social roles and occupations (Figure 5.2). In such societies, individuals enjoy more rights and greater autonomy. Because all people are interdependent, individual differences in attitudes and aspirations—or what we might call individualism—are not a threat to society as they are in primitive "mechanically integrated" groups. In modern society, the individual, rather than the collective, becomes the center of public and private rituals holding society together, a function once performed by religion in premodern societies. Durkheim termed this attitude the "cult of the individual": "Thus very far from there being the antagonism between the individual and society which is often claimed, moral individualism, the cult of the individual, is in fact the product of the society itself. It is the society that instituted it and made of man the god whose servant it is" (1974: 59).

FIGURE 5.2   Charlie Chaplin in what, in my humble opinion, is his greatest film, *Modern Times* (1936). Although he certainly appears to be brimming with organic solidarity in this picture, once those gears start turning, he's going to experience alienation *big time*. © AF archive/Alamy.

In contrast to Marx, who saw the division of labor as resulting in greater social conflict between classes, Durkheim viewed industrial society as a stable, self-renewing entity. Indeed, Durkheim believed that conflict in modern society persisted to the extent that organic solidarity remained incomplete. With the continued development of this process, however, he believed that such conflict would diminish over time; indeed, he expressed a great deal of optimism about the ability of technology, science, and industry to bring about a more ordered and peaceful society. Here there is also an interesting implied contrast with Marx. Durkheim predicted that the ties of mutual dependence would grow over time, meaning that society's hold over the individual would actually increase in tandem with the division of labor. This contrasts with Marx's prediction that in a future communist society, the state would wither away, leaving the individual free to act independently of social restraint.

We can also see an implicit contrast with Marx in how Durkheim accounted for the division of labor in modern society. Economists from Adam Smith in the eighteenth century onward, including Marx, agreed that the division of labor developed because greater specialization of labor allowed for the cheaper production of goods (indeed, as we saw, this argument was key to Marx's notion of how capitalists responded to competition for markets). But the main thrust of Durkheim's work was to reject this notion, which he called "economic determinism" (i.e. *materialism*). The greater productivity of labor under specialization is a beneficial consequence of the division of labor, but it is not why the division of labor occurs, according to Durkheim. Note that there is also a significant difference between Marx and Durkheim in terms of the effects of the division of labor. Durkheim claimed it would lead to greater solidarity based on interdependence. Marx claimed that the complex division of labor in capitalist society separated each worker from identifying with the product of his/her labor. Because each worker's contribution to the overall product was almost indiscernible, s/he was alienated from that product. Alienation was thought to be a major contributor to the emergence of class consciousness as all workers found their labor reduced to the same unskilled, repetitive actions.

Durkheim argues by analogy from Darwin's *Origin of Species* that a complex division of labor reduces conflict among people. The basis of this argument was Darwin's observation that in the natural world competition was most acute between members of the same species, and that specialization was one evolutionary response to this competition. Darwin famously illustrated this with the proliferation of finch species that he observed on the Galapagos Islands. The birds were apparently descended from a common ancestral species on the South American mainland, but as they competed for survival on the islands, the finches adapted to distinct food sources. Over time, then, the species ceased to compete as they specialized for separate niches. Durkheim similarly noted that the threat of competition in human societies grows with population density and possible conflict over resources. Human societies resolve this competition through organic solidarity, i.e. by members of those societies occupying specialized roles in the division of labor. This explanation gives you an idea of how far (even absurdly far) Durkheim sought to replace the economic arguments of Marx with a non-materialist explanation. The division of labor develops not to increase productivity, but to reduce competition. In other words, the function of the division of labor is to enhance social solidarity.

So Marx and Durkheim brought very different preliminary assumptions to the analysis of social life. Many of these assumptions stemmed from the differing political values that each held. Where Marx stressed the contradictions inherent in society, Durkheim emphasized the integrative functions of social facts. Marx viewed the industrial capitalist social order as one of class struggle; Durkheim perceived organic solidarity in the same society. Marx perceived modern society as one of exploitation of the vast majority of its members; Durkheim examined the same factors and perceived a complex division of labor in which employers and employees depended upon each other. Marx emphasized that material factors ultimately determine the relationships and values to which people subscribe, while Durkheim strove to disprove the notion that ideas were reducible to economic causes. Instead, beliefs are collectively-held values that are essential to society's maintenance by ensuring conformity to norms. Ultimately, Durkheim expressed faith that a capitalist social order would result in greater integration of its members with one another, while Marx predicted greater alienation and conflict, resulting in its utter transformation.

The birth of functionalism, or why Emile knows best

Function is a notion inherent in Durkheim's sociology, and is shared by all social theorists influenced by him. In explaining what he called "social facts," or those cultural rules and practices that have a binding or coercive effect on the individual, social scientists should look for the functions they provide. As in the division of labor, these functions are *not* the immediate ends or practical purposes that they serve for individuals.[1] Indeed, Durkheim argued that society's collective representations usually prevent its members from viewing the causes of their behavior in the "objective" terms employed by the social scientist. Durkheim was emphatic that a science of society be concerned with society as a collectivity, and not with the psychology or interests of the individuals that make it up. In this sense, he challenged the ideas of his English predecessor Herbert Spencer (1820–1903) and contemporary Edward Burnett Tylor (1832–1917), who tried to explain social practices in terms of the needs and desires of the individual. As we'll see in a later chapter, Tylor famously argued that the origins of religion lay in the need of people to account for the universal experiences of dreaming and death, and arose through a process of rational thought about each experience. For Durkheim, religious belief and participation were instead an expression of society's hold over the individual. Participation in common religious ritual and adoption of a common moral code provide the means by which social cohesion among the members of a given religion is achieved; in other words, the function of religion is to enhance social solidarity (starting to sound familiar?).

One of the problems with this perspective (although it is not unique to Durkheim or functionalism) is that the social theorists' categories and concepts become the motivating force for the behavior they seek to explain. When someone participates in a religious ceremony, they typically offer up a variety of reasons for their involvement; they may say that they are worshipping God, celebrating a change in their or someone else's spiritual status (e.g. through First Communion or Baptism), or seeking divine guidance. I have never personally met anyone who states that they attend church because it enhances their sense of cohesion with society, although many people may mention the benefits of a particularly cohesive congregation. Yet functionalist social theorists claim to know the "real" factors motivating the behavior of those they study, even though these subjects of study are unaware of these factors or their influence on their behavior. The problem here is one of *reification*. This means that a model is created to describe the workings of society, and then is given a real force of its own. What starts out as an abstraction designed to help the theorist understand society ends up being viewed as a real determinant of people's behavior.

From Durkheim's view, society cannot be equated with the individuals that make it up because social facts often do not correspond or fulfill the desires of individuals; in fact they are often opposed to them. For example, many people might secretly wish to engage in theft, promiscuity, or murder, but society imposes constraints on these desires to make it possible for people to live together with a minimum of conflict. By the same token, social facts may be useful for individuals, but they should be explained sociologically in terms of their social functions. The function of social facts is to make collective life possible. This is how Durkheim looks at the division of labor; it provides benefits for industrialists, but its social function is to reinforce social solidarity:

The division of labor appears to us otherwise than it does to economists. For them, it essentially consists in greater production. For us, this greater productivity is only a necessary consequence, a repercussion of the phenomenon. If we specialize, it is not to produce more, but it is to enable us to live in new conditions of existence that have been made for us.

(1933: 275)

Society imposes tremendous force on individual behavior through what he called its "*collective conscience.*" This is a society's shared system of beliefs and values, which shapes and directs human behavior. Durkheim's conception here is similar to what modern anthropologists call culture, although he himself did not use that term. Indeed, the principal test that something is a "social fact" is the "coercive effect" that it exerts over an individual. Consider, for example, what causes a soldier to die for a scrap of fabric (a flag) in battle. This was literally the case in much warfare prior to the twentieth century, when the flag bearer was unarmed and marched at the head of his unit in the most exposed position possible. Despite the fact that flag bearers suffered extremely high casualty rates, the duty to carry the flag was considered an honor. In the soldier's mind, the flag symbolizes society and has real power over him and the decisions he makes. Indeed, Durkheim argues that when the coercive power of society over the individual is loosened, the individual may lose the will to live.

The importance of social solidarity in Durkheim's world view is reflected in his work on suicide (his book *Suicide*, 1951, originally published in 1897). In explaining what is usually seen to be a supremely individualistic action (the taking of one's own life), Durkheim argued that social facts were actually the critical determinants of suicide rates. He argued that the most common form of suicide, which he described as both a social and individual pathology, is related to a breakdown of society's hold over the individual. His work was devoted to showing the relationship between suicide rates and religious denomination: predominately Catholic regions of Europe exhibit lower suicide rates than those which are mainly Protestant. Before Durkheim, most people looked at this question in theological terms, noting that suicide in Roman Catholic doctrine was considered a mortal sin, one that denies a person the possibility of salvation after death. Durkheim, however, claimed that the differences in suicide rates cannot be ascribed to differences in the way each denomination looks at suicide, because both condemn the practice (although Catholicism's more explicit doctrine on the matter is likely to have skewed some of the national-level evidence on which Durkheim relied, as we'll see below).

Instead of explaining differences in suicide rates in terms of belief, Durkheim argues that the difference lies in the social organization of the churches. Catholicism, according to Durkheim, is a more strongly "integrated" church because it is formed around a traditional hierarchy whose authority over the individual is binding. From a hierarchy of clergy extending up to the Pope (and beyond him to God), Catholics receive an authoritative understanding of what must be done to achieve salvation (through faith, good works, and sacraments, including the confession of sin). In Protestantism, however, the individual stands comparatively alone before God, and is compelled to interpret many matters for himself. The Calvinist doctrine of predestination (in which the individual is unsure whether he is part of the Elect who are destined for salvation) and the doctrine of grace received from faith alone introduce much uncertainty into the minds of Protestant believers, a point which Max Weber was also to raise in his classic analysis of the Protestant work ethic. In contrast, Catholicism offers believers the doctrine of the communion of saints (which stresses the intervention of saints on behalf of the believer), religious sodalities (voluntary associations of laypeople within the church who devote themselves to the veneration of particular saints), and a clearly established hierarchy extending from the believer to God and the saints. For these reasons, Durkheim contends, Catholicism is more highly integrated in terms of providing social solidarity than is Protestantism. Of course, as we already know, Durkheim—an agnostic Jew—was not writing as any sort of Christian believer. For a period of time as a youth he studied Catholic doctrine, however, and appears to have had an intricate knowledge of both the intellectual and social components of Catholicism.

Durkheim argued that the "cult of the individual" is characteristic of Protestantism, and under its conditions, the individual is not sufficiently restrained by social forces. *Egoistic suicide*, which he viewed as characteristic of predominately Protestant nations, resulted from the individual's lack of integration with society. This sense of estrangement ultimately leads him to question his very reason for existence and, in extreme cases, to kill himself. This is not the only form of suicide found in modern societies, however. There is also *anomic suicide*, resulting from a state of *anomie*. This term describes a gap between expectations and reality. When social instability or uncertainty about the future exist and one's traditional expectations can no longer predict social conditions, anomie or disorientation result. Anomic suicide, Durkheim contends, occurs in situations of rapid and unpredictable social change. The implication of this is that revolutionary social change is actually pathological for the individual (order and progress, anyone?).

While Durkheim devoted most of his attention to egoistic and anomic suicide, he also noted two other less common variants in passing: *altruistic* and *fatalistic*. Altruistic suicide occurs in societies with exceptionally high levels of integration, where the individual is deemed less important than the larger social group. It occurs when the individual willingly surrenders his life for the well-being of society (e.g. a willing victim in a rite of human sacrifice, or giving up one's life in order to save another person).[2] Fatalistic suicide occurs in exceptionally oppressive situations, where the individual seeks to end his or her life to escape continuous abuse (say, in a prison setting, where suicide attempts are common).

Sociologists continue to debate Durkheim's interpretation of suicide as being related to religious orientation. The aggregate data that he assembled did indeed suggest that suicide rates were higher in predominately Protestant than Catholic regions of the same countries (e.g. Germany), although the association becomes less clear when data are compared cross-nationally. From the outset, many of Durkheim's critics faulted his tendency to take official statistics at face value. The reason for this was that in Catholic regions police and coroners were less likely to record suicide as the official cause of death even when it was fairly apparent that someone had taken his/her own life. To register a death as suicide would prevent the use of Catholic funeral rites (a requiem Mass) and the burial of the person in consecrated ground. Today, when active religious affiliation of any sort in most of Western Europe is much less common than in Durkheim's day, official statistics may be much more accurate. And such evidence does indeed suggest that suicide rates are higher in traditionally Protestant than in Catholic areas. Does that bear out Durkheim's argument? Personally, I don't think so. Consider that modern Europe is overwhelmingly secular, especially compared with the United States. With church attendance throughout Western Europe at less than 20 percent, just how likely is it that religious differences still account for such differing levels of suicide, if they ever did? At the risk of invoking the spirit of Montesquieu and his climatic theory of behavior, I would maintain that the key here may be more geographical, climatic, and ultimately psychological than Durkheim was willing to acknowledge. Traditionally Protestant areas such as Sweden, northern Germany, and Denmark receive substantially less daylight than traditionally Catholic areas such as Spain and Italy. During the winter, most of northern Europe receives seven hours or less of sunlight each day. Could Seasonal Affective Disorder and behaviors relating to its depressive effects, such as alcoholism—which is more widespread in northern than southern Europe—be among the factors that Durkheim neglected to mention?

Durkheim's comparatively sanguine view of modern society and its potential was eventually shattered by the events of World War I, during which he avidly supported the French cause as a bulwark against German nationalism and anti-Semitism. He saw most of his students, among them the most promising young intellectuals of the time, recruited into the French Army. Other than his nephew Marcel Mauss, who provided a critical link between Durkheim and Lévi-Strauss and who went on to influence the field of economic anthropology, few of Durkheim's students returned alive from the trenches. In 1915 Durkheim learned that his own son, André, who had been a promising scholar in his own right, had been listed as missing in action during fighting in Serbia. He died heartbroken two years later, soon after the news of his son's death in battle had been confirmed.

Although very few of Durkheim's own students survived the war, his ideas were to be enormously influential in several later theoretical schools in anthropology. As already noted, Durkheim directly influenced a school of anthropology that developed decades later in Great Britain (that of structural functionalism). But he also advanced some arguments that were to inform an important theoretical perspective on the continent of Europe, that of French structuralism. This viewpoint, as we'll see, is most closely associated with the work of Claude Lévi-Strauss (1908–2009; yes, you read that correctly, he lived to 101). Durkheim's argument, developed in *The Elementary Forms of the Religious Life* (2002, orig. 1912) was that religion leads people to classify the world around them into opposing categories (good/evil, right/wrong and, most importantly, "sacred" and "profane"), which are then extended beyond the religious realm into all areas of life. While its influence in the modern world has waned, Durkheim noted, religion created the very categories by which people understand the world, including those of a scientific world view. "If religion gave birth to all that is essential to society," he wrote, "that is so because the idea of society is the soul of religion" (2002: 48). While not specifically developing Durkheim's theory of religion, Claude Lévi-Strauss adopted his ideas about the human tendency to dichotomize and applied them to the analysis of ritual, myth, and kinship in numerous societies.

Weber also answers Marx

The other major school in social theory to develop around the time of Durkheim was associated with the German sociologist Max Weber (1864–1920). Weber's social thought breaks with the dominant positivist tradition in nineteenth-century social theory, and for that reason he was less prone to generalize across cultures and time periods than either Durkheim or Marx (although the latter is typically not regarded as a positivist). Because Weber didn't seek invariant "laws" of social systems, some social scientists consider him to be "unscientific." The Weberian tradition is one of *naturalistic* (rather than positivist) accounts of behavior. The naturalistic tradition denies that there is a cause of behavior other than those causes that can be understood by the human agent. Naturalistic explanations start from the agent's own stated reasons for behavior, and try to account for how a particular cultural setting gives rise to the individual's desires and beliefs.

Although positivists might disparage the naturalistic approach, some of the most important work in the social sciences has adopted this orientation. Weber argued that the individual's explanation of his behavior cannot be considered incidental to it. Indeed, Weber argued that social scientists should seek not generalizations about human behavior but *Verstehen*, or a deeper "understanding" of the specific historical and cultural circumstances that give rise to it. By this he means an empathetic identification with those whom one studies to better understand their motives and the meaning of their behavior. This contrasts sharply with positivist approaches that tend to dismiss, or at least diminish, peoples' stated motives for their action.

Weber's approach closely corresponds to a set of philosophical principles known as *phenomenology*. This sets out to understand human experience as it is lived rather than as "objective" data. The German phenomenologist philosopher Edmund Husserl referred to a mode of knowing as *Einfühlung*, literally meaning "feeling into" (we would translate it as empathy) as an attempt to "get inside" the experience of another human being and to know and experience the world the same way he or she does. In other words, Weber, like the phenomenologist philosophers, tried if you will to put himself into another person's shoes.

As explanations, Weber's analyses are sophisticated and strike many modern readers as highly plausible. The naturalistic mode of analysis is reflected in Weber's most frequently cited work, *The Protestant Ethic and the Spirit of Capitalism* (2005, originally published after his death, in 1930). Weber tried to account for the simultaneous rise of capitalism and Protestantism in northern Europe in the 1500–1600s. While Weber concurred with Marx that capitalism entailed unprecedented transformations in social and economic relations—focusing on the creation of a class of landless producers with only their labor to sell—he suggested that Marx's own explanation of capitalism's origins was insufficient. In dialectical fashion, Marx had argued that "contradictions" (class conflict) arose within feudalism between an urban, increasingly profit-oriented merchant class and a broader society governed by feudal lords who controlled most of society's land and labor resources. These lords were allied with the Church, which restricted avenues for investment and profit through the imposition of strict usury laws, which prohibited the lending of money at interest. Under the feudal mode of production, the landlord would take a portion of the harvest from the peasant population under his control. As serfs, peasants themselves remained in contact with the means of production (land) and therefore were not "free" in the sense of being a readily available source of wage labor. Hence (we're still following the Marxist argument here), urban merchants came into conflict with both feudal lords over the control of labor and with the Church over the free use of money as capital as a source of investment. Capitalist exploitation requires that the laborer be separated—or "alienated"—from the means of production so that he could be exploited as a wage laborer, rather than as a chattel of the lord. It thus became necessary for the existing feudal relationships to be broken down in order to produce a pool of free laborers that the capitalist could employ under the new mode of production. Marx saw this change in the nature of the servitude of the laborer as a historical progression, abolishing as it did serfdom, and creating the free laborer who was not bound to the economic structure of feudal society. The former serf has thus "become a free seller of labor-power," free from the demands of the landlord. Similarly, urban merchants supported the growing Protestant Reformation, freeing society from the dominion of the Catholic Church and its impediments on lending and investment. In *The Communist Manifesto*, Marx praised the incipient capitalist bourgeoisie for having destroyed "the isolation of rural life"[3] that he associated with traditional peasant communities.

While Weber did not disagree with Marx's analysis of the origins of capitalism, he also claimed that it was not by itself a complete explanation. Most importantly, why had capitalism developed first in some places in Europe, and literally centuries later in others? Weber was particularly interested in the fact that modern capitalism had arisen in the Protestant regions of Europe, and that even in the late nineteenth century, most industrialists remained Protestants rather than Catholics. Weber argued that this was because Protestantism prescribed a life of disciplined, hard work and a rejection of worldly pleasures as the ideal life for a pious individual. Obviously these values are compatible with the capitalist work ethic. But why do Protestants feel so obliged to work hard; why do they view recreation as virtually sinful? Weber noted that Catholics were not so burdened by guilt about not working continuously. Indeed, by the late Middle Ages, when all of Europe remained Catholic, nearly one-quarter of the annual calendar was taken up with various holy days and saints' feast days during which work was discouraged. (Nothing like those rollicking, carefree Middle Ages!)

In accounting for the Protestant work ethic, Weber turned to the doctrines developed by the French Protestant reformer John Calvin (1509–1564) in the sixteenth century. Calvin substituted the notion of "predestination" for Catholic ideas that had provided Christian believers with more clearly defined routes to salvation. Although Catholics believed that the basic nature of humanity tended toward sinfulness, they also believed that a whole host of saints could intervene for the individual before God, that penance and absolution could remove the stain of grave ("mortal") sin, and that works of mercy (charity) could also win God's favor. Indeed, the selling of "indulgences" by the Church to those seeking absolution for the sins they had committed (or planned to commit!) was one of its most offensive practices in the eyes of Protestant reformers. The Calvinist doctrine of predestination, on the other hand, is the idea that one's eternal destiny is forever established even before birth, and that only a small number of people, known as the "Elect," could expect to go to heaven. Those who accepted the doctrine of predestination had no way of knowing whether or not they were destined to go to heaven, and there was nothing that they could do to change their fate. You might expect that this would lead to a certain passive fatalism: if there's nothing that I can do to improve my chances of salvation, then why should I bother going to church? Weber argued differently.

Under the doctrine of predestination, according to Weber, the individual was consumed with a burning desire to know whether or not he was among the Elect. This led him to constantly look for "signs" of God's favor. Non-attendance at church was taken as evidence of sinfulness, and certain proof that the person was not of the Elect. A visibly pious life, on the other hand, was but one sign from God that you just might be predestined for heaven. Similarly, worldly success was considered a sign of God's favor—in other words, if you were blessed with material prosperity, you were probably a member of the Elect. Because of the uncertainty and anxiety that this doctrine produced in the minds of its believers, Protestants had an intense desire to learn of their eventual fate. One way that they could learn if they were "saved" was to accumulate evidence of God's favor. That meant they worked hard—in fact, were driven by uncertainty and fear—to amass wealth, which might indicate that they were destined for salvation. From these anxieties arising from predestination emerged the "Protestant Ethic" of disciplined hard work, savings and investment, and a virtually religious commitment to the accumulation of wealth.

This is how Weber explained the conjunction between Protestantism and capitalism. His explanation took the stated motives of the people of that society and accounted for why those motives exist. He did not suggest that there is a cause of behavior any different from one that would make sense to a member of that society. And he certainly didn't disregard people's own explanations as irrelevant or seek some universal principle that would explain their behavior. Yet his explanation strikes us as reasonable. Notice, too, that Weber's explanation breaks from the materialism of Marx's explanation of historical change. Calvinists were driven by religious motives to accumulate wealth as a sign of their personal salvation; the accumulation of wealth was not an end in itself, and capitalism arose as a by-product of their pursuit of

BOX 5.1 Comparative religion and economics: St. Francis vs. the gospel of prosperity

Although predestination is de-emphasized in some modern Protestant denominations and entirely rejected by others, it still plays a major role in some variants of Protestant theology. Jehovah's Witnesses, for example, believe that there are just 14,400 "spaces" in heaven, while a study commissioned in the 1990s by the Southern Baptist Convention determined that less than 30 percent of the US population was destined for salvation—based entirely on Americans' stated denominational identity. If you happen to be Muslim, Jewish, Catholic, Orthodox Christian, or liturgical Protestant, such as Lutheran or Episcopalian— much less Wiccan, agnostic, or atheist—you can pretty much forget it, according to the SBC. The so-called "prosperity gospel" that emerged from Calvinism continues to find expression in some evangelical forms of American Protestantism today. It is the reason that ministers who preach this message feel no remorse in displaying their wealth ostentatiously in the manner of fine clothes, large homes, luxury cars, etc. In fact, they feel compelled to do so as evidence of the "grace" that God has bestowed upon them. Congregants flock to these churches in the hope that they, too, will accumulate good fortune by following such obviously successful ministers. After all, what ambitious person who aspires to wealth and success would follow some homeless, wandering carpenter who hangs out with paupers and prostitutes and then ends up executed beside a couple of criminals? Loser.

FIGURE 5.3   St. Francis renouncing his earthly father and worldly goods, 1437–44 (tempera on panel), Sassetta (Stefano di Giovanni di Consolo, c.1392–1450). © National Gallery, London, UK/The Bridgeman Art Library.

continued ...

Box 5.1 continued

Jesus said to his disciples, "I was hungry and you fed me. I was naked and you clothed me. I was thirsty and you gave me a drink. I was in prison and you visited me." His disciples asked, "but Lord, when did we do these things for you?" Jesus said, "whatever you do for the least among us, you do also for me."

(Matthew 25)

It is easier for a camel to pass through the eye of a needle than for a rich man to enter the Kingdom of God.

(Luke 18)

The Lakewood Church (Figure 5.4) is headed by Pastor Joel Osteen, a modern-day proponent of the "prosperity gospel," and his wife Victoria. They preach that those who are blessed by God will enjoy material abundance as a sign of His favor, just as they have. Having earned tens of millions of dollars from the sale of their books and videos, the Osteens recently moved into a $10.5 million, 17,000 square foot mansion in the suburbs of Houston.

Quick quiz: which of the theologies above is most compatible with capitalism?

FIGURE 5.4   The 30,000-seat Lakewood megachurch in Houston, Texas, the largest single church in the United States. Photo courtesy of the author.

personal salvation. Notice, too—although Weber doesn't acknowledge this—that adopting Protestantism had the added bonus of freeing the incipient bourgeoisie from the Catholic Church's restrictions on usury.

There are differences as well between Durkheim and Weber in their approach to religion, and the motives for behavior in general. Durkheim would argue, as would most positivists, that people are mostly unconscious of the underlying reasons for their actions. The function of most values and practices is to maintain social solidarity, yet people usually offer more pragmatic motives for their behavior. Asked why they go to church, most religious people would say something about their belief in God, or their need for hope, consolation, or moral guidance. But this is simply a justification, from Durkheim's point of view; what they are actually doing is enhancing their social relations with one another through increased social solidarity. God is in fact a representation of society's power over the individual. The goals and the values of the faithful are secondary to the needs of society. In fact, their behavior is unconsciously motivated by society's needs.

The problem with structural dopes

Why do people need religion? Why don't they develop a rational understanding of the world around them and their place in it? From Durkheim's point of view, the reason is that society is too complex to be understood by the participant without the aid of an objective social science. The individual realizes that a superior power impinges upon him. He experiences a powerful enthusiasm when participating in collective life. But he does not understand these phenomena clearly enough to represent them in "real" terms, so religion becomes a way to represent society's awesome power over the individual. Notice here that Durkheim says nothing about the content of any particular religion and why it appeals to the believer. Indeed, he assumes that despite their varying belief systems and teachings, all religions fulfill the same social function.

Weber would argue that people's values and interests aren't secondary to their actions. In fact, he criticized the Durkheimian approach for its failure to actually account for differences in behavior. If all religions fulfilled the same function, then why aren't they all the same? For Weber, the kind of faith that people expressed and acted on was of supreme interest and importance, and not something to be considered incidental to its social function. For example, Weber asked under what conditions religious prophets preaching redemption gain a following, as opposed to religions that legitimate an existing social order. Usually prophets acquire followers among the poor and oppressed, in part because the poor feel a right to be compensated in the hereafter for suffering in the here and now. Usually, messianic beliefs are adopted by those having little or no stake in the existing order, or who are actively opposed to it. This tends to be true whether we are considering the earliest Christians who defied Roman authorities, participants in the Ghost Dance of the Plains Indians, or more recent messianic movements such as Jim Jones' People's Temple. On the other hand, religions that preach that hard work is a virtue and material success a sign of divine blessing acquire followings among the wealthy and fortunate, or those who emulate them. Weber writes:

> The fortunate are rarely satisfied with the fact of being fortunate. Beyond this, they need to know that they have a right to their good fortune. They want to be convinced that they "deserve" it, and above all, that they deserve it in comparison with others…Good fortune thus wants to be legitimate fortune.
>
> (1970: 283)

Weber's work also differs sharply from Durkheim's in that he does not employ the concept of an organismic analogy or the concept of function to explain culture. Weber rejected the idea that society could be seen as some kind of smoothly operating and self-regulating unit whose members were bound together through solidarity. Rather, it is comprised of a variety of competing social strata, which he called "status groups." These are groups of people who share a set of moral ideas that guide their conduct, world view, and identity. These are not necessarily social classes in the sense that Marx recognized them, but might be thought of in modern terms as "subcultures." Examples of status groups in the modern US would include Christian fundamentalists, academics, African-Americans, etc.

Needless to say, someone can be (in fact, almost always is) a member of more than one status group as Weber defined them, so unlike social classes, these identities aren't mutually exclusive. On the other hand, from Marx's point of view, the salient distinctions in modern society were bourgeoisie and proletariat, and as Marx characterized them, you could not belong to both categories at once.[4] Indeed, to the extent that proletarians identified themselves primarily in terms of ethnicity, nationality, race, religion, gender, etc. rather than social class, they experienced what some Marxists have conventionally called "false consciousness," which leads them to act in ways contrary to their class interests (how's that for disparaging people's reasons for their behavior?). Unlike Marx, as well, Weber argued that the conflict between such groups arose more commonly over its status (position) in society rather than economic interests. Indeed, he said that only rarely did the social classes of the bourgeoisie and proletariat in the Marxist sense actually act cohesively, a fact that Marx was pained to acknowledge as well after the inability of workers to come together as a class and challenge the conditions of their existence. While differing from Marxist notions of class, Weber's notion of status groups is also no more compatible with Durkheim's notions of solidarity. Unlike Durkheim, who perceived the modern social order as one grounded in interdependence (organic solidarity), Weber argued that status groups were more often competitive than mutually dependent.

The naturalistic explanation emphasizes an understanding of behavior by understanding the social determinants of people's reasons for their behavior. This is a minority viewpoint in the social sciences today. In *The Rise of Anthropological Theory*, Marvin Harris hardly accords any attention to Weber, except to criticize his reluctance to generalize: "Unless one can specify the conditions under which now religion, now art, or then again subsistence comes to the fore, the principles involved will be valid for only one case at a time, much as if mass and gravitational force were related in one way on the earth but in a different way on the moon. A generalization which applies in only one case is a contradiction in terms" (1968: 285). Of course in writing this, Harris neglects the fact that it is his, and not Weber's, goal to produce generalizations about society. I think that naturalism offers some logical advantages over the positivist explanations that traditionally dominate the social sciences (this would obviously exclude more recent postmodern approaches, which reject the idea of any kind of "totalizing" social theory in its entirety).

The British sociologist Anthony Giddens (1979) has elucidated some of the logical problems and inconsistencies of positivist explanations of behavior, among them that most positivist explanations are "dehumanizing." If behavior is accounted for in terms of general laws, then there has to be a corresponding reduction in the role of human *agency* (meaning deliberate, purposive action understood by the individual). Giddens contends that in determinist (by which he means functionalist and materialist) theories of social science, people are little more than "social and cultural dopes" who are pushed and pulled around by social factors beyond their control or comprehension (Figure 5.5). In a sense, we become robots or automata enacting a program written for us by society in general. In addition to the structural functionalists, this assumption is represented in the work of many modern-day cultural materialists, who argue that the validity of a scientific explanation is completely independent of whether it makes sense to the people being studied.

The logical problem with this perspective is this, Giddens adds: under positivist explanations, the social scientist's concepts and categories become the motivating

FIGURE 5.5   Socio-cultural dopes, pushed and prodded by structural forces beyond their comprehension. No wait, these are zombies. In the end, I suppose they're roughly the same thing. Photo courtesy of the author.

force of behavior. When the Yanomamo practice warfare, they state that they do so to kidnap women or to avenge previous losses in warfare. But according to some anthropologists, the motivating force for their warfare is not women, but the need to maintain their population size within the limits of the region's carrying capacity. This kind of explanation introduces a logical problem. The anthropologist claims to possess knowledge of the "real" factors motivating behavior. These things are not apparent to members of the society, who are only conscious of their own cultural categories. But how can you act in terms of the analyst's categories, concepts that you are not aware of?

Although Weber is not usually mentioned among the forebears of anthropology, his work has had longstanding influence. The naturalistic (non-positivist) mode of explanation that he championed was also that adopted by the founder of American cultural anthropology, Franz Boas (although not by his students who introduced psychological theory in anthropology, as we'll see in a later chapter). Weber's ideas on religion seemed to be borne out by anthropological analyses of millenarian movements and cargo cults in the years after World War II, as such movements typically occurred among dispossessed colonized people experiencing rapid social change. A leading anthropological theorist of religion, Anthony F.C. Wallace (2003), made prominent use of Weber's ideas in his analysis of American Indian revitalization movements of the nineteenth century, as did Peter Worsley in his volume *The Trumpet Shall Sound* (1968), the authoritative anthropological study of Melanesian "cargo" cults. Weber's emphasis on *Verstehen* as a method of understanding was adopted as well by symbolic and interpretive anthropologists, who emphasized empathetic understanding of the meanings of symbols in the daily lives of people (it is similar to Clifford Geertz' argument that anthropologists adopt "thick description," an empathetic, almost novelistic description of cultural scenes).

Finally, Weber's ideas on the Protestant ethic became the basis for some post-World War II development anthropology and sociology that looked at how spiritual beliefs and religion in general affected economic activity. Inspired by Weber, many Cold War era sociologists argued that before economic development could occur, there had to be in place cultural values that promoted investment and profit, a viewpoint known as "modernization theory" (see, for example, Rostow 1960). This had a very significant role in economic development programs instituted by the US government during the 1950s–70s, which emphasized cultural change as a mechanism and precondition for economic development. It even led to the creation of an influential journal at the University of Chicago (*Economic Development and Culture Change*), which was for many years the leading social science journal dealing with questions of development. This perspective, however, is one vehemently opposed by scholars working in a Marxist tradition, for whom imperialism rather than "premodern" cultural values are seen as the major source of underdevelopment and poverty in the world today (Frank 1969, De Janvry 1981).[5] But that's a chapter for another book!

Quiz yourself

Answer True or False to each statement

1 Durkheim's notion of mechanical solidarity—that people in "primitive" societies are largely alike in their personalities and outlooks—is a viewpoint widely accepted among modern anthropologists.

2 Like Franz Boas, but unlike most nineteenth-century social thinkers, Durkheim believed that race was not a determinant of one's behavior.

3 Durkheim believed, like Marx, that an increasingly complex division of labor in modern industrial society would lead to growing conflict between classes.

4 The primary function of social facts, Durkheim argued, is to make collective life possible by promoting social solidarity.

5 Durkheim's views of religion were conditioned by the fact that, like many generations of his family before him, he was a practicing Rabbi.

6 Suicide was most likely in Protestant societies such as Sweden rather than Catholic countries such as Italy or Spain, Durkheim believed, because the Catholic Church taught that the practice was a mortal sin.

7 Weber subscribed to a naturalistic orientation, which tried to account for the desires and beliefs of individuals based on the specific social and historical context in which they lived.

8 According to Weber, Protestantism developed primarily because a rising bourgeoisie (capitalist class) wanted to free itself from the restraints of the Catholic church on money lending.

9 Although Weber disagreed with Marx over the origins of capitalism, he agreed with him that the primary source of conflict in modern society was between the proletariat and the bourgeoisie.

10 Anthropologists who have studied messianic religious movements, such as the Native American Ghost Dance or Melanesian Cargo Cults, have drawn more heavily from the ideas of Durkheim than from Weber.

6

SPENCER, DARWIN, AND AN EVOLUTIONARY PARABLE FOR OUR TIME

Salvaging evolution after the Enlightenment

This chapter examines the role played by evolutionary theories of culture in nineteenth-century anthropology. Those who are casually acquainted with the history of anthropology assume that the first self-identified anthropologists—Edward Burnett Tylor and Lewis Henry Morgan—were directly influenced by Charles Darwin's publication of *The Origin of Species* in 1859. But we've already seen that the Enlightenment thinkers developed social evolutionary ideas nearly 100 years before *Origin*. And the terminology used by Enlightenment philosophers such as Ferguson, who argued that cultures evolve through savagery, barbarism to civilization, is no different from that of the first evolutionary anthropologists. So clearly the first anthropologists *did not* draw their inspiration from Charles Darwin, however highly they thought of his work.

In contrast to earlier theories of evolution developed by Lamarck and Erasmus Darwin, *The Origin of Species* created a storm of controversy when it appeared, but much of this furore could be attributed to the times in which it appeared. Notions of cultural evolution and the environmental conditioning of behavior that had seemed so commonsensical to Enlightenment thinkers had been suppressed for decades by the time of *Origin*'s publication. For most mid-nineteenth-century scholars, the concept of degeneration was widely accepted; i.e. the notion that the condition of most human beings had degenerated since the time of the Tower of Babel. Similarly, the idea that human behavior is the product of a social environment had become considered politically unacceptable. As you recall, Locke's notion that we acquire all of our behavior from "experience" implies that humans have equal abilities and intellects, and that any inequalities between people result from their social environments. By the mid-nineteenth century, in contrast, most scholars who addressed the question of human behavior did so from an overtly racist perspective.

The rejection of evolution in the conservative era of the 1820s–1850s led to a resurgence of a much older theological dispute about the origins of humanity. Almost every publication in this period that dealt with the causes of racial differences in humans argued either for a *monogenist* or a *polygenist* theological interpretation. The monogenist interpretation was most compatible with traditional scriptural authority: this was the belief that all humans share an ancestry with Adam and Eve. Increasingly, toward the middle of the nineteenth century, the pendulum swung to polygenist interpretations. Among American "race scientists" of the time, such as Samuel G. Morton (1799–1851) and the Swiss-born Louis Agassiz (1807–1873), human races were believed to be different and unequal *species*. Theologically, polygenists suggested that God created the various races of the world at different times, and created them as inherently unequal. In an age of ubiquitous racism, polygenists were its most vehement proponents, both Morton and Agassiz arguing that their doctrine justified the slavery of Africans. They also suggested that because of the innate inequality of the races, that whites (who were believed to have been created in God's image) would always and inevitably possess superior characteristics to non-whites. One might think that monogenists would be more likely to accept human equality, but in practice they weren't that much more tolerant in their sentiments. Many believed that the ultimate ancestors of today's Africans, Asians, and Native Americans had been white, but these distinct races "degenerated" due to the effects of climate, disease, diet, or mode of life. Some monogenists held out the prospect that with changes in these conditions, the "degeneracy" of non-whites could be alleviated or even reversed. This often took the form of a practical theological difference between monogenists and polygenists, with the former promoting Christian missionization of non-white races as a mode of "improving" these races and the polygenists believing conversion to be pointless or even contrary to the "divine" purpose by which God created "inferior" races to serve whites.

Concepts of degeneration were also applied to culture. It was thought that as certain human groups physically degenerated from their white ancestors, their intellects deteriorated as well, which in turn accounted for the cultural practices of primitive societies. John Lloyd Stephens, who provided the first English-language description of Mayan ruins in Central America, forcefully argued that such monumental architecture had been created by the ancestors of modern Maya whose culture had deteriorated to a more "savage" state over time (1841: 442). The degeneration paradigm argued that there was no progression or evolutionary movement of culture, at least among non-Europeans. In contrast to Enlightenment thinkers, most early nineteenth-century speculation on human differences emphasized that primitive cultures were highly degraded versions of a past "golden age." On the other hand, the advances of "civilized" peoples were viewed as evidence of God's grace.

But among scholars of the early nineteenth century, there were some who rejected this belief in cultural degeneration, one of them being Auguste Comte, as we have seen. One of the most strenuous opponents of "degenerationism" was the Englishman Herbert Spencer (1820–1903; Figure 6.1), who was the foremost—if one of the only—social evolutionary thinker writing in the mid-nineteenth century. Spencer was

FIGURE 6.1 Herbert Spencer, looking a bit irritated that he hasn't gotten the credit for the theory of evolution that he deserves. ©The Print Collector/Alamy.

exceptionally important in the history of anthropology in that he kept alive the idea of cultural evolution at a time when it had been attacked by theological conservatives, providing a link between Enlightenment thinkers and the first anthropologists at the end of the nineteenth century. More importantly, and less widely appreciated, is the fact it was from Spencer's theories of cultural evolution that Darwin directly developed his notions of natural selection.

Yes, you read that correctly: it was Darwin who was inspired by theories of social evolution, not the other way around. In 1842, 17 years before the appearance of Darwin's *Origin*, Spencer published the first of several works dealing with his "laws of human development." Spencer argued that human nature was an evolutionary product: not only is human nature changeable, but it is perfectible as well. Spencer's evolutionary theory did not specify universal stages through which human society would evolve (in other words, he was not an advocate of the savagery–barbarism–civilization stage theory). But he did argue that different points in social development were characterized by their own versions of human nature. For Spencer, like most scholars of his time, one of the most important contributions of the Enlightenment was all but forgotten; contrary to Locke, he didn't see behavior as something learned, but as largely innate in that one's biological nature generally determined one's behavior. Yet he also believed that biological characteristics of the individual were molded directly by the natural and social environment. While he assumed (like most of his contemporaries) that non-whites were inferior in intellect and temperament, he also believed that *all* people underwent evolutionary change and therefore had some capacity for eventual progress. This was what passed for a liberal perspective at the time.

What caused evolution to take place? Spencer's work incorporated the earlier claims of the Rev. Thomas Malthus (1766–1834) that limited food supplies could not keep up with a growing population (we'll revisit this argument later in our examination of modern materialist theories). Malthus believed that an "inexorable passion between the sexes" led to population growth, resulting in hunger and other "positive" checks on population, including war and disease. Spencer built upon this argument to assert that population growth resulted in competition for limited resources, in which the "weak" would lose out while the most resourceful and intelligent members of society would survive. Hence, while Malthus predicted increasing misery over time, Spencer argued that the same principles described by Malthus would lead to a gradual perfection of human society through progress (an interesting illustration of how the same assumption about people could lead to dismal pessimism on one hand and considerable optimism on the other). Spencer's notion directly influenced Darwin. It was Spencer who first coined the expression "survival of the fittest," a term that Darwin later borrowed for his description of natural selection. This notion is the most important "universal law" of human development, according to Spencer.

Social Darwinism: a pernicious, persistent paradigm

Spencer's views have often been labeled *"Social Darwinism."* (This is really a misnomer; given the chronological order of influence, as it would be more accurate to refer to Darwin's work as "Biological Spencerism"!) Social Darwinism involves the idea that competition is the natural order of human society, and that this competition results in evolutionary progress by eliminating society's weakest members. Those who survive would be superior representatives of human society, since the weakest, least intelligent or least skillful people would be unable to survive. Although this process might be cruel (at least to those who find themselves unable to compete!), over the long term it would culminate in the improvement of human nature.

If you hold this kind of view, what kind of policies or politics would you support? Spencer was nothing if not consistent in his social and political views. He was an avowed enemy of socialism in general or any sort of social welfare program that might be instituted in an otherwise capitalist society. He considered any social arrangement that did not involve a purely competitive market economy to be a violation of "natural law." He was opposed to free public schools, public libraries, public hospitals, compulsory vaccination and public health provision of all kinds. His opposition to such measures was not born of callousness, he said, but a belief that these social interventions would only increase the suffering of the poor in the long run, in a sense prolonging their misery.

Spencer's was not only a powerful argument in the nineteenth century, but variants of it are frequently heard today among proponents of laissez faire capitalism—the notion that the state should do little or nothing to regulate the workings of the economy to lessen the severity of business cycles or poverty. In his day, Spencer's "scientific" arguments were often cited by governing officials when they debated policies toward the poor. During the early 1800s, the English Parliament debated whether to continue "Poor Laws," which for centuries had established a minimum provision of food aid for the destitute. Spencer, citing Malthus, argued vehemently that the laws should be abolished as they simply ran contrary to the naturally competitive nature of society, permitting many who were "unfit" to survive. Quoting Malthus' earlier claim that hunger is the "best inducement to labor" (Ross 1998: 12ff.), Spencer argued that the Poor Laws discouraged productive work on the part of the poor. Spencer's ideas were amenable to the era's powerful industrial investors, who could point to their own accumulation of wealth as the end-product of a "natural" process. As the Scottish-American steel magnate Andrew Carnegie (1835–1919) stated in *The Gospel of Wealth*:

> [W]hile the law [of competition] may be sometimes hard for the individual, it is best for the race, because it ensures the survival of the fittest in every department. We accept and welcome, therefore, as conditions to which we must accommodate ourselves, great inequality of environment; the concentration of business, industrial and commercial, in the hands of the few; and the law of competition between these, as being not only beneficial, but essential to the future progress of the race.
>
> (1901: 4–5)[1]

What assessment might we make of this doctrine today? Although the term itself is rarely used by its proponents, Social Darwinism remains the ideological basis of free market capitalism and is more widely embraced by today's officeholders and political commentators than many people realize. It would come as no surprise that former Louisiana State Senator and ex-Ku Klux Klansman David Duke (who we met in an earlier chapter) employed Social Darwinist arguments when he advocated that those receiving government welfare should be subjected to involuntary sterilization so that the "unfit" do not reproduce (presumably by "welfare" recipients he means black mothers receiving food stamps, *not* investment bankers whose firms are bailed out after making bad loans). But it is also the basis of more "mainstream" arguments opposing government regulation in the economy: many members of Congress justified their votes against the federal economic stimulus package in 2009 on this basis. Similarly most of the same officeholders opposed the extension of unemployment benefits a year later because, in their view, the extravagant benefits received by the jobless (about one-third of their previous earnings) discourage them from seeking work. And while noting that it's unfortunate that millions of people can't afford health care, most of them oppose a government-run health service or insurance system because it runs contrary to the "laws of the market."

Over the years, I have encountered not a few college students who seem taken with libertarian philosophy, the notion that government should exercise minimal influence over the behavior of society's members. One aspect of libertarianism that they find appealing is its advocacy of decriminalization of many personal behaviors that are illegal today, such as recreational drug use, and the lack of interest of most libertarians in "legislating morality." While it is true that libertarians (such as the quirky Texas congressman Ron Paul, who has a surprisingly large following among young voters) favor a reduced role for government in the realm of personal behavior, they also are strongly in favor of laissez faire capitalism, including the abolition of minimum wages or social welfare programs such as social security or unemployment insurance. Ultimately, these arguments can be traced back to Spencer, but there are more influential modern advocates of these positions, among them the late Russian-American writer Ayn Rand (1905–1982, Figure 6.2) and her philosophical perspective known as "objectivism." The fundamental argument in objectivism is, in Rand's words, that "man—every man—is an end to himself, not the means to the ends of others. He must exist for his own sake...The pursuit of man's own rational self-interest and of his own happiness is the highest moral purpose of his life" (1962: 35). Much of the political lobbying against health care reform in the US during 2010 was mounted by an organization called the Ayn Rand Institute. Its namesake advocated, according to the title of one of her many books, *The Virtue of Selfishness*. From her perspective, government has no role to play in ameliorating poverty, discrimination, or in providing even fundamental public services such as education, all of which should be provided by the private market. According to Rand, that which is moral is that which the individual deems to be most in his or her interests. During her lifetime, Rand justified her own

FIGURE 6.2 Ayn Rand, founder of the philosophy of "objectivism." For a sampling of her thinking, you might read *The Virtue of Selfishness* or her best-selling novel, *Atlas Shrugged*. It weighs a ton, but by the first few pages you get the general message: society has no right to restrict in any way the behavior of the ruthlessly ambitious individual. Here she is seen testifying against "Soviet propaganda" as a friendly witness before the US House of Representatives Un-American Activities Committee in 1947. © Bettmann/CORBIS.

often outrageous behavior with this doctrine. Now, I don't like making *ad hominem* arguments, which attack an idea based not on its merits or lack thereof (after all, nobody's a saint—unless you happen to actually be one) but on the personal foibles of its advocates. As Rand cited her amoral philosophy as justification for a string of open adulterous affairs and other flagrant behavior, however, the old *ad hominem* may be warranted in this case. Interestingly enough, Ayn Rand and her modern-day followers would lead Durkheimians as well as Marxists to make common cause!

It's not my intention here to paint a uniformly negative view of Spencer, as his ideas about competition were actually typical of most nineteenth-century social theorists. Despite his ardent defense of laissez faire doctrines, Spencer also articulated ideas that were surprisingly progressive for the time. While favoring capitalism as the most "natural" economic system of the time, he also abhorred imperialism: what he found particularly appalling was the callous way in which European nations lay claim to the resources of colonized peoples while hypocritically promoting among them a religion (Christianity) based on love and charity. Clearly, Spencer's arguments in favor of unfettered capitalism did not mean that he accepted all of the reigning political doctrines of his time.

Darwin's dilemma

It is interesting to consider that Darwin's view of the natural world as one of incessant competition (a "struggle for existence" within "nature, red in tooth and claw") was very likely influenced by Spencer. In other words, Darwin "naturalized" Spencer's view of capitalist society, assuming that, just like a market economy, nature itself was a place of intense and incessant competition. More recent scholars have noted that Darwin overlooked many instances of non-competitive forms of adaptation. As early as 1890 the Russian naturalist Petr Kropotkin observed that, for many species, the individuals that survived were those that cooperated with others. "Mutual aid" (cooperation), he said, was found at all levels of existence. By the 1960s biologists were noting many instances in the real "jungle" where animals—presumably unfettered by conscience and not corrupted by liberal views of the sort rejected by Spencer and Rand—were engaged in forms of cooperative symbiosis. (Just as Darwin ignored the role played by altruism and symbiosis in evolution, below we'll consider the views of a doctrinaire Soviet scientist, Trofim Lysenko, who rejected Darwinian principles altogether because they did not correspond to politically correct communist thought in Stalin's Russia.)

How do the ideas of Spencer and Darwin (Figure 6.3) relate to those of the first anthropologists, Tylor and Morgan? In many cases, histories of anthropology treat Spencer, Darwin, Tylor, and Morgan as little different from one another. It's assumed that Tylor and Morgan were simply doing for culture what Darwin had done for biology. But in fact the ideas of Tylor and Morgan differed substantially from those of Spencer and Darwin. Neither Tylor nor Morgan retained the idea of competition as a motor of evolutionary change, and neither invoked the concept of the "survival of the fittest." They were not, in other words, Social Darwinists. In Spencer's and Darwin's

FIGURE 6.3   A photograph of Darwin taken late in life, around 1870. Courtesy of the Library of Congress.

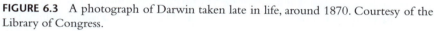

work it was *competition* that caused some individuals to survive and reproduce while others perished. Over time this resulted in changes in the characteristics of species, with variations that enabled individuals to better adapt surviving while other, less adaptive variations were eliminated. For both Darwin and Spencer, evolution was a progressive process. Darwin argued that evolution resulted in "higher and higher levels of perfection in the natural world." It's often thought that because Tylor and Morgan also talked about progress that they must have gotten this idea from Darwin, but their concept of progress differs from Darwin's.

   The evolutionary theory of the early anthropologists is not a direct application of Darwinian notions to society. In general, Tylor and Morgan argued for a unilinear conception of social evolution. This is the idea that all societies will pass through a consistent sequence of stages, from savagery to civilization. This notion has a counterpart in biology, but it is not Darwinian natural selection. The counterpart is known as *orthogenesis*—the notion that organisms will follow a particular line of development irrespective of selective forces. This was a pre-Darwinian belief common to Jean Baptiste Lamarck and other eighteenth-century scholars. For example, Lamarck argued that once an organism acquired the "will" to change, it would develop the corresponding physical structures. He offered the famous illustration of a horse-like animal straining to reach the leaves at tree tops. As each generation stretched higher for leaves, it passed on these acquired characteristics and became a giraffe in the process. As we have all known since the rediscovery of Mendelian genetics in the early twentieth century, genes don't work that way. Famously, of course, Darwin was unaware of the principles of Mendelian genetics, even though Mendel's experiments with sweet peas had been conducted some 30 years before publication of *Origin*. But he did reject the Lamarckian idea that physical characteristics acquired during the lifetime of the individual could be inherited by its offspring.

Darwin's ignorance of the principles of inheritance remained a source of great frustration throughout his life, as the popular belief in heredity at the time was one of "blended inheritance" rather than dominant and recessive genes. If individuals were simply a blend of their parents' traits, Darwin's critics asked, how could favorable variations be passed on rather than being gradually diluted? *Darwin never had an answer for this.* There is the amazing story that the scientific journal containing Mendel's results of his pea-breeding experiments was found among Darwin's belongings after his death. He had never read it, however, judging from the fact that the journal's pages—which were bound together in the fashion of the time—had never been separated. Consequently, he never found the "missing piece" of the puzzle that would have resolved the major scientific (as opposed to theological) criticism of evolution that he faced during his lifetime.

The Lamarckian notion of evolution by the inheritance of acquired characteristics is contrary to how Darwin viewed evolutionary change, which was that variations arise *randomly* among organisms and are *selected for* by natural conditions. In Darwin's view, depending on the variations that develop, there would be many possible evolutionary pathways for a given organism. Darwin conceived of evolution as a branching tree, with each branch forming a line leading to a separate species. He did not see evolution as a straight line down a predetermined path. The idea that all organisms—or societies—would undergo development in the same way is one that was foreign to Darwin's thinking. As we'll see in the following pages, Tylor and Morgan's way of thinking has much more in common with Enlightenment ideas of social progress than Darwinian notions of adaptation and change.

The first generation of anthropologists

By 1870, anthropology was recognized as a social science discipline distinct from sociology. It had carved out its niche as research on "primitive" nonwestern societies. The recognition of anthropology's distinct status also corresponded to the creation of the first academic programs. The leading figures associated with anthropology during the period 1870–1900 are the Englishman Edward Burnett Tylor (1832–1917; Figure 6.5) and the American Lewis Henry Morgan (1818–1881). There are many shared assumptions about their theoretical perspective, which has become known as *unilinear evolution*. Because of these common elements, when the evolutionary paradigm was later attacked (most vociferously by Boas and his students), both scholars were typically mentioned (or more accurately, denounced) in the same breath. This conflation overlooks the fact that there were many substantive differences in the ideas of the two evolutionists, especially in what they sought to explain through evolutionary theory.

Born into a middle class Quaker family, Edward Burnett Tylor was precluded by his religion from attending the leading British universities of the time. In his day, Cambridge and Oxford only granted degrees to students who were members of the

BOX 6.1   A cautionary evolutionary tale for our times

There follows an historical digression regarding Lamarckian evolution, which serves as a warning for our times. During the 1930s, as Communist Party General Secretary Joseph Stalin consolidated his control over the USSR, Darwinian notions came to be held in disrepute by Soviet officials, who linked them to capitalism. This equation of natural selection with capitalism arose because of Darwin's notion that competition (a notoriously "capitalist" form of behavior) fueled evolutionary change. There also emerged an attack on Mendelian genetics for its implication that an organism's characteristics were inherited rather than infinitely changeable in response to a conditioning environment. At the time, the USSR claimed to be forging a socialist "New Man" of collective spirit in place of the cut-throat competition inspired by capitalism. Stalin, like most communists, came down strongly on the "nurture" side of the "nature/nurture" debate.[2]

A ruthlessly ambitious plant scientist by the name of Trofim Denisovic Lysenko (1898–1976; Figure 6.4) rose to prominence by exploiting these "nurturist" ideologies (yes, I know that "ruthlessly ambitious" and "plant scientist" do not go together in most people's minds). Lysenko gained the notice of the Communist Party leadership by promoting agronomic practices based on Lamarckian ideas of the inheritance of acquired characteristics. He believed that instead of breeding higher yielding varieties of crops through hybridization, one could achieve higher yields by simply exposing seeds to extreme environmental conditions, such as soaking them in freezing water. His

FIGURE 6.4   Trofim Lysenko, the Rasputin of Soviet agronomy, examining grain on a collective farm. © Hulton-Deutsch Collection/CORBIS.

continued …

Box 6.1 continued

beliefs, which emphasized the direct environmental influence on organisms rather than the influence of genetic inheritance, were deemed to be more in accordance with the official Stalinist "line" than were Mendelian and Darwinian principles. From 1938 onwards, Lysenko's political influence became impossible for serious Soviet biologists to ignore, who found themselves increasingly unable to challenge his scientifically absurd doctrines. As he gained political support within the Communist Party, he used his growing prominence to vilify geneticists as "enemies of the people." Before long, many of them were sent to the *gulags* (forced labor camps in Siberia, from which few returned alive), or otherwise "disappeared," with Lysenko's followers taking their places.[3] Lysenko's arch detractor, the leading Soviet geneticist Nikolai Vavilov, was arrested in 1940 and died in prison three years later.

Meanwhile, Lysenko and his followers continued to make fantastic claims, with the editors of Soviet scientific journals fearing to publish anything that deviated from his theories. According to historian Zhores Medvedev in *The Rise and Fall of T.D. Lysenko*:

> In nearly every issue of [the Soviet agricultural journal] *Agrobiologiya*, articles appeared in which were seriously reported transformations of wheat into rye and vice versa, barley into oats, peaches into vetch, vetch into lentils, cabbage into swedes, firs into pines, hazelnuts into hornbeams, alders into birches, sunflowers into strangleweed. All of these communications were utterly without proof, methodologically illiterate, and thoroughly unreliable. The authors had one leading thought—to please Lysenko.
>
> (1969: 171)

Lysenko's beliefs amounted to a dogmatic merger of Lamarckism with Stalinism: the infinite malleability of man was mirrored by the malleability of plants. Lysenko even claimed that if you grew plants incrementally farther north each year, they would gradually adapt to the climate until eventually anything could be grown in the Arctic. The existence of chromosomes and genes was denied altogether in Lysenko's biology, these being denounced as "bourgeois constructs." Stalin himself had argued for the promotion of "proletarian" over "bourgeois" science, extending class-struggle doctrine into biology. Lysenko's persecution of scientists also merged with Stalin's paranoid persecution of political opponents.[4] In 1948, Lysenko laid a trap for his remaining opponents. During a conference of the Lenin All-Union Academy of Agricultural Sciences, his agents encouraged the remaining independent Soviet biologists to speak in favor of neo-Darwinian genetics on the premise of a "free and open dialogue." On the final day of the conference, Lysenko presented an address which he said had been approved by Stalin himself. He denounced as enemies of the state the very scientists who had been invited to speak in previous sessions.

From that day forward, the official biology of the Soviet Union was to be Lysenko's, as his few remaining opponents were hauled off to prison. Mendelian genetics was banned as "bourgeois science" from Soviet agricultural policy, textbooks, and college curricula until the mid-1960s. The rediscovery of genetics in the USSR came only after officials in the country's economic and agriculture ministries recognized that Lysenkoism had been responsible for more than two decades of stagnation in Soviet agricultural production. Not until Nikita Khrushchev was removed from power as Soviet leader in 1964 did Lysenko finally lose favor. This is a powerful example of the dangers inherent in subordinating scholarship to a political agenda.

Can't happen here, you think? Consider the struggles that occur in school systems over the teaching of evolution, one in which politicians regularly seek through legislation to give non-scientific explanations of life an equivalent standing with the accepted scientific principle of natural selection. Many a beleaguered high school biology teacher, fearing angry parents and intrusive school board members on the one hand, and knowing that they will receive little backing from fearful principals on the other, simply avoid mentioning evolution altogether. No doubt they feel the same sense of frustration and defeat as Lysenko's critics who threw in the towel because of his bullying and threats. Until 2005 the Alabama Board of Education required "warning labels" in high school biology textbooks to advise students about the "controversial" nature of the theory of natural selection. Among other things, the label warns students that:

> The theory of evolution by natural selection is a controversial theory that is included in this textbook. It is controversial because it states that natural selection provides the basis for the modern scientific explanation for the diversity of living things. Since natural selection has been observed to play a role in influencing small changes in a population, it is assumed that it produces large changes, even though this has not been directly observed.
> (Alabama State Board of Education)

The label raises the claim that the theories of Darwin are less scientifically robust (and therefore more subject to debate) than those of Copernicus, Newton, and Einstein. No credible biological scientist would contend that natural selection is "controversial" or that it continues to be subject to legitimate scientific debate. To say that the theory remains debatable because we have never directly observed speciation—a process requiring many generations to occur—is comparable to claiming that uniformitarian geology is "controversial" because no one living today saw the Grand Canyon or Rocky Mountains being formed.

FIGURE 6.5 Sir Edward Burnett Tylor in a photograph taken around 1880, an era of most impressive beards. © Bettmann/CORBIS.

Church of England. Ironically, although he hadn't attended university himself, Tylor went on to hold the first university professorship in anthropology at Oxford and also wrote the first anthropology textbook. Tylor's comparatively liberal upbringing led him to agnosticism in matters of religion, yet it is his evolutionary theories of religion for which he is best remembered, and occasionally criticized. Notably, it is sometimes said that he viewed religious belief more as an intellectual system for understanding the world rather than in terms of its other roles in providing meaning and consolation in times of stress or uncertainty.

A common, if overstated, criticism of both Tylor and Morgan is that their research was devoid of direct field experience, but was rather based on library research and correspondence with missionaries and colonial administrators. The notion here is that the first practitioners of the discipline were "armchair anthropologists" rather than fieldworkers. This claim, as we'll see, is patently not the case for Morgan, but does seem to fairly characterize Tylor. His travels outside Europe were limited to a single four-month trip to Cuba and Mexico taken in his early twenties on the advice of his doctor, who had diagnosed symptoms of tuberculosis. This trip seems to have greatly stimulated his anthropological interests, leading to his first published book, consisting of observations of modern Mexico. Yet it was never followed by any subsequent travel outside of Europe over the course of his long life. Following his return home, he avidly went through missionaries' accounts, explorers' journals, and colonial government reports to search for similarities in human cultures. "When similar arts, customs, beliefs or legends are found in several distant regions, among peoples not known to be of the same stock," Tylor asked, "how is this similarity to be accounted for?" (1865: 5). He admitted two possible explanations: *independent invention* ("the like working of men's minds under like conditions") or *contact*, direct or indirect, between two societies, leading to the *diffusion* of cultural knowledge. Yet, as his inquiries into culture progressed, Tylor spoke less and less of diffusion, and increasingly of evolution (independent invention) as the cause of cultural similarities in different places.

It was in his 1871 volume *Primitive Culture* that Tylor laid out his evolutionary theory aimed at reconstructing human history. I quote the following passage at length because it reveals some of the key underlying assumptions about evolution entailed in Tylor's theory, as well as the not-so-quaint paternalism of the time:

> [T]he phenomena of Culture may be classified and arranged, stage by stage, in a probable order of evolution…To general likeness in human nature on the one hand and to general likeness in the circumstances of life on the other, this similarity and consistency may no doubt be traced, and they may be studied with especial fitness in comparing races near the same grade of civilization. Little respect need be had in such comparisons for date in history or for place on the map; the ancient Swiss lake-dweller may be set beside the medieval Aztec, and the Ojibwa of North America beside the Zulu of South Africa. As Dr. [Samuel] Johnson contemptuously said when he had read about Patagonians and South Sea Islanders in *Hawkesworth's Voyages*, "*one set of savages is like another." How true a generalization this really is, any Ethnological Museum may show*. Examine for instance the edged and pointed instruments in such a collection; the inventory includes hatchet, adze, chisel, knife, saw, scraper, awl, needle, spear and arrow-head, and of these most or all belong with only differences of detail to races the most various. So it is with savage occupations; the wood-chopping, fishing with net and line, shooting and spearing game, fire-making, cooking, twisting cord and plaiting baskets, repeat themselves with wonderful uniformity in the museum shelves which illustrate the life of the lower races from Kamchatka to Tierra del Fuego and from Dahome to Hawaii. Even when it comes to comparing barbarous hordes with civilized nations, the consideration thrusts itself upon our minds, how far item after item of the life of the lower races passes into analogous proceedings of the higher, in forms not too far changed to be recognized, and sometimes hardly changed at all. Look at the modern European peasant using his hatchet and his hoe, see his food boiling or roasting over the log fire, observe the exact place which beer holds in his calculation of happiness, hear his tale of the ghost in the nearest haunted house, and of the farmer's niece who was bewitched with knots in her insides till she fell into fits and died. If we choose out in this way things which have altered little in long course of centuries, we may draw a picture where there shall be scarce a hand's breadth difference between an English ploughman and negro of Central Africa. These pages will be so crowded with evidence of such correspondence among mankind, that there is no need to dwell upon its details here, but it may be used at once to override a problem which would complicate the argument, namely, the question of race. For the present purpose it appears both possible

and desirable to eliminate considerations of hereditary varieties or races of man, and to treat mankind as homogeneous in nature, though placed in different grades of civilization…[S]tages of culture may be compared without taking into account how far tribes who use the same implement, follow the same custom, or believe the same myth may differ in their bodily configuration and the color of their skin and hair.

(1871: 5–6; emphasis added)

In this extended passage are laid out most of the underlying assumptions of Tylor's evolutionary theory. Notable among these is the argument that *race does not explain cultural differences*. Toward the end he claims that stages of culture may be compared without consideration of human physical traits. This was a remarkably liberal argument for the time, although one that would be shared by most of his fellow Quakers, who were mostly known for their tolerance and strenuous anti-slavery sentiments. This does not mean, however, that Tylor considered "savagery" as equal to "civilization" in its moral and scientific progress, as suggested by his agreement with the curmudgeonly eighteenth-century writer Samuel Johnson ("one set of savages is like another").

Secondly, societies with similar cultural traits represent similar stages in the development of human society. Tylor noted the similarities in technology found at each level—the tools for farming, hunting, cooking, etc.—but also pointed out similarities in mythology and other aspects of cultural life. These parallels reflect the fact that similar cultures have attained comparable stages of development along the pathway from savagery to civilization. Tylor believed that the "laws of the mind" are uniform at any particular stage of development, an assumption that has been deemed the *psychic unity of mankind*: at any given stage of cultural development, people's minds work in a like fashion, leading them to invent similar practices in response to their environment.

Third, Tylor assumed that nonwestern "primitive" societies preserve earlier stages of cultural development. This is the assumption of the *comparative method*. Note, for example, Tylor's equation of a prehistoric "Swiss lake dweller" with the more recent Aztec. The comparative method allowed the evolutionists to reconstruct the past of their own now-civilized societies by examining extant "primitive" peoples, who are presumably still at a stage that Europe surpassed long ago. The comparative method is common to most evolutionary approaches to culture, but had some pernicious implications, as we will see.

Finally, Tylor argued that cultural practices may arise during a given stage, but persist even as the society that invented them evolves. This is the notion of *survivals*, cultural practices that continue through their own inertia beyond the stage that gave rise to them. Notice his reference to modern European peasants who "cling" to forms of mythology or ritual that presumably arose during an earlier stage of evolution. Survivals are essential to the evolutionary paradigm because they help us understand why some practices that we might deem as "primitive" are found in "civilized" societies. Tylor defined survivals as "processes, customs, opinions, and so forth, which have been carried by force of habit into a new state of society different from that in which they had their original home and they remain as proofs of an older condition of culture out of which a newer has been evolved" (1871: 16).We say "God bless you" when someone sneezes because it is a survival, not because we believe, as our medieval forebears did, that the soul is leaving the body. We celebrate Halloween because it is a survival, not to placate ghosts on the night before All Soul's Day. We shake hands as a greeting, not, as was originally the case, to show that we are unarmed. Similarly, magical practices such as palmistry or the use of talismans ("lucky charms") persist in "civilized" societies even though by and large magic has been supplanted there by religion.

Human history, Tylor argued, was the story of progress. In technology, the development of firearms showed a progression from matchlock to wheel lock to flint lock to percussion cap to machine gun (of course, some might question whether new and more efficient ways of killing people actually constitute "progress"). The order of technological change is obvious, Tylor stated, as one innovation leads to another. Similarly, other dimensions of culture can be seen in progressive or linear terms, showing "that the main tendency from primeval up to modern times has been from savagery to civilization." Patterns of human thought and reasoning can also be arrayed in linear terms; as human societies evolve, their capacity for reasoned understanding improves as well: "Acquaintance with the physical laws of the world, and the accompanying power of adapting nature to man's own ends, are, on the whole, lowest among savages, mean among barbarians, and highest among modern educated nations" (Tylor 1871: 24). The "physical laws" to which Tylor referred are clearly those of western science; other ways of knowing are error-prone and less logical inferences about the world that have been abandoned (more or less) by civilized societies. Similarly, other nineteenth-century scholars, such as Sir James Frazer, spoke of the evolution from magic to religion to science in glowing terms as the triumph of progress and reason over dark superstition.

Tylor's attempt to account for the development of religion was a prime illustration of the intellectual progress that, he said, accompanies evolution. The religion of "savages," he contended, could be understood and rationally explained, in contrast to most western observers of the time who consigned primitive religion to the realms of "superstition," "nonsense" and "fallacy." In fact, Tylor's imaginative attempt to explain "primitive" religion attributed some degree of rationality and logic to its adherents. The original religious impulse, one he termed *animism*, arose as people tried to find an explanation for the universal experiences of dreaming and death. When dreaming, the individual thinks that he is in a waking state, moving about and interacting with others (both living and dead). Upon waking, however, he discovers that he was unconscious and inert while experiencing these things. How is he to explain these vivid experiences when the body was immobile? This paradox would lead people to invent a belief in the "soul," defined by Tylor as "an immaterial entity which animates the body and which can leave it far behind" (1871: 429). Obviously, because the soul of a living person who is dreaming often encounters people who have died (deceased family members and friends who appear during dreams), people reason that the soul has the capacity to persist beyond death.

Tylor argued that as people continue to think about unexplained events, their religious concepts will develop accordingly. As people perfect their reasoning powers, they develop more sophisticated religious beliefs to explain the workings of the world. Thus, we could perceive a movement from animism, a belief in the human soul, to *animatism*, the belief that plants, animals, and other features of the natural world also possess animating forces, which he called spirits. Spirits of the natural world could be propitiated through worship or manipulated through magic in order to ensure success in hunting, fishing, or farming. From this emerged the idea of species deities, or gods that controlled entire species or categories of phenomena. This led inevitably to the idea of polytheism, or an array of gods directing the workings of specific areas of the natural world. Finally, from this pantheon of deities emerges one more powerful God (for example, in the classical tradition, Zeus or Apollo, who presided over lesser gods in their respective pantheons). Eventually, as major gods eclipse all others in importance they replace them in their entirety, resulting in the monotheism characteristic of modern civilization.

Thus, as people reason about their experiences in the world, their intellects move in a linear pattern from a belief in the soul to spirits to polytheism and eventually to monotheism. Societies could be placed on a unlinear scale according to their dominant belief system, which represented a particular stage in the ongoing evolutionary trend toward increased command of rational thought. In Enlightenment fashion, Tylor argued that this process would culminate in advanced civilizations where science would replace religion altogether. While he clearly regarded science as superior to the beliefs in animism and animatism by which "savages" understood the world, Tylor's theories of religion acknowledged that even savages possessed some capacity for logical thought, and that the beliefs in spirits and souls were sensible enough given the limits of understanding at such stages. At the same time, Tylor's theories of religion have been criticized for depending too heavily on the intellect, as if suggesting that the original and continuing religious impulse is simply born of a need to understand the world. Like earlier Enlightenment philosophers, Tylor conceived of religion as simply an inferior and less logical form of scientific thinking. Clearly, he neglected the transcendent nature of religion, which is to provide meaning and guidance to the believer and to resolve existential questions of life and death; in other words, to answer precisely those questions that science is incapable of resolving. Durkheim later took vehement exception to Tylor's explanations, not only because they had nothing to say about religion's social functions, but also because they implied that religion was born of individual and not societal needs. Of course, it might be said that Durkheim ignored the intellectual dimension of religion altogether.

Tylor is notable as the first anthropologist to provide a definition of culture: "Culture, or civilization, taken in its wide ethnographic sense, is that complex whole which includes knowledge, belief, art, morals, law, custom, and any other capabilities and habits acquired by man as a member of society" (1871: 1). This definition, while widely quoted, has also been subject to some debate since Tylor's time. A.L. Kroeber, one of Boas' first students, credited Tylor with being the first scholar to define culture in "its modern technical or anthropological meaning" (Kroeber and Kluckhohn 1952: 9). But others, such as L.L. Langness, note that Tylor actually appears to be using the term "culture" more ethnocentrically, as synonymous with "civilization"

(2005: 25). If so, that implies that "savages" and "barbarians" can aspire to culture, but only to the extent that they become "civilized."

Morgan and kinship

Let us turn to Tylor's US contemporary, Lewis Henry Morgan. Trained as an attorney and residing in western New York State, Morgan developed close personal and professional ties to the Seneca Nation, a tribe of the Iroquois Indians. It has become commonplace to deride the Victorian-era anthropologists as cloistered scholars who rigidly imposed their preconceptions on second-hand, often inaccurate accounts of nonwestern cultures.[5] This characterization of "armchair anthropology," however, does not fully apply to Morgan. He conducted intensive, albeit brief, periods of fieldwork among Native American tribes in Kansas and Nebraska (1859–60), the upper Missouri valley (1862), and the Southwest (1878). With the support of the Smithsonian Institution and US State Department, he sent out a printed questionnaire requesting information about local kinship systems to consular officials, missionaries, and scientists around the world. From his own research among Native Americans and the completed questionnaires, he gathered information on 139 different cultures from North America, Asia, and Oceania. Using this bank of information, he was the first to grasp many essential features of nonwestern kinship systems that remain accepted principles in anthropology today.

From his ties to the Seneca of upstate New York, Morgan learned of the seemingly peculiar distinction between cross and parallel cousins made by the Iroquois. Recall from your introductory anthropology class that your parallel cousin is your father's brother's or mother's sister's child. Your cross cousin is your father's sister's child or mother's brother's child. The Iroquois call parallel cousins "brother" or "sister," while cross cousins are called "cousin." Even more amazing to Morgan was the fact that sexual relations with a parallel cousin are deemed incestuous, while cross cousins are often viewed as preferred marriage partners. So much for regarding kinship as simply a matter of biology! Morgan realized that this unusual cultural trait had wider significance when he found the same practice among the Ojibwa of Wisconsin. The result of his research into kinship was contained in his first book, *Systems of Consanguinity and Affinity of the Human Family* (1997, orig. 1870). Here Morgan stated that all systems of kinship terminology are reducible to six varieties, and he attempted to account for the variation that existed. (Morgan's original names for these kinship systems were replaced in the early twentieth century by names identifying them after particular cultures: Eskimo, Hawaiian, Iroquois, Crow, Omaha, and Sudanese. Despite the fact that Morgan's original terms for them are no longer used, his basic descriptions for how each of them operates are still accepted today.) Iroquois terminology is shown in Figure 6.6 for a matrilineal society; typically in such a society, where my father belongs to a different lineage, his kin receive a term equivalent to "father's family."

Morgan argued that these terminology systems reflected distinctions based on marriage. Claiming that forms of marriage evolve through sequential stages, he said that it would be possible to arrange kinship terminology systems in an evolutionary

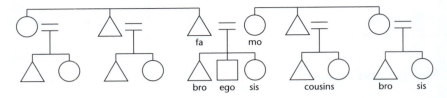

FIGURE 6.6 Iroquois kinship terminology.

sequence as well. Over the course of cultural evolution there was a shift from "classificatory" to "descriptive" systems of kinship (these were his terms). That is, the "lower" stages of cultural development have kinship systems in which all or some collateral relatives are "merged" with one's lineal relatives (i.e. one's direct ancestors and descendants). An Iroquois system, for example, would be considered classificatory because mother's sister's son and father's brother's daughter receive the terms brother and sister, i.e. they are merged with one's lineal relatives. On the other hand, the system found in industrialized societies like the United States or Britain (the Eskimo) is considered descriptive in that all collateral relatives are distinguished from lineal relatives.

As family forms change, Morgan argued, so do terminology systems and, in fact, terminology systems provide a clue to the relationships between people. He postulated the existence of family forms that would account for the different kinship systems existing in various cultures. One of the systems he investigated was what he called Malayan, and what is today known as Hawaiian. This is the most classificatory system of kinship terminology, where all cousins receive terms equivalent to "brother" or "sister" and all aunts and uncles are called the equivalent of "mother" or "father." Morgan postulated that this kinship system was a survival from a state of "group marriage"[6] in which consanguines (blood relatives) regularly mated with one another. Hawaiian kinship thus implied, in Morgan's words, "an antecedent condition of promiscuous intercourse, involving the cohabitation of brothers and sisters, and perhaps of parents and child; thus finding mankind in a condition akin to that of the inferior animals, and more intensely barbarous than we have been accustomed to regard as a possible state of man" (1871: 581). Elsewhere, Morgan referred to this theoretical antecedent state as "the lowest conceivable stage of savagery" as "the bottom of the scale. Man in this condition could scarcely be distinguished from the mute animals by which he was surrounded. Ignorant of marriage and living probably in a horde, he was not only a savage but possessed of a feeble intellect and a feebler moral sense" (1909: 507). Hawaiian terminology, or, if you prefer, a survival of "promiscuous sexual communism" is shown in Figure 6.7.

Morgan's attribution of promiscuity to "savages" was very much part of the Victorian times in which he worked, when despite a general inhibition on discussing sexual matters, people couldn't seem to overcome their obsession with them.

In a state of indiscriminate promiscuity, Morgan argued, people are unable to distinguish their siblings from more distantly related individuals; hence one

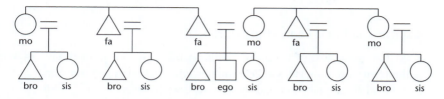

FIGURE 6.7 Hawaiian kinship terminology.

would apply sibling terms to all members of one's generation. Now, it was apparent to Morgan that there were no existing societies in which this form of "promiscuous intercourse" actually took place. All human societies prohibit incest between siblings, a fact that Morgan recognized.[7] Faced with the fact that no human societies actually permitted nuclear family incest, Morgan suggested that wherever Hawaiian terminology was practiced, it was a persisting practice (again, a *survival*) corresponding to a family form that no longer existed. This was what he called the consanguineal family and it corresponded to the stage of "lower savagery."

Of course Morgan's argument about an earlier state of promiscuous mating is entirely speculative, although there is a certain perverse logic in his claim. Because the use of Hawaiian terminology is a survival from an earlier stage in which it described actual relationships between people, those societies that have it must be only recently evolved out of lower savagery. Morgan provided "evidence" from the Polynesians for this claim. For one thing, he cited the well-documented absence of sexual inhibition among Polynesians that had so excited the early European explorers of the region (although by the time of his writing, Methodist missionaries had taken care of that, insisting that Polynesian women cover themselves completely with long dresses then known as "Mother Hubbards"). Morgan also cited the absence of the bow and arrow among Hawaiians. For Morgan, single cultural traits could be evidence of evolutionary stages. The American Indians, such as the Iroquois, are cited as examples of "lower barbarism" because of this trait and because of their distinctive kinship system, which is more "advanced" than the consanguineal family of the Hawaiians. Since the Iroquois are at the lowest stage of barbarism, the Hawaiians with their even more classificatory kinship terminology and absence of the bow and arrow could only be lower. We now recognize, however, that the Hawaiian chiefdom existing prior to European contact was a politically and economically more complex society than most precontact societies in North America. This of course illustrates the fallacy of identifying a culture specific trait such as the bow and arrow as diagnostic of an evolutionary stage and then judging other cultures accordingly.

In addition to discerning the six basic types of kinship terminology, Morgan also made some valid observations on the relationship between terminology and descent. At the stage of barbarism, Morgan argues that the "gens" comes into existence because of the growing importance of property belonging to the kinship group. By gens, he referred to unilineal descent groups (that is, what we today call *lineages*), which do have the function of administering property. He notes that members of the

BOX 6.2　Our fun-loving Victorian forebears

A fun fact to know and tell of our Victorian heritage: Our present-day use of the term "white meat" and "dark meat" when referring to the parts of a turkey actually originated during the Victorian period, when it was considered indelicate, if not obscene, to ask for a "breast" or "leg" or "thigh" when at table. But this is a relatively minor instance of the Victorian-era prudery that prevailed on both sides of the Atlantic. A widespread (if now thoroughly discredited) belief was that nineteenth-century Americans even covered the legs of their furniture with skirts out of a sense of sexual modesty. The idea originated with the publication of Captain Frederick Marryat's *Diary in America* in 1839. Marryat, a visiting Englishman, noted the American propensity to replace the word "leg" in conversation with the less suggestive "limb." At a boarding school for young ladies in New York state he saw a "square piano-forte with four limbs the mistress of the establishment had dressed all these four limbs in modest little trousers, with frills at the bottom of them"! These covers, Marryat's American guide confided, were necessary to preserve the "utmost purity of ideas" among the impressionable young girls (Sweet 2001: xv).

Nothing like the good old days, eh?

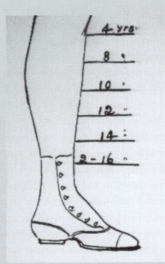

FIGURE 6.8　"The proper length for little girls' skirts at various ages," a chart published in *Harper's Magazine* in 1868. Notice that all traces of visible leg disappeared by about age 15.

same gens, because they are sharing property equally, treat one another as siblings. This is reflected in their kinship terminology, where members of the same lineage are automatically classified as parallel cousins and given the same kinship term as "brother" or "sister." This also accounts for the fact that members of the lineage must "marry out," for marriage to another lineage member is considered tantamount to incest. Morgan's analysis of the relationship between unilineal descent and Iroquois terminology is accepted to this day.

What drives evolutionary change?

In comparison with Spencer and Darwin, who identified competition as the motive force of evolution, Tylor and Morgan were less explicit about what causes a culture to evolve from one to the next. I would argue that they both adopt *idealist* explanations of this change; i.e. they both argue that rational thought causes change, although overall Morgan is more ambiguous about causality than is Tylor. On the one hand, he mentions that evolutionary stages (what he calls the "ethnical periods of man") could be best classified by "arts of subsistence." He also points out that each of the family forms in human evolution coincides with these subsistence bases.

Considering the important role that they play in his work, Morgan's notion of the evolution of subsistence forms represents the empirically weakest part of his argument. The earliest form of subsistence identified in his scheme ("subsistence on fruits and roots") is entirely speculative. As Morgan acknowledges that no extant examples of societies at lower savagery exist, he offers no evidence for societies at this stage. The second stage ("fish based subsistence") is nearly as speculative as the first. Again, we know from prehistory that some societies had such maritime adaptations, but they were a matter of local specialization and could hardly be considered a general stage that all cultures pass through. Notice too that he infers that because of the uncertainty of subsistence throughout savagery, people would be forced to adopt cannibalism at these levels. Only the discovery of agriculture with the arrival of barbarism saved people from the "scourge of cannibalism."

The emphasis on subsistence and the one acknowledgment that subsistence corresponds to certain kinds of family form has been interpreted as a materialist theory of history. Marx and Engels read Morgan with great enthusiasm and suggested that he had independently corroborated their materialist ideas. I would suggest that you can only reach that conclusion if you ignore other aspects of Morgan's work, where, for example, he talks of men working their "way up from savagery to civilization through the slow accumulations of experimental knowledge" (1909: 3). On the following page he refers to the "gradual evolution of their mental and moral powers through experience" (ibid.: 4). This is really no different from the notions of Enlightenment thinkers such as Adam Ferguson, who stressed that people think themselves out of savagery to civilization.

Morgan's evolutionary scheme was an ambitious effort to interrelate aspects of subsistence with kinship practices, and even material culture such as hunting implements and house styles. In at least one area, however, he expressed the idea that evolutionary theories simply could not explain cultural practices. As he memorably put it, *"all primitive religions are grotesque and to some extent unintelligible"* (Morgan 1909: 5, emphasis mine). Consequently, Morgan made no effort whatsoever to explain or document "primitive" religion, which, as we have seen, was the major preoccupation of his contemporary, Tylor. The ironic aspect of this quote is that Morgan, with his much greater field experience, never attempted to discuss native belief systems, while Tylor, who had little exposure to nonwestern cultures, "explained" them at great length!

In evaluating the evolutionists, we're left with the question of how they differ from earlier evolutionists such as Spencer. It was apparent that Spencer was a racial determinist, although his beliefs along these lines were more nuanced than most nineteenth-century racists. Believing that the different races were differentially equipped to develop civilization, he also argued that biological changes determining intellect could occur over time, so that given proper conditions and sufficient time, non-whites could attain some degree of sophistication in thought. How did such notions correspond with ideas of Tylor and Morgan? As in Morgan's scheme, the major force in human history for Tylor is thought. Both Morgan and Tylor adhere to the psychic unity of mankind, which is essential to unilinear theories of evolution. To argue that people develop similar solutions to similar problems you must assume that their minds work in comparable fashion.

Does the assumption of *psychic unity* mean that the evolutionists accepted the inherent equality of races? Tylor, as we've already seen, did not accord race any significance in terms of influencing behavior, a position that was exceptionally liberal-minded for his time. The anthropologist Eleanor Leacock claimed that Morgan, because of his acceptance of psychic unity, was also an advocate of racial equality. Her interpretation of this doctrine is that *all* people have similar intellectual abilities. To my mind, this is a very selective reading of both the assumption of psychic unity and of Morgan, whose other writings suggest that he subscribed to many racist beliefs of the time. He advocated the abolition of slavery as an economic system, but nonetheless repeatedly wrote that blacks were intellectually inferior to whites.[8] So while Morgan's evolutionary scheme required him to postulate that all minds pass through a consistent series of stages, that doesn't mean that he thought all minds are equal. At any one stage, the innate mental conditions of people tend to be the same. But these mental conditions are also the result of biological evolution. As people move from savagery to civilization, their biologically-based mental capabilities improve. In fact, with no evidence whatsoever Morgan claimed that as human society evolved through successive "ethnical periods," so too did human brain size increase! (as Langness [2005: 54] points out, the belief that whites had larger brains than non-whites was widespread at this time). We now turn to the interesting question of why such ethnocentric, if not overtly racist, evolutionary theories were so ubiquitous in the Anglo-Saxon intellectual landscape of the late nineteenth century.

Quiz yourself

Answer True or False to each statement

1   Among early nineteenth-century "race scientists," polygenists argued that God created the human races as inherently separate and unequal.
2   The idea that competition fuels evolution through "the survival of the fittest" was one that originated with Charles Darwin.
3   Social Darwinism involves the idea that competition is the natural order of human society, and that this competition results in evolutionary progress by eliminating society's weakest members.
4   Unlike Lamarck and other evolutionary predecessors, Darwin rejected the notion that physical traits acquired during the life of the individual would be passed on to their offspring.
5   Soviet agronomist Trofim Lysenko rejected Darwinian evolutionary theory and Mendelian genetics, and used his position to persecute Soviet scientists who disagreed with him.
6   E.B. Tylor argued that the behavioral differences between people in civilized and "savage" societies were due to the racial differences between their members.
7   According to Tylor, the earliest impulses for religious belief developed as people sought to explain what happened during dreaming and death.
8   Unlike many "armchair anthropologists" of the nineteenth century, Lewis Henry Morgan conducted original fieldwork with a number of Native American societies.
9   Morgan's recognition that there are six basic systems of kinship terminology used by all of the world's cultures is still accepted as valid today.
10   While Tylor attributed some logic to primitive religion, Morgan claimed that "all primitive religions are grotesque and to some extent unintelligible."

7

BOAS AND THE DEMISE OF CULTURAL EVOLUTION

Imperial uses of the evolutionary paradigm

Almost every anthropological volume published in the United States and Britain between 1870 and 1910 employed some kind of evolutionary scheme in which white Anglo-Saxon cultures were ranked "higher" than the non-white colonized parts of the world. These rankings so closely coincided with skin pigmentation that invariably the "lighter" the population, the "higher" it was ranked. This was a time of pervasive racism, in which it was widely believed among white Anglo-Saxons in the United States and Europe that non-whites lacked the intellectual capacities of whites. Evolutionary theories provided a purportedly "scientific" rationale for the evident racial disparities in wealth and living standards within countries and across the globe, but also served a convenient purpose at a time of imperial expansion (Figure 7.1).

Why was racism so prevalent at this time? By the late 1800s there were a handful of colonial powers in the world, all but one of them (Japan) identified as "white" European or North American powers. Great Britain and the United States, the two most powerful countries of the time, officially promoted the principles of democracy at home while building Empires abroad. Britain had consolidated control over most of sub-Saharan Africa, Southern Asia, the Caribbean, and much of the Southwest Pacific. Although residents of Britain represented just 1/25th of the world's population in 1900, in its imperial holdings the country ruled over one quarter of the world's people. Unofficially, the United States controlled most of Latin America, whose governments enjoyed only nominal sovereignty and were regularly removed from power by US troops if they challenged American interests in the region. During the 1890s, America annexed Western Samoa and Hawaii. These acquisitions were followed by the 1898 Spanish American war, in which the US won control over the former Spanish colonies of Puerto Rico, Guam, and the

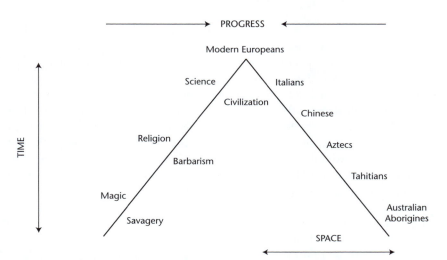

FIGURE 7.1   Chart of evolutionary progress, reproduced from Langness' *The Study of Culture* (2005). Notice that Italians are ranked lower than "modern Europeans"!

Philippines (and briefly, Cuba). At various times between 1910 and 1930, US troops also occupied the Dominican Republic, Nicaragua, Panama, and Honduras, all in order to install compliant governments and to protect US property and interests.

These occupations put the colonizing powers in an ambiguous position. Officially, democracies aren't supposed to maintain colonial holdings in which native people are denied the right to decide their destiny. Yet, that was precisely what was taking place in most of Latin America and the Philippines. Needless to say, if militarily occupied people were given the choice, it is hard to imagine that many would vote to remain occupied! This is where the evolutionary paradigm served a useful political purpose. The only way to justify democracy at home while maintaining actual or de facto colonies in which it is denied to native people is to postulate some fundamental difference between yourself and the people you have colonized. The contradiction in which the US and Britain found themselves led almost inexorably to racist explanations of human difference. The non-white native populations in Britain's and America's colonies were not ready for self-governance, according to such schemes. From this point of view, imperialism is rendered as a kind of benevolent force, one that is helping native peoples to politically and socially "mature" so that, at some indefinite point in the future, they might be able to govern themselves.

Portrayals of Latin Americans, Caribbean Islanders, and Philippinos in popular publications of the time represent them as disobedient dark-hued children, almost always with exaggerated physical features found in racist depictions of blacks. The United States, represented in the figure of Uncle Sam, is either a firm or exasperated but always well-meaning parent. George Black, author of *The Good Neighbor: How the United States Wrote the History of Central America and the Caribbean* (1988), assembled a large array of editorials and cartoon images from the time of the Spanish-American war, when the US found itself a de facto colonial power. Figure 7.2 shows images from the early 1900s, derived from Black's book.

In 1899, the English poet Rudyard Kipling (of *Jungle Book* fame) authored the poem *The White Man's Burden: The United States and the Philippines Islands*. In it, Kipling, an ardent apologist for the British Empire, welcomed the United States to the exclusive club of imperial powers in the wake of the Spanish-American war. The White Man's Burden became a reference to what many supporters of imperialism viewed as their central mission: to bring the benefits of civilization to "savage peoples," most of whom failed to appreciate the benefits bestowed upon them by altruistic white colonizers. His verses reflect the same portrayal of colonized people as disobedient children as that in the cartoon in Figure 7.2:

> Take up the White Man's burden –
> Send forth the best ye breed –
> Go bind your sons to exile
> To serve your captive's need;
> To wait in heavy harness
> On fluttered folk and wild –
> Your new-caught, sullen peoples,
> Half devil and half child...
>
> Take up the White Man's burden –
> The savage wars of peace –
> Fill full the mouth of Famine
> And bid the sickness cease;
> And when your goal is nearest
> The end for others sought,
> Watch Sloth and heathen Folly
> Bring all your hope to naught.
>
> (Kipling 1919: 377)

The reference to famine here is ironic, given that the state of Bengal in Kipling's India suffered a severe famine in 1943 brought on by British mismanagement. While hundreds of thousands died, Prime Minister Winston Churchill refused to send aid, blaming India's problems on natives who were "breeding like rabbits" (Greenwald 2010).

The cartoon in Figure 7.3 gets at the crux of a dilemma facing US policymakers as they acquired colonies—should these new colonial acquisitions be granted statehood, and if so, what representation would they have in Congress? Black analyzes the implications of the United States' occupation of foreign territory as seen by editorial writers immediately after the Spanish-American war:

> Editor and Senator Carl Schurz posed the following dilemma: If Caribbean countries were annexed, the logic of American democracy would mean

FIGURE 7.2   Cartoon with the caption:"Cutting a switch for a bad boy" (Black 1988: 26). Nicaragua had recently resisted US demands for a reduction of banana export taxes, a "request" put to that government by the United Fruit Company (present-day Chiquita). Because of Nicaragua's refusal to grant the company's demand, the country was about to be invaded by the US Marines. In this cartoon from 1910, Nicaragua is portrayed as a disobedient, churlish child who deserves to be punished by Uncle Sam. The "Monroe Doctrine" woodshed is an allusion to President Monroe's 1823 declaration that Europe had no right to interfere in the internal affairs of the Americas. A later US President, Theodore Roosevelt, reinterpreted the doctrine to grant the United States the exclusive right to intervene throughout the hemisphere, a claim about which the residents of those countries were never consulted, obviously.

> granting them statehood. But that would contaminate the American system. "Have you thought of it, what this means?…Fancy ten or twelve tropical States added to the Southern States we already possess; fancy the Senators and Representatives of ten or twelve millions of tropical people, people of the Latin race mixed with Indian and African blood; …fancy them sitting in the Halls of Congress, throwing the weight of their intelligence, their morality, their political notions and habits, their prejudices and passions, into the scale of the destinies of this Republic…Tell me, does not your imagination recoil from the picture?"
>
> (1988: 17)

Widespread concern about "absorbing semicivilized Catholic states" into the United States repeatedly prevented American presidents from seeking annexation of Central American and Caribbean territories, even though this would be the logical consequence of the American principle of representative democracy. Black continues:

FIGURE 7.3   In this 1904 cartoon from the St. Paul (Minnesota) *Pioneer Press,* "San Domingo" (the Dominican Republic) is portrayed as a child (again with stereotypical racial features) having a temper tantrum while waving a straight razor on which is written "revolution." A concerned Uncle Sam looks on and comments, "Maybe I'll have to bring that boy into the house to keep him quiet." The cartoonist implied that the Dominican Republic should be annexed as a US state in order to prevent revolutionary upheaval there.

In cartoons, [Uncle Sam] appeared in a variety of stern and kindly guises as the dispenser of punishment and reward: parent, policeman, and baby-sitter; guardian, schoolteacher, and sentry. Whether Uncle Sam's new charges exasperated him or moved him to compassion, there was little disagreement that they were helpless. According to the partisans of empire, the United States had a moral duty to uplift them…The few anti-imperialists of 1898, on the other hand, were convinced that incompetent savages had no place in the American system. For both sides, the ultimate concern was less the welfare of the colonized than the constitutional health of the United States. The country already had a "black elephant" in the South, said a *New York World* editorial. Why should it get mixed up with a "brown elephant in Porto Rico [*sic*] and perhaps a yellow elephant in Cuba?" These arguments had been heard before…When the administration of Chester Arthur tried to acquire rights to a Nicaraguan canal, E.L. Godkin, editor of the *Nation*, was alarmed at the prospect of fifteen million "slightly catholicized savages" becoming US citizens. Central America, he believed, contained "more rum, Romanism, and rebellion to the square mile than probably any other part of the world."

(Black 1988: 16)

Administrators in Britain's Colonial Office, which oversaw the running of that country's vast Empire, similarly denied colonized people the right to represent themselves in Parliament. Instead, they spoke of colonialism as a form of extended "tutelage," in which natives were to be exposed to British economic and political institutions as a long-term (a *very* long-term) prelude to being allowed to manage their own affairs. This argument was first used when Parliament abolished slavery throughout the British Empire in 1834. Although former slaves in Britain's Caribbean colonies were nominally "free" at that point, Parliament required them to continue working for their masters without pay for another four years, a period of "adjustment" to freedom that was euphemistically called "Apprenticeship."

Political and civil rights were to be granted to America's and Britain's colonial subjects only as they were judged ready for them. When the United States returned "self-rule" to the Philippines under colonial Governor (later US President) William Howard Taft, he allowed the formation of only one political party and limited voting to 3 percent of the population. In the British Empire of the late nineteenth century, only a tiny minority of well-connected and propertied "colored" (mixed race) residents had the right to vote for elected representatives in any of the colonies' Legislative Councils. These Councils typically consisted of a group of three appointed ("official") and three elected ("unofficial") officeholders who were supposed to advise its Governor, an Englishman appointed by the Colonial Office in London, on the administration of the colony. Such "representation" was almost meaningless, as the votes of the unofficial representatives in each colony could be overturned by the veto of the colony's Governor. Of course, it was not until Britain was forced to surrender its Empire through widespread local resistance, beginning with India in 1948, that colonized people finally gained the right to meaningful representation and self-determination. Soon thereafter, by about 1960, most of the Empire had been swept away.

The cartoon in Figure 7.4 was published just after US forces withdrew from Cuba and granted that country independence. In 1901, American forces were bogged down in the third year of a savage occupation of the Philippines, where the military attempted to crush an independence movement. Between 1898 and 1902 the occupation cost an estimated 250,000 Philippino lives, the vast majority of them civilian noncombatants.[1] The American military remained in the Philippines until the Japanese invaded the islands in World War II. As James Bradley points out in *The Imperial Cruise* (2009), the Japanese attack was profoundly ironic, as the US had earlier supported Japanese expansion in the Pacific to counter other rising powers. Having been deemed "Honorary Aryans" by US policymakers and journalists, the Japanese were thought to have legitimate imperial ambitions in Korea and China (ibid.: 183). As we will see in a later chapter, this relatively favorable characterization of the Japanese was immediately replaced by a much more negative racial stereotype after 1941. Notice that both figures in the cartoon above have the same exaggerated racial features, even though the Philippines has no populations of African descent! As Bradley writes, even US diplomats sent to oversee the occupation referred to Philippinos as "negroes," when they were not using another n-word.

FIGURE 7.4   In this *Minneapolis Tribune* cartoon from 1901, the Philippines and Cuba are having a conversation. Caption:
The Philippines: "What yer got?"
Cuba: "Pie" (a tag is hanging from the pie marked "independence")
The Philippines: "Where'd yer git it?"
Cuba: "Mah Uncle Sam gin it to me. An' maybe if you was half way decent he gin you some." (Black 1988: 22)

What accounts for these persistent representations of colonized people as children? In the *Study of Culture*, L.L. Langness mentions that the comparative method gave rise to what has become known as the "biogenetic law" of "ontogeny recapitulates phylogeny" (2005: 42). What this means is that the development of the individual prior to birth and during growth and maturation resembles the development of the species. This "law" came about when the nineteenth-century German embryologist Ernest Häckel observed that human fetuses seem to repeat the evolutionary development of the species (at one point, the fetus has visible gill slits, like a fish; at another, it has a tail). Sometimes, the strong grasp of very young children is described as a "simian reflex," in effect suggesting that children are passing through an ape-like stage of development. In the hands of late-nineteenth-century psychologists, Häckel's argument was extended to mental capabilities as well. The thought processes of adult "savages," it was argued, resemble those of children in "civilized" societies. Indeed, this is the origin of the common reference to misbehaving children as "little savages." As Langness points out, the argument was soon extended to women and the mentally ill as well. The notion that "children = savages" was obviously a potent rationale for those seeking to deny civil and political rights to colonized people (as did "children = savages = women" for those who wanted to deny women in western societies the right to vote). In disparaging the abilities of women, the nineteenth-century physiologist Gustave LeBon argued that

> All psychologists who have studied the intelligence of women…recognize today that they represent the most inferior forms of human evolution and that they are closer to children and savages than to an adult, civilized man. They excel in fickleness, inconstancy, absence of thought and logic, and incapacity to reason. Without doubt there exist some distinguished women, very superior to the average man, but they are as exceptional as the birth of any monstrosity, as, for example, of a gorilla with two heads; consequently, we may neglect them completely.
>
> (quoted in Langness 2005: 55)

In the popular press, people in the newly acquired territories were not only represented as misbehaving children, but occasionally as less evolved primates. Perhaps the most graphic use of the evolutionary paradigm occurred in the lavishly illustrated, best-selling 1899 volume *Our Islands and Their People*, which introduced American readers to their new Pacific possession, the Philippines. The text represented islanders as intermediate in evolutionary development between apes and humans. In one of the volume's photographs of "natives near Manila," the caption reads, "When at rest, these people neither stand or sit down, but on the contrary, squat like animals, this peculiarity being one of the indications of their low state of civilization…These people represent the lower orders and mixed races. Their squatting positions, similar to the monkey's favorite attitude, indicate a no-distant removal from the 'connecting link.'" (in Black 1988: 16).

Evolutionary thinking persists today among psychologists and others who rank types of thinking or tasks in a hierarchical fashion. Such hierarchies imply that those activities rewarded by developed industrialized societies reflect a "higher order" of intelligence than those tasks favored in non-industrialized societies. Among the administrators of colonial powers, this kind of evolutionary ranking of cultural capacity only died with colonialism itself many decades later. Yet within anthropology itself, a field that had first embraced unlinear evolution, by the end of the 1800s the paradigm was in crisis. It was apparent that many of the schemes were contradictory: for example, in his 1861 book *Das Mutterrecht* the German evolutionist J.J. Bachofen proposed that the earliest stages of society were promiscuous (as in Morgan's scheme). From this, matrilineality developed, giving way to patrilineality. In the same year, Henry Maine's *Ancient Law* appeared, suggesting that the original family form had been patrilineal and patriarchal! Given the information available at the time, there was no way to evaluate these conflicting claims. That was true for most of what the evolutionists attempted to explain; their schemes rested on speculative judgments concerning the sequence of cultural practices. Anthropology's impending shift from speculative, grandiose theorizing to careful empirical data-gathering was to be accompanied by an abandonment of cultural evolution for more than four decades.

The Boasian revolution

The first generation of anthropologists to follow the evolutionists represented a sea change in the way scholars looked at "primitive" culture. Applying Kuhn's notion of scientific revolutions, we might refer to this as a fundamental shift in paradigms. By about 1900, the evolutionary paradigm, which had guided social theory back to the Enlightenment, was pronounced dead in anthropology (but not in colonial policy, where it lived on for generations). The evolutionary anthropologists had fit virtually everything then known about primitive society into this paradigm. They accounted for the evolution of kinship systems, political organization, subsistence, and religion through independent invention. In doing so, they had agreed upon a methodology: the comparative method. They had accounted for the consistent and universal stages of cultural development with the principle of *psychic unity*. They also provided a way of accounting for observed discrepancies between theory and fact: the notion of *survivals*.

These assumptions were criticized most directly in the early work of Franz Boas (1858–1942). In his 1896 paper, "The Limitations of the Comparative Method," Boas addressed what he saw as the logical and empirical shortcomings of unilinear evolution. Among these, he argued that unilinear evolutionary rankings were arbitrary and simple-minded. He asserted that it was impossible to abstract single traits from contemporary cultures and order them in a verifiable sequence. While some practices in specific cultures may be organizationally simple, other traits in the same culture may be quite complex. Indeed, he noted that entirely different rankings would be achieved if different traits were selected as criteria for ranking. Complex ideational or ritual practices, for example, were often found in conjunction with extremely simple subsistence technologies. The central Australian hunter-gatherers have perhaps the most elaborate form of marriage prescriptions ever documented: their social groups are divided into eight sections which determine where one can find a marriage partner. Yet this is associated with a Paleolithic technological base.

Boas also argued that similar practices in different places do not demonstrate the principle of psychic unity. Similarities between cultures are often superficial, he noted, and do not indicate similar causes at work. Masks, for example, might exist in many different cultures, something that Tylor attributed to a certain stage of religious sentiment. But for this theory to hold true, masks would have to have the same function wherever they are found. But in some cultures, they are used as disguises so that harmful spirits do not recognize the wearer; in others, they are worn to commemorate a deceased relative; elsewhere, they may be used during Carnival or other time of social license to conceal the individual's identity from others. How can a constant mental principle be at work, Boas asked, if the same item in different cultures fulfills different goals?

Finally, even if the same trait exists in different cultures and fulfills the same function, that does not prove independent invention as the evolutionists argue. Wherever cultures are in contact, it is easier to borrow a useful trait than to invent it independently. That's why we see the rapid spread of maize cultivation through the Americas after its initial domestication in Mesoamerica. But in the case of other cultural practices, for example, creation stories with similar motifs, it is more difficult to know where traits come from. Given the existence of diffusion, it is probably impossible to determine whether the creation story was independently invented or borrowed.

Boas countered the evolutionists with a relatively modest thesis. Instead of civilization being determined by rational processes leading to uniform development, each culture has its own history, the product of both independent invention and diffusion. Comparison of those histories will reveal that cultures exhibit much more variation than the evolutionists believed. Where neighboring cultures were highly similar, the probable explanation for those similarities was diffusion.

By the time that Boas was honing his critique of unilinear evolution, a strongly anti-evolutionist orientation had already developed among anthropologists in Britain and Germany. This perspective was associated with *diffusionism*, the notion that cultural similarities result from a borrowing of traits by one group from another. As a student in Germany, Boas was well acquainted with geographers, such as Friedrich Rätzel, who promoted diffusionism under the guise of the *Kulturkreis* (culture circle) school. This perspective sought to map the distribution of similar traits in all of the cultures found within a geographic area, with the assumption that a given trait originated in an area in which it was most widely distributed. That is, if a particular religious motif or folktale is found among 90 percent of the cultures in an area, it is assumed to have more likely originated there than in a region where it is found among only 10 percent of the resident cultures. Using this procedure, the German *Kulturkreis* scholars Frobenius and Gräbner claimed to be able to reduce all of the world's cultural diversity to just four major *Kreise*, or "circles" of origin.

The English diffusionist school, led by G. Elliot Smith and William Perry, was even more zealously reductive. Impressed during a trip to Egypt by the complexity of the process of mummification, Smith concluded that the procedure could only have been invented once. This led him, on the basis of no evidence whatsoever, to conclude that almost everything else associated with Egypt could have been invented only once (this list was extended to agriculture, control of fire, polytheism, writing, clothing, housing, and medicine). He and his protégé William Perry (neither of whom had any anthropological training, such as it then existed) proceeded to argue that at about 4000 BC the Egyptians began to travel widely around the world in pursuit of resources to build their civilization. In their travels they everywhere encountered "natural men," who lived without any of the benefits of domestication, housing, clothing, or even fire. These and other "gifts" of civilization were diffused around the world by the beneficent Egyptians. The evidence of Egyptian transoceanic travel is "obvious," they said, pointing to the existence of pyramids in the valley of the Nile as well as Mesoamerica (such as Mayan sites in the Yucatan and Central America, as well as Aztec and earlier sites in the Valley of Mexico) and North America (e.g. Cahokia and Moundville).

From an anthropological point of view, the basic problem with diffusionism (apart from a lack of evidence for its most sweeping claims) was that it failed to

BOX 7.1 Diffusion in popular culture

Contrary to Smith and Perry's imaginative thesis, there is no credible evidence that the Egyptians ever visited the New World. Nonetheless, these are amazingly persistent ideas, variants of which are often reflected in popular culture. During the 1950s, the Danish adventurer Thor Heyerdahl tried to "prove" the theory of Egyptian diffusion by building a raft of papyrus and floating across the Atlantic from the Mediterranean. Heyerdahl's ability to do so, with modern navigational equipment, maps, a convenient supply ship following him, as well as the certain knowledge that he wasn't venturing off the edge of the earth, obviously proves nothing about the Egyptians accomplishing the same crossing 3,000 years ago. But the most extreme diffusionist arguments were advanced a decade later by the Dutch author Eric von Daniken. In *Chariots of the Gods* von Daniken argued that the achievements of ancient human civilizations actually represented *extra-terrestrial* diffusion. His idea was that "ancient astronauts" from other galaxies brought the benefits of their civilizations to the inhabitants of earth who, just as Smith and Perry had argued 80 years before, were too dimwitted to invent anything on their own. In turn, these ancient space travelers were worshipped as gods by grateful earthlings. His diffusionist ideas are still occasionally featured in what I call "supermarket anthropology," the sensationalist tabloids you are forced to read while waiting in line at the supermarket check-out.

Where, I wonder, did this strange notion come from that extra-terrestrials are somehow well intentioned, and will come to earth to help hapless humanity solve our problems? Eminent British physicist Stephen Hawking has recently argued that we should immediately cease any ongoing efforts to contact or communicate with other intelligent life forms in the universe. Given that extra-terrestrials who have the capacity for space travel are probably seeking new planets and resources to exploit, it is very unlikely, he argues, that we humans are going to fare very well from that contact. According to Hawking,

> We only have to look at ourselves to see how intelligent life might develop into something we wouldn't want to meet. I imagine they might exist in massive ships, having used up all the resources from their home planet. Such advanced aliens would perhaps become nomads, looking to conquer and colonize whatever planets they can reach...If aliens ever visit us, I think the outcome would be much as when Christopher Columbus first landed in America, which didn't turn out very well for the Native Americans.
>
> (quoted in Leake 2010)

Hawking's belief is that aliens would likely be along the lines of the legendary *Twilight Zone* episode "To Serve Man" rather than the benevolent visitors from advanced civilizations encountered in much science fiction literature (Figure 7.5).

FIGURE 7.5   From a 1962 episode of *Twilight Zone:* a member of the Kanamits, a nine-foot tall alien race that arrives on earth with seemingly benevolent intentions to eradicate famine, disease, and war. *To Serve Man*, a mysterious book in the Kanamit language that the visitors regularly consult, reveals that their actual motives are far less generous. Courtesy of CBS Photo Archive/Getty Images.

answer the question that the evolutionists had tried to answer, albeit in ethnocentric fashion. Even if you accept the diffusionists' assumption that culture traits are more often borrowed than independently developed, every culture trait still had to develop *somewhere*. But diffusionism was unable to account for the origins of cultural practices, nor could it explain why some traits diffuse and others don't.

Both evolutionism and diffusionism set out to account for cultural similarities and differences but they did so with contrasting assumptions about human nature. For the evolutionists, psychic unity and independent invention were necessary to account for how different peoples would develop similar traits. These assumptions are well suited to explaining cultural similarities for geographically distant groups, but become problematic for people who have a history of contact. For the diffusionists, the comparable assumption was that people are fundamentally unimaginative. According to the diffusionists, if the same thing is found in two places, it is evidence for culture contact and migration. This argument works well for cultures in close proximity, but becomes less plausible if cultures are some distance from each other (although Smith and Perry weren't restrained by this inconvenient fact). So, just as Thomas Kuhn would predict, when a new paradigm comes into existence, there are some things that it cannot explain. Diffusionists could not explain cultural similarities between groups that were never in contact, either directly or through intermediaries. Also, as Kuhn would suggest, this explanatory problem led diffusionists to view their data in a way different from evolutionists. When they examined cultures in close proximity or for whom there was probable historical connection, members of the *Kulturkreis* school described them as being similar. But when they analyzed cultures located on different continents, they described the traits as not remotely similar either in form or function. Their very descriptions of data, then, sought to minimize possible problems for the diffusionist paradigm.

Boas and relativism

A number of myths were started about Boas by latter-day interpreters, including some of his first students. It is sometimes thought that he favored diffusion as an alternative to evolution in explaining cultural similarities. This idea was advanced by his students Alfred Kroeber and Clark Wissler, who became associated with the American diffusionist school of Culture Area studies. This approach was roughly patterned after the *Kulturkreis* school, although it was more rigorous in its data collection and much less grandiose in its pronouncements. Another of Boas' early students, Robert Lowie, promoted diffusionism primarily as a way of attacking evolutionary assumptions. Contrary to such claims, Boas simply argued that it was impossible to determine whether diffusion or independent invention accounted for similar traits in different places, due to our inability to know the histories of each culture. And he emphasized that what he opposed in the schemes of Tylor and Morgan was their reliance on orthogenesis, not their use of evolutionary concepts. In fact, Boas' student Alexander Lesser argued that Boas followed an approach closer to Darwin than Tylor and Morgan did. This was because he regarded cultural development as a process of branching, divergent histories rather than unilinear movement through universal stages.

Unlike most social scientists of the late 1800s, Boas' doctoral dissertation was not in philosophy, law, or history, but it did touch on questions that informed his later anthropological thinking. Boas (Figure 7.6) completed his PhD in Physics in 1881, submitting a dissertation entitled "Research into the Perception of the Color of Sea Water." His dissertation research inclined him to issues that were to occupy the remainder of his life's work. Boas came to recognize that the color of water, which could be measured precisely with scientific instruments, was perceived differently by the Inuit, whose color perception in turn differed from his own. Two years later, while conducting postdoctoral work in geography, Boas went to Baffin Island, Canada, to study how the Inuit understand the geography of the regions over which they migrate. It is usually assumed that this marked a radical break with his background in physics, but in fact his anthropological career was a continuation of these earlier interests. Throughout his life, Boas was concerned with questions that deal with epistemology, which, as you eagerly recall, is the branch of philosophy relating to claims to knowledge. Above all, he was always concerned with how the individual and cultural characteristics of people affect their perception of reality.

Boas' work was heavily influenced by the German philosophical tradition in which he was educated. This was a tradition that revived the philosophy of the eighteenth-

FIGURE 7.6 Franz Boas, ca. 1900, in the aggressive stance of a Kwakiutl dancer. He posed for a large number of such photographs, as well as collaborating in the field with the great photographer of Native Americans, Edward Curtis. I would conduct my classes in this way, except for the likelihood that people would run screaming in horror for the exits as soon as I remove my shirt. Courtesy of the National Anthropological Archives, the Smithsonian Institution.

century German scholar Immanuel Kant (1724–1804), who held that a real world is unknowable apart from the perceptions of those who try to know it. These perceptions are constrained by preexisting categories of mind, such as moral ideas and individual concepts of space and time. Not surprisingly, Kant's ideas are often seen as the ultimate precursors of some currents of postmodern philosophy; indeed, Michel Foucault's doctoral dissertation dealt with Kant's theory of knowledge. This relativity of perspective is something that Boas maintained throughout his work, and it is reflected in his enunciation of the principle of *cultural relativism*, which we will explore in a few pages. But first, relativity lends itself to two great jokes, courtesy of our philosopher friends Cathcart and Klein (2006: 173–175):

> A snail was mugged by a turtle. When the police asked him what happened, he said, "I don't know. It all happened so fast."

I hope I don't have to explain this, but for those who are a little slow on the uptake, the above joke is about the relativity of our time perspectives. While to a human, a turtle seems like a slow animal, to an even slower animal, like a snail, it seems fast.

A second contribution to Boas' thinking also derived from his German academic background. In the 1880s the Kantian philosopher Wilhelm Windelband formulated the difference between the social and natural sciences in terms of their "idiographic" and "nomothetic" orientations. The natural sciences are nomothetic in that they seek facts in order to draw generalizations (the term is derived from the classical Greek word *nomos*, meaning "law"). A nomothetic study, then, is interested in facts primarily as a means to producing theory. An idiographic study is one that is particularizing, seeking individual facts to understand them more fully within context. The field of history (and anthropology, according to Boas' reading of Windelband) is a discipline that cannot and should not be made to produce generalizations. You can probably see by now that Durkheim and other positivists such as Tylor and Morgan share a nomothetic orientation (despite disagreeing about everything else!), while Boas shared an idiographic approach with another German contemporary, Max Weber.

Boas' career in anthropology was a long one. Following his research with the Inuit, he worked at the Berlin Ethnological Museum until 1886, when he traveled to coastal British Columbia to collect museum materials. The following year, he immigrated to the United States in part because anti-Semitism prevented him from acquiring a university position in Germany. Boas established the first academic department of anthropology in the US at Clark University, but financial turmoil at that institution led to a mass faculty resignation in 1892. After working on the anthropological staff of the Chicago World's Columbian Exposition to celebrate the 400th anniversary of Columbus' travels to the New World, he moved to New York's Columbia University (then College) in 1896. There he dominated the anthropology program until his death in 1942, and it was while at Columbia that he single-handedly trained an entire generation of American anthropologists. (Indeed, almost every American cultural anthropologist—assuming that they have been taught by US-trained anthropologists—can trace their "intellectual heritage" back to Boas. This is because it was Boas' students who fanned out across the country and established new programs in their own right.)

Over the course of his career, Boas grew increasingly adamant that the goal of anthropology should be strictly idiographic and historical. Before his first trip to Baffin Island he had adopted a geographical determinist position, suggesting that features of geography would be directly reflected in a culture's settlement size and mobility. By 1890 he retreated from this position, arguing that geography affects cultures in complex ways, and this relationship can be understood only with an understanding of the psychology of the members of a culture. In his 1896 publication "Limitations of the Comparative Method," Boas criticized the evolutionists for their methods, not for their claim that cultures can be explained with general laws. His point was simply that data had to be more carefully collected than it had been by earlier anthropologists. He favored an *inductive* orientation, suggesting that only after assembling large amounts of carefully collected ethnographic data would anthropologists successfully derive laws of culture.

In a later book *The Mind of Primitive Man* (1963, orig. 1911), Boas rejected any kind of causal relationship between culture and the natural environment or subsistence practices. The influence of the environment on culture is entirely unpredictable, he said. He pointed to a number of hunter-gatherer cultures to illustrate the tremendous diversity of belief systems among people practicing the same way of life. This was evidence, he said, that cultural traits could not be regarded as simply responses to the environment, subsistence resources, or other material factors. "Even among the Eskimo," Boas wrote, "who have so marvelously well succeeded in adapting themselves to their geographical environment, customs like the taboo on the promiscuous use of caribou and seal prevent the fullest use of the opportunities offered by the country" (1963: 175). In what might serve as a refutation of Marxian claims that a culture derives its character from its economic basis, he wrote:

> There is no reason to call all other phases of culture a superstructure on an economic basis, for economic conditions always act on a preexisting culture and are themselves dependent upon other aspects of culture. It is no more justifiable to say that social structure is determined by economic forms than to claim the reverse, for a preexisting social structure will influence economic conditions and vice versa...The claim that economic stresses preceded every other manifestation of cultural life and exerted their influences on a group without any cultural traits cannot be maintained. Cultural life is always economically conditioned and economics are always culturally conditioned.
>
> (ibid.: 177)

With the publication of *The Mind of Primitive Man*, then, Boas had staked out the position with which he was to become associated for the remainder of his career: culture is a thing *sui generis*, a "thing in itself" that cannot be "reduced to" (that is, explained in terms of) other factors of life, be they economics or the physical environment. Culture, in a word, can only be explained in terms of itself. By the final decade of his life, in the 1930s, Boas had become strident in his opposition to *any* generalizations about culture. The search for lawful regularities between cultures is futile, the aims of anthropology should not be to discover such laws, and no amount of additional research could lead to their discovery:

> In my opinion a system of social anthropology and "laws" of cultural development as rigid as those of physics are supposed to be are unattainable in the present stage of our knowledge, and more important than this: on account of the uniqueness of cultural phenomena and their complexity nothing will ever be found that deserves the name of a law excepting those psychological, biologically determined characteristics which are common to all cultures and appear in a multitude of forms according to the particular culture in which they manifest themselves.
>
> (1966b, orig. 1936: 311)

What is notable about this passage is Boas' developing interest in psychology, reflected in a belief that anthropologists should examine how each culture affects its individual members. In this respect, he came to embrace a psychological orientation to culture that was already being explored by some of his better-known students (among them, Edward Sapir, Paul Radin, Margaret Mead, and Ruth Benedict). On the other hand, Boas' growing interest in the relationship between the individual and culture led to a persisting dispute with Kroeber (1876–1960; Figure 7.7). Kroeber earned his doctorate at Columbia under Boas in 1901 (the first anthropology doctorate conferred in the United States) and went on to establish the Department of Anthropology at the University of California, Berkeley, where he spent the remainder of his professional life. Kroeber argued that individuals were entirely subordinate to their culture, which he contended had a "superorganic" existence. That is, culture existed apart from the people who participated in it; indeed, even "great men" who supposedly changed history through their inventions or actions were little more than the vessels for cultural expression. Their ideas found expression and acceptance only because cultural conditions were appropriate for them. As proof of this, Kroeber delighted in pointing out the many coincidences that occurred with so-called "world-changing" discoveries, such as Leibniz' and Newton's simultaneous invention of calculus in the 1690s and Wallace's and Darwin's simultaneous discovery of the principle of natural selection in the 1840s.

FIGURE 7.7 Alfred Kroeber, the first of Boas' students to receive a doctorate in anthropology. Kroeber was also the father of the celebrated science fiction and fantasy writer Ursula K. Le Guin (born 1929), many of whose works explore themes in anthropology as well as feminist theory. Her book *The Dispossessed* is one of my favorite sci fi novels. It is an extraordinary story about the tensions between the civilizations of two planets, one having been settled by egalitarian revolutionaries fleeing from an earth-like neighbor characterized by extremes of wealth and poverty. If I could combine fiction and anthropology, this would be it! Courtesy of the National Anthropological Archives, Smithsonian Institution.

A profile in courage

It is not hard to account for Boas' opposition to anthropological generalizations. Partly it stems from the German philosophical tradition in which he was steeped, leading him to regard anthropology as akin to history in seeking to understand particular cultures in detail. Partly, too, it was the neo-Kantian relativism that pervaded his view of culture. His work is remarkable for the time in that he was the first anthropologist (and one of the only scholars of the time) to treat nonwestern cultures in a respectful, non-condescending fashion. His reluctance to generalize was partly due to the grandiose, racist speculations behind most anthropology until 1900. As a Jew in Bismarck's Germany, and as an immigrant in the United States, no doubt he was especially sensitive to issues of prejudice, a concern that he extended to Native Americans and blacks. In his respect for the people he studied, and for the integrity of the data he collected, Boas stood head and shoulders above his contemporaries. For the sake of comparison with what passed as anthropology in his early career, six years into Boas' appointment at Columbia University, William McGee was appointed first president of the American Anthropological Association. Despite his total lack of anthropological training or fieldwork (or perhaps because of them), McGee engaged in the most sweeping racist pronouncements on human difference. Arguing that white America was the pinnacle of evolutionary perfection, he had nothing kind to say about American Indians and other indigenous people, who at the time were being decimated by colonial expansion in "the struggle for survival": "The savage stands strikingly close to sub-human species in every aspect of mentality as well as in bodily habits and bodily structure" (McGee 1901: 13).

In contrast, Boas was a vocal champion of civil rights for minorities, a founding member of the National Association for the Advancement of Colored People (NAACP), and an outspoken opponent of imperialism. As early as 1910, Boas raised his voice in support of racial equality in the US and denounced the failure of legal authorities to enforce what anti-lynching laws were then on the books. This was a nearly unprecedented position for a white academic to take at the time. Boas' peace activism during World War I attracted a storm of criticism, notably after he questioned the morality of patriotism in the pages of the *New York Times* in 1915. He adamantly opposed US entry into World War I, regarding the conflict as a struggle between imperialist powers. To underscore this point, in 1918 Boas declared his membership in the Socialist Party USA, whose leader, Eugene V. Debs, had just been sentenced to 10 years in prison after a speech denouncing US participation in the war. Boas also criticized the anti-German sentiments that were whipped up in the US during the war itself, in which German-speaking Americans were ordered by law to assimilate. (Remember "freedom fries" and "freedom toast" of a few years ago, as everything French was ridiculed when that country opposed the invasion of Iraq in 2003? In Boas' time, after the US entered WWI in 1917, it was "liberty cabbage" in place of sauerkraut.) At that time, Americans of German ancestry came under intense suspicion for speaking their native language, which was banned in public in many locales.[2]

Soon after the war, Boas learned that several American archaeologists had conducted espionage against German targets while ostensibly engaged in research in Central America and Mexico. In a 1919 article in the *Nation*, Boas criticized the men (without naming them) for having "prostituted science by using it as a cover for their activities as spies" (1974b, orig. 1919: 336). For this act of "disloyalty," Boas was censured by the American Anthropological Association by a vote of 21 to 10. Most of the dissenters were Boas' former students and close associates (Patterson 2001: 55). The author of the resolution, W.H. Holmes, even alleged that Boas had spied on behalf of Germany during the war; the accusation led to an investigation by the US Attorney General, who later exonerated him. Nonetheless, the controversy that swirled around Boas and the censure vote forced him to withdraw his candidacy for a seat on the powerful National Research Council, whose findings had a major effect on US immigration policy during the 1920s (ibid.: 54). These changes to policy, restricting immigration from Southern and Eastern Europe, as well as "non-white" parts of the globe, would no doubt have been strenuously opposed by Boas.

The perils of induction, or why you can't get there from here

In his early career, Boas stated that there were two reasons why anthropologists would have to indefinitely postpone generalization. First, he argued, there simply isn't enough known about primitive cultures to generalize about them. He criticized the work of his contemporaries not only for their racism, but also for the fact that they didn't know anything about primitive culture. This gave way to ludicrous speculations such as "promiscuous intercourse among siblings" or world-wide travels by ancient Egyptians. Second, Boas recognized that primitive cultures were rapidly disappearing or losing their traditional practices. Under these circumstances, Boas argued that anthropology should adopt the goal of "salvage ethnography": documenting native cultural traditions before they were lost completely. It was as if he felt that theorizing and imposing order on his findings would diminish the time available to him to gather data. With indigenous cultures everywhere disappearing, theory could wait until all the "facts" had been collected.

Boas' opposition to generalization resulted in an exhaustive but unsystematic collection of ethnographic information. One of his first students, Paul Radin, said of Boas that "the essence of his method was…to gather facts, and ever more facts… and permit them to speak for themselves" (quoted in White 1947: 406). Marian Smith, an archaeologist who trained under Boas, observed that "This exhaustive collection of data which seems at the time to have little or no connection with any specific problem is peculiarly a feature of [Boas'] natural history approach…There is a fascination in following the details of a subject just for its own intrinsic interest" (Smith 1959: 49). Boas himself published almost 10,000 pages on the Kwakiutl Indians, with whom he lived on-and-off over a 20-year period beginning in 1890. But the absence of any theoretical program meant that there was no guidance to his research. Boas might encounter an informant well versed in dance, and collect as much data as possible from that person; from another he might collect a large number of folk tales; from a third a tremendous amount about building fish traps. There was no method to his data collection, and he published the primary data in unedited form with minimal commentary. One of his texts contains almost 40 pages of Northwest coast blueberry pie recipes!

In essence, Boas attempted to follow the canons of inductive reasoning that Bacon laid out in the early seventeenth century, but he was never able to derive any generalizations from his meticulous ethnographic evidence. This should not surprise us, or most philosophers of knowledge for that matter. As philosophers from Hume to William James pointed out in their critiques of induction, without a theoretical or conceptual framework to guide our observations, it is impossible to make sense of the world. Yet, Boas' extensive publications on the Kwakiutl did prove inadvertently helpful to the tribe itself decades later. At the time of Boas' fieldwork with the Kwakiutl, they were coming under intense pressure by Canadian authorities to assimilate, culminating in a ban on potlatching and confiscation of numerous potlatch valuables. By the 1950s, Kwakiutl tribal members sought to recover some aspects of their culture and language that had been lost in the years since Boas' work with them in the 1890s, and they turned to Boas' texts in order to help them reconstruct some aspects of their lost culture.

Nonetheless, considering the many recipes and other ethnographic trivia compiled by Boas, it was hard even at the time for some of his students to understand the relevance of much of his ethnographic data. The bulk of Boas' years of work among the Kwakiutl was concerned with folk tales, mythology, food preparation, and material culture. Scholars who have tried to reconstruct the subsistence practices, kinship, and political organization of the Kwakiutl have found this material largely wanting. After reading this, I know you want to sample some of Boas' rich ethnographic data, so here it is. Below I present a portion of a lengthy recipe for Kwakiutl "salmon stomachs" as transcribed by Boas in the 1890s. Enjoy, but be sure to observe the warning about not boiling them too long!

> After the woman has cut open the silver-salmon caught by her husband… she squeezes out the food that is in the stomach, and the slime that is on the gills. She turns the stomach inside out; and when she has cleaned many, she takes a kettle and pours water into it. When the kettle is half full of water, she puts the stomach of the silver-salmon into it. After they are all in she puts the kettle on the fire; and when it is on the fire, she takes her tongs and stirs them. When (the contents) begin to boil, she stops stirring. The reason for stirring is to make the stomachs hard before the water gets too hot; for if they do not stir them, they remain soft and tough, and are not hard. Then the woman always takes up one of (the stomachs) with the tongs; and when she can hold it in the tongs, it is done; but when it is slippery, it is not done. (When it is done,) she takes off the fire what she is cooking. It is said that if, in cooking it, it stays on the fire too long, it gets slippery. Then she will pour it away outside of the house, for it is not good if it is that way. If it should be eaten when it is boiled too long, (those who eat it) could keep it down only a short time. They would vomit. Therefore they watch it carefully.

No doubt you are asking why I included this recipe. The answer is fairly obvious. By now, you know that this would not be a legitimate anthropology textbook unless there was *at least* one passage about local food practices intended to make you queasy.

A major shortfall of his perspective, then, was the collection of facts that would not permit generalization (most of the world's cultures, I suspect, lack recipes for salmon guts). A second feature was that Boas sought out examples that would disconfirm those generalizations that did exist. Later critics argued that Boas and his students tried to suggest that cultural practices are chaotic and unpredictable. For example, one of the valid generalizations made by nineteenth-century anthropologists (following the Jesuit ethnographers of the seventeenth century) was that hunter-gatherers tended to have communal hunting territories rather than individualized land tenure. To Morgan and Marx this seemed logical since there is no conceivable way that people could get wild game to confine themselves to one part of a territory. One of Boas' first students, Robert Lowie, tried to demolish this "myth" and to disprove the Marxist notion of "primitive communism" by citing a number of hunting-gathering societies for which individual land tenure was reported. He discussed, for example, the Algonkians of Labrador, eastern Canada, who were studied by Boas' student Frank Speck in 1915. At the time that Speck worked in the area, the Algonkians had been involved in beaver trapping for well over 100 years, having long since given up their caribou hunting past. Speck found that in some areas individuals did claim rights to trapping territories. Neither Speck nor Lowie apparently asked whether that was the aboriginal (pre-contact) pattern. In the 1950s Eleanor Leacock conducted an ethnohistorical study using early fur trappers' records and Jesuits' diaries and found considerable evidence for communal hunting territories. It was the introduction of a cash economy that undermined this communal land tenure, causing land to be divided into individually or family owned parcels. Lowie did not mention this history, but every one of his "exceptions" cited to "demolish the myth of communal hunting territory" can be analyzed in the same way.

What we see here is not just an aversion to producing theories of culture. The Boasians' assumptions that culture could not be explained led them to examine those areas of culture that could not be generalized about. It also led them to emphasize the differences between cultures in their descriptions. Whereas evolutionists (and to an extent the diffusionists) had overemphasized similarities in accounting for cultural laws, the Boasians played up the seeming unpredictability of culture. Far from resulting in useful generalizations, their reliance on inductive procedures contributed to this fragmented view of randomly associated cultural traits.

Contributions of the Boasian school

There are a few who argue that Boas was a reactionary. Leslie White, for example, said that Boas set back the course of anthropology an entire generation due to his refusal to build on the theories of the past (those of the unilinear evolutionists, of whom White considered himself a disciple). I don't accept that at all. We should by now recognize from Kuhn that when a new paradigm appears it overthrows everything in the preceding paradigm, regardless of its merit. The Boasian perspective was a radical break with the past. Despite its failure to develop a coherent theory of culture, it left us with significant, indeed defining contributions that anthropologists today continue to accept.

Prior to Boas, few researchers had collected original ethnographic data, and those who did were usually government agents or missionaries with explicit agendas for controlling, pacifying, or converting Native Americans. As early as 1830, Henry Schoolcraft, one of the founders of the Bureau of American Ethnology, recorded primary ethnographic data from American Indians, as did John Wesley Powell several decades later on the western frontier. By the 1860s, Christian missionaries were engaged in ethnographic research along the western frontiers of the US and Canada, often working in conjunction with government Indian agents (Higham 2000). What elevated Boas above his peers was that ethnographic fieldwork became not just an optional, short-term activity performed by a few anthropologists but the single most important professional criterion for all anthropologists. Further, unlike most previous ethnographic research, his work and that of his students emphasized primary data collection independent of the agendas of government and the church. He required original fieldwork of all his PhD students, a requirement that has since been institutionalized in every graduate program of cultural anthropology in the United States. When Boas found it, anthropology was speculative theorizing; when he left it, it was a strong empirical study.

A second significant contribution was Boas' separation of the concepts of race and behavior. He single-handedly resurrected the Enlightenment notion that human groups owe their entire behavioral repertoire to their social environment. As we have seen, Durkheim and E.B. Tylor could be characterized among Boas' immediate predecessors or contemporaries who were also non-racist in their theoretical pronouncements. Yet, for them, these sentiments were made only in passing, and not wedded to active engagement with political struggles for social justice and equality. Meanwhile, the large majority of their contemporaries remained overtly racist in their explanations of human behavior. Boas, however, was emphatic there were no biological or racial determinants of social behavior and he staked his professional career on alleviating racial injustice. In 1894, Boas wrote that "the variations inside any single race are such that they overlap the variations in another race so that a number of characteristics may be common to individuals of both races" (1974a, orig. 1894: 227). This assertion, a radical dissent from the prevailing notion of races as immutable and discrete categories, closely anticipates the position of modern physical anthropologists, who have questioned the utility of race as a biological construct. His work in this regard was extremely progressive for the day, when the reigning attitudes of most educated people were much more closely aligned with the aforementioned William McGee.

Finally, Boas is credited with developing the concept of cultural relativism. Boas was the first anthropologist (and perhaps the first Euro-American scholar of his time) to refer to small-scale nonwestern cultures in a way that was empathetic, tolerant, and respectful. Despite his non-racist beliefs, Tylor certainly saw "savages" as inferior to "civilized" people in their reasoning ability. Durkheim, too, entertained stereotypes about "mechanically" rather than "organically integrated" societies. None of this condescension is present in Boas' work. In contrast, Boas wrote home during his first trip among the Inuit (1883):

> Is it not a beautiful custom that these "savages" suffer all deprivation in common, but in happy times when someone has brought back booty from the hunt, all join in eating and drinking? I often ask myself what advantages our "good society" possesses over that of the "savages." The more I see of their customs, the more I realize that we have no right to look down on them. Where amongst our people would you find such true hospitality?
>
> (quoted in Stocking 1982: 148)

But what exactly do we mean by cultural relativism? While all anthropologists continue to hold the principle of cultural relativism as an ideal, this goal has been understood in varying ways by different scholars. Some of these interpretations have troubling ethical connotations. Cultural relativism is frequently stated in several variants, each of which has differing implications:

a) that cultural values can only be understood within their cultural context of local history and traditions. This, I would argue, is closest to Boas' original meaning.
b) that because cultural values cannot be understood outside their cultural context, they are all equally worthy of respect. This phrasing of cultural relativism seems to have first arisen in the concluding chapter of Ruth Benedict's best-selling book *Patterns of Culture* (1934).

In variant (a) above, cultural relativism might be considered an important methodological principle. Just as social theorists going back to Durkheim, Comte, and Montesquieu recognized that cultural practices are integrated, Boas argued that they must be seen in the context of their relationship to other traits and practices. Anthropologists who failed to do so, he warned, would gravely misinterpret the cultural behaviors and materials that they sought to understand. Although (b) may appear to have a similar meaning, its implications are actually quite distinct. It means, by implication, that outsiders may make no judgments about cultures other than their own. Like epistemological relativism, it has been argued that this definition is illogical because it contradicts itself, in addition to posing troubling implications for our ethical and political stance toward cultural practices that entail human rights violations. How is this? In the former case, if we consider all cultures equally valid, and some cultures subscribe to the belief that other cultures are not valid, then we should consider as valid the belief that not all cultures are equally valid. (My head hurts.) Of perhaps greater importance, a tendency to regard all cultural practices as equally worthy of respect implies that anthropologists should refrain from denouncing genocide, racism, and sexism in those cultures whose members deem these to be acceptable. My argument is that it is possible to examine, for example, the 1994 Hutu genocide of Rwanda's Tutsis within the cultural and historical context of that society (as in the first meaning of cultural relativism), without embracing the morally objectionable stance of the second meaning.

The image of Boas which was upheld by his students was that of a professional scientist who had raised anthropological research methods to a level comparable to that of the natural sciences. In doing so, he established fieldwork as a fundamental professional requirement for cultural anthropologists and thereby rid the discipline of the quacks, cranks, racists, and armchair theorists that had earlier dominated it. Margaret Mead, probably Boas' best known student outside of academia, stated that "there are no methods named after Boas, just as there is no Boas school." There was simply a driving compulsion to conduct careful, thorough ethnographic research. Yet, his emphasis on compiling long lists of cultural traits, his emphasis that each culture had a unique history reflecting both diffusion and independent invention, did imply some assumptions about human societies overall. There was a tendency among Boas and his students to emphasize the parts over the whole, to describe individual traits and ignore the way in which they might be related to one another. Indeed, if a culture borrows trait x from another culture, independently invents trait y, and borrows trait z from yet another culture, there would be no necessary relationship between x, y, and z. Although these traits are shared by the same set of people, they come from different sources and are unrelated. Hence, the Boasian view of individual cultures is that they are fragmented, not integrated in the sense that Montesquieu, Comte, Durkheim (or, for that matter, Marx) had earlier suggested. This view is best expressed in the work of one of Boas' first students, Robert Lowie, who wrote in *Primitive Society*:

> To that planless hodgepodge, that thing of shreds and patches[3] called [culture,] its historian can no longer yield superstitious reverence. He will realize better than others the obstacles to infusing design into the amorphous product; but in thought at least he will not grovel before it in fatalistic acquiescence but dream of a rational scheme to supplant the chaotic jumble.
>
> (1920: 331)

Culture then, from the Boasian viewpoint, is a "planless hodgepodge," a "thing of shreds and patches," an "amorphous product," a "chaotic jumble." Culture was essentially random, and each society the product of a historical accident. If the Durkheimian analogy is one of a living, breathing organism with interrelated parts, the Boasian model of culture was one of a patchwork quilt whose parts bore no relationship to one another at all. It is simply an amalgam of unrelated scraps whose owner plucked from other places or sewed himself. It is this model of culture that the next generation of anthropologists was to reject, both in the United States and Britain.

Quiz yourself

Answer True or False to each statement

1   US and British colonialism in the nineteenth century was based on the idea of bringing democracy to people living in the colonized parts of the world.

2   Widespread concern about "absorbing semicivilized states" into the United States repeatedly prevented American presidents from seeking annexation of Central American and Caribbean territories.

3   According to Langness, one of the implications of Ernest Häckel's "biogenetic law" is that the thought and behavior of "savages" is like that of children in civilized societies.

4   Boas criticized the notion of "psychic unity" by pointing out that the same trait in different cultures often served quite different purposes.

5   The idea that all great inventions originated just once, in ancient Egypt, was a claim advanced by the German *Kulturkreis* school of diffusion.

6   Eighteenth-century German philosopher Immanuel Kant claimed that our perceptions of the world are constrained by preexisting categories of mind, such as moral ideas and individual concepts of space and time.

7   Boas argued that in principle there were no differences between the goals of the natural sciences and the social sciences.

8   The goal of Boas' "salvage ethnography" was to engage in as much theoretical debate as possible so that the pressing anthropological questions of evolution vs. diffusion could be settled once and for all.

9   Boas might be considered an early proponent of the deductive approach in anthropology, allowing his theory to guide his collection and interpretation of data.

10 Boas basically shared Comte's and Durkheim's "organismic" view that all the elements of a culture stood in some kind of functional relationship to one another.

8

CULTURE AND PSYCHOLOGY

Shredding the patchwork quilt

Recall that one of the assumptions of Durkheim had been an organismic analogy, by which he assumed that institutions contribute to the maintenance of society. It becomes possible to explain these institutions in terms of their functions and their relationship to each other. What Boas had proposed was quite different. His view of culture, as expressed by his student Robert Lowie, was not of a living organism, but of a patchwork quilt. Each patch had a different origin and was unrelated in any way to the patch sewn next to it. A given system of kinship bears no relationship to the type of subsistence practiced by the same culture, and these have no relationship to that culture's religious concepts. Regardless of the famous differences between Malinowski and Radcliffe-Brown (to be explored in the next chapter), this "fragmented" view of culture was rejected by British anthropologists in the first half of the twentieth century. In this chapter, we examine a perspective in American anthropology that also rejected this idea of culture as a hodgepodge of unrelated traits. This is the perspective of *Culture and Personality* (later known as *Psychological Anthropology*), which dominated American anthropology between 1930 and the 1950s. This perspective was more or less contemporary with British functionalism.

As his career progressed Boas developed an interest in the effects of culture on the individual, particularly how culture shapes the behavior of the individual and how individuals leave their mark on culture. Boas imparted this interest to many of his students, who in turn took this line of inquiry in different directions. Among them, Paul Radin (1883–1959) worked with the Winnebago Indians of the Great Plains for over 40 years. Radin attempted to show how individuals can be both the product of their culture as well as a factor influencing its development. He did this not by writing ethnographies of entire societies, but biographies of selected members. In 1926 Radin published *Crashing Thunder: The Autobiography of an American Indian*. This was the first time the life history method had been used in ethnographic writing; Radin used the experiences of a prominent Indian chief to illustrate the effects of culture and history on the individual. Radin began an ethnographic approach that has been embraced by many subsequent anthropologists who published life histories of members of the cultures with whom they resided (notable examples of this are Oscar Lewis' *Five Families* [1959] and *The Children of Sanchez* [1963], Andrew Strathern's *Ongka: A Self-Account of a New Guinea Big Man* [1979], and Marjorie Shostak's *Nisa: The Life and Words of a !Kung Woman* [1990]).

Two of Boas' most prominent students, Ruth Benedict (1887–1948) and Margaret Mead (1901–1978), turned an interest in psychology into the Culture and Personality orientation. Both set out to discover how culture shapes the personality of the individual. You might consider how the biographical details that I provide of each scholar (below) informed the way in which they viewed anthropology and its relationship to their own society. In short, their dissatisfaction with the gender role expectations of American society led them to embrace a fairly strong form of cultural relativism. Benedict and Mead might be considered excellent illustrations of Thomas Kuhn's point that our research interests are influenced by our paradigms, which we often adhere to for highly personal reasons.

Benedict (Figure 8.1) entered graduate school at Columbia University and studied with Boas from 1919 until 1923, when she joined the faculty there in the Department of Anthropology. She had earlier majored in English at Barnard College and had earned some literary success as a poet, publishing under the pseudonym Anne Singleton. Benedict entered the field of anthropology in her early 30s, after an unfulfilling experience in social work and an unhappy marriage persuaded her to

FIGURE 8.1   Ruth Benedict. © Bettmann/CORBIS.

return to college. She went on to become one of the first American women to hold a university teaching position. It is said that her determination to establish herself in an academic career arose from the dismissive attitude of one of her undergraduate professors, who told his female students that women were "unsuitable" for academic life. Largely because her graduate advisor Franz Boas challenged such ideas and encouraged his female students to seek academic careers, and because of his towering influence in the discipline in its early decades, anthropology has always been a more congenial place for women than most of the social sciences.[1]

Although Benedict's efforts were supported by her mentor, her husband was not supportive of Ruth's career in the slightest way. Stanley Benedict discouraged her from returning to college or taking up a profession. If this wasn't bad enough, the fact that she was "Mrs. Benedict," wife of a successful biochemist, actually prevented her from being paid for her teaching at Columbia. University administrators considered her "financially supported" by her husband and therefore *ineligible* for a salary! This status changed when, after 16 years of marriage, the couple separated. As a consequence, Ruth was finally appointed as an Assistant Professor of Anthropology in 1931, her first salaried faculty appointment after nine years of unpaid teaching. It was also at about this time that she discovered her "feminine nature," according to her letters, and fell in love with her former student, Margaret Mead. Mead at the time was married to her second husband, the New Zealand anthropologist Reo Fortune. Reflecting the norms of the times, the relationship between the women was concealed from others, but became widely known from the exchange of letters that were made public after Mead's death. One of Benedict's most famous poems, "In the Hour after Love," concludes by asking "what can compete/With sleep begotten of a woman's kiss?" Few readers of the time could have known that these lines were spoken of a same-sex relationship.

Margaret Mead arrived at Columbia in 1924 and earned her doctorate after studying with Boas and Benedict. Benedict's initial fieldwork was with the Zuni Pueblo of Arizona, while Mead went to Samoa and later New Guinea. Their close professional relationship turned amorous after Mead finished her PhD in 1929. Although Mead was married three times (to three different anthropologists), her romantic relationship with Benedict continued until the 1940s. Her critics, such as Derek Freeman, have argued that she employed her anthropological findings as a means to indirectly critique those aspects of American gender roles that she found inhibiting. Whether or not criticism of western cultural norms was her intention, it seems plausible, as Kuhn might claim, that Mead's personal life drove many of her scholarly concerns.

Ruth Benedict's *Patterns of Culture* probably best exemplifies the Culture and Personality school. Reflecting her training as a poet and writer, Benedict brought to her work a literary quality and evocative style rarely seen in most anthropological publications, and the book's readability and beauty have won it perennial popularity. Widely read by anthropologists and non-anthropologists alike after it was published in 1934, it is still in print today and has been translated into 12 languages and sold millions of volumes. Benedict's book contrasted three societies that exhibit strikingly different norms of behavior: the Southwestern Zuni and Hopi (based on Benedict's own fieldwork in the late 1920s), the Dobuans of the Southwest Pacific (based on the field research of Mead's second husband Reo Fortune), and the Kwakiutl and surrounding Northwest Coast tribes of North America (based on Franz Boas' ethnographic work). The book argues for the extreme plasticity of human behavior, implicitly challenging the notion that the norms of American society are either widely-shared or somehow more "natural" to human groups than are the contrasting norms found in other cultures.

The central theme of *Patterns of Culture* is that people are faced with an infinite array of behavioral possibilities, from which each culture will select only a limited range as acceptable and normative. In one of her most famous passages, Benedict quotes a chief of the Digger Indians of California who said, "In the beginning… God gave to every people a cup, a cup of clay, and from this cup they drank their life" (1934: 21). With this metaphor she emphasized the uniqueness of each culture and its associated values. The behaviors that are selected are those conforming to the culture's *configuration*, by which she meant its overall psychological orientation. The term configuration is derived from the then-popular notion of Gestalt psychology (*Gestalt* being German for "form" or "shape"). Psychologists of the time applied this idea to experiments which suggested that people learn in response to underlying patterns called forth by a specific event rather than by a direct stimulus response. For example, when we learn as children that unruly behavior is unacceptable in one ritual setting (a church or synagogue), we extend that knowledge to other scenes and sites of ritual behavior, such as museums, weddings, funerals, etc. Even when we enter new situations we follow previously learned instructions because the new situation summons forth an earlier learned pattern.

Benedict's essential argument in *Patterns of Culture* contains, according to Margaret Mead's Preface, a "view of human cultures as 'personality writ large'" (1934: xiii). Each culture chooses from "the great arc of human potentialities" (ibid.: viii) only a few characteristics which become the leading personality traits of the members of that culture. These traits suffuse an interdependent constellation of aesthetics and values in each culture which together add up to a unique *Gestalt*. It would be possible to discern some cultures as having an overtly aggressive configuration; others might be passive; others cooperative, and so on. All aspects of a given culture, in terms of its interpersonal behavior, mythology, aesthetic styles, and conceptions of the supernatural, are thought to reflect its distinct configuration. In somewhat circular fashion, the rituals, beliefs, and personal preferences among the members of each culture then encourage the formation of a distinct personality. In contrast to the Boasian notion of a "planless hodgepodge," Benedict's argument is that all aspects of a given culture reflect a given psychological configuration; culture is "individual psychology thrown large upon the screen" (1934: 32).

Among Pueblo cultures of the American Southwest, Benedict describes an overriding emphasis on the value of restraint, contrasting that with the emphasis on *abandon* in the Native American cultures of the Pacific Northwest. Rather than using psychological terms (i.e. aggressive or passive or neurotic) to characterize individual

FIGURE 8.2   Friedrich Wilhelm Nietszche. Courtesy of the Library of Congress.

cultures, *Patterns of Culture* borrows concepts used by the nineteenth–century German philosopher Friedrich Nietzsche (1844–1900; Figure 8.2) to contrast character types in his study of Greek drama, *The Birth of Tragedy*. Benedict employs the Nietzschean opposites of "Apollonian" and "Dionysian" "psychological types" to characterize the two Native American cultures featured in her work. Nietzsche had described how in ancient Greece, the worshipers of Apollo emphasized order and restraint in their celebrations. In contrast, the worshipers of Dionysus, the god of wine, engaged in wild abandon.

Benedict was attracted to some of the complex philosophical notions of Nietzsche long before entering the field of anthropology. In her 1989 biography *Ruth Benedict: Stranger in the Land*, Margaret Caffrey writes that Nietzsche "advocated the destruction of conventional morality and conformity because they suffocated creativity. He affirmed physical joy…All of these were qualities Ruth believed most important…" (1989: 54–55).Yet, given Nietzsche's exceptionally misogynistic views, as well as his repudiation of egalitarianism or any form of democracy, it is somewhat surprising that she was drawn to his philosophy. But Nietzsche may be one of those complex thinkers for whom everyone can find something that is affirming. Decades after his death, the Nazis revered him for his conception of the *übermensch*, or "superman," which they mistook for the German "master race." To force this interpretation, the Nazis had to ignore Nietzsche's denunciations of anti-Semitism and German nationalism, which had even led him to sever his friendship with the composer Richard Wagner, perhaps the leading figure in German cultural life at the time. Nietzsche was given to outrageous claims, particularly where women were concerned, and his interpreters still debate how much of these statements were sincere and how much he uttered them simply for their shock value. As Nietzsche wrote famously in his most heavily-read work, *Also Sprach Zarathustra*, "[E]verything about woman has one solution: pregnancy…Man should be educated for war, and woman for the recreation of the warrior; all else is folly" (Nietzsche 1976: 178).

Using Nietzsche's character types, Benedict portrays the Zuni as having an Apollonian configuration, emphasizing emotional restraint, an aversion to excesses, and an emphasis on perfection. The Zuni perform celebratory dances in precise and careful formations that betray little emotional expressiveness. Intoxication and loss of emotional control are considered repulsive and shameful. On the other hand, the Kwakiutl are prone to exuberant Dionysian excess, reflected most dramatically in the hyper-competitive rhetoric and exchange associated with the potlatch. Ostensibly an exchange of gifts, the goal of the potlatch is expressed in the term "p'asa," or to *flatten* one's adversaries with a level of extraordinary generosity that cannot be reciprocated. These competitive exchanges of wealth are conducted by strutting, megalomaniac chiefs who taunt their visitors by pointing out their comparative poverty. Dionysian excess carries over into winter initiation ceremonies, when young men transition from boyhood to adult status. The initiates dance ecstatically for days on end, inducing a trance state in which they fling themselves at one another and bite the living flesh from each others' arms. Benedict writes:

> The Dionysian…seeks to attain in his most valued moments escape from the boundaries imposed upon him by his five senses, to break through into another order of existence. The desire of the Dionysian, in personal experience or in ritual, is to press through it toward a certain psychological state, to achieve excess…The Apollonian distrusts all this, and has often little idea of the nature of such experiences…He keeps to the middle of the road, stays within the known map, does not meddle with disruptive psychological states. In Nietzsche's fine phrase, even in the exaltation of the dance he "remains what he is, and retains his civic name."
>
> (1934: 72)

The Melanesian society of Dobu presents a different picture altogether in its cultural configuration, one in which jealousy and supernatural means of retaliation dominate. Benedict characterizes the Dobuan as

> dour, prudish, and passionate, consumed with jealousy and suspicion and resentment. Every moment of prosperity he conceives himself to have wrung from a malicious world by a conflict in which he has worsted his opponent. The good man is the one who has many such conflicts to his credit, as anyone can see from the fact that he has survived with a measure of prosperity. It is taken for granted that he has thieved, killed children and his close associates by sorcery, cheated whenever he dared…Sorcery and witchcraft are by no means criminal. A valued man could not exist without them.
>
> (1934: 168–169)

Indeed, Reo Fortune, who supplied Benedict with ethnographic material about Dobu, mentioned that a Dobuan friend gave him a magical incantation so that he could make himself invisible. The value of this spell, the Dobuan explained to the puzzled anthropologist, was that "now you can go into the shops in Sydney, steal what you like and get away with it unseen" (ibid.: 122). He went on to explain how he had frequently used the spell himself to steal food from neighbors and to harm enemies without detection.

The Dobuans appear to represent a paradox in sexual terms: "It is significant that prudery should be as extreme in Dobu as it was among our Puritan ancestors" (ibid.: 121). Hence, bodily functions are always performed in private and both they and sexuality are taboo topics of conversation. Yet, Benedict goes on to note that prudery in public is associated with considerable sexual tension and activity in private. Men are intensely jealous of the sexual attentions that other men pay their wives; such concerns are indeed warranted, Benedict notes, as all men regard any unaccompanied woman as fair game for their sexual prowess. "In Dobu dourness and prudery go along with prenuptial promiscuity and with a high estimation of sex passion and techniques…The stock sex teaching with which women enter marriage is that the way to hold their husband is to keep them as exhausted as possible. There is no belittling of the physical aspects of sex" (ibid.: 155).

From her own life experience, Benedict recognized that not all individuals can comfortably accommodate the accepted norms within their culture. By the time she began graduate study in anthropology, she realized that she could no longer conform to the prevailing gender expectations for married American women. Benedict assumed that similar conflicts between individual values and cultural expectations could be found in other societies as well. One of her students, Ruth Landes, affirmed that Benedict "pursued anthropology to answer her own private questions about the individual's fate" (quoted in Cole 2002: 533). Human nature is not fixed, nor are people entirely devoid of free will. The sanctions for defying the values of one's culture are so severe, however, that most people ultimately conform, at least on the exterior, to the core values of their society. Yet not everyone finds the values of their culture to be "equally congenial." Benedict described deviance as essentially a clash between the individual's personality and their culture's values. A person honored and respected in a Dionysian culture would be a despised outcast in an Apollonian one. Among the Dobuans, a deviant would be the person who exhibits friendship and sincerity to others, attributes that would be valued elsewhere. Hence, not only are cultural values relative and not absolute, but so is the definition of deviance.

Because of the beauty and vividness of Benedict's writing, her book remains one of the two or three most widely read ethnographic studies ever published. For millions of non-anthropologists it represents what cultural anthropology is about. Yet it is not without its intensely controversial aspects. In her concluding chapter, Benedict carried Boas' methodological principle of cultural relativism into a plea for the acceptance of all cultural differences. The argument set forth in the final sentences of her book approaches that of moral relativism that I posed in my discussion of Boas in the previous chapter:

The recognition of cultural relativity carries with it its own values, which need not be those of the absolutist philosophies. It challenges customary opinions and causes those who have been bred to them acute discomfort…As soon as the new opinion is embraced as customary belief, it will be another trusted bulwark of the good life. We shall arrive then at a more realistic social faith, accepting as grounds of hope and as new bases for tolerance the coexisting and *equally valid patterns of life* which mankind has created for itself from the raw materials of existence.

(1934: 257)

Having ended her book with a recognition of the "equally valid patterns of life" found among the world's cultures, Benedict adroitly side steps the moral quandaries posed by tolerating cultural practices that may oppress or harm others. Many anthropologists then and since would take exception to Benedict's closing argument that all cultures are equally valid; unfortunately, because her book has become associated in the minds of many with cultural anthropology, her controversial understanding of cultural relativism is one which is often attributed to anthropology as a whole.

Mead employed the notion of configuration to produce a similar study based upon her fieldwork with Reo Fortune in northern Papua New Guinea during 1931–33 and published two years later as *Sex and Temperament in Three Primitive Societies.* Here Mead contrasted three societies in terms of their sex role expectations: the "gentle mountain-dwelling" Arapesh, the "fierce cannibalistic" Mundugumor, and the "graceful headhunters" of the Tchambuli. Mead described her study as "an account of how three primitive societies have grouped their social attitudes toward temperament about the very obvious facts of sex-difference" (1950: ix). Her goal was to show that the sex-specific roles we in western society consider appropriate and "natural" are not universal, and that gender expectations are subject to as much variability as is personality. Mead's portrait of the Arapesh suggested that in this culture men and women act in a largely similar fashion. Men have as much of a role in childrearing as women do, while women are accorded as many rights and responsibilities within the family as men. The Arapesh, Mead wrote, "regard both men and women as inherently gentle, responsive, and cooperative, able and willing to subordinate the self to the needs of those who are younger or weaker and to derive a major satisfaction from doing so" (1950: 134).

The Mundugumor are presented as a stark contrast: according to Mead, both men and women are aggressive, both acting according to an extreme variant of the competitive relations existing between men in our culture. Mundugumor men are "born into a hostile world, a world in which most of the members of his own sex will be his enemies, in which his major equipment for success must be a capacity for violence, for seeing and avenging insult" (ibid.: 189). Similar attitudes are shared among women, who "are believed to be just as violent, just as aggressive, just as jealous. They simply are not quite as strong physically, although a woman can put up a very good fight and a husband who wishes to beat his wife takes care to arm himself with a crocodile jaw and to be sure that she is not armed" (ibid.: 210).

Finally, men and women among the Tchambuli act in a manner largely opposite to the gender expectations of western cultures. Women are the energetic managers of households and farms. They are largely uninterested in self-expression or adornment, devoting most of their efforts to fishing and manufacturing. Men, on the other hand,

> may be said to live principally for art. Every man is an artist and most men are skilled not in some one art alone, but in many: in dancing, carving, plaiting, painting and so on. Each man is chiefly concerned with his role upon the stage of his society, with the elaboration of his costume, the beauty of the masks that he owns…and upon other people's recognition and valuation of his performance.
>
> (ibid: 255)

For their part, women look at men's self-absorption with "kindly tolerance and appreciation" (ibid.).

Sex and Temperament, like *Patterns of Culture*, was widely read by a non-academic audience, and indeed Mead herself stated that her purpose in publishing the work was far broader than simply influencing anthropological debates. With it she challenged dominant ideas in the United States regarding the fixity of gender roles. Most Americans then believed that the male role as breadwinners and domestic role of women were the inevitable outcome of biological differences between the sexes. Mead countered this assumption with the ethnographic claim that gender was just as malleable and culturally-determined as Benedict had suggested for personality in general. Mead's ability to discern such immense cultural differences among neighboring societies prompted skepticism among other anthropologists, however. The first to raise questions about the accuracy of her reporting was her former collaborator and husband, Reo Fortune, whose marriage to Mead unraveled while the two of them worked with Cambridge anthropologist Gregory Bateson in the Sepik valley.[2] In the 1950 edition of her book, she acknowledged that "many readers felt that her analysis was too pretty" and that "I must have found what I was looking for" (Mead 1950: 170). The differences in gender role patterns that Mead identified in three adjacent cultures may have seemed, she acknowledged, "too good to be true," but she reasserted the objectivity of her account and that she had not simply reported what she had wanted to find.

Before we turn to the criticisms that soon emerged of the Culture and Personality school, we might acknowledge that one of the reasons why *Patterns of Culture* and *Sex and Temperament* were so persuasive in their day was that they described cultures in ways that made sense to many readers. When describing other people, we tend to offer generalizations about their personalities. We don't typically describe people in terms of how they behave ("I saw him looking around frantically in a crowded room" or "I saw her hold the door open for someone in a wheelchair"); instead, we say, "he's anxious," "she's considerate," etc. And the idea that each culture has a unique set of personality traits certainly didn't originate with Benedict and Mead. It's found in the ethnographic observations of the ancient Greeks; whose writings of course tended to describe other groups in exceptionally negative terms. This was unlike the much more respectful—if not romanticized—portraits offered by Benedict and Mead. Despite this significant difference, the Culture and Personality school just made explicit what was a widespread tendency anyway when describing other people.

What one does not see in Benedict's and Mead's work was any accounting at all of *why* one culture's configuration is different from another. It was apparently just an arbitrary group decision of the Zuni to be passive and restrained, while for their part the Kwakiutl gave themselves up to excesses and competitiveness. Presumably, the Tchambuli had agreed among themselves to reverse the standard gender roles associated with western culture, while Mundugumor men and women alike had decided to act in the competitive spirit of western men. While the popularity of *Patterns of Culture* has made it an important source of student recruitment into the profession of anthropology, the book fails to offer any explanation for why a particular configuration of culture exists in one place and another elsewhere. Its central claim, expressed in the simplest possible terms, is just that some cultures are similar, and others different. Needless to say, many anthropologists since have found this argument highly unsatisfying.

Patterns and *Sex and Temperament* dissented (gently) from the view of "Papa Franz" (as Benedict addressed him) that each culture was a "planless hodgepodge," asserting instead that it was patterned along a configuration of personality and psychological traits held in common by the members of that culture. This seems like a mild enough dissent from the Boasian view, and yet even then Benedict felt the need to qualify it, as if anticipating her mentor's objections to her *Gestalt* view of culture. She wrote in the penultimate chapter:

> All cultures of course have not shaped their thousand items of behavior to a balanced and rhythmic pattern. Like certain individuals, certain social orders do not subordinate activities to a ruling motivation. They scatter. If at one moment they seem to be pursuing certain ends, at another they are off on some tangent apparently inconsistent with all that has gone before, which gives no clue to activity that will come after. This lack of integration seems to be as characteristic of certain cultures as extreme integration is of others… Tribes like those of the interior of British Columbia have incorporated traits from all the surrounding civilizations. They have taken their patterns for the manipulation of wealth from one culture area, parts of their religious practices from another, contradictory bits from still another. Their mythology is a hodge-podge of uncoordinated accounts of culture heroes out of three different myth cycles represented in areas around them… Like certain individuals who have been indiscriminately influenced in many different directions, their tribal patterns of behavior are uncoordinated and casual.
>
> (1934: 206–207)

(Notice her no doubt intentional use of the term "hodge-podge" while describing the British Columbian tribes in Boasian terms.)

From "configuration" to Freudian psychology

Notwithstanding Benedict's view that (at least most) cultures are integrated according to a central theme and configuration, she shared with the Boasian tradition the notion that culture just "happens." Later anthropologists in the culture and personality school sought to move beyond ethnographic description to actually explain cultural variation. In one of his most widely-read essays, Edward Sapir (1949) pleaded for anthropologists to embrace the insights and methods of psychoanalytic theory to understand the dynamics of culture. Accordingly, many anthropologists turned their attention to the work of Sigmund Freud (1856–1939; Figure 8.3), for whom childhood, sexual, and family experience loomed large as determinants of personality. As we'll see, most anthropologists have rejected much of Freud's work, but they have also retained some important aspects, notably the role of child rearing in personality formation.

Although he practiced almost exclusively among middle- and upper-class Viennese (until the end of his life when the 1938 Nazi *Anschluß* forced him to flee his native Austria), Freud wrote extensively about "primitive" culture, particularly in his early work. The reason why this work is rarely mentioned in anthropology is that it was prone to the worst excesses of nineteenth-century evolutionary speculation. Freud published a number of wide-ranging conjectures as theories of the origins of culture traits. In his 1913 work *Totem and Taboo*, he attempted to account for the

FIGURE 8.3 Sigmund Freud. Asked once whether the cigar that he smoked was not a phallic symbol, Freud replied, rather anxiously, "sometimes a cigar is just a cigar." Cigars were to prove his undoing, as late in life he endured 30 often excruciating operations for recurrent oral cancer. Indeed, he was already in the terminal stages of cancer when he left Austria for England so that he could "die in freedom." Courtesy of Time & Life Pictures/Getty Images.

origins of religion. The earliest societies, Freud wrote, were those in which a single patriarch held exclusive sexual privileges over his sisters and daughters. His sexually deprived sons resented this monopoly to the extent that they eventually killed the old man and devoured him in a cannibalistic orgy. Afterwards, however, the brothers were overcome with guilt, and so they repressed their desire for sexual relations with their mothers and sisters. At the same time, to rid themselves of this guilt, they created the religious idea of the totem, which is regarded as their father but is symbolically represented as an animal species. By worshipping the totem, which they honor by refusing to kill and eat it, they hope to alleviate their guilt over their earlier murderous deed (Freud 2001: 152).

From this original act of sexually-inspired murder, according to Freud, we see the creation of the universal nuclear family incest taboo. We also see origins of the Oedipal complex: the universal but usually repressed desire of males to kill their fathers and sleep with their mothers (c'mon guys…fess up!). And finally, we also see the origins of religion. Isn't this a great all-purpose theory? Indeed, it renders obsolete and unnecessary the work of Tylor, Morgan, Frazer, Durkheim, Weber, and probably many others!

Freud's evolutionary speculations in *Totem and Taboo* were widely criticized by early twentieth-century anthropologists. Upon his return to England from his Trobriand fieldwork, Malinowski read Freud for the first time and immediately wrote a paper to "disprove" the notion of a universal Oedipal complex with evidence from the Trobriands. Freud had argued that the father–son relationship was always an ambivalent, competitive love–hate relationship because of the son's latent sexual interest in his mother, over whom his father had a sexual monopoly. The Trobrianders, unlike Freud's Viennese clients, are matrilineal, and like many matrilineal societies, a young male has relatively distant relations with his father. The most important relationship in a young man's life is with his mother's brother, his matrilineal kinsman who acts as an authority figure. It's with that individual (his maternal uncle) that a young man has an ambivalent love–hate relationship, not with the man who has sexual rights to his mother.

Now here's a very interesting side-light on the relationship between Malinowski and Freudian ideas. As you recall, while he was in the Trobriands, Malinowski kept the infamous journal that was published after his death as *A Diary in the Strict Sense of the Term*. In several passages, he reported being tormented by nightmares of witnessing or causing his father's death and subsequently having sex with his mother. This was *before* he encountered Freud's work on the Oedipal complex! How, then, are we to interpret Malinowski's later eagerness to "disprove" the Oedipal complex? Psychologists have a term for this: *denial*.

That is exactly how a prominent psychological anthropologist interpreted Malinowski's position on the Oedipal complex. One of the relatively few anthropologists to remain a doctrinaire Freudian, the Hungarian scholar Geza Roheim (1891–1953) even dedicated his 1950 volume *Psychoanalysis and Anthropology* "to the memory of Sigmund Freud." Roheim argued that if anthropologists challenged the universality of the Oedipal complex it could only mean one thing: they had unresolved and repressed Oedipal complexes themselves! Indeed, for Roheim, the Oedipal complex underlay almost every single one of the cultural phenomena minutely described in his massive 496-page volume. Among the Arunta, an Australian hunter-gatherer group, he claimed that the mother slept with her young male child under her in order to keep him warm in an arrangement resembling the male position during coitus (Roheim 1950: 44). This, he said, produces marked sexual confusion and Oedipal anxieties in the male child, which receives later institutional expression and resolution in the famous initiation rite of sub-incision. This involves an operation on a young man in which the base of his penis is sliced open its entire length all the way up to the uretha (do I detect some squirming out there?). Sub-incision is required of all aboriginal males during the process of initiation to adulthood, which occurs at about the age of 15. In an earlier psychoanalytic study of the Australian Arunta, Roheim declared—in a rather awkwardly written passage—that the sub-incision rite represents an attempt by men to possess both a vagina and a penis and is rooted in their earlier sexually ambiguous sleeping arrangement with their mothers:

> Religion and society are erected as walls of defense against libidinal dangers inherent in the infantile situation. The mother lies on her son—women must be kept at a distance from the [male initiation] rites. The bleeding vagina is a mystery fraught with attraction and anxiety—women must not be presented at the periodical bleeding of men. The child must not witness parental coitus—the demons are those who are "stuck together"—the rite represents the copulating father. And finally, the central mystery is a penis that is also a vagina (sub-incision).
>
> (Roheim 1945: 176)

Lest such Freudian thinking be dismissed today as something archaic, you can imagine my surprise when, in 1996, my former dissertation advisor at UCLA, Allen Johnson, published a volume with fellow anthropologist Douglass Price-Williams entitled *Oedipus Ubiquitous*. The two of them scoured folklore and mythology in over 200 cultures, encountering Oedipal themes in each. The book went on to win a prestigious award for scholarship in psychoanalysis. So the debate started by Freud, answered by Malinowski, and continued by Roheim, persists today! Perhaps the best known (and best-selling) recent volume to apply the Oedipal complex is a 2007 book by Justin Frank, a Professor of Psychiatry at George Washington University, entitled *Bush on the Couch*. In it, Frank argues that President George W. Bush's arduous relationship with his parents betrayed an active Oedipal complex. The younger Bush's determination to overthrow Saddam Hussein, who his father left in power after the first Gulf War, his repudiation of most of the advisers who had served in his father's administration, and his determination to be re-elected at all costs (the senior Bush, you recall, was a one-term president) are all offered to suggest that he regarded his father in a harshly competitive light. Also mentioned as evidence for his Oedipal inclinations is his apparently compliant behavior toward his mother. The book is entertaining, but as serious scholarship it has been widely criticized. Most ethical psychiatrists would say you can't make a personality assessment without at least having spoken to the patient!

In addition to Malinowski, anthropologists like Margaret Mead also criticized Freud. Freud argued that all children undergo similar developmental stages during which they exhibit certain types of behaviors and fixations on particular parts of the body (the so-called oral, anal, and genital stages). Mead attempted to document child-rearing practices in a variety of cultures to show that there were no universal developmental stages rooted in biology.[3] Instead, development was determined by the child-rearing practices to which children were exposed. While Malinowski, Mead, and most others rejected the more speculative theories of Freud, there was also much in his work that they found worthwhile. Many of the particular processes that Freud identified in the human psyche continue to be recognized among those who study and treat personality disorders and other forms of mental illness (not to mention the generations of Psych majors who selected that field to self-diagnose and to diagnose the "issues" of those around them).

Freudian psychodynamics, or sometimes a cigar is *not* a cigar

Following the early culture and personality work of Benedict and Mead, later anthropologists drew more explicitly on some of the psychological processes identified by Freud. Among these is *repression*, the tendency to suppress or deny emotions experienced during a period of stress. Pushed down (often with great effort) into the sub-conscious, these emotions often lead to later pathological symptoms, such as compulsive behavior, addiction, neurosis, and personality disorders. Repression, for example, is the root cause of Post Traumatic Stress Disorder (PTSD), which in turn is implicated in a whole host of behavioral problems from substance abuse to domestic violence and suicide.

Following Freud, psychological anthropologists also recognized the relationship between frustration and aggression. That is, frustrated desires may lead to later aggressive, destructive behaviors externalized toward others or internalized toward the self. The boss reprimands you unfairly or humiliates you in front of others and when you come home you kick the dog or punch a hole in the wall. Another psychological process is that of *projection*, the attribution of one's emotions or beliefs to another person, especially externalization of one's own blame or guilt to another party. This kind of behavior of turning the tables and blaming others for your own bad behavior would be familiar to anyone who has experienced domestic violence. ("You gave me no choice but to hit you.")

In addition, Freud recognized the process of *transference*, the unconscious redirection of your feelings for one person to another. It is often defined as the inappropriate repetition in the present of a relationship that was important earlier in the person's life. Hence, we might transfer the emotions generated by a parent during our childhood to a later relationship with a spouse (don't we all bring parental "issues" into our marriages?). Or someone who resembles a childhood friend may be trusted inordinately. Or someone who resembles a person who mistreated us in the past may be disliked and distrusted without cause. However, cases of transference also often occur among adult relationships, as I explore in this chapter's text box.

Finally, there is *parapraxis*, or the "Freudian slip." This is an error in speech, memory, or physical action that occurs due to the interference of some unconscious ("dynamically repressed") wish, conflict, or train of thought. As a common pun goes, "a Freudian slip is when you mean one thing, but you say your mother." Here's a good parapraxis joke:

> Question: How many Freudian psychiatrists does it take to change a light bulb?
> Answer: Two. One to screw it in, and one to hold the penis… *I mean, ladder*!

Neo-Freudians in anthropology recognize that many of the above factors implicated in the formation of adult personality arise during childhood. What they have attempted to do is to illustrate how culturally-specific child-rearing practices lead to differing adult personalities. This refinement of the culture and personality school emphasized the importance of early childhood experience in affecting personality formation. Anthropologists in this orientation hypothesized that such factors as toilet training, nursing, weaning, sibling rivalry, sexual discipline, and body contact would be significant variables accounting for differing personality types found in different cultures. The most influential work in this regard was undertaken by Abram Kardiner (1955), a psychoanalyst and anthropologist working from the 1930s to 50s. As a scientific theory, Kardiner's work was an important advance over the earlier culture and personality work of Mead and Benedict. This was because it offered explicit hypotheses relating child-rearing practices to cultural personality. In other words, it attempted to explain the origins of personality differences with a testable hypothesis, something that eluded the earlier culture and personality formulations of Benedict and Mead.

Kardiner began with the assumption of a "basic personality structure"; that is, that most members of a given culture would exhibit a similar personality typical of that society. This is basically analogous to the configuration that Benedict and Mead posited. Then he divided the institutional aspects of culture into two categories. *Primary* institutions were those responsible for forming the basic personality structure. These practices would be most concerned with disciplining, gratifying, and inhibiting infants and young children. Kardiner did not compile a universal list of these institutions, because he believed that different behaviors might serve these functions in different cultures. But in general, research on primary institutions would focus upon family organization, feeding, weaning, neglect of children, sexual training, and toilet training. *Secondary* institutions were those that "satisfy the needs and tensions created by the primary or fixed ones" (Kardiner 1955: 471). Secondary institutions reflect features of personality development, or are necessary to manage the tensions that arise in our personalities. These include systems of taboos, religion, rituals, folktales and aesthetic culture. As Freud would say, these are *projections* of our psyches into culture. Projections are ways of viewing the world that correspond to

BOX 8.1 Freud goes to the movies

At the time that anthropologists were adapting Freudian theory to cultural analysis, Freud's ideas were also becoming widely disseminated in American popular culture. The years after World War II evidenced a growth of the film genre known as the psychological thriller, into which screenwriters and directors often incorporated Freudian theory. Many of these films featured characters with emotional problems as well as the psychiatrists who treated them, offering many filmgoers their first (fictional) acquaintance with psychotherapy.

An excellent film portrayal of the psychodynamic process of transference was Alfred Hitchcock's[4] gorgeously filmed 1958 technicolor release *Vertigo*, starring James Stewart and Kim Novak. Stewart plays a detective ("Scotty") who is forced to leave the San Francisco police because of his disabling acrophobia (fear of heights). After learning of Scotty's retirement, an old friend, Gavin, hires him to trail his wife, Madeline, because he is afraid that she is contemplating suicide. Madeline periodically passes into a trance state, spending hours at a time frequenting the locales of a nineteenth-century heiress, Carlotta Valdes, who went mad and committed suicide. Each time Madeline emerges from these trances, she is unable to recall where she has been or what she did. Gavin reveals to Scotty that Carlotta was Madeleine's great-grandmother, whose spirit Gavin fears has possessed his wife. Yet, Madeleine, he says, has no knowledge of Carlotta. Trailing Madeline across the city, and rescuing her from an apparent drowning attempt, Scotty soon falls in love. Yet, because of his fear of heights he is unable to stop her from a second suicide attempt, in which she (apparently) leaps off the bell tower of a Spanish mission. There ensues a long period of depression, during which Scotty is hospitalized and treated by a psychiatrist. Sometime after his release, he meets another woman, Judy, who resembles Madeline in appearance but not in behavior or speech. In a classic case of Freudian transference, Scotty becomes obsessed with her and insists that she dress and style her hair in the same way as Madeline, as if trying to recreate her. Soon Scotty is again in love.

A carelessly hidden necklace (formerly worn by Madeline) causes Scotty to realize that Judy and Madeline are in fact the same person. Taking an increasingly anxious Judy to the scene of Madeline's death, he learns from her that Gavin hired her to play the part of his wife, knowing that Scotty would be unable to climb the tower to prevent her death. In what appeared to be a suicide, Gavin had actually flung the body of his already-murdered wife from the tower. Forcing Judy to revisit the scene of the crime at the top of the bell tower, Scotty suddenly discovers that he has conquered his fear of heights. Judy tearfully asks his forgiveness, proclaims her love for him, and the two embrace. The sudden appearance of a nun at the top of the tower causes Judy to step back, losing her balance and falling from the tower to her death. Scotty looks down in despair and shock at his second loss.

FIGURE 8.4   Scotty and Madeline proclaim their love as the Pacific crashes behind them. Set against the San Francisco of the 1950s, *Vertigo* is both haunting and beautiful. The score by Bernard Herrmann, in my humble opinion, is the most atmospheric film music ever composed. © AF archive/Alamy.

the development of our personalities. For example, in his 1927 volume *The Future of an Illusion* (1989), Freud argued that there was a correspondence between our childhood relationships with our parents and the ways we approach and manipulate the supernatural. The Judeo-Christian God is the projection of western culture's patriarchal and occasionally punishing father. The idea is that the same kinds of behaviors that bring about gratification with our parents will be gratified by the supernatural: if you have to beg your parents in order to get something, you will probably approach the supernatural the same way. On the other hand, Freud believed that those who enjoyed an indulgent relationship with their parents were likely to view God as an indulgent, generous figure.

Kardiner's idea was that primary institutions determine a culture's basic personality structure, which in turn determines its secondary institutions. This is a causal theory which provides testable explanations of cultural traits:

primary institutions → basic personality structure → secondary institutions

One of the first applications of this theory was in the 1944 study *The People of Alor*, by Harvard anthropologist Cora Du Bois (1903–1991). Alor is a society in Island Southeast Asia that Du Bois studied with the help of numerous psychological techniques. While in the field, she used Rorschach test protocols (inkblots), collected children's drawings, assembled life histories emphasizing childhood experiences, and compiled accounts of dreams. After returning, she analyzed the emotional content of the materials, and she also submitted them to Kardiner and her colleague Emil Oberholzer to independently analyze them. All three reached similar assessments of Alorese adult personality; they identified "a sense of bewildered insecurity and suspicious distrust" (Du Bois et al. 1944: 52).

Du Bois concluded that the major factor leading to these observed personality traits was maternal neglect experienced by the Alorese infant. When women go to work on farms, they leave their children with relatives who are often unable to accord them much attention. Further, the Alorese fed their children only sporadically, gave them little verbal training, and seemed to enjoy shaming and humiliating them. (This sounds remarkably like my Midwestern childhood, except that the Alorese probably were *not* subjected to a daily diet of fish sticks and green Jello.)

How were these linked up to the culture's secondary institutions? Du Bois showed how the Alorese project their childhood experiences into ambivalent, insecure relationships with the supernatural. One of the collected folk tales told of a boy who is sent by his parents to retrieve water with a pot. He finds that the pot has a hole in it and is forced to laboriously repair it. When he finally does and returns with the water, he discovers that his parents have moved away. Du Bois showed that the Alorese make effigies of spirit beings, which are used to contact spirits for assistance in times of need. These effigies are made in a slipshod fashion; they are used in a perfunctory manner and then thrown away. She argued that this failure to develop elaborate ritual art was due to a low expectation of rewards from supernatural sources. In turn, this apathy toward the supernatural could be traced to the relationship between children and their mothers: "That a child can be indulged and placated one moment and struck or deserted in the next can hardly create an image of a secure outer world" (ibid.).

Anthropology goes to war

One of the most controversial uses of neo–Freudian culture and personality theory was related to wartime developments in the 1940s.[5] When the US entered World War II, American war planners knew virtually nothing about the Japanese. A number of social scientists were put to work in compiling ethnographic information on the Japanese in order to better direct US military and propaganda policy. Among these were the British researcher Geoffrey Gorer and Ruth Benedict, both of whom were involved in "national character" studies. They joined other anthropologists, including Margaret Mead, Alexander Leighton, Gregory Bateson, and Clyde Kluckhohn as analysts in the Foreign Morale Analysis Division of the Office of War Information (OWI). Gorer and Benedict, in particular, extended the basic personality structure concept to the populations of nation–states comprising tens of millions of people. While some of these efforts resulted in lasting contributions to anthropological scholarship (notably Benedict's 1946 volume *The Chrysanthemum and the Sword*), others were widely ridiculed for their flights of speculative and ethnocentric fancy.

Gorer argued that Japanese behavior in wartime could not be understood apart from the purportedly compulsive nature of the Japanese people. He set out to account for the apparent paradox of "the all-pervasive gentleness of Japanese life in Japan, which has charmed nearly every visitor, and the overwhelming brutality and sadism of the Japanese at war" (quoted in Barnouw 1963: 121). Most psychologists of the time concurred that a preoccupation with cleanliness, order, and ritual—themes that supposedly pervaded Japanese life at home—were symptomatic of obsessive compulsive disorder. Such was Gorer's claim of the Japanese population as a whole, an assertion shared by anthropologist Weston La Barre, who called the Japanese "the most compulsive people in the world ethnographic museum" (quoted in Barnouw 1963: 122).

On the other hand, supposed cultural attributes of cruelty and treachery were exhaustively propagated in wartime films such as *The Sands of Iwo Jima* as well as print propaganda.[6] Gorer and La Barre attributed such brutality to traumatic aspects of Japanese childrearing, specifically severe and early toilet training, with Japanese infants punished and shamed when they made mistakes. In an influential report written for the OWI in 1943, Gorer asserted that Japanese parents compelled infants to control their sphincter muscles before they had acquired an appropriate level of emotional and muscular development. Repressed rage at severe toilet training leads to adult personalities characterized by compulsiveness and outbursts of sadism (an illustration of the Freudian frustration–aggression hypothesis), while at the same time creating an obsessive need for order and extreme cleanliness in one's immediate surroundings. In an outstanding study of wartime propaganda and stereotypes, John Dower summarizes the Freudian reading of Japanese national character adopted by wartime anthropologists:

> Japanese aggression and barbaric behavior abroad derived from the value system and national character, which in turn were profoundly influenced by forced control of the sphincter muscle in early childhood. Alien and unfamiliar situations were terrifying to the Japanese, for there were no clear rituals of behavior to follow. By the same token, however, in such contexts the collapse of customary prescribed rituals…meant the collapse of the subliminal restraints against aggressive impulses, with catastrophic consequences. Frustration and rage pent up by the regimented rituals of social interaction within Japan exploded with appalling savagery against enemies abroad.
>
> (1986: 126)

Dower demonstrates how such "expert" assessments, when conveyed to the broader population through popular media outlets, such as feature films and magazines, suggested that the Japanese were collectively mentally ill. With their intellectual and emotional development blocked at an infantile (anal) stage, the Japanese represented little more than compulsive, neurotic, but ultimately dangerous children. We have seen how similar characterizations of nonwestern populations flourished in an earlier imperial context; during World War II they rapidly resurfaced to serve a similar purpose. The characterization of the Japanese as a whole as mentally ill, childlike, or subhuman contrasts notably with wartime depictions of Germans, who were typically viewed as recognizably human and adult, albeit deeply deceived by their Nazi leaders. How useful such "expert" analyses proved to war planners is debatable; even among Gorer's colleagues in the OWI, some, like Clyde Kluckhohn, dismissed his explanation as the "Scott Tissue interpretation of history," after the popular US brand of toilet paper (quoted in Dower 1986: 122).

Anthropologists continued to work for the government during the early years of the Cold War. Some 32 anthropologists were employed by the Navy to gather data for the administration of Micronesia, which was occupied by US forces (Patterson 2001: 113). Others who had formerly conducted wartime analyses of Japanese personality now turned their attention to the Russian national character, reflecting the emergence of the west's new adversary of the time. Margaret Mead and Gorer collaborated on work suggesting that the Russian national character could be understood as the result of long and severe infant swaddling, thought to be practiced in the Soviet Union. When babies are swaddled they are confined to tight wrappings that immobilize their arms and legs and prevent them from fully turning their heads. According to Gorer, swaddling among Russian infants leads to a manic depressive personality stemming from the alternating restraint when swaddled and freedom experienced when the bandages are removed. The swaddling produces a pent up rage which is indiscriminately directed outward, since the baby is handled in a very impersonal way. The baby is also made to experience guilt for its emotional outbursts. Gorer attempted to show that many aspects of recent Soviet history— everything from tearful, guilt-ridden confessions of "treason" during the Stalinist show trials to aggression directed toward neighboring countries—were related to the rage and guilt built up in the Russian character.

Bear in mind that all of these theories about national character and child-rearing practices were made without the benefit of field research. To the extent that anthropologists interviewed people of Japanese heritage during World War II, it was mostly with the Japanese Americans interned in detention camps in the western states. Many of these people were second or even third generation American citizens, so many were thoroughly acculturated to American norms. After World War II, when social scientists conducted actual research in Japan, it was determined that the toilet training hypothesis of the Japanese character was seriously in error. Japanese children differ little from American children in terms of the age or severity of toilet training (in fact, the interned Japanese Americans were largely "Americanized" in terms of child-rearing practices, although this fact seemed to escape those scholars who emphasized its "primitive" and "severe" nature!). In the same sense, Gorer didn't have any ethnographic evidence concerning the extensiveness of swaddling in Russia. In actuality, this practice is primarily confined to rural peasants, not the urban governing classes whose behavior Gorer was trying to explain. We might also point out that both of these societies underwent rapid change in the postwar period without any corresponding change in child rearing.

There was something of use that came out of the Japanese national character studies that had direct application at the end of the war. As the war was drawing to a close, a debate arose concerning the eventual fate of the Emperor Hirohito. The allies knew what they would do with the Nazi high command (Hitler, Goering, Goebbels, etc.), as well as the Japanese high command at the end of the war: they would be charged and tried for war crimes and punished if found guilty. But what were they to do with the Emperor of Japan, who was considered a God on earth and the most important emblem of Japan in the minds of its citizens? Anthropologists pointed out what they had learned from military intelligence, which was that the conduct of the war was largely directed by the general staff, not Hirohito. They predicted that it would be virtually impossible for allied troops to occupy Japan without intense resistance if Hirohito were executed. Ruth Benedict specifically recommended to President Roosevelt that Hirohito be retained on the throne as a constitutional monarch, almost as a means of indirect rule by the victorious allies. They figured that if the allies could get Hirohito to urge his subjects to cooperate with occupation forces, keeping him in his imperial position would be a great asset. This was a recommendation that the US Armed Forces high command accepted, and is widely considered to have been the correct decision for postwar planning.

Problems with psychological anthropology

The many problems with wartime national character studies illustrate problems with culture and personality theories in general. Most anthropologists' characterizations of personality, whether of the early culture and personality school or later Freudians, tended to be highly simplistic. The early culture and personality school argued that each culture is characterized by a single "theme" or "pattern" and that all behaviors among all members of that culture reflect that theme. It is now known that Benedict's *Patterns of Culture* omitted evidence contrary to that idea. The Zunis were portrayed as conforming to an Apollonian ideal: they were noncompetitive, retiring, even passive. According to Benedict, they found drunkenness repulsive because it signified a loss of personal control. But Benedict was not able to observe all facets of Zuni culture, or if she did, she selectively reported them. Zuni communities are still often divided into factions, corresponding to divisions between Catholics and Protestants within the tribe. In the early 1900s, faction fights often resulted in violence and even death. The Zuni medicine societies in Benedict's day were known to have dramatic and sometimes masochistic initiation rituals. Initiates were required to flog themselves, often until strips of skin hung from their backs. Adult members of the medicine societies walked on red hot coals or swallowed swords. These acts are not consistent with Benedict's portrayal, nor is the fact that alcoholism was endemic on Zuni reservations.

What this suggests is that the idea of a consistent set of behaviors, which psychologists tend to reject for individuals, is no more applicable for a group of people. *Personality disorders*, which afflict tens of millions of people in the US alone, tend to be characterized by simultaneous or sequential disparate behavior traits (e.g. bipolar, passive-aggressive, histrionic, and borderline). Indeed, probably the most popular text examining borderline personality disorder directly alludes to the disparate attitudes that it entails. The book bears a title that anyone who has lived with such a person can relate to: *I Hate You. Don't Leave Me!* (Kreisman and Straus 1989). Critics of the culture and personality school contend that what was being done in the name of identifying a "basic personality structure" was just simpleminded stereotyping. Indeed, the approach might be characterized as an updated, if less disrespectful, version of the crude ethnic stereotypes that people have made about others since time immemorial.

Second, there is much more variability within cultures than culture and personality and psychological anthropology theorists were prepared to acknowledge. Most of the studies discussed so far made generalizations about group personality without benefit of standardized psychological tests. Most suffered from problems of operationalization (that is, how do we measure something like neurosis or a "Dionysian" configuration?) and intersubjectivity (that is, would a second observer arrive at the same conclusions?). In the early 1950s, Anthony F.C. Wallace addressed the first of these problems when he conducted a psychocultural study of the Tuscarora band of Iroquois Indians. He employed Rorschach tests administered to a statistically significant sample of Tuscarora, and assessed personality types for each informant along 21 dimensions (Wallace 1952). By this approach, Wallace found that only 37 percent of his sample fell within the modal (most common) personality. In other words, only a little more than a third of the members of this small (fewer than 3,000 members) society exhibited the tribe's "basic personality structure." When cross-cultural studies with this kind of methodology are conducted of personality, it is usually found that the differences between cultures for most variables are less than the differences within cultures. In other words, we can't say that one personality is representative of a culture, nor that the members of different cultures are radically different from one another in personality type.

After encountering these criticisms, readers might think that culture and personality and Freudian psychological anthropology expired with little or no lasting influence. In fact, they have been among the most influential anthropological theories *outside* of academia, albeit in an indirect way. As this perspective was getting underway in the 1920s and 30s, there were many child psychology "experts" who lectured American mothers about the "correct" way to raise children. They warned that unless certain benchmarks were achieved by a certain age and that unless certain feeding patterns were systematically followed, children would grow up with behavioral problems or even psychoses. The problem was that the experts rarely agreed with one another, so that parents worried about the effects of following the "wrong" advice. American women were so obsessed with following "modern scientific" advice regarding the raising of children that, by the 1930s, breast-feeding had virtually died out, at least among white, middle and upper class women who were eager to follow their doctors' advice to use the newly available formulas.

Margaret Mead documented that there are many different ways to raise children, and yet there are no societies populated entirely by adult neurotics and psychotics. She communicated this fact to a friend of hers, New York pediatrician Dr. Benjamin Spock, who incorporated Mead's findings into his own work with children. Indeed, Spock became Mead's own pediatrician after the birth of her daughter, Mary Catherine Bateson (currently an anthropologist in her own right). Mead produced quite a stir by not only breast-feeding her baby—a practice then discouraged by many pediatricians—but insisting on the right to do so in public. Mary Catherine's father, Gregory Bateson, had pioneered the use of motion pictures in anthropological research, and shot thousands of rolls of film as Bateson was growing up. She had, in her later words, probably the "best documented childhood on earth."

In the late 1940s, Spock published the first edition of *Baby and Childcare*, which became the "bible" for childrearing in the United States. His advice to mothers: every child is an individual, they do not go through uniform stages and benchmarks, and you should trust your instincts. Spock's book has gone through *eight* subsequent editions, and even those parents who have never read it have been influenced by it because our societal notions of parenting have become so tied to his advice over the years. So there you have it; Margaret Mead may have ultimately made you the person you are!

Quiz yourself

Answer True or False to each statement

1   Boas' student A.L. Kroeber focused his attention on how exceptional individuals influence and reshape the cultures in which they participate.
2   Following her research in Samoa, Margaret Mead engaged in a prolonged, fierce debate with Derek Freeman over her ethnographic research on the island.
3   Benedict's *Patterns of Culture* suggested that the interpersonal behavior, mythology, aesthetic styles, conceptions of the supernatural, all express the dominant psychological orientation of a given culture.
4   Benedict's notion of cultural relativism entailed the idea that cultural practices must be understood in the context and traditions within which they occur, but not the idea that all cultural practices are equally valid.
5   Among the Tchambuli of New Guinea, Margaret Mead claimed to have found a society in which western standards of gender roles were essentially reversed.
6   Malinowski argued that the Oedipal complex was absent in the matrilineal Trobriand Islands, where a young man has an ambivalent relationship with his mother's brother, not his father.
7   According to Geza Roheim, the Australian practice of sub-incision was rooted in the Oedipal complex as expressed in that culture's sleeping arrangements between mothers and their male children.
8   In the film *Vertigo*, when Scotty falls in love with Judy, who resembled the deceased Madeline, he is exhibiting the psychological process of transference.
9   Psychological anthropologists during the 1940s attempted to explain Japanese atrocities in wartime in terms of Japanese infant toilet-training practices.
10   Anthony F. C. Wallace's research shows that personality types in small-scale societies are indeed largely homogeneous, but that the notion of a basic personality structure does not hold for large-scale industrialized societies.

9

STRUCTURE AND FUNCTION

Low-stakes politics

In this chapter, we turn to the other major school that rejected the Boasian idea of culture as a hodgepodge of unrelated traits: functionalism, which dominated British anthropology from the 1930s to the late 1950s. During this time British social anthropology centered around two powerful and charismatic individuals: Alfred Reginald Radcliffe-Brown (1881–1955; Figure 9.1) and Bronislaw Malinowski (1884–1942). They and their students were responsible for training almost all the professional anthropologists of Britain until about 1960. Much has been made of the dispute between them concerning their differing interpretations of functionalism (Malinowki's "psychological" or "pure" functionalism versus Radcliffe-Brown's "structural functionalism"). Today, we tend to view the differences between them as grossly exaggerated. At the time, the differences were phrased in theoretical terms, but the basic conflict between the two men was at least equally political; that is, they vied for control of British academic anthropology. Given the small resource base of students and funding in Britain at the time, and the enormous egos of the men, it's not surprising that they were to struggle over differences that to us seem inconsequential. Indeed, the feud between Radcliffe-Brown and Malinowski is an excellent illustration of Henry Kissinger's memorable observation that "*academic politics are so vicious because the stakes are so low.*"

Although Alfred Reginald Brown's family was of modest origins, he managed to enter the elite Trinity College at Cambridge University. Over the course of several university appointments following World War I, his professional bearing reflected increasingly aristocratic pretensions; in 1926, he legally changed his name to Alfred Reginald Radcliffe-Brown. During a later appointment at the University of Chicago, he dressed in elegantly tailored English suits and regularly sported a monocle and cigarette holder. Malinowski, on the other hand, was a Pole who had

FIGURE 9.1 A.R. Radcliffe-Brown. Courtesy of the Royal Anthropological Institute.

not had the elite training of Radcliffe-Brown and as a foreigner was regarded as an outsider from the elite British universities. He earned his doctorate at the less prestigious London School of Economics, which was where he spent most of his academic career as a lecturer. As if to set himself apart from his aristocratic competitor, he was known for his occasionally vulgar humor and outbursts of obscenities in conversation.

The two men were also quite different in their attitudes toward field research. Malinowski set a standard for anthropological field research that few anthropologists since then have equaled. During the four years he spent in enforced exile, he became fluent in Trobriandese and compiled a massive ethnographic record dealing with almost every aspect of Trobriand culture. In contrast, Radcliffe-Brown's ethnographic contributions were slight. His primary work was conducted in 1906–08 with Australian aborigines on the Andaman Islands, which were a British penal colony. Radcliffe-Brown apparently never acquired fluency in any field language; he worked entirely through interpreters, and in some cases had his informants brought to him, where he interviewed them on his veranda. Radcliffe-Brown is usually cited as the founder of the structural functional viewpoint in British social anthropology.

Radcliffe-Brown and structural functionalism

Radcliffe-Brown's structural functionalism was a largely unaltered version of Durkheim's sociology as applied to "primitive" societies (although interestingly, he made no use of Durkheim's notion of "mechanical" integration). Recall (for the millionth time) that one of the contributions of Durkheim had been an organismic analogy, in which the institutions that contribute to the maintenance of society were seen as analogous to the organs of a living thing. Radcliffe-Brown was responsible for a few additions to these Durkheimian concepts, one being that the study of society should be directed toward what he called "social structure," and emphatically not culture. Social structure in Radcliffe-Brown's usage encompasses two different phenomena. The first of these is what anthropologists call *corporate groups*, social entities that persist in time despite changes in their membership. These persisting social groups would include nations, tribes, kinship groups, or voluntary associations. Hence, if a structural functionalist were conducting a study of a university, the study would address the institution rather than the flesh-and-blood members of any particular class. Although university faculty hold positions of employment from which they hopefully retire (some day!—or more likely simply die), and students take classes and graduate, while administrators promulgate new policies justifying their existence and collect paychecks, the university persists beyond any one group of people who participate in it at any given time. Second, social structure comprises the rules governing relations between people belonging to these groups. All individuals occupy social *roles* as members of a group; these are positions such as father, husband, clan elder, shaman, etc. At the same time, as the occupant of a role, a person has a certain *status*, i.e. the rights and responsibilities he or she enjoys relative to other people.

The focus of study for Radcliffe-Brown was this social structure, which might be thought of as an abstraction from many individual cases of behavior. It is something akin to an organizational chart. To continue our university example, the *roles* that people occupy in the University can be arranged hierarchically, from the President to the various Vice Presidents (or Provosts) below him or her, to the Deans of the various Colleges, to the Chairpersons of various Departments, then to the lowly faculty and staff who carry this top-heavy, parasitic edifice on their shoulders by doing all of the actual work. Each of these roles persists despite changes in their personnel over time. Their statuses would be revealed by consulting various university documents. At my university, for example, there is a Faculty Handbook that lays out in detail professors' responsibilities with regard to teaching, research, and service, as well as more mundane matters such as scheduling office hours, grievance procedures, and benefits. Most workplaces have something comparable; they are typically called "job descriptions."

Radcliffe-Brown claimed that his approach to studying society was explicitly scientific. The comparative study of *social structure* would generate universal laws applicable to all societies. Radcliffe-Brown set himself apart from his contemporaries in the United States (as well as his nemesis Malinowski) with his sweeping pronouncement that a scientific study of *culture* was not possible. It is largely because of his enduring influence in British academe that the subfield became known in Great Britain not as cultural anthropology (as it is called in the US), but as *social anthropology*. It was because of his aversion to studying culture that Radcliffe-Brown had little good to say about the work of Boas and his students in the US. He referred to the Boasian and culture and personality approaches as "worse than useless," a withering epithet that he also flung at Malinowski with some regularity. There was little love lost between the two camps, with most American anthropologists of the time finding Radcliffe-Brown insufferably arrogant. Margaret Mead described him as aloof when not openly rude. Ruth Benedict wrote that Radcliffe-Brown "seemed to me impenetrably wrapped in his own conceit" (1973: 327). Leslie White deplored in his English counterpart "the tendency to assume originality for himself and to ignore or depreciate the work of others" (1966: 32).

Radcliffe-Brown was never entirely clear what he meant by culture, but he seemed to have used it in a sense distinct from that of American anthropologists. As Audrey Richards, one of Malinowski's former students (and therefore, as you might expect, an adversary of Radcliffe-Brown) once put it: "he argued that social structure should be clearly separated from the other aspects of man's social heritage. These came to be subsumed under the title 'culture,' a word which has often been used…almost in a pejorative sense to describe a sort of rag-bag of odds and ends in which to thrust all facts and ideas in which the social anthropologist was not at the moment interested" (1957: 29). Whereas anthropologists after Boas generally agreed that culture consisted of the learned traditions, values, and rules that guide behavior (with some including behavior as well in that definition), Radcliffe-Brown contended that culture was only "thoughts." Because "thoughts" can't be observed, it would be impossible to formulate a scientific study of them, he argued.

This assertion is curious for two reasons. First, even if culture is just considered to be only the beliefs and rules that people carry within their heads, there's no reason why those thoughts can't be studied because they're not "visible." How do we find out about thoughts? Just ask! Second, while Radcliffe-Brown argued that social structure is somehow more "real" than culture, he was not addressing actual behavior with that concept or any other. Indeed, Radcliffe-Brown said that it *is* permissible to study "logical fictions," which he described as "not itself a real entity, but valuable in describing phenomenal reality" (1957: 44).

Social structure is one such abstraction, consisting of the rules (statuses) that people are supposed to follow and the responsibilities they hold relative to one another. Yet, do these abstractions reveal their actual behavior? To continue our previous example, however specific a "job description" is, it is usually a poor guide to what people *actually* do on the job. Most people learn all kinds of shortcuts and alternatives that make their jobs easier than the formal procedures set out in the description. What do we do with the time we save through such shortcuts? *We goof off in all kinds of ways that are completely incompatible with our job description!* Sometimes, in fact, if workers want to express displeasure with their managers but are afraid to strike for fear of being fired, they may "work by the book." That means they follow every step exactly as outlined in their job descriptions, which usually slows the pace of work to a virtual standstill. Since they are not violating work rules, they can't be fired, but by the same token, they affect production in the manner of a strike. *But in Radcliffe-Brown's world, we need not study behavior because he assumed that people follow the rules to a letter; all that is needed then is a complete knowledge of social rules.*

Radcliffe-Brown's approach to understanding social structure was *non-evolutionary*. Like the Boasians in the US, he rejected the explanation of cultural traits in terms of evolution. But unlike the Boasian view of culture as a fragmented "hodgepodge" and a "thing of shreds and patches," the organismic analogy favored by Radcliffe-Brown regarded institutions as interrelated and mutually-reinforcing. Thus, his argument was that you simply did not have to seek the origins of social practices because they could be understood in terms of how they operate at a single point in time. For example, the evolutionist Lewis Henry Morgan explained the peculiarities of the Hawaiian kinship terminology system (where all cousins are called brothers and sisters) by suggesting that this was a survival from an earlier stage of promiscuous incest, where people simply didn't know who their actual siblings and parents were. Radcliffe-Brown would say that such explanations in terms of speculative historical reconstruction are both wrong and superfluous. The brother/sister term refers to a kinship relationship that is defined like that of siblings because of the degree of social and economic interdependence between these relatives, which approximated that of siblings. Hence, there is no need to dig back into an essentially unknowable past in order to figure out how a social practice operates today.

The structural functionalists adopted what they called a *synchronic* perspective on society: the anthropologist resides in a society for about a year or so, studying. Does this limited period of study prevent us from knowing the past or the future of that society? Not according to Radcliffe-Brown, who assumed that the synchronic "snapshot" made at the time of the anthropologist's residence provides a portrait that would be of lasting relevance. The reason for this, following Durkheim, is that a properly functioning society is one that resists change. The Andaman Islanders whom he studied in 1908 were assumed to be little different from their predecessors 100 years before or what their society would be 100 years hence. Indeed, when Radcliffe-Brown finally published a book-length study of them in 1922, he confidently stated that the society was little changed from the time of his residence there, even though he had not set foot on Andaman since the time of his research 14 years earlier.

The basis of the synchronic point of view was the Durkheimian concept of "function," which was directly appropriated into anthropology by Radcliffe-Brown (we'll see later how this differs from Malinowki's use of the term). He argued that institutions "functioned" to perpetuate the social structure. Like Durkheim, he claimed that they did so by promoting social solidarity among society's members. We've already seen how Durkheim regarded social change in a negative light, even implying that social change is pathological because of its purported relationship to anomic suicide. Similarly, Radcliffe-Brown assumed that societies had a tendency toward *equilibrium*; because of this resistance to change, the synchronic snapshot did not just "freeze" a society in time, but offered a view of it that was essentially timeless. The synchronic perspective revealed it as it existed for all time.

This idea that behaviors contribute to maintenance of the social structure introduces an important distinction between the motive of a behavior and its function. The function of a rain dance is not to bring rain, but to enhance social solidarity through common participation in ritual. The function of marriage is not to produce a family, but to enhance social solidarity by creating alliances between lineages. The function of sorcery is not to retaliate against an enemy, but to enhance social solidarity by punishing deviants and anti-social people. And so on. I like to think of structural functionalism as "fill in the blank" anthropology. For the structural functionalists, then, the motivating force for peoples' behavior is not their goals, interests, or values, but the "needs" of "social structure." And yet, even Radcliffe-Brown would admit that social structure is not real, but is the anthropologist's abstract model of society, his "logical fiction." As noted earlier, the key problem here is one of *reification*: creating a concept that helps to understand a society and then attributing real force to that concept in peoples' actions, even though they themselves are unaware of the concept.

Feeble findings for the colonial office

Some of the "laws" of social structure that Radcliffe-Brown developed from this approach are remarkably feeble:

> There is a necessity for stability and continuity in the social structure.

> Rights and duties need to be defined in a way that conflicts can be resolved without destroying the structure.

And my favorite:

> There is a universal sociological law though it is not yet possible to formulate precisely its scope, namely that in certain specific conditions a society has a need to provide itself with a segmentary [lineage] organization.
> (Radcliffe-Brown 1952: 44–45)

The problem with these "laws" is that they are truisms. They are incapable of accounting for why a certain set of institutions exists in one place, and a different set in another (after all, isn't our goal as anthropologists to understand cultural similarities and differences?). As Robert Lowie, a Boasian and one of Radcliffe-Brown's American critics, sarcastically responded to the last "law" (above), "Whoever heard of a universal law with an as yet undefinable scope, of a law that works in certain specific *but unspecified* conditions? Is it a law that some societies have clans, and others have not? Newton did not tell us that bodies either rise or fall" (quoted in Langness 2005: 108–109).

One of the earliest and classic statements of the structural functionalist approach also highlights many of the problems with it. In 1940, British anthropologists Meyer Fortes and E.E. Evans-Pritchard edited a volume entitled *African Political Systems* (Radcliffe-Brown himself wrote the Preface to the book), which consisted of a survey of eight African societies, each compiled by a different anthropologist working within the structural functionalist framework. The work was commissioned by the British Colonial Office in an effort to learn something about the African societies they were then administering. The purpose of the study was not benign information gathering or "basic research," but to provide administrators with information that would ultimately make these colonial societies easier to govern.

Since the late eighteenth century, the British had adopted a policy throughout their Empire of *indirect rule*. In this practice, they converted the existing leaders of African and other colonized societies into functionaries of the colonial government, turning once independent leaders into what were essentially "puppets" of the colonial administration, responsible for collecting taxes and recruiting labor for colonial projects. British anthropologists collaborated in this effort; indeed, prior to World War II the Colonial Office was one of the few major sources of research funding that England's anthropologists could consistently rely upon. Many anthropologists probably justified this collaboration in their own minds with the rationale that colonial rule was a foregone conclusion anyway, so the government might as well have accurate information on which to base it.[1]

African Political Systems is a survey of eight societies dealing with their forms of political organization and providing brief sketches of their economy and society. Fortes and Evans-Pritchard categorized these societies as either Group A, "those societies which have centralized authority…in short, a government" or Group B, "those societies which lack centralized authority" (Fortes and Evans-Pritchard 1940: 5). The former are "primitive states" and the latter are "stateless societies." This distinction was key to the initiative of indirect rule, for in Group A societies there were already leaders who could be co-opted as colonial functionaries. In Group B societies, there would be a need to either appoint such leaders or solidify whatever positions of authority that do exist in the person of a headman (Figure 9.2).[2]

One of the observations that Fortes and Evans-Pritchard offer in their introductory chapter is that "a large population in a political unit and a high degree of political centralization do not necessarily go together with great density" (ibid.: 8). They note that some state societies are found in sparsely populated areas while in others there are "stateless" societies associated with densely populated areas. This argument challenges much of what was then already known from archaeology and cultural anthropology about the relationship between population density and political complexity. In actuality, this is a fallacious assertion reflecting the synchronic viewpoint of the contributing authors, which led them to ignore the effects of colonialism on the societies they studied. The editors included the South African Zulu among those societies with a state-level political structure but low population density. Yet they ignored the fact that the Zulu had been ravaged by nearly 200 years of colonial warfare (first with the Dutch Boers and then the English) and then forced labor in European-owned mines and plantations. Conversely, the relatively egalitarian Tallensi of West Africa were seen as having a surprisingly high population density for a stateless society. Yet the authors would have been less surprised had they examined the demographic impact of British administration of the Gold Coast,

FIGURE 9.2   During my doctoral fieldwork, I became good friends with the late Victor Lewis. He was the last *alcalde* to serve in Hopkins, Belize, before the *alcalde* system was replaced by an elected village council in the 1960s. Here, from a 1986 photo, is Victor holding a ceremonial staff of office used by the village's *alcaldes* going back to the late nineteenth century. Photo courtesy of the author.

which forced many Tallensi off their land and into more marginal and crowded areas (thus artificially raising the population density). Such displacements were ignored by the contributing anthropologists, who treated these societies as they encountered them in the late 1930s as if they had always been that way. In fact, they were studying the often disorganized remnants of cultures that had been thoroughly transformed by colonialism. Indeed, the fact that over the previous three centuries some 14 million Africans may have been swept up in the Atlantic slave trade, and their societies irreparably altered as a result, passes unmentioned by any of the volume's contributors.

What led the anthropologists to deny this colonial history? Was it their naïve belief in social equilibrium—that they were observing societies in the late 1930s that had been unchanged by European contact? Possibly, but it is hard to imagine that they were unfamiliar with at least some of these changes. Was it ignorance of colonial history? This latter point seems almost certainly impossible, as the British authorities kept excellent, detailed records of their interactions (and wars) with native peoples throughout the world.[3] Rather, it seems likely that the anthropologists denied the readily evident effects of colonialism because of their dependence on the British Colonial Office for funding and access to the field. As we all know, you don't bite the hand that feeds you, a major reason that doubts are often cast on medical research funded by pharmaceutical companies. Similarly, raising the possibility that British colonialism might have been anything other than a benign presence could very well have ended any possibility for future research support.

To be fair, it bears mentioning that when Radcliffe-Brown put aside his sweeping if sometimes vapid theoretical pronouncements, he was capable of much insight in analyzing ethnographic data. He offered a cross-cultural analysis of totemism (the worship of the mythical ancestors of kinship groups) that anticipated Lévi-Strauss' approach by several decades. Elsewhere, as in a 1945 lecture on "Religion and Society," he sought to account for the circumstances that give rise to ancestor worship, in which deceased ancestors are venerated and propitiated by the members of a clan or lineage. The living often make offerings of food and drink to their ancestors in a ritual act viewed as sharing a meal with them. Ancestor worship also entails a relationship of mutual support between the living and the dead; ancestors will provide abundant crops, healthy children, and well-being if they are honored, but will send misfortune if they are ignored. Radcliffe-Brown notes that ancestor worship is most prevalent in societies where unilineal descent is practiced:

> For the individual, his primary duties are those of lineage. These include duties to the members now living, but also to those who have died and to those who are not yet born. In the carrying out of these duties he is controlled and inspired by the complex systems of sentiments of which we may say…are centered on the lineage itself, past, present and future. It is primarily this system of sentiments that is expressed in the cult of the ancestors. The social function of these rites is obvious: by giving solemn and collective expression to them the rites reaffirm, renew and strengthen those sentiments on which the social solidarity depends.
>
> (Radcliffe-Brown 1977: 114)

One of the notable things that Moore (2009: 157) observes about this passage is that Radcliffe-Brown here proposed a relationship between belief and social structure that can be tested cross-culturally, unlike the Boasians who claimed that cultural practices were largely random and *sui generis* assortments of diffused and independently invented traits. The argument that ancestor worship arises from lineage-based kinship systems, that they are associated with dependent relationships, and that ancestor worship would decline with a lessening of "traditional social forms" may all be evaluated as scientific hypotheses.

House arrest: Malinowski in the Trobriands

Ironically, while Radcliffe-Brown was of modest origins but adopted aristocratic pretensions, Bronislaw Malinowski (1884–1942) was born to a family with an aristocratic background, but struck an earthier public image than his English contemporary and competitor. He was born in Kraków, a part of Polish Galicia that had been controlled by Austria since the mid-1800s. His father was a renowned professor of Slavic languages and his mother the daughter of an estate-owning family. As a child, he was frail, often suffering from ill-health, and yet he excelled academically. While attending the university in Kraków, Malinowski became ill and took to reading James Frazer's *The Golden Bough* to distract himself during his recuperation. At Leipzig University in Germany, he studied under the economist Karl Bücher and psychologist Wilhelm Wundt. They inspired a life-long interest in both economics and psychology, to which many of Malinowski's anthropological publications on the Trobriand Islands were devoted. In 1910, he went to England to pursue anthropological studies at the London School of Economics under C.G. Seligman and Edward Westermarck.

In 1914, Malinowski traveled to Melanesia, where he conducted fieldwork at Mailu, Papua (in what would later become Papua New Guinea) and then in the Trobriand Islands. World War I had broken out by the time of his arrival in the region, putting him in a severe predicament. As an Austrian citizen in a British colony, he was considered an enemy alien and briefly interned. After the intervention of British anthropologist and colleague R.G. Marrett, Malinowski was released on the condition that he remain in Australia's Melanesian territories for the duration of the war. During this enforced but accidental exile from Europe, Malinowski went on to complete two full years of residence in a native village on the Trobriand Islands, yielding the most intensive ethnographic research completed until that date. The sexual frustrations revealed in his field diaries and his later intensive study of Freud inspired research into the sexual practices of the Trobrianders, which he documented in the volume *The Sexual Lives of Savages in Northwest Melanesia* (Malinowski 2010). Following its publication in 1929, it quickly became an anthropological bestseller, challenging as it did western notions of sexuality and conception. Like Mead's work in Samoa, Malinowski wrote of a society in which premarital intercourse with numerous partners was widely practiced and accepted. More astonishingly, Malinowski reported that the Trobrianders saw no relationship between sex and pregnancy, the islanders even pointing out to the author why western beliefs linking the two were entirely illogical. Despite the best-selling status of *Sexual Lives*, English university students who wanted to read it were out of luck if they looked for it on campus. Because of its subject matter, it was kept in a secured location in most British university libraries until the 1940s, and could only be accessed with the written permission of the Dean.

Like Radcliffe-Brown, Malinowski's method sought to identify the structure of society as revealed in relationships between kinship, economics, religion and magic, and other institutions. This structure however provided only the skeletal outlines of society, for he was always most interested in what he called "the imponderabilia of actual life" (Malinowski 1984: 20). By this he meant the subjective knowledge and specific behaviors and dispositions of people taking part in daily activities. In conspicuous contrast to Radcliffe-Brown's more aloof manner of field research, Malinowski argued that the ethnographer should not stand apart from the society he or she studies, but should "try to find himself...in the midst of an assembly of human beings, who behave seriously or jocularly, with earnest concentration or bored frivolity, who are either in the same mood as he finds them every day, or else are screwed up to a high pitch of excitement…" (1984: 21). This involvement in daily life reminds the ethnographer that his subjects are living humans and not museum specimens, individual actors rather than the mere enactors of cultural rules. Whereas earlier anthropologists often ignored ritual or considered it some form of superstitious if not nonsensical behavior, Malinowski paid it intense attention, arguing that it ultimately served a utilitarian function in meeting the deep-felt needs of individuals and the groups to which they belonged.

Malinowski's monumental study of the Trobriand Islanders, *Argonauts of the Western Pacific*, was published in 1922 but remains an anthropological classic today, with a depth of ethnographic detail matched by few researchers since then. Much of Malinowski's work focused on the *kula* ring, famously showing how Trobriand men undertake perilous ocean voyages of hundreds of miles to exchange shell armbands (*mwali*) and necklaces (*soulava*) with trading partners on other islands. The Trobriands are a coral island chain located east of New Guinea and consisting of four primary islands and a dozen or so smaller ones forming a ring in the Southwest Pacific. The outermost islands are 210 miles apart from north to south and 190 miles from east to west.

Every shell item exchanged in the kula ring was known by name and had an elaborate "genealogy" that chiefs could recite, stating where it had been, which chiefs had owned it, and the items they had exchanged it for. The ornaments could only be exchanged in specific directions: *mwali* (shell armbands) were always exchanged in a clockwise direction among the islands in the kula ring, while *soulava* (shell necklaces) were traded only in counterclockwise direction. *Mwali* could only be exchanged for *soulava*, and vice versa. These "ornaments" were actually prestige goods; Malinowski referred to them as the Trobriand equivalent of the Crown Jewels, which function as insignia of rank and wealth for the English nobility.

In visiting his partner on an adjacent island, each man received a shell ornament of only one type, which the recipient was then obliged to pass on to his partner on the next island in the chain. Ornaments had high prestige value and long histories, but they were not exchangeable for any other good. Trobriand men derived prestige from the types of objects they returned with from a trading expedition. But since these were life-long partnerships, they were also expected to be generous and fair in their dealings with partners. Chiefs in particular tried to accumulate as many partnerships as they could, because it increased the amount of prestige wealth that passed through their hands. Chiefs usually initiated a partnership by making a utilitarian gift (e.g. pigs or axes) to a prospective partner, eventually building up to an exchange of kula items. Malinowski pondered why the Trobrianders risk their lives in such open ocean voyages to exchange merely symbolic wealth, shell "valuables" with no utilitarian purpose that are in most instances too fragile to wear. Indeed, he describes the items as unimpressive in appearance, and even ugly in the view of outsiders. Again, Malinowski invokes a comparison with the English Crown Jewels in observing that the shell prestige goods were valued not for their intrinsic properties or aesthetics but for their emotional and historical associations: "However ugly, useless and—according to current standards—valueless an object may be, if it has figured in historical scenes and passed through the hands of historic persons, and is therefore an unfailing vehicle of important historical associations, it cannot but be precious to us" (1984: 89).

Malinowski sought to challenge then-dominant notions of economic behavior by contending that such exchanges were undertaken with the goals of prestige and alliance, rather than material self-gain. His publications on the kula are considered foundational documents in the field of economic anthropology, which continues to grapple with the question—first posed by Malinowski—of the applicability of formal economic theory to nonwestern and nonmonetary economies. As you can probably tell from Malinowski's take on the kula, his view was that formal economics was not applicable to societies such as the Trobriands. Many anthropologists have disagreed with Malinowski since then, claiming that he misunderstood economics' basic assumptions about human behavior. The "economic man" that Malinowski criticized (that is, an actor whose sole motivation is one of material gain) is recognized by most economic anthropologists today as an oversimplified "straw man." We'll revisit this argument when we deal with transactionalism in Chapter 10. Malinowski also mentions that while chiefs were trading in these prestige goods, they also carried with them valuable cargo traded in separate transactions, including pigs, sago palm, and stone for manufacturing axes. This cargo was essential to islanders back home and provided the material basis of the chief's power over them. In other words, the trade in prestige goods was accompanied by and set the stage for more utilitarian exchanges between men, including those that enabled chiefs to exert power over commoners.

Was Malinowski the objective scientific observer of island life that he purported to be in the introduction to *Argonauts*? As we've already seen, his diaries reveal a man of great complexity, occasionally given to intense anger toward his hosts. Yet, in recent years, we've also come to recognize that, like other male ethnographers, Malinowski either ignored or overlooked the gendered nature of island politics and economics. More than five decades after his fieldwork in the Trobriands, the islands were visited by anthropologist Annette Weiner (1933–1997), who performed her research near the very site at which Malinowski had conducted his. Weiner found that many aspects of island economic and social organization continued little changed from Malinowski's day. Men still took to the seas in kula exchanges, chiefs still strutted haughtily in public and commoners bowed before them, and men still provided their brothers-in-law with annual *urigubu* payments of yams.[4] Yet on her very first day in the field Weiner also discovered a dimension of Trobriand life that Malinowski had overlooked: the critical economic importance of women as expressed in ritual exchanges, especially during mortuary ceremonies. For five hours she watched as women gathered boisterously in the center of a village, exchanging bundles of dried banana leaves and decorated fiber skirts while men looked on from the sidelines. Weiner reported that some women would distribute some 30,000 such bundles in a single day, each equivalent in value to one Australian cent. The day's events came to an end when women presented fiber skirts and men offered objects of male wealth to the father and spouse of the deceased person.

Such rituals demonstrate the significance of complementary yet distinct female and male domains of power. Through their exchange of female-specific wealth, Weiner states that women symbolically free the dead person from all reciprocal claims to others and thereby secure a person's "pure" matrilineal identity. Men who are related to the deceased, on the other hand, control the physical body of the deceased by their payments to all who were important members of the dead person's social network. Trobriand women are said to control immortality through the regeneration of matrilineal identity in a timeless continuum across generations. In contrast, male power, based on land and knowledge of the history of property, are situated in much closer and more limited horizons of time and space. Participating in both the social and cosmic dimensions of Trobriand society, women enjoy a dimension of social power inaccessible to men: "Trobriand women, with their complete control over the continuity of life and death, never confront a possible loss of their control. The structure of time and space that women control must be seen as fundamental to the organization of the Trobriand universe…The fact of matrilineality gives women a domain of control that men can neither emulate successfully nor infiltrate with any degree of lasting power" (Weiner 1976: 234). Weiner's ethnographic work, conducted a generation ago, provided one of the first glimpses into how an analysis informed by concerns of gender could provide a corrective and complement to a famed if partial ethnographic record of the past.

Malinowski and magic

Malinowski regarded magic as an attempt to control events in which there is high risk or uncertainty and an inability to control those events by other, more direct means. This conception transcended the views of earlier anthropologists, such as Tylor, that it was simply a flawed system of knowledge and a "primitive" counterpart to science. Magic, he writes, "is always strongest…where vital interests are concerned, where violent passions or emotions are awakened, when mysterious forces are opposed to man's endeavors; and when he has to recognize that there is something which eludes his most careful calculations, his most conscientious preparations and efforts" (Malinowski 1984: 395–396).

He notes, for example, how the incidence and use of magic differ among Trobriand fishermen depending upon where they are working. Within the inner lagoon, the waters were calm and clear, fishermen were safe, and fish were caught in a straightforward manner with a minimum of ritual preparation. But when they had to venture beyond the reefs, out into the deep ocean—with all the dangers of the open sea, high waves and sudden storms, as well as sharks, unpredictable yields, and other difficulties—fishermen then resorted to magical ritual to assuage their fear and assert some sense of control. To Malinowski, it did not matter that such rituals had no effect on the phenomena they were supposed to control (that is, that they would not actually calm waves or ensure a good catch). What mattered most was that they empowered the islanders to do what needed to be done when events were beyond their direct control. Thus ritual and magic maintained the psychological well-being of tribal members, and allowed members to better participate in the necessary social and economic functions of the community.

Most importantly, in his analysis of magic, Malinowski argued that the mind of "primitive" people is essentially no different from that of people in "civilized" society, an argument completely at odds with previous scholars who had argued that there was a qualitative, hierarchical difference between them. Everyone from Tylor and Morgan to Frazer and Durkheim had assumed that the mind among civilized people was more rational and logical than the primitive mind, which was generally equated more with the thinking of children. From his own experiences with illness, Malinowski writes, "the sick man, primitive or civilized, wants to feel that something can be done. He craves for miracles" (2001:199). This perspective helps us understand why forms of magic (whether astrology, palm reading, tarot cards, "lucky" charms or prayers for a saint's intercession) persist in "modern" societies wherever people face uncertain circumstances or anxiety. Malinowski's view is far more plausible than the early evolutionists' belief that magical thinking is simply an illogical "survival" from an earlier stage of society. One anthropologist, George Gmelch (2009), has even used his insights to show how baseball players, many of whom are considered famously "superstitious," engage in magical thinking no less than Malinowski's Trobriand fishermen. He mentions, for example, that before every game that he was to pitch, Dennis Grossini of the Detroit Tigers tried to repeat everything that he had done on the first day that he pitched a winning game. He would awaken at the same time, eat the same meals, wear the same clothes prior to the game, and drive the same route to the ballpark. Grossini never deviated from his "winning" routine. He did not always win, of course. But the failure of magic to bring about desired effects, Malinowski observes, never falsifies the belief in its efficacy. Rather, when magic doesn't work, it is assumed that it was not performed properly.

"Hyphenated" vs. "pure" functionalism

Upon his return to Britain from the Trobriands, Malinowski taught for a number of years at the University of London. In 1941, he took a position at Yale University in the US, where he soon died of a heart attack as he was preparing for a new project in Mexico. Malinowski's ethnographic contributions are obviously considerable, but his functional theory—which was derived from psychology and emphasized how cultural practices met the needs of the individual—was heavily debated during and after his lifetime. Much of this debate arose in conjunction with Radcliffe-Brown, whose Durkheimian assumptions emphasized society's needs over those of the individual. From the 1920s until 1937, there had been relatively little direct contact or competition between the men; indeed, their few references to each other's work suggested that they viewed their approaches as different, yet compatible and not conflicting. During this time, Radcliffe-Brown held appointments at the University of Cape Town, the University of Sydney, and the University of Chicago. In Radcliffe-Brown's absence, Malinowski essentially controlled social anthropology in Great Britain, having trained most of the country's anthropologists, and exerted

BOX 9.1 Magical thinking from the opera house to the White House

While living in Los Angeles during my graduate school years, I was struck by the number of well-educated people there who made use of palm readers, horoscopes, and tarot cards. At first I just attributed this to southern California's love of eccentricity and "New Age" thinking, but Malinowski helped me to understand the proliferation of such forms of magic among local residents. As we all know, Los Angeles is the center of the American film industry, and it seems that every other person there is an aspiring actor or screenwriter. Many of these people are indeed very talented, but haven't gotten the "right break" yet to land that important role. On the other hand, we always hear of actors and actresses being "discovered" in LA, often accidentally while they were simply doing their day jobs to support themselves. Hence, much like Trobrianders fishing in open water, for a prospective actor, establishing oneself in show business is an extremely uncertain undertaking. Accordingly, much of the audience for palmists and astrologers consists of people hoping to find a lucky break that is going to bring them some success. Indeed, I knew a number of people who were trying to get into the movies, and they all frequently consulted their horoscopes or tarot readers.

My more recent experiences as an opera chorister (Figure 9.3) confirm that singers act in a similar way. However much you rehearse your part, there are many circumstances beyond your control on the night of a performance. Will you be up to par, or will you be experiencing some congestion or a sore throat? Will the auditorium be too hot or too cold or the air too dusty or dry? Audiences, too, have their own personalities, which can affect your confidence on stage.

FIGURE 9.3 Your author, dressed as a pastry chef who appears in the final scene of Mozart's *Don Giovanni*. The stage makeup tends to make us look a bit…embalmed. During that performance I went on stage wearing my "lucky socks," as always. Photo courtesy of the author.

Will the "house" be warm and responsive or cold and indifferent? Every opera singer I know has some personal ritual that he or she performs before going on stage. Many wear a "lucky" garment—a certain pair of underwear or socks beneath their concert dress or costume—to guard against misfortune. Before going on stage, we often turn to the person next to us and exchange the same Italian expression: "in bocca al lupo" ("into the wolf's mouth"). The appropriate response, which every singer knows, is "crepi il lupo" ("may the wolf die"). The "wolf" is a euphemism for the house. These sayings are comparable to the English expressions "break a leg" and "knock 'em dead" before performers go on stage. Aren't we singers a uniquely primitive and superstitious tribe?

Years of teaching have convinced me that students also engage in magical thinking. On the day of an exam, many of my students become quite upset if they are unable to sit in the seat they have customarily occupied that semester, while others insist on using a certain "lucky" pen or pencil to write their exam. Again, many have recourse to a "lucky" garment of some sort, worn only on exam days. But it turns out that athletes, performers, and students are not alone! On September 10, 2009, the morning after US President Barack Obama delivered a much-anticipated speech on health care reform to a joint session of Congress, Alex Koppelman, a contributor to Salon.com observed that during his speech the President sported the same red striped tie that he had worn on other important occasions (Figure 9.4). These included his Summer, 2008

FIGURE 9.4   President Barack Obama sporting his lucky red and silver striped tie during his health care reform speech to Congress, 09/09/09. Could it be that Obama selected this date for his speech because of its "lucky" implications? And what are we to make of the fact that Vice President Biden (in the background) wore the same blue tie on both occasions that the President addressed Congress that year? Mere coincidence? I don't think so! Courtesy of www.whitehouse.gov.

continued...

Box 9.1 continued

address to the Democratic Convention, his third debate with John McCain, his "closing argument" speech just before the election, his victory speech in Chicago's Grant Park on election night, and his first address to Congress in January, 2009. Koppelman concluded that this is "nearly conclusive proof that we have a superstitious president...though he seems to be an urbane, empirically-minded sort, Barack Obama has a lucky tie for the big speeches" (ibid.).

considerable influence over research funding. It was not until Radcliffe-Brown's return to England in 1937 to take a position at Oxford that sparks began to fly. Suddenly the two men were drawn into direct competition for control of British anthropology and its limited pool of graduate students and resources. This competition was heightened by a basic difference in their demeanors, which was soon expressed in open hostility. By 1939, Radcliffe-Brown was deriding Malinowski's "so-called functionalism" in print as "worse than useless". Malinowski mocked Radcliffe-Brown's "hyphenated functionalism" and Durkheimian approaches in general that "neglect the individual and disregard biology" (1939: 939). Since the personal and professional differences between the men were expressed in terms of their theories, these theoretical differences merit some greater attention.

Malinowski's functional approach argued that culture exists to meet the universal biological, psychological, and social needs of the individual. While agreeing with Durkheim (and therefore Radcliffe-Brown) that solidarity is an essential precondition for social life, he went far beyond him by postulating seven basic human needs that underlie all cultural practices. In Malinowski's scheme, no cultural trait has a simple or singular function. Instead, he argued that cultural practices are complex, integrated, and often indirect responses to these seven needs, which he outlined as in Table 9.1.

Malinowski described each of these needs and cultural responses in detail, but a few examples will serve to illustrate his argument. The first human need, metabolism, refers to the processes of food consumption, digestion, and elimination. The cultural response he labeled "commissariat," the literal meaning of which is the military unit that supplies an army with food. The corresponding cultural practices include how food is grown or obtained, prepared, and consumed; where food is consumed and in what social groups; the economic and social organization of food distribution (such as reciprocal exchange, redistribution, or trade); the legal and customary rules that ensure the steady operation of food distribution, and the authority that enforces this rule. Another basic need, safety, refers to the prevention of injuries by accident or attack, whether by animals or other human beings. Straightforward as this might sound, it is implicated in a host of seemingly unrelated cultural responses. These might include the manner of constructing houses to prevent damage from flooding; the organization of armed defense against aggression; patterns of socialization

TABLE 9.1   Malinowski's seven basic human needs

Basic needs	Cultural responses
1. Metabolism	1. Commissariat
2. Reproduction	2. Kinship
3. Bodily comforts	3. Shelter
4. Safety	4. Protection
5. Movement	5. Activities
6. Growth	6. Training
7. Health	7. Hygiene

in young men to render them potential combatants; the magical recruitment of supernatural forces for defense or vengeance against enemies, and a host of other derived responses. Obviously, then, each one of these basic needs is implicated in a wide array of cultural practices; the job of the ethnographer is to view customs, beliefs, and institutions in the context of these underlying needs. Culture, he said, was a "vast instrumental reality" created by people to satisfy their basic needs. Malinowski criticized those anthropologists who would view single traits in isolation without seeking to understand their relationship to one another and the underlying needs of people. Hence, he objected to the Boasian "shreds and patches" analogy in much the same fashion as Radcliffe-Brown, whose functional theory also emphasized the relationship between institutions. On the other hand, Malinowski did not arbitrarily dictate, as Radcliffe-Brown had, that "culture" or any other aspect of human society was off-limits for study. Indeed, virtually nothing was off-limits as virtually all things that people did could be related to our seven basic needs!

Because a complete functional analysis of culture required data on everything from material culture to subsistence to beliefs and ritual, the corpus of evidence that Malinowski expected of his students was *enormous*. Not surprisingly, many of Malinowski's students went on to become as dedicated and thorough in their fieldwork as he did, while others became disillusioned with his high expectations. As Langness notes, "one reason many of the British anthropologists entered the camp of Radcliffe-Brown rather than follow Malinowski lay in the sheer bulk and richness of the ethnographic materials that had to be presented in Malinowski's approach to culture. They felt it was unmanageable and thus they chose to abstract one important feature, social structure, and attempted to make it the prevailing and only legitimate anthropological interest" (2005: 102).

Radcliffe-Brown and his students sharpened their attacks on Malinowski during the few years that both worked in Britain, prior to Malinowski's departure for Yale. Many then and since argued that his theory was tied too closely to the Trobriand case to merit the kind of generalizations about culture that he made for all human societies. From the single case of the Trobrianders, Malinowski made more abstract pronouncements about all human societies, which, interestingly enough, bore a striking resemblance to the Trobrianders! This criticism, I would add, is not one that should be confined to Malinowski, and therefore should not be taken as a challenge to his particular brand of functionalism. We've already seen how Oscar Lewis' studies of societies as varied as Mexico, Puerto Rico, New York City, and India tend to emphasize similar qualities of social disorganization and alienation. Most cultural anthropologists claim expertise with just one region of the world, and in many instances, just one culture in that region. Naturally, though, we seek to extrapolate our findings to a broader range of societies with which we have much less direct familiarity as, after all, we are seeking to answer some broader questions about human behavior. It then falls to the specialists in other cultures to correct our misconceptions or errors.

More specifically, Malinowski's approach was criticized with the same argument that Durkheim had used against Tylor and others who had devised utilitarian theories of culture in the nineteenth century. Is it not possible that societies require things of individuals that are counterproductive or even contrary to their needs? Some practices such as human sacrifice or even altruism (the willing sacrifice of one's own interests for another party's benefit) could obviously not be easily accommodated by a theory that reduces all cultural practices to the needs of the individual. More prosaically, as Durkheim pointed out, people are always forced by society to rein in their desires and interests—whether for material gain, sexual satisfaction, vengeance and any other wants—in order to make social life possible. Since the late 1950s, all variants of functionalism have fallen out of favor in anthropology, for which there are both scholarly and social historical reasons (the latter to be examined in the next chapter).

Among the critiques that have been made of functionalism, whether of Malinowski's or Radcliffe-Brown's varieties, is that functionalism has limited explanatory power. One problem with all functionalist theories is that *constants*— whether universal laws or universal needs—cannot explain *variables*. All varieties of functionalism "explain" a particular cultural practice without showing why another practice could not do the same thing. For example, they might explain the social or individual functions of a particular religion without answering the more interesting question of why people adopt the specific religious practices that they do. They identify the functions of unilineal descent without showing why some societies trace descent through the male line and others through women. It is often said in this sense that functionalism is non-falsifiable in that it postulates explanations for phenomena that cannot be disproven. Secondly, functionalism is unable to account for change and conflict. These issues are much more pronounced and problematic for structural functionalism than for Malinowski's perspective. If social practices function to promote social solidarity and to maintain the social order, there is an implicit assumption that all societies tend toward harmony and equilibrium. As we'll see in our next chapter, this fatal assumption was perhaps the most significant reason that most British anthropologists came to abandon the functionalist perspective during the 1950s, a period of great tumult throughout the rapidly diminishing British Empire.

The Panglossian fallacy

Functionalism has always been associated with conservative political implications, whether we situate them in Durkheim's rejection of Marxism, the myopia of British anthropologists in colonial Africa, or the assertions of American functionalist sociologists during the 1950s. Ultimately, these implications stem from the underlying, if unstated, assumption that all cultural practices are desirable because of the benefits they provide to individuals or societies. If an institution or cultural practice exists, it is assumed that it functions to fulfill individual or societal needs. Therefore, the reasoning goes, that practice is necessary and any deviation is likely to be disruptive. Obviously this serves as a strong defense of the status quo and a warning against any attempt to alter it in social, political, or economic terms. In the late 1940s, two American anthropologists referred to functionalism as a "dismal science" (Gregg and Williams 1948), adopting a dismissive term usually applied to classical economics.[5]

In her classes at the University of Iowa, my undergraduate professor Dr. June Helm often described this as the "Panglossian fallacy," after the character Dr. Pangloss in Voltaire's satirical picaresque novel *Candide*. First published in French in 1759, the novel depicts the sufferings and adventures of the young hero Candide after his beautiful fiancé Cunegonde is kidnapped. She is repeatedly sold into slavery, raped, and even killed (a death from which she later, miraculously, recovers) while Candide and his teacher, Dr. Pangloss, travel across the globe to try to liberate her from her captors. Along the way they witness horrific tragedies, including acts of senseless violence, wars, and natural disasters that claim thousands of lives. Among the most terrible of these was one that preoccupied theologians of all time: what has been called "the problem of evil." If God is beneficent and merciful, why does He allow horrible suffering to happen to good people? This question was hotly debated at the time of Voltaire's book because of a natural disaster that befell Lisbon, Portugal, on All Saint's Day, 1755. An earthquake leveled the city at precisely the time that most of the population was at church. At least 30,000 people were killed in the wreckage, the tsunami, and fires that followed (an event described in detail by Voltaire). Yet, throughout their travels and in the face of such horrors, Pangloss assures his young charge that "this is the best of possible worlds," finding redeeming, elaborate but ultimately (to the reader) ridiculous reasons for all of the tragedies that they have witnessed. In most interpretations of Voltaire's novel, Pangloss' character is said to satirize the then-prevalent argument associated with the seventeenth-century German philosopher Gottfried von Leibniz that everything that happens does so for a reason and is therefore not only unavoidable but ultimately desirable. In this respect, Pangloss might be considered the original functionalist. Here is a representative "explanation" by Pangloss of why things are the way they are:

> It is demonstrable…that things cannot be otherwise than as they are; for as all being created for some end, all is necessarily for the best end. Observe, for instance, the nose has been formed to bear spectacles, thus we have spectacles. Legs are visibly designed for stockings—and thus we have stockings.
>
> (Voltaire 1918, orig. 1759: 2)

How might this line of thought be identified in the work of functionalist anthropologists? E.E. Evans-Pritchard's classic study of *Witchcraft, Oracles and Magic among the Azande* (1937) set out, in hyphenated structural-functionalist fashion, to identify the functions of witchcraft beliefs in this East African society. The Azande believe that there is no such thing as a death due to natural causes; indeed, most misfortunes are attributed to the actions of witches. Consequently, when misfortune strikes the group, a diviner may be called to identify the cause of that misfortune. Usually he will identify someone by name as a witch, and depending upon their infraction, that person may be required to make a sacrificial offering or, in more extreme cases, may be banished from the group or even killed. Evans-Pritchard noted that those individuals identified as witches usually were considered eccentrics or "loners." Of course, if an individual who exhibits such behavior knows that he may be punished by being identified as a witch, he or she will conform more closely to society's expectations. Thus, the social function of witchcraft is that it promotes adherence to social norms, reduces deviance, and reinforces social solidarity through such reinforcement and by creating common cause among the members of the community against someone who has violated its expectations for behavior. What this analysis omits, of course, is why "deviance" is considered such a danger to society that eccentrics must be punished and even killed. Were the McCarthy hearings and anti-Communist witch hunts of the 1950s similarly functional for US society, notwithstanding their cost in careers, marriages, and even lives?

The absurdity of the syllogism "if something exists it does so for a good reason" becomes even more apparent when we consider functionalist analyses undertaken by sociologists of contemporary society. Although functionalism was not widely represented in cultural anthropology in the US, other than among Radcliffe-Brown's students at Chicago, before and after World War II it dominated American sociology under the influence of the Harvard scholar Talcott Parsons. In 1937, the Harvard-trained sociologist Kingsley Davis published a paper entitled "The Sociology of Prostitution." While prostitution is identified as vice in the popular mind and often thought of as a threat to stable marital and family life, Davis argued differently. Prostitution, he said, enables both married and unmarried men[6] to satisfy sexual needs that they are unable to within marriage. Instead of an enduring emotional relationship that might threaten the bonds of marriage (as would, for example, a long-term extramarital affair that may lead to divorce), prostitution is a one-time transaction that is purely physical and monetary. Davis backed up his claim with evidence from at least one other society; in Italy, a visit to a prostitute did not constitute adultery in the eyes of the law because it was not seen as an emotional betrayal as would the keeping of a mistress.

Now, of course, Davis could have examined many other consequences of prostitution, such as the degradation and abuse of women by pimps and clients, the trafficking of impoverished women and minors across borders as virtual slaves, the spread of sexually transmitted diseases to the broader population, including the clients' wives, the fact that prostitutes are often the victims of violence and that they are frequently prone to drug abuse, which in turn leads to even greater vulnerability to violence and exploitation (see Sterk 1999). But instead of mentioning any of these *dys*functional or dangerous aspects of the sex trade, Davis attributes to prostitution—rather counter-intuitively—the function of actually salvaging marriage, and thus delivers an argument that this cultural practice is ultimately desirable![7] Dr. Pangloss could not have said it better! By the way, early in the novel *Candide*, Pangloss himself is infected with syphilis after a sexual encounter with the "pretty wench" Paquette but he is completely unperturbed by his affliction. As he expresses it:

> ... it was a thing unavoidable, a necessary ingredient in the best of worlds; for if Columbus had not caught in an island in America this disease, which contaminates the source of life, frequently even hinders generation, and which is evidently opposed to the great end of nature, we should have had neither chocolate nor cochineal.
>
> (Voltaire 1918, orig. 1759: 15–16)

Quiz yourself

Answer True or False to each statement

1   Radcliffe-Brown largely agreed with Boas and Malinowski that anthropology should focus on the study of culture.
2   Assuming that all people in a particular society follow social rules in the same fashion, Radcliffe-Brown claimed that it was only necessary to know the rules of society in order to understand the behavior of the people who belong to it.
3   To understand social structure, according to Radcliffe-Brown, it was necessary to understand how it evolved and changed over time, leading him to adopt a "multi-chronic" perspective on society.
4   The edited volume *African Political Systems* examined in great detail how colonialism had altered African societies.
5   Reflecting prevalent theories of the time in archaeology and cultural anthropology, *African Political Systems* showed that stratified societies in Africa were those with the highest population densities.
6   In analyzing the trading partnerships of the kula ring in the Trobriand Islands, Malinowski set out to show how the assumptions of western formal economics apply everywhere.
7   Malinowski viewed magic as an attempt to control events in which there is high risk or uncertainty and an inability to control those events by other, more direct means; as such, he said, it was found in both "primitive" and "civilized" societies.
8   Malinowski argued that cultural practices develop to satisfy seven individual needs universal to all humans.

10

DECOLONIZATION AND ANTI-STRUCTURE

A painting used to hang in the ante-room of former [Ghanian] President Kwame Nkrumah. The painting was enormous, and the main figure was Nkrumah himself, fighting, wrestling with the last chains of colonialism. The chains are yielding, there is thunder and lightning in the air, the earth is shaking. Out of all this, three small figures are fleeing, white men, pallid. One of them is the capitalist, he carries a briefcase. Another is the priest or missionary, he carries the Bible. The third, a lesser figure, carries a book entitled *African Political Systems*: he is the anthropologist.

Johan Galtung, "Scientific Colonialism: The Lessons of Project Camelot," p. 13)

An imploding empire and the problem of change

By the 1950s, functionalism had been the dominant theory in British anthropology for nearly 30 years, but increasingly many anthropologists recognized that it was unable to provide a plausible account of society. The years between 1955 and 1960 entailed great experimentation in British social anthropology, a period which saw the abandonment of functionalism. This rapid demise was due in large part to the changing political circumstances in which ethnographic research was conducted. As suggested by the anecdote above, British anthropologists were heavily associated with colonialism in Africa, Asia, and the Pacific. Many worked in conjunction with colonial administration in societies that had experienced devastating changes from colonialism. Yet, as we saw in our discussion of *African Political Systems*, structural functionalism treated these cultures as if they were unchanging and as if they were isolated entities, having little or no connection to the surrounding colonial societies of which they were a part.

Given his Durkheimian assumptions of equilibrium, Radcliffe-Brown simply had no way to account for or even acknowledge conflict and change, which were regarded as pathological conditions that arose only in a situation of social disintegration.

With his focus on the needs of the individual, Malinowski was unburdened by such assumptions. Indeed, he published one of the first anthropological volumes to deal with culture change (a collection of his writings on the topic, *The Dynamics of Culture Change*, was published posthumously in 1945). Most of Malinowski's work along these lines took the form of an early variety of applied anthropology, in which he identified the contributions that anthropologists should make in situations of European contact with African cultures.[1] He argued that anthropologists were well-positioned to identify basic needs that were inadequately met by indigenous institutions and should advise colonial governments on how to satisfy those needs with their administrative policies. Malinowski presumed that Europeans and Africans were involved in a reciprocal relationship that should balance out in the long run. Europeans provided the benefits of their political and technological practices to Africans, in return for which Africans gave the benefit of their labor and resources. Anthropologists should mediate between the two sides, informing colonizers of those areas in which they failed to give as much as they had taken from Africans. While doing so, however, Malinowski warned anthropologists against indulging in "an outburst of pro-native ranting." In an earlier work, "The Life of Culture," Malinowski noted that functionalism was particularly helpful as a tool of colonial administration: "The practical value of functional theory is that it teaches us the relative importance of various customs, how they dovetail into each other, how they have to be handled by missionaries, colonial authorities, and those who economically have to *exploit savage trade and savage labor*" (1927: 40–41; emphasis added).

Neither Malinowski nor the anthropologists who contributed to *African Political Systems* considered why Africans—who after all had been invaded and enslaved by Europeans—owed *anything* to their colonizers. Instead, they accepted the premise that Europeans had a right to govern them, and that Africans had benefited from this process. As suggested by his rejection of "pro-native ranting," Malinowski advised that anthropologists should avoid inciting feelings of nationalism or self-governance among natives, which would upset this symbiotic relationship. Considering its sullied history in Africa, it is little surprise that social anthropology is regarded with suspicion in much of the continent. Indeed, to this day, few African universities offer degrees in social anthropology, although sociology is widely taught.

Lest US readers believe that American researchers' intentions were "purer" than those of their British counterparts, allow me to direct you to the subtitle of the journal article (Galtung 1967) from which I've taken the anecdote about Kwame Nkrumah. *Project Camelot* was a social science project designed by the US Army in 1964, at the peak of our government's obsession with "communist subversion" in the Americas (the Cuban revolution had taken place just five years earlier, and the US had already sought several times to overthrow Castro). The goal of the project was to identify the causes of social unrest and the actions a (pro-US) Latin American government could take to undermine political opposition. Project Camelot was to recruit social scientists to gather data for the US Army in "politically unstable" societies that could then be used to prevent revolutionary change. In most of Latin

America at the time, that meant gathering information on human rights activists, peasant organizations, labor unions, and other social movements; this information could then used by military dictatorships to crush such opposition and remain in power.[2] Chile was to be the test case for the project. The Norwegian sociologist Johan Galtung, who had been invited to participate in the project, instead alerted Chilean social scientists of Camelot's real purpose.

Other social scientists, however, were willing to offer their services to the Army. Among those who accepted an assignment in Chile was a prominent American cultural anthropologist. While in Chile he allegedly concealed Camelot's real goals, but its objectives were soon unmasked by Galtung's statements to the Chilean press. Protests arose from Chile's government, which, unlike many of Latin America's governments in the mid-1960s, had been democratically elected and had even attempted moderate economic and political reforms. Chile lodged a diplomatic protest with the US Ambassador. After Congressional hearings in 1965, Project Camelot was officially canceled, *not* because it violated the sovereignty of another country but because Galtung had "compromised" its clandestine nature. But the end of Camelot did not bring to an end covert US intervention in South and Central America. Throughout the 1950s and 60s, numerous US social scientists worked in government-sponsored projects under the guise of "modernization theory," a set of policy prescriptions to spur capitalist development and to create "an environment in which societies which directly or indirectly menace ours will not evolve" (Millikan and Rostow 1954: 41).

When development policy based on modernization theory failed to achieve such goals, a heavier diplomatic and military hand served as backup. In 1970, five years after the collapse of Project Camelot, Chilean voters narrowly elected the Socialist "Popular Unity" government, one that pledged to nationalize the American-owned copper companies that dominated the Chilean economy. In response, the Nixon administration initiated Operation Make the Economy Scream, a clandestine effort to undermine newly-elected Chilean President Salvador Allende.[3] The US government instituted a trade embargo, vetoed Chile's loan applications to multilateral agencies such as the World Bank, stepped-up military training of the Chilean army, and directed the CIA to subvert the transport of consumer goods in Chile. These efforts culminated in a military coup in Chile on September 11, 1973 (Figure 10.1),[4] resulting in Allende's death by suicide. Besides killing virtually all of the leaders and officeholders in the Popular Unity government, the military government brought to an end Latin America's longest lasting constitutional democracy, one that had seen democratic transitions of power since the 1840s. What replaced it was the dictatorship of General Augusto Pinochet, a government with one of the worst human rights records in the hemisphere. Pinochet presided over a government that killed or "disappeared" some 3,000–5,000 of its citizens and forced into exile another 800,000–900,000 over the 15 years that it held power.

US intervention in Chile during the Allende years was no aberration in American foreign policy. Instances of a similar nature include the Marine invasion of Nicaragua and installation of the Somoza government in the 1920s (a family dictatorship that

FIGURE 10.1 At right, Dr. Salvador Allende Gossens (1908–1973) standing next to General Augusto Pinochet at a ceremony in which the general was appointed Army Commander-in-Chief. Pinochet overthrew Allende's government less than three weeks later. © AFP/Getty Images.

remained in power until 1979); the overthrow of Guatemala's reformist government in 1954 (resulting in 40 years of dictatorships whose brutality exceeded even Pinochet's); the CIA's promotion of a military coup against a democratic government in Brazil in 1964 (resulting in a dictatorship lasting until the late 1980s); US training of the Argentine officers who oversaw that country's "dirty war" against leftists during the 1970s and 80s;[5] the 1980s "contra" war against the Sandinista government in Nicaragua, during which the Reagan administration financed attacks that left at least 40,000 dead, and US support of a 2003 coup attempt against Hugo Chavez in Venezuela. As Kathleen Gough (1968) once observed, given the involvement of some anthropologists in counterinsurgency programs such as Project Camelot, "modernization" research, and outright espionage, it is little surprise that many people in developing countries view anthropologists as part of the apparatus of foreign domination. I have often been asked myself by skeptical informants in the Caribbean and Central America whether I was working for the CIA, most recently in 2010. Such beliefs are not without reason. In *Threatening Anthropology* (2004), an exhaustively researched volume based on declassified government documents, David Price shows that anthropology has often been used as a cover for espionage. And, as we saw earlier, when Boas and Wolf criticized anthropologists for spying, it was they, not the accused spies, who were censured or criticized by the American Anthropological Association (AAA). Such awareness of and discomfort with the relationship between anthropology and colonialism has led many anthropologists

FIGURE 10.2 Mohandas ("Mahatma") Gandhi (1869–1948); the little man whose movement of non-violent civil disobedience brought down an empire (and inspired Martin Luther King to adopt the same methods in pursuit of civil rights). His resolve earned him the hatred of colonial authorities; during the early 1940s, Winston Churchill fumed that he "ought to be lain bound hand and foot at the gates of Delhi and then trampled on by an enormous elephant with the new [British] Viceroy seated on its back" (Greenwald 2010). © Pictorial Press Ltd/Alamy.

in recent decades to embrace the kind of advocacy that is a hallmark of Marxist and postmodernist approaches.

I think we can explain anthropologists' acceptance of functionalism in the 1920s–50s in part because it did not threaten the colonial system that sponsored anthropological research. British social anthropologists understood, quite accurately, they would enjoy little institutional support if they highlighted the adverse effects of colonialism. Functionalism, whether Malinowski's or Radcliffe-Brown's version, served as part of this denial. But denial, as Kuhn (or Freud, for that matter) would point out, can only last so long. By the 1950s, it became impossible to ignore the political consequences of colonialism. The largest single British colony (India) won its independence in 1948 (Figure 10.2). Much of Africa was rebelling in various ways against colonial control of their societies and resources. Decolonization of much of the British Empire occurred peacefully, in part because a succession of Labor Governments in the 1940s and 50s came to recognize the heavy cost of maintaining an Empire over the ardent wishes of native people for self-rule. Recall that in 1955 almost all of Africa was governed as South Africa was until the end of Apartheid in 1990. These were white settler regimes, in which Europeans alone enjoyed electoral and civil rights. Uprisings such as Kenya's Mau Mau rebellion in the late 1950s sought to violently assert Africans' sovereignty over their own lands. Rebellions against minority rule required the far-flung deployment of expensive garrisons, destroyers, and battleships. Britain, then seeking to rebuild after World War II and repay its wartime debts to the United States, could no longer afford the expensive machinery of empire. With these dramatic movements for independence across the British empire, it was no longer possible for anthropologists to pretend that "tribal" societies don't change.

During the period of decolonization, as that empire gave way to newly independent countries, a remarkably rapid change took place in social anthropology. As late as 1955, most British anthropology was still based on the notions of "social structure" and "function"; by 1960, these concepts were considered outmoded. Anthropologists sought ways to account for the change and conflict that they observed in decolonizing societies. This experimentation also owed much to the increased independence of researchers, who could count on greater financial support for their research from public foundations and universities. This enabled them to sever ties with the Colonial Office, which had underwritten most British anthropology prior to World War II.

By the early 1950s, some anthropologists (most of them Malinowski's students) were trying to accommodate some role for social conflict into functionalist theory. Max Gluckman (1911–1975), whose work took place in southern and western Africa in the 1940s and 50s, was among these transitional figures. He saw that conflict and rebellion against authority were regular themes in the ritual life of many African societies. Conflict from Gluckman's perspective was not some kind of pathology, but seemed to contribute to the integration of society. Certain kinds of ritualized conflict are functional, in other words.

In his volume *Order and Rebellion in Tribal Africa* (1963), Gluckman dealt with rituals of rebellion found in many stratified African societies, in which the social order is, for a brief time, symbolically inverted. In these rituals, which take place on a given day each year, the hereditary leader (a king or chief) must dress like a pauper or fool. He is marched through his subjects' villages at the point of a staff. People throw things at him, and they subject him to humiliation and slander. An effigy of the king is mutilated and burned. Similar rituals are common in Latin America and Southeast Asia as well. In highland Guatemala, for example, some Maya communities engage in mock enactments of the Spanish conquest designed to ridicule the Spanish Conquistadores and their Mestizo descendants. During *Semana Santa*, or Holy Week, Christ's passion is re-enacted by Indians, with his "Roman" persecutors dressed like Mestizos or Spanish soldiers. In other societies such ritualistic inversions of the social order took the form of Carnival (Mardi Gras) or John Canoe, an annual celebration in the pre-emancipation Caribbean in which slaves openly mocked their masters.

Radcliffe-Brown would have had no way of accounting for practices that invert the symbolic order that helps maintain the social structure. Gluckman, however, stressed that these were *ritual* rebellions and not actual revolutions, in that they did not alter the social structure in any lasting way. Indeed, he argued that such ritualized rebellion prevented the real thing from happening. For one, such rituals are cathartic, offering a psychological release of the frustrations and resentment that people feel toward their rulers throughout the rest of the year. For another, they restrain the actions of leaders by serving as a warning against their abuse of power. Rituals of rebellion asserted the primacy of political institutions over individual leaders. The institution of kingship was more important than any one person who occupied it at a given time. If an overly ambitious king violates the rules of that institution, he knows that ritualistic rebellion can become an actual rebellion to replace him with someone who will respect its rules.

Anthropologists realize that people don't always follow the rules

For other anthropologists during this time, accounting for social change meant a shift from the abstraction of social structure to the actual behavior of individuals. Remember that social structure is a model derived from behavior, not the behavior itself. For Radcliffe-Brown, the assumption was that social structure provided rules for behavior, which people follow uncritically and with little variation. From the structural functional point of view, there was no need to study actual behavior because they assumed that *rules* and *behavior* were identical. It should be readily apparent that people don't always follow rules to the letter (you only have to get on the highway to see that!). But the way people interpret rules differently and use them to their advantage is neglected in structural functionalism, which regards variation from rules as a kind of deviance.

Much as Gluckman and others were exploring the topic of social conflict during the 1950s, another of Malinowski's students, Sir Edmund Leach (1910–1989), examined the relationship between individual action and social structure. Carrying out fieldwork in Burma under challenging circumstances before and into World War II (during which he saw military service), Leach experienced that worst nightmare of all anthropologists when his fieldnotes were lost (Sanjek 1990: 37). He managed to salvage enough information to assemble the monograph *Political Systems of Highland Burma* (1981, orig. 1954), which has become a classic in political anthropology. The volume was a critical transitional work in that it remained within Malinowski's functionalist framework while examining how the strategies of individuals are reflected in political structures. In the Burmese highlands, individual Kachin villages ranged along a continuum from nearly egalitarian to much more hierarchical. Leach argued that these different forms actually represented phases in a long-term fluctuation from egalitarianism to hierarchy and back again. He showed how political leaders manipulate kinship and property rules in their political conflicts, and suggested that the structural outcome of these manipulations was only visible if the entire highland region was viewed as a whole. His framework for analyzing the strategies of leaders conformed to Malinowski's earlier argument that kinship and myth were not morally binding norms (as structural functionalists claimed), but "charters for action" that actors manipulate and reinterpret in accord with their interests.

FIGURE 10.3 Sir Raymond Firth in his office at the London School of Economics during the 1960s. Firth not only lived to almost 101, but published a major article just months before his death! Courtesy of the London School of Economics and Political Science Archives.

As Leach was publishing his ethnography of Kachin villages, his professor (and another of Malinowski's famous students), the New Zealand-born Sir Raymond Firth (1901–2002; Figure 10.3) also came to acknowledge that people don't follow social rules blindly. Instead, they "play" with rules, bending them to the greatest extent they can in pursuing their own interests. He saw this willful use of social rules as an important source of structural change. Firth worked on the island of Tikopia in the Southwest Pacific in the early 1920s, returning three decades later to encounter a tremendous amount of social change. Not all of this change was externally imposed by colonial authorities or the global market; much had instead come about as people recombined and reorganized existing cultural elements.

In accounting for this change, Firth's work during the 1950s and 60s introduced a critical distinction between *social structure* and *social organization*. Social structure is defined much as Radcliffe-Brown defined it as social roles, statuses, and rules for behavior. In Firth's usage, it makes up a "framework for action." Social organization is the "action" or behavior itself, which he called "role playing": "…circumstances provide always new combinations of factors. Fresh choices open, fresh decisions have to be made, and the results affect the social action of other people in a ripple movement which may go far before it is spent" (Firth 1964: 35). Notice that he is implicitly dissenting from the idea of people as "structural dopes," as Giddens referred to functionalism's implicit assumption that individuals blindly follow the dictates of society.

Allow me to provide a somewhat extended example of the way that people manipulate the rules that are supposed to govern society. This has to do with the uses of divination, and derives from the work of anthropologist Eugene Mendonsa (1982) among the Sisala, a horticultural people of Northern Ghana.

To determine the causes of illness or misfortune, the Sisala employ divination, a ritual practice for determining the truth or predicting the future. Like many African societies, the Sisala also engage in ancestor worship, and believe that the spirits of the deceased are critical to protecting the well-being of the living. Most misfortune is thought to be caused by tiny malevolent spirits ("bush fairies"), which are invisible but constantly seek to harass people. Usually the worst effects of the bush fairies don't occur because the spirits of the ancestors protect the living from hostile intent, at least as long as the ancestors are remembered with periodic sacrifices and society's taboos and normative expectations are observed. When a community member violates a social norm or fails to make an offering to the ancestors, they are angered and withdraw their protection. This allows bush fairies to attack the living, resulting in illness, drought, or crop failure.

When problems become severe enough, Sisala elders may decide that a supernatural remedy is in order. They call on a diviner to determine what caused their ancestors to withdraw their protection. A procedure known as *vugun* is employed to determine the source of their displeasure. The diviner uses a dried goat's stomach in this process, while the members of the community gather around him to observe the process and learn of his verdict. From the goatskin the diviner withdraws a number of seemingly ordinary objects: a cowrie shell, a ceramic effigy, a dried plant root, a feather, an arrow point, and so on. The types of items he removes, and the sequence in which he removes them, are then interpreted to identify the ancestors' sentiments. Ultimately, the diviner pronounces the cause of the problem, and what the ancestors want to be done to restore their protection. Invariably what happens is that someone within the group is identified as deviant; for example, someone was observed violating a food taboo or a rule of social etiquette. Before the divinatory process, the practitioner has already learned of this violation, so divination is really a foregone conclusion to make public an accusation of a breach of conduct. The diviner indicates who is at fault, the nature of their violation, and what they have to do to repair the breach. This usually means a sacrifice of livestock on the lineage's ancestors' shrine. Only after the sacrifice is made is it believed that the misfortune or illness will go away.

As you might expect, the first attempt at divination often does *not* resolve the problem. Livestock may continue to die, crops wither, or children sicken, despite efforts to identify the ancestors' displeasure. But the Sisala don't reject their belief in divination because of this. They consider divination a *perfect* procedure for identifying why the ancestors act the way they do. The procedure, though, is controlled by fallible humans. When it fails, it is repeated again and again, until the misfortune disappears. When failures do occur, they are attributed to improperly performed ritual, not to underlying belief system themselves. *This is not unlike laboratory scientists who fail to obtain the results they expect on the first attempt, and chalk it up to "experimental error" until they finally do manage to confirm their expectations.* And this is one reason why

FIGURE 10.4   E.E. Evans–Pritchard among the Azande in the late 1920s. This photo nicely evokes the colonial context of structural functionalism. Notice the Azande boys in the background saluting in the fashion of British soldiers. I love the look on the face of the young man directly behind Evans-Pritchard. It's as if he's thinking to himself, "oh, brother!" Courtesy of the Pitt Rivers Museum/University of Oxford.

critical philosophers of science such as Paul Feyerabend have suggested that science is a lot closer to magic than many people would believe!

How would a structural functionalist analyze this institution? In other words, what are the social functions of divination? As we saw in the last chapter, E.E. Evans-Prichard's *Magic and Witchcraft among the Azande* (1937) asserts that divination is a mechanism to control deviance (Figure 10.4). Those who violate rules encounter social pressure to conform in the future. If we view this practice in the terms of structural functionalism, we see that divination insures that people follow social rules, insuring that social structure is unchanged over time. And because all people are expected to partake of these behavioral rules, social solidarity is reinforced.

What's missing from the structural functional analysis is that social rules are not impartially enforced on behalf of society's "needs," but are interpreted and applied by active, conscious agents whose interests often conflict. What is considered deviance is up to the individuals doing the defining (or in this case, the divining!). From the perspective of Firth's social organization, we see people pursuing their individual interests by using rules to their advantage. In *The Politics of Divination*, Mendonsa starts with the observation that divination is not a neutral process, but is controlled by lineage elders, who use it to support their own position in Sisala society. The diviner is himself an elder, and elders determine when divination will be performed. They also determine what acts will be identified as offenses against the social order and the identities of those who have committed such acts. The elders' base of power in the past was that they alone controlled the resources that young men needed to get married. To marry in Sisala society, a young man must make a bride wealth payment of up to 20 cattle to his prospective parents-in-law. Traditionally, young men were able to obtain livestock only from lineage elders, who would make it available to young men on the condition that they work for them for a period of years and provide them with "gifts" of grain. In actuality, this constituted a loan at usurious rates of interest, with young men ultimately paying back to elders as much as eight times the amount of wealth they earlier borrowed. Young men were virtually enslaved to elders under these traditional arrangements, until of course they became elders themselves, able to exploit the next upcoming generation.

With the expansion of a cash economy in the form of nearby commercial farms, Mendonsa reported that young men were going outside the community to earn wages and buy cattle themselves for bride wealth. Bypassing the elders completely, young men undermined the elders' political and economic control and their elevated status in society. Elders resorted to supernatural retaliation to restore their power over young men. When misfortune struck the community, men who worked outside the village were those identified as the ultimate cause, with their disobedience to the elders identified as the reason the ancestors were upset. When young men's "selfishness" was seen as the cause of dying livestock or epidemic illness, tremendous social pressure could be brought on the men to conform. They were required to make sacrifices on the ancestors' shrines, and if they refused they were ostracized from the community, making it impossible for them to marry local women. What we see here is that divination is not a practice by which social structure maintains itself. It is a *political process* that the powerful use to maintain their power and to punish their opponents. Cultural rules are manipulated, bent, and broken for personal interest, *not enacted* in some neutral way to perpetuate social structure.

Transactionalism and the pursuit of naked self-interest

One consequence of the innovative ideas of Leach and Firth during the 1950s was a shift away from analyzing the functions of institutions to examining the interactions of individuals. The Norwegian-born Fredrik Barth (1928–) was educated at both the University of Chicago and Cambridge University (where he studied with Leach), and was therefore steeped in both the American and British anthropological traditions. Presently, he is a Professor of Anthropology at Boston University, and has held appointments at Harvard, Emory, and the University of Oslo. (Yes, that's right: we're finally talking about a living, breathing anthropological theorist.) During the 1950s and 60s, Barth became the best known advocate of a perspective in anthropology known as transactionalism.

Transactionalism considers social behavior as a series of exchanges between individuals who are pursuing their self-interest, a view of behavior in stark contrast with that of structural functionalism. For anthropologists like Radcliffe-Brown, society consisted of a group of people sharing a moral consensus, that is, a general agreement about the rules of society and their desirability. Since it was assumed that all people follow these rules uncritically, society perpetuates itself with little or no change.

For Barth, there is no such thing as moral consensus underlying peoples' behavior, however much they may state their agreement with society's expectations. In their actions, people are guided much less by the needs of society than by their individual wants and desires. Society was considered to be the sum total of exchanges and interactions between individuals, all of whom seek their self-interest. According to Barth, this view of behavior would allow anthropologists to analyze those things that structural functionalism could not. For one, transactionalism provides a way of accounting for behavioral variability in that people were seen as manipulating, redefining, and even breaking cultural rules rather than obeying them slavishly. Transactionalists recognized that intra-cultural variation was much more common than structural functionalists acknowledged. In other words, what Durkheim and Radcliffe-Brown considered "deviance" was really the norm. In addition, transactionalism provides an insight into change. In defining social rules to their own benefit, people innovate and develop new rules. Unlike structural functionalism, this perspective recognized that society was not in equilibrium but was constantly in flux, which arises from the innovative, strategic behavior of its members.

There is an older anthropological antecedent of Barth's work, and that is *The Gift* (2002, orig. 1950) by Marcel Mauss (1872–1950; Figure 10.5), the student and nephew of Emile Durkheim. Mauss claimed that a gift is never entirely free to its recipient, but invariably contains some expectation of return; "gifting" is a means of establishing reciprocal relationships. He argued that all behavioral interactions

FIGURE 10.5 Marcel Mauss, who appears to have dozed off in one of Professor Durkheim's lectures! Courtesy of Musée du quai Branly/Scala, Florence.

involve some kind of exchange between people. Yet, there is a critical difference in the goals of exchange in "primitive" versus industrialized societies. In small-scale societies, goods are exchanged primarily to cement social relationships (much as Malinowski argued for the kula ring), with their material or economic value being secondary or even inconsequential to the importance of the relationship they create. In industrialized societies, goods are no longer the means to an end, but often become the end in themselves and, indeed, a social relationship may be compromised or violated in order to get something of value from another party (Marshall Sahlins went on to deem this *negative reciprocity*). Mauss admitted that this is not always the case in industrialized societies, especially where close social ties exist between people. Consider two friends who go to a tavern, during which each person in turn buys a round of drinks. Why would I buy a round instead of simply paying for my own drinks? I probably spend the same amount of money in the end, but Mauss would say that by buying rounds, I have cemented a social relationship, through exchange, with my companion.

Although Barth's *Political Leadership among Swat Pathans* (1959) did not allude to any sociological antecedents, his approach also reflected developments in American "interactionist" sociology at about the same time. The most famous application of this perspective was in Erving Goffman's 1960 book *The Presentation of Self in Everyday Life*. During his studies at the University of Chicago in the 1950s, Barth met Goffman (then a member of Chicago's Sociology faculty) and was apparently influenced by his views of social interaction. In *The Presentation of Self*, considered a modern classic in sociology, Goffman argued that almost all social interaction entails individuals trying to influence others in order to obtain their goals. Interpersonal behavior involves "impression management" designed to shape others' perceptions of you. People use stealth and "false advertising" when they interact with others to further their careers, reputations, romances, or other objectives (it's too bad that Goffman was writing in the pre-Facebook, pre-online dating days, when impression management was still limited by face-to-face interaction!). We all play parts in the drama of everyday life, according to Goffman, with our actions divided between our "onstage" behavior, in which we enact those roles that we want others to witness, and our "backstage" behavior, which represents our "real selves." Our backstage behavior is hidden from view, even occasionally from those with whom we live. Goffman's world is very different from that of Emile Durkheim and Radcliffe-Brown. Here there are no sincere motives, solidarity, or value consensus, but only the unbridled ambitions of individuals.

Everyone does this in innumerable ways every day. Consider the student who decides he would rather spend the day at the beach than take an anthropology midterm exam. The student would have two choices: he could just take off, without notifying the professor. Or he could make up some plausible excuse, and then take off. Goffman would say that conscience is less likely to determine the choices that people make than their notions of self-interest. And most students recognize that an unexcused absence (or much worse, telling the truth in this instance) will not be in their self-interest. So the student needs an excuse, and he knows that going to the

FIGURE 10.6 "Hello. You've reached the voicemail of Professor Moberg. If your excuse for missing today's exam is that your car broke down, please press '1.' If your excuse is that you had psychological problems, please press '2.' If your excuse is that your grandmother died, please press '3.' If your excuse is …" Courtesy of the artist, April Hopkins.

beach is not an acceptable one. Two legitimate excuses come to mind: illness or a death in the family. And it is extraordinary to see how many outbreaks of flu there are and how many grandmothers die immediately before a midterm exam.[6] In order to substantiate their excuse, the student who wants to go to the beach has to call his professor and play the appropriate "onstage" role, by either acting very sick, or grieved by his family member's death (Figure 10.6).

The ultimate inspiration for this view of social behavior as self-interested exchange was the classical economic theory of the Scottish social philosopher and economist Adam Smith (1723–1790). In his famous volume *The Wealth of Nations* (1776), Smith argued that the economic behavior of individuals was (and should be) governed exclusively by their pursuit of self-interest. There are three critical assumptions about human behavior in Smith's economic theory that are in turn adopted by Barth. Among these is the claim that people are free to make choices between alternatives. Think of the multitude of everyday choices available in our society; you can brush with Crest or Colgate, you could drive a Chevy or a Toyota, you could date Karen or Bob. Indeed, in our late capitalist, market-based society, we regard the individual as a sovereign consumer faced with literally millions of choices with regard to action and (above all) consumption.

Secondly, Smith assumed that people everywhere attempt to maximize their self-interest (however this is defined by the individual). Contrary to Malinowski's characterization of "economic man" in *Argonauts of the Western Pacific*, economists do not claim that all people set out just to maximize wealth, although obviously that is a goal for many of us. Rather, they maintain that "actors" maximize their "utility," meaning that people seek to get the most of whatever they consider to be desirable. That could be praise, leisure, home runs, winning hands at poker, shell armbands and necklaces, or whatever else it is that a particular person seeks. Since most economists work in the financial industry, however, what this means, in practice, is that they look for ways to maximize wealth. Finally, Smith assumed that people are "rational." This doesn't relate to sanity or lack thereof, but that people can clearly calculate the costs and benefits of a particular course of action, and in doing so, seek the maximum benefit for the least cost. In the supermarket, the rational actor will be the shopper who, when faced with two identical quantities (gallons) of milk, one selling for $4.29 and the other for $3.35, would select the milk selling for least cost. Rationality would also entail somewhat higher order calculations, so that a rational actor would select the gallon selling for $3.35 over two half-gallons selling at $1.75 each.

Barth discovers Adam Smith

When they were formulated in the late eighteenth century, Adam Smith's ideas were revolutionary in that they broke with earlier ideas about economics, which were informed by mercantilism (discussed in Chapter 3). In the same sense, Barth's ideas broke with earlier assumptions that the functionalists had made about society; i.e. that people had little free will in their behavior, but were compelled to act according to social rules.

Prior to Smith, it was widely accepted that a strong state was necessary to restrain peoples' pursuit of self-interest. English political philosopher Thomas Hobbes (1588–1679), writing at the time that King Charles I had been deposed and executed, argued (much like Smith) that people were inherently, even ruthlessly self-interested. However, he concluded from this that selfishness led to incessant conflict between people and that, in the absence of a strong government to rein in this conflict, people would experience the "war of all against all." Given humanity's selfish inclinations, until government forced people to set aside their bloodthirsty quarrels, life "in a state of nature" was, in Hobbes' memorable phrase, "solitary, poor, nasty, brutish and short."[7] Hobbes' argument, needless to say, was a defense of monarchy against the rising tide of anti-monarchical sentiments and civil war then occurring in England.

Does the fact that people act in terms of their self-interest create conflict between individuals? Smith rejected this view and, implicitly, much as Locke had argued before him, he rejected Hobbes' argument for a powerful state that would intervene in and regulate people's behavior. Smith believed that if people were free to pursue their self-interest, conflict would in fact *not* occur. Instead, as everyone entered a free, unregulated market either as producers or consumers of goods, everyone would also be able to assure their own best interests: "It is not from the benevolence of the butcher, the brewer, or the baker that we expect our dinner, but from their regard to their own interest" (Smith 2005: 19). From Smith's point of view, capitalism creates relationships in which there are no losers. The ability of the market to automatically

BOX 10.1 The limits to rationality

On the surface, the assumptions of economic rationality appear reasonable, and they are presented as axiomatic in economics classes. But consider for a minute the limits of rationality in our actual daily decision making. Imagine the case of a shopper who goes to a certain store not to secure the best deal on the half-gallon of milk that she is planning to purchase but to seek a date with that hot junior assistant produce manager. In this instance, of course, the economist's "out" would be that having a date with the produce manager has greater utility for that customer than saving money, so she is still acting rationally. Critics point out that since economists always define "utility" with reference to the person's actual choices, this is a non-falsifiable proposition, as the following classroom exchange might suggest:

> Student: Why did she select a date over choosing lower-priced milk?
> Economics professor: Because a date had greater utility for her than cheap milk.
> Increasingly skeptical student: But how do we know that a date had greater utility?
> Increasingly evasive professor: Because that's what she selected!

There's another complication as well even when we act strictly in terms of price, one which supermarkets have long used to their advantage. Rarely do we go to the market and buy just one thing, although one thing may be foremost when we set out for the store. For example, I might need bananas and milk, but while I'm there I also pick up cat food, diapers, chicken, canned soup, and apples. Consequently, supermarkets compete with one another on the basis of price for only a limited range of items. Have you ever noticed how newsprint and television ads for supermarkets consistently highlight their savings on bananas, eggs, or milk, three items that are most frequently on shopping lists? Often these items are actually sold at a loss (they are what are known in the supermarket trade as "loss-leaders") in order to lure you into the store where you end up buying things that are not so favorably priced. What appears to be rational decision-making on the part of the consumer actually has irrational outcomes (at least, where the shopper is concerned).

Cross-culturally there is an even more vexing problem: rationality in economic behavior requires some ability to use numbers and to calculate, for example, the unit cost of a particular item. Now most of us can do this and sometimes we are assisted in this by supermarket shelf labels, which often provide unit prices (e.g. the cost in cents per ounce of rival brands of strawberry jam). But what if we still lived in the Middle Ages, when people used Roman numerals, which are notoriously difficult to add and subtract, much less multiply and divide? In his book *Revolution in Time*, David Landes talks about the computational limits of that long expanse of European history:

> Medieval man…was innumerate as well as illiterate. How much reckoning could he do in a world that knew no uniformity of measurement? Units of distance were linked to physical characteristics that varied as people do (the English foot, for instance, and the French inch, called a *pouce*, which means thumb); while weights typically were converted to volume standards (a bushel of grain) that inevitably varied from place to place and mill to mill. Even the learned were not accustomed to using numbers. The schools offered little if any training in arithmetic, and the very persistence of Roman numerals was both symptom and cause of calculational paralysis. All of this began to change in the twelfth and thirteenth centuries. This was a period of growing trade, and he who trades must reckon. So must clerks and functionaries who count taxes and expenditures, and these were years of rapid development of royal power and government apparatus.
>
> (2000: 81)

Even greater limits to computation (and hence, rationality from the economist's definition) are found among small-scale societies. The entire numbering system among the Yanomamo consists of "one," "two," "three" and "more than three," a numerical limitation more or less common to many Amazonian languages (see Everett 2008 for a fascinating illustration of this). Notwithstanding such constraints on calculating costs and benefits, economists consider rationality to be an attribute of all decision-making everywhere.

satisfy everyone's needs even while they pursued their own interest was what Smith called the "invisible hand of the marketplace."

How does this happen? Let's say that in order to increase the profits on the goods that I manufacture, I begin to cut corners and rely upon cheaper, but inferior, raw materials. Before long my customers will abandon my shoddy goods, giving their business instead to my competitors. In the end, I will either be forced out of business or forced to improve the quality of my goods in order to survive. Greed is restrained by competition; hence, an economy based on freely competing individuals would be the optimal means of averting the unrestrained exercise of power that Hobbes identified in a "state of nature." As Smith expressed it, "The real and effectual discipline which is exercised over a workman is…that of his customers. It is the fear of losing their employment which restrains his frauds and corrects his negligence"

(2005: 112). So an additional, critical assumption that is carried over from economic theory to transactionalism is that exchanges between individuals result in *social harmony*. That is, Barth, like Smith, assumed that interactions occur between people who are each getting equivalent value from their interactions.

What exactly is exchanged between people when they interact, according to transactionalism? Barth argues that the object of interaction between people is a "prestation," a term coined by Mauss in *The Gift* to refer to any social or material reward given by one person to another. These could be such things as praise, respect, honor, support, or help. Money and sex are probably up there on the list of prestations, too. Barth argues that we implicitly evaluate the costs and benefits of any social relationship before entering into it. People attempt to get as much or more from a relationship than what they invest in it. In his *Models of Social Organization* (1966), Barth argues that all social relationships correspond to this form: where individual A offers prestation x and B responds with prestation y; for A, $x \leq y$; for B, $y \geq x$. In other words, "each party consistently tries to assure that the value gained is greater than the value lost" (ibid.: 13). Barth goes on to argue that if these conditions do not hold, then A and B do not sustain a relationship over the long term.

The idea here is that all social relations are reciprocal: people receive from others something of equal or greater value than what they give themselves. That doesn't mean that people are exchanging the same thing; in most cases they don't. The CEO provides a big political contribution to a legislator in exchange for regulations favorable to his company. The waiter provides exceptional service in exchange for a tip. The Assistant Professor writes a journal article, and makes the Department Chair co-author in exchange for a tenure recommendation to the Dean. And so on; everything in our interactions with others, Barth suggests, is governed by *quid pro quo* ("something for something"). (On the other hand, have you ever been in a relationship in which you give and *give* and *give*, but the first time that you ask for something in return, that person refuses your request? Of course you have. And don't most of us after a few such disappointments decide that it's not worth it to stay in that relationship? Well, we would if we were rational; that's really all that Barth is saying. We all know of instances in which this rational calculation breaks down and we stay in an imbalanced or even exploitative relationship because our fears, insecurities or emotional needs get in the way.)

Barth's insights have been widely applied to the study of politics in both small-scale and contemporary societies. The idea that reciprocity is the basis of all enduring relationships certainly helps us understand how legislative politics operates. (I think it also helps us understand how marriages operate, both those that endure and those that don't!) A good example of this legislative process was the passage of NAFTA, the North American Free Trade Agreement, by the US Congress in 1993. The bill, which was designed to rescind tariff barriers to trade between the United States, Canada, and Mexico, had been supported by Republican President George H.W. Bush and almost all Republicans in Congress. When President Bill Clinton came to office at the beginning of 1993, he signaled that he would sign the bill into law, but it was assumed that it would not pass the Democratic-controlled Congress. Because

Democrats count among their most important constituents the members of labor unions, and unions were adamantly opposed to the prospect of manufacturing jobs leaving the country under NAFTA, most members of Congress expressed opposition to the bill. Yet, in the end it passed as a result of President Clinton cutting enough deals with lawmakers to change their votes. Because the President himself controls some discretionary spending and can make recommendations to his cabinet secretaries for the use of spending in their departments that would benefit particular Congressional districts, he managed to change enough Democrats' votes in order to gain a majority to pass the bill.

Reciprocity. That's how politics is done. And since NAFTA, as its opponents anticipated, hundreds of thousands of jobs have in fact moved south of the border. It seems that everyone got something except working people, contrary to expectations of the invisible hand. The assumption of social behavior as exchange of equivalent rewards raises an interesting question. Under what circumstances are there losers? Is social behavior between individuals always consensual and mutually beneficial?

Can inequality be consensual?

This is the issue that looms large in Barth's *Political Leadership among Swat Pathans* (1959), considered a classic of post-functionalist political anthropology. Swat is an autonomous state that is presently a part of northern Pakistan (this is a region that has become heavily involved with the Taliban since the 1990s, so as Edwards [1998] points out, Barth's description of events and alliances should be considered more than a little anachronistic). The people of the region are Islamic in orientation, but their culture has also been shaped by aspects of Hinduism (notably, its caste system). The state is ostensibly under the leadership of a prince, known as the Wali. Yet, the Wali has relatively little sway in rural areas; this is a feudal society in which landlords command most local political and economic power. According to Barth's data, most of the land in this society is owned by members of the Pakhtun caste (leaders known as *khans*), who make up only 5–10 percent of the Swat population. The vast majority of the population is landless, and depends on these powerful landlords for access to land. They are essentially a class of sharecroppers, paying up to 80 percent of their harvests as rent to the khans whose land they occupy. We might assume that this group of tenant farmers is completely dominated by their landlords, so much so that they have no choice in any aspect of this system. Barth argues otherwise.

Applying his theory of transactionalism, Barth argues that everyone in this system, tenant farmer and landlord alike, makes choices about their political allegiance, not unlike the choices made by consumers in the market: "All relationships implying dominance are dyadic relationships of a contractual or voluntary nature" (Barth 1959: 3). In other words, tenants and khans have implicit contracts in which they each seek something of value from the other. Further, these relationships are freely entered into or broken off as circumstances warrant: "In Swat, persons find their place in the political order through a series of choices, many of which are temporary or revocable" (ibid.: 2). The peasants need khans for economic benefits, such as meals, credit, and future assistance, all of which they obtain when they visit a khan's men's house:"The relationship between a villager and a Pakhtun leader, whereby the former gains regular access to a men's house and becomes a member of the clique-like group that habitually congregates there, thus has the nature of an informal contract. In return for the numerous pleasures and benefits of membership, the villager must submit to the presiding chief's authority and thus forfeit an unspecified part of his political freedom" (ibid.: 56).

What does the khan get from his relationship with peasants? By the mere act of visiting a khan's house, the peasant expresses his political loyalty to the khan. In effect, peasants offer their political loyalty to khans in exchange for food and material goods. According to Barth, khans constantly compete with each other for the allegiance of peasants, whose support is needed because the khans are incessantly feuding with one another over land. One khan will attempt to seize a portion of the land belonging to another, leading to retaliation. The only way a khan can survive in this situation of feuding is if he assembles a large political following. For this reason, Barth asserts that powerful khans actually have to bargain for the support of seemingly powerless peasants. Barth contends that anyone in this system can switch his allegiance from one khan to another depending on the kind of deal that he is able to negotiate. So what appears on the surface to be a relationship of extreme domination actually is mutually beneficial.

Needless to say, some anthropologists have expressed skepticism about these claims. Talal Asad, who himself grew up in Pakistan and teaches anthropology at the City University of New York, questions the plausibility of transactionalism in this context at a number of levels. Asad (1972) argues that Barth's imposition of the "market model" of social relations casts a situation of extreme inequality into one of unlikely reciprocity. The significant conflict in Swat Pathan society is not among landlords, but between landlords and small farmers, with most of the latter having lost their holdings to landlords over the years and becoming landless tenants as a result. Further, Asad questions how much freedom of choice tenants can actually exercise in this system:"The economic evidence shows that for all practical purposes the tenant has no choice whether to take up a tenancy or not, and that the taking up of a particular tenancy involves the subordination of a tenant to his landlord" (1972: 87). If I rent land from one owner, how likely is it that I could express my political support for another landlord (potentially his rival) by sitting in his men's house? Isn't it probable that my landlord would punish me for such "disloyalty" by evicting me from his land?[8] Barth argues, rather implausibly, that "economic" and "political" contracts are independent of one another, and that tenants are free to give their allegiance to whomever they want, even those landlords who are adversaries of their own.

I would venture that Barth's description of landlord–tenant relations as reciprocal probably has much to do with Barth's outsider identity as with his "market model" of social relations. His research took place over a relatively short period of fieldwork and was conducted through translators. As a non-Pakhtun speaker and educated outsider, Barth most likely would have associated with higher caste individuals (that is, landlords) who provided him with his introductions and much of his information about political relations. Like many upper class individuals in class stratified societies, these informants probably viewed the system in which they participate as much fairer than do lower caste members of the same society. They would represent political relations with their subordinates as "just" and "reciprocal," views that are probably not held by lower caste tenants (I'm reminded of the very disparate polling results given by whites and African-Americans when they are asked about the "fairness" of American society). Swat tenant farmers, if interviewed at all, probably said little to an educated outsider that might challenge their superiors' views of society, especially if they have seen that educated outsider associating with their landlords. Thus, while Barth's model of political relations is coherent and internally logical, it has little grounding in a Pathans' reality in which social class, rather than reciprocity, is the salient feature. Clearly, the distribution of wealth and land—in other words, the structure of economic inequality—severely constrain the free will of Swat tenants.

It bears mentioning that the same circumstances that cause Barth's model to fail also lead to a failure of classical economics. Adam Smith argued that competition between producers created the invisible hand of the market, ultimately benefiting all members of society. But what if one producer is able to monopolize a market, because their greater economic power allows them control over the resources required for production? Can they not then dictate the terms of their exchange with the buyers of their products? On the face of it, ours appears to be a competitive market economy along the lines that Smith advocated. Consider, for example, the incredible proliferation of consumer products on supermarket shelves, displaying dozens of brands of toothpaste, deodorant, soap, etc. Yet, underneath that surface appearance, much of the so-called competition between producers is illusory; if you check the labels, you may find that these many "competing" brands are manufactured by the same corporation. In addition, retailers control the marketing of soap, soft drinks, etc., by controlling which manufacturers have access to their shelves. (Rarely, for example, will you find more than one brand of a given type of fresh produce available in a given store, and, as we all know, almost the entire selection of soft drinks in US supermarkets is divided between Coke and Pepsi products.) And a situation of severely restrained competition among two or three firms means that the consumer enjoys few of the benefits of price competition that Smith referred to in a free market.

Similarly, Barth describes a situation in which a phenomenally wealthy caste controls the basic resources that a large majority of Pathans require to survive. Much as the invisible hand breaks down when there is no longer competition, when there is inequality in status and wealth, Barth's assumptions of social harmony and reciprocity appear much less plausible. Like Smith's ideas, Barth's notions appear to work where there is genuine equality and free choice. The long-term trend in capitalism, however, has been one of growing consolidation of wealth in fewer and fewer hands, approaching monopoly in the case of some commodities. None of these criticisms alter the fact that I consider *Political Leadership among Swat Pathans* to be one of the true classics of political anthropology. What I love about it is the relentless way Barth applies his model, and that he does so with such complete, even joyous abandon! As I have often said over the course of my career, I love a theory— even one that is dead wrong—when it is applied with gusto!

From Barth to Bourdieu

While it is apparent that Barth was directly influenced by both American interactionist sociology and the social anthropology of Gluckman, Firth, and Leach, there is no evidence of a direct link between Barth's transactionalism and the later theories of French anthropologist Pierre Bourdieu (1930–2002). Yet there are enough parallels between Bourdieu and the "methodological individualism" discussed in this chapter that this seems the logical place to turn to his ideas, especially as Bourdieu addresses (and by many accounts, resolves) the problem of free will associated with actor-oriented perspectives. Like Barth, Bourdieu rejects those aspects of Durkheimian sociology that emphasized social solidarity and the reproduction of social structures through the normative behavior of society's members. Like him, as well, Bourdieu emphasizes the creative role of social actors (for Bourdieu, agents) in both reproducing and transforming society, although unlike Barth, he rejects the assumption that agents base their actions on rational economic calculations.[9] In developing *A Theory of Practice* (1977), Bourdieu denies that behavior is simply an acting out of cultural rules. Instead of a market metaphor, Bourdieu views society as game-like in that it involves rules, individual behavior (including what might be differential ability on the playing field), and strategy, all of which taken together comprise a particular social *field*. Just as a player integrates all three seamlessly, rules must not be seen as prior to their enactment and interpretation by the individual. Society as a whole is comprised of numerous distinct social fields, examples of which might be politics, the arts, bureaucracy, education, the workplace (and, of course, sports!).

Within society as a whole, the individual is not only defined by social class membership, but by every kind of "capital" he or she can exercise in relations with others. To Bourdieu, capital not only refers to wealth but also includes the value of social networks (*social capital*), which, as he showed in his volume *Distinction: A Social Critique of the Judgement of Taste* (1984), can be used to produce or reproduce inequality. In addition, agents may be able to deploy *cultural capital* (such as education or cultural knowledge) and *symbolic capital* (such as social honors or recognition) in advancing their social mobility. For example, people who deploy cultural capital in the form of familiarity with classical music or appreciation of fine wine may be thought by others to be of a wealthy or educated background and are accorded more opportunities as a result, despite the fact that there is no necessary relationship between cultural and material capital in this sense. Bourdieu's extension of the notion of capital into the symbolic, cultural, and social realms has been highly influential in the social sciences. His recognition of the importance of aesthetics in marking the individual stems from his own background, growing up in a provincial rural village of southern France. Arriving in Paris without the requisite cultural knowledge and polish, he experienced some prejudice from fellow academics and intellectuals.

Within a given social field, the individual develops a certain *habitus* that is typical of his position with regard to class, capital (in all its variants), and "feel for the game," or particular ability to operate within that field. Bourdieu views habitus as the set of socially learned dispositions, skills, and ways of acting that are often taken for granted, and which are acquired through the activities and experiences of everyday life. Habitus resembles anthropological concepts such as enculturation, but it does not primarily operate at the conscious level. In addition, unlike culture, habitus is highly individualized in that it develops according to an agent's social position and particular mix of social, symbolic, and cultural capital. Habitus contributes to society's reproduction by generating and regulating the practices that make up social life. Through habitus, agents internalize not only values, but taste, opinion, and even bodily dispositions such as tone of voice or mannerisms. The entire set of these attributes might be what we think of when we distinguish, for example, a working class person from someone who is upper class. Through the internalization of all these attributes, individuals learn to want what their social position makes possible for them, and do not seek what is not available to them. Indeed, they may regard the preferences of other classes with revulsion.

Regarded by the International Sociological Association as one of the ten most important sociological studies of the twentieth century, *Distinction* reveals how social inequality is perpetuated in French society. Drawing upon surveys of French citizens from various economic and educational levels, Bourdieu reveals how social class influences a person's likes and interests, and how distinctions corresponding to class are reinforced in daily life. He observes that even when lower classes have their own idea of good taste, "the working-class 'aesthetic' is a dominated 'aesthetic' which is constantly obliged to define itself in terms of the dominant aesthetics" (Bourdieu 1984: 41). Likes and dislikes for certain kinds of food, art, and music are learned at an early age and guide children to their later appropriate social positions, by internalizing in them a preference for items and behaviors suitable for their social position and an aversion toward the objects and behaviors preferred by other classes. When an individual encounters the culture (or especially the food) of another class, he or she feels "disgust provoked by horror or visceral intolerance ('feeling sick') of the tastes of others" (Bourdieu 1984: 56). Because tastes are learned early and heavily internalized, they are difficult to change and so tend to permanently stigmatize people of certain classes and block their social mobility. In this way, the tastes of the dominant class dominate those of other classes, leading individuals in lower classes to appear vulgar or tasteless in the view of dominant classes.

Bourdieu's ideas, while admittedly complex, provide one resolution of a longstanding division between theories that stress the determinism of social structure and those that emphasize the agency of social actors. With this model of society and action, Bourdieu steers between the extremes of free will (as it was embraced by Barth's transactionalism) and determinism of the structural functionalist variety by showing that the individual both creates and acts in accordance with the rules of every social field in which he or she participates. As we have seen in so many instances in this volume, Bourdieu's theories, particularly relating to the creation and perpetuation of class distinctions, also stem from his personal experience and attempt to make sense of it, a reflection of the ultimately personal and political basis of paradigmatic ideas.

Quiz yourself

Answer True or False to each statement

1 Malinowski argued that his functionalist theory would be of great use to the colonial administrators and missionaries who "need to exploit savage trade and savage labor."

2 Launched during the Cold War, Project Camelot sought to employ social scientists to identify the causes of social rebellion and the actions pro–US governments could take to undermine their political opposition.

3 Lacking any way to analyze conflict from a functionalist perspective, the anthropologist Max Gluckman simply ignored the "rituals of rebellion" that regularly occur in some African societies.

4 From Raymond Firth's perspective, "social organization" consists of the actual behavior of people, as opposed to the rules for behavior prescribed by social structure.

5 Marcel Mauss argued that no gift is entirely "free" to the recipient, but always contains the expectation of some return.

6 Anthropologists who study economic behavior in non-capitalist societies tend to agree with economists that rationality is universal to all human societies.

7 Adam Smith agreed with Hobbes in claiming that when people act in terms of their self-interest, the result is conflict, abuse, and tyranny.

8 Frederic Barth argued that his theory of transactionalism—and its assumption of reciprocity in social relationships—applies well within families or egalitarian societies, but breaks down in unequal situations like the Swat Pathans.

9 Talal Asad argues that Barth's view of khan–tenant relations as reciprocal probably reflected the fact that he interacted the most with relatively powerful individuals and internalized their view of Swat Pathans society.

10 According to Bourdieu, an individual's position in society was determined not just by his or her wealth, but also by symbolic, social, and cultural capital.

11

ECOLOGICAL AND NEO-EVOLUTIONARY APPROACHES

Cold War panics and persecutions

All materialist theories in anthropology share an assumption that the features of cultural systems can be explained in terms of the material conditions of life, meaning those behaviors and technologies related to satisfying human subsistence needs. Materialists concur that a society's "material base" ultimately—either directly or indirectly—affects the other, non-economic aspects of culture, such as its social structure and beliefs. Among the factors that all such theorists would include in society's material base are the natural resources available to human populations, the knowledge of how to use those resources, and technology used in exploiting those resources. Beyond this point of agreement, there are significant differences among materialist approaches. Two broad varieties of materialism emerged in mid- to late-twentieth-century anthropology: ecological approaches (including cultural ecology, human ecology, cultural materialism, and political ecology) and Marxism (including dialectical materialism and structural Marxism). Most ecological approaches include within a given society's material base its population size, density, and growth rates. Dialectical materialism does not include these demographic characteristics in the base, but adds to the list above a society's organization of labor in production and the social distribution of resources and the products of labor. Finally, structural Marxism rejects the base–superstructure distinction altogether!

Because ecological and Marxist approaches share some assumptions about the nature of social life, the two perspectives are often confused. Sometimes this confusion has been intentionally fostered as a way of dismissing any materialist theory by linking it with Marxism. In response to a 1950s article by Betty Meggers (1921–) outlining the neo-evolutionary perspective that she developed with her professor Leslie White, fellow anthropologist Morris Opler (1907–1996) observed that "it is curious that our neo-evolutionists constantly acknowledge their debt to

Darwin, Tylor and Morgan and never have a word to say about the relation of their ideas to those of Marx, Engels, Bukharin, Plekhanov, Labriola, Suvovrov, Lenin, Stalin, et al. Yet it is patent that their formulations are a great deal closer to those of [Marxist economist Nikolai] Bukharin than they can ever be to those of Tylor or Morgan" (1961: 13). Opler's attempt to link Meggers and White to Marxism revealed not just scholarly disagreement, but a willingness to expose them to the anti-communist passions of that time. Such allegations were known as "red-baiting," and in the 1950s and early 60s they were as damaging as accusations of "terrorism" today or "witchcraft" in bygone centuries.

Julian Steward (1902–1972), a materialist pioneer in anthropology, was well aware of the dangers of being directly associated with Marxist thought. Steward was subpoenaed to testify before the House [of Representatives] Un-American Affairs Committee (HUAC) about leftwing politics at Columbia University, although he himself was largely apolitical. In a 1969 letter, Steward recalled how country's socio-political environment shaped his academic career in the 1930s:

> ...the key factor of the national intellectual climate was the Depression, which started after I finished my studies at Berkeley in 1928. I had taught at Michigan two years, 1928–30, and Utah 3 years, by the time the Depression became so acute that everyone was asking Why?...and thinking generally took a sharp Marxist turn. It was during the thirties that Columbia became a communist cell far more than people knew, and curiously many adopted the political and economic orientations yet remained thorough-going [Boasian] relativists in their anthropological work. I too read Marx and others but it was dangerous to proclaim a Marxian position.
>
> (quoted in Price 2004: 31)

Such dangers escalated after 1945, when the United States entered into a Cold War with world communism. Relying on investigatory records accessed through the Freedom of Information Act, David Price's book *Threatening Anthropology: McCarthyism and the FBI's Surveillance of Activist Anthropologists* (2004) showed that allegations of leftist beliefs were taken very seriously by the FBI, which maintained files on hundreds of academics. During the 1950s and 60s, the FBI followed and harassed anthropologists Melville Jacobs, Paul Radin, Elman Service, Oscar Lewis, Margaret Mead, and Cora Du Bois, less for their theoretical pronouncements than for their support of civil rights and freedom of speech. (Bear in mind that the FBI's director, J. Edgar Hoover, regarded the civil rights movement as "communist-inspired" and ordered extensive surveillance of Martin Luther King, Jr.) One of the period's most heavily published anthropologists, Ashley Montagu, was fired from Rutgers University after he delivered a speech criticizing Senator Joseph McCarthy, then the chief anti-communist crusader in Congress. After holding a lecturer position at Columbia for 17 years, anthropologist Regina (Gene) Weltfish was fired for refusing to answer whether she was a communist before Senator McCarthy's Internal Security Committee. Similar fates awaited Richard Morgan and Morris

Swadesh, neither of whom was able to teach again in the United States. In response to such dangers, most anthropologists during the 1950s expunged any terminology or ideas from their work that could be identified as Marxist.

On the other hand, some notable scholars, such as George Peter Murdock at Yale University and Karl Wittfogel at Columbia, became FBI informers and reported to the agency on colleagues whom they suspected of leftist leanings. Murdock corresponded with J. Edgar Hoover to name 12 anthropologists that he believed were communists. During the 1950s, the FBI directly pressured universities to fire such individuals. Since the 1970s, as Marxist analysis more openly entered anthropology and the political constraints on academic inquiry have lessened, attacks such as those mounted by Opler on Meggers and White have largely disappeared. Yet, even as late as the 1990s, Napoleon Chagnon was employing similar tactics against his adversary Marvin Harris, whose ideas he dismissed in his popular ethnography *Yanomamo: The Fierce People* as "vulgar Marxism." As we'll see, there are such significant differences between Harris' cultural materialism and dialectical materialism that it would be misleading to identify Harris as a Marxist.

From diffusion to ecology

Ecological approaches, which are at the root of today's cultural materialism, derive from an earlier environmentalist tradition in geography and history. This is a tendency to attribute types of cultural practices to features of geography or climate. We can see elements of this way of thinking going back to the Enlightenment. In terms of its impact on anthropologists, environmentalist thinking was most influential in the work of German geographer Friedrich Rätzel (1844–1904), who related cultural practices to their geographical distribution. Rätzel initiated the anthropogeographical school of human geography, which attempted to plot out the distribution of cultural traits by region, leading to the idea that different regions were associated with certain types of cultures. Rätzel and his students believed that differences in "habitat" could explain most cultural diversity, although why this was so was not explained.

Rätzel's work was influential in geography and arrived in the United States through Franz Boas, who was a product of his school. Boas disputed the idea that the environment directly caused particular features of culture. He argued instead that the association between geographic region and culture occurred because cultural practices diffused over large areas and were blocked by the natural features (mountains, coastlines, rivers) that demarcate one region from another. In bringing this orientation with him to the US, Boas revolutionized the museum display of ethnographic materials. Until then, artifacts had been classified in evolutionary terms, with items from hunter-gatherers classed together with other "savages," materials from "barbarous" societies classed together, and so on, completely divorced from their cultural or geographical origin (Patterson 2001: 47). At the American Museum of Natural History in New York City, Boas reorganized ethnological collections into a system of classification that persists in museology today, one in which collections are organized by region (e.g. "Southwestern Indians," "Peoples of Mesoamerica," etc.). This was an antecedent of the "culture area" concept, by which Otis Mason (1838–1908) and other American anthropologists mapped areas of North America in terms of the cultures that dominated within each geographic region.

In 1895, Mason, then a Curator at the Smithsonian Institution, published the article "Influence of Environment upon Human Industries and Arts." Here he identified 18 American Indian culture areas between the Arctic and Patagonia at the tip of South America. Each culture area is a region in which a majority of cultural traits are shared by the societies within its borders. To take, for example, the culture area identified as "the Plains of the Great West," we would find that cultures within this region share horse-based hunting of herd animals, teepees, and similar kinds of basketry, clothing, and weaponry. Like Boas, Mason rejected the idea that the environment directly determined culture; rather, he argued that cultural similarities in a given region were due to diffusion.

While the culture area concept delineated the relationship between the environment and cultural practices, it soon came under criticism. Alfred Kroeber disputed the idea that there was a consistent association between region and culture type, pointing out that many different kinds of cultures were found within a single region. We can readily see this in the case of Southwestern Indian tribes, which exhibited distinct forms of economic and social organization in the same region. In historic times, the plateau region of Arizona has been occupied by three groups. The sedentary Hopi Indians practiced irrigated maize agriculture associated with a stratified social system whose leaders derived power from control of irrigation. The Hopi maintained symbiotic relations with their neighbors, the pastoral Navaho, who were egalitarian sheep farmers. Both societies were regularly raided by their neighbors the Apaches, who were mobile horse-based hunters. Many aspects of these cultures were indeed similar, particularly with regard to their mythologies and much of their material culture. But these similarities were superficial and almost certainly the result of diffusion. In their economics and political and social organization, the Hopi, Navaho, and Apache were highly dissimilar. This indicates that the environment by itself doesn't determine cultural features. Following Boas, Kroeber argued that any similarities between such cultures were due to diffusion rather than a direct result of the environment.

In his 1939 work *Cultural and Natural Areas of North America*, Kroeber characterized the relationship between culture and environment as *possibilism*. This is the idea that the environment sets broad limits on cultural possibilities and does not directly determine the traits that will develop. For example, Kroeber showed that maize cultivation was restricted to American Indian groups living where there was a summer season of at least one month and adequate precipitation. Maize was thus able to diffuse from Mexico to the Southwest, but not to California, where sufficient water did not exist. In coastal California, however, many other subsistence practices are possible, including offshore fishing, hunting of marine animals, seed collecting, and hunting of terrestrial animals. Reflecting the Boasian position, Kroeber argued that which of these strategies is adopted is largely a matter of local

TABLE 11.1 Subsistence practices associated with North American culture areas

Food area	Culture area
Caribou	Eskimo
Salmon	North Pacific Coast
Bison	Plains
Wild seed	California
Eastern maize	Southeast, Eastern woodland
Intensive agriculture	Southwest, Central Mexico, Inca

history: "the interactions of culture and environment become exceedingly complex when followed out. And this complexity makes generalization unprofitable, on the whole. In each situation or area different natural factors are likely to be impinging on culture with different intensity" (Kroeber 1939: 205).

Another of Boas' students, Clark Wissler (1870–1947), persisted in seeking an association between the environment and culture. After overlaying a map of dominant subsistence practices with North American culture areas, Wissler recognized that the boundaries of the two largely corresponded. His reclassified culture area scheme made the associations shown in Table 11.1.

Wissler's *food area* concept, laid out in his volume *The American Indian* (1938), anticipates a materialist idea of culture; i.e. that there is some causal relationship between a geographical region, the dominant food sources within it, and the cultural practices that develop there. The major problem with Wissler's idea remained his association of large geographical areas with a single subsistence practice. The scale of the environmental zones in Wissler's culture area concept was much too large to allow for meaningful analysis. All eight million square miles of the Americas were divided into just 12 culture areas (Figure 11.1). Within a single culture area, there was so much environmental variation that it could not be assumed that a single practice existed.

In the late 1930s, Kroeber's student, Julian Steward (Figure 11.2), found a way out of the impasse between environmental determinism and possibilism with his theory of *cultural ecology*, which holds that cultural practices provide people with the means of adapting to the environment. Cultural ecology, as Steward later described it, "distinguishes different kinds of sociocultural systems and institutions, it recognizes both cooperation and competition as processes of interaction, and it postulates that environmental adaptations depend on the technology, needs and structure and on the nature of the environment. It includes analysis of adaptation to the social environment" (1968: 337). Key to this process of adaptation was what Steward called the *culture core*, consisting of those cultural practices most closely related to meeting the needs of a population. These would obviously include a society's subsistence technologies and patterns of behavior involved in obtaining food. But Steward also recognized that certain social, political, and ritual practices might influence subsistence activities. For example, he might include within the

FIGURE 11.1 Wissler's eight food areas of the New World, taken from *The American Indian.* Courtesy of Oxford University Press, Inc.

culture core religious beliefs that imposed a taboo on hunting certain kinds of game, as these beliefs would clearly influence subsistence practices. For Steward, the environment and culture core jointly determine other aspects of culture. Hence, while the Hopi are not like their neighbors, they do closely resemble other societies having similar subsistence practices based on irrigated agriculture in an otherwise arid environment. The culture core provides a key element missing from Wissler's and Kroeber's earlier formulations of the relationship between environment and culture. Steward postulated that given two societies that have adapted to similar environments with similar culture cores, other aspects of their cultures should be similar as well. Cultural ecology provided testable hypotheses about the causes of cultural similarities and differences, one that suggested a functional relationship between culture and the natural environment.

FIGURE 11.2   Julian Steward contemplating a hominid fossil. Courtesy of the Library of Congress.

Steward's first application of this theory was in the influential 1936 paper, "The Economic and Social Basis of Primitive Bands." This was the first attempt to explain the organization of an ethnographically known society in terms of its material basis. Steward argued that similar environmental and technological conditions would lead to similar kinds of social organization among hunter–gatherers. This distinct form of social organization is the *band*, a small group consisting of several nuclear families enjoying equal rights of access to land. He argued that because of the band's reliance on hunting, which is a male activity, there will be an emphasis on patrilocal postmarital residence. Patrilocality insures that related men stay in the vicinity of their birth as their wives marry in from other groups. The effect of this is that related men—brothers and cousins—live in proximity to one another throughout their lives. Patrilocality thus enhances cooperation among men, improving their hunting success and their ability to defend territory against outsiders. Steward's effort to explain (if you will, "reduce") cultural practices in terms of material determinants represented a big step over Boasian perspectives which held that culture was the result of historical accident.[1]

Interestingly, Steward's first attempt to publish this work was rejected by the discipline's leading journal, *American Anthropologist*, as "too speculative." His initial difficulties with publication stem from the fact that he operated well outside the confines of the then-dominant paradigm of American cultural anthropology. His fieldwork was what we would today consider "problem-based," rather than seeking a "complete" ethnographic description of a single culture. At a time that Boasian induction held sway among most American anthropologists, Steward's explanatory approach was considered to be preconceived and biased. In addition, Steward was not interested in cultural traits, styles or "configurations," typical concerns of anthropologists of the time, and instead focused on the issue of how cultural practices helped solve adaptive problems. Finally, to the extent that Boasian anthropology operated with any theoretical preference at all, Steward's work implicitly challenged it. In arguing that regular patterns existed among hunter-gatherers who were geographically remote from one another and had never been in contact with one another (such as the Shoshones and the Australian Aborigines), Steward emphasized parallel developments due to adaptation. In rejecting diffusion and migration as factors in cultural similarity, he seemed to argue for an evolutionary view of culture that was then unpopular among American anthropologists. Indeed, Steward was a key figure in the reintroduction of social evolutionary theory in cultural anthropology, after nearly two generations of Boasian anthropologists had rejected it.

Hunter-gatherers: hardship or "affluence"?

Steward's ethnographic work focused on the Shoshone and Northern Paiute of California, hunter-gatherers who ranged through the Great Basin from arid desert zones to mountainous piñon groves. His research established some notions about nomadic foragers that remained influential for decades until the revolutionary work of Richard Lee among the !Kung San in the 1960s. Steward noted that the marginal environment occupied by the Shoshone resembled those of other hunter-gatherers, such as the Australian Aborigines, the San of the Kalahari, and the Semang of Malaysia. He claimed that all exhibited similar adaptations resulting from low population density, foot transportation, and hunting of non-migratory game. By the time of Steward's research among the Shoshone in the mid-1930s, the Indians had long before ceased to be hunter-gatherers. Through interviews with tribal elders—then in their 70s and 80s—Steward attempted to reconstruct Shoshone life during the 1880s, when a few bands remained active foragers. The resulting work, *Basin Plateau Aboriginal Sociopolitical Groups* (1938), was notable for what has been described as its "gastric" view of the Shoshone, who were so consumed with securing food in a difficult environment that they failed to produce anything notable in the way of material culture or ritual: "The nomadic hunters and gatherers barely met minimum subsistence needs and often fell far short of them...To them, adequacy of production meant physical survival, and they rarely had surplus of either products or time" (Steward and Faron 1959: 60). This view was extrapolated to hunter-gatherers in general in Melville Herskovits' *Economic Anthropology* (1952), which drew heavily on Steward's 1930s work with Shoshone foragers.

Steward's reconstruction of Shoshone life from nearly 60 years before his arrival in the Great Basin may indeed have been an accurate portrayal for the 1880s. Today, however, we know that the few remaining foragers of that time were not living in anything resembling precontact conditions. In his ethnohistorical research on the nineteenth-century Paiute, anthropologist Richard Hanes revealed that the world into which Steward's informants were born had already been transformed by traumatic contact:

> Epidemics of smallpox, cholera, and other diseases swept through Paiute communities in the 1830s and 1840s. The limited contact with Euro-American explorers, fur trappers, and settlers changed abruptly when large-scale migration over the Oregon Trail began in the mid-1840s...The rapid influx of miners and ranchers into the region led to hostilities with Northern Paiutes, which escalated to the Pyramid Lake War...By 1866 the military took the offensive to end the Paiute resistance to white incursions...Though several large reservations (Moapa, Pyramid Lake, Walker River, Duck Valley, and Malheur) were established for the Paiutes in Nevada, Oregon, and Idaho between 1859 and 1891, by the turn of the century tribal lands had been reduced to less than 5 percent of their original territory...Typical of many reservations throughout the nation, the General Allotment Act of 1887 carved up tribal lands on the larger Paiute reservations into small allotments allocated to individual tribal members and then sold the "excess" to non-Indians...Around the turn of the century, many of the Owens Valley Paiutes were restricted to areas far too small to support their former way of life as the city of Los Angeles acquired former tribal lands to control water rights to the Owens River.
>
> (Hanes and Collier Hillstrom n.d.)

In another publication, Hanes (1982) mentions that even those Shoshone who retained some access to land in the late 1800s found it contaminated by toxic mine tailings and unable to provide them with the game and plants necessary for survival. What we should infer from this is that Steward's portrayal of the Shoshone as being constantly at work simply in order to survive reflects the dire straits that their surviving members had fallen into by the 1880s. Forced onto marginal, poisoned lands that were a fraction of their former size, the Shoshone were militarily defeated, undernourished, and depopulated fragments of their former selves. We now know that every one of the cases mentioned by Herskovits in his 1952 volume decrying hunting-gathering as a way of life involving severe hardship focused on people who had lost most of their land and thereby their livelihoods.

When new research among relatively unacculturated groups came into print in the 1960s and 70s, Steward's portrait of hunter-gatherer hardship was supplanted by a different understanding. Among the Hadza of Southern Africa, Woodburn found that people spent on average less than two hours per day in productive labor. Working with Australian aborigines at Hemple Bay, McArthur determined that both women and men worked an average of four hours per day (1960: 92). How does that compare with the United States? According to Richard Lee, !Kung hunter-gatherers in the South African Kalahari experience a "subsistence" work week of 16.2 hours (Lee 1969: 67), compared with the US weekly average of 43 hours spent at the workplace (Schorr 1992: 43ff.). If we consider all work, including childcare, food preparation, household maintenance, etc. (in other words, all non-leisure waking hours), the comparable figures are 42 hours for the !Kung (Lee 1969: 67) and 83 for the US (Schorr 1992: 43ff.). Sociologists such as Juliet Schorr (*The Overworked American* [1992]) and Robert Putnam (*Bowling Alone: The Collapse and Revival of American Community* [2000]) have observed that working time in the United States has actually increased over the past generation. This is despite the proliferation of "labor saving" technologies that, back in the 1950s, were claimed to usher in a new life of leisure. The average American worked only about 38 hours per week in 1955, but is now working nearly one full day more per week than in that year.

Do hunter-gatherers suffer materially for putting so little labor into making a living? Lee notes that !Kung foragers consume more than enough calories and protein for their metabolic needs, a finding echoed in Margaret McArthur's research among the Arunta (Australian) aborigines (see Sahlins 1972: 18). Compared with people in industrialized societies, there is substantial childhood mortality (as there was in the developed countries until about a century ago), and many people in hunter-gatherer societies also die or are injured in accidents as adults. Despite these hazards, Lee observes that once they have passed the age of childhood, many !Kung live to an advanced age. In fact, the percentage of !Kung over the age of 60 is about the same as the percentage of Americans over 60. The two greatest sources of mortality in our society (coronary disease and cancer, both of which are related to diet and lifestyle) occur at much lower rates in hunter-gatherers. So if hunter-gatherers spend so little time working, and are not suffering for their low expenditure of labor, what do they do with their remaining time? I'll answer this in a few pages. But first, a little digression in Box 11.1.

The return of evolution

Boas' role in shaping early twentieth-century American anthropology can hardly be overstated. Through his pronouncements on culture and his training of the entire first generation of American cultural anthropologists, he left an impact across the discipline that persisted even after his death in 1942. In condemning the ethnocentrism and speculative nature of unilinear evolution, Boas had also consigned to academic oblivion all that was insightful in the theories of Morgan, Tylor, and Marx. The first students trained by Boas assumed as their mission the critique of evolutionary theory as applied to culture. After Robert Lowie's anti-evolutionary volume *Culture and Ethnology* was published in 1917, an enthusiastic early reviewer, Berthold Laufer, endorsed Lowie's position with the claim that "the theory of cultural evolution [is] to my mind the most inane, sterile, and pernicious theory ever conceived in the history of science (a cheap toy for the amusement of big children)" (1918: 90). Considering the strength of such sentiments and Boas' evident approval of them, it is not surprising that cultural evolution became a taboo topic among anthropologists, one raised only for purposes of ridicule.

Leslie White (1900–1975) was among the first anthropologists to dissent from this view, and he often did so with a stridency that his peers found abrasive. White

BOX 11.1   What happened to leisure?

The technologies that have been promoted as "labor saving" have actually been used to increase our productivity rather than our leisure. The average American worker today produces in 11 hours what his or her 1950 counterpart needed 40 hours to produce. Rather than contenting ourselves with producing the same amount in a shorter time, we have used these technologies to generate more output in the same time. Your new software allows you to process as many reports as you had previously in half the time, but the boss doesn't tell you to leave early because your work is done. Further, the ever expanding range of products available to us means that people are working more to procure these items. Finally, Americans have experienced declining real wages since the early 1970s, with the result that more people have had to work more than one job in order to support themselves. Schorr and Putnam argue that the increasing length of the work week over the last generation has come at a heavy cost in terms of the quality of our lives and society in general, identifying time pressure as the primary reason for our lack of civil engagement. At the domestic level, the cost is even more dramatic: a study conducted of American married couples in the late 1990s showed that husbands and wives communicated an average of 12 minutes per day. Can we be surprised that slightly more than half of all US marriages end in divorce?

In compiling evidence for hunter-gatherer work and diet in his 1972 volume *Stone Age Economics*, Sahlins made the point that there are two routes to "affluence," or a state in which all of one's material needs are satisfied. One's needs may be attained either by producing much or desiring little. In capitalist society, we make the assumption that our needs are great, even infinite, so that we must seek to satisfy them by producing much. This claim reflects a basic assumption of economics: all people's wants are greater than the means to attain them, therefore all people experience "scarcity" and must choose among alternative ends. Ironically, by producing an infinitely expanding array of goods, we guarantee that we will never feel that our needs are fully satisfied. We often assume that many things that people spend their money on are not really necessary, but I think it is fallacious to assume that "wants" can be easily distinguished from "needs." The reason for this is that technological "advances" are quickly transformed from a novelty into a necessity in order to function in the workplace and daily life. In 1980, no academic that I knew of used a computer; all relied on the typewriter to produce article and book manuscripts. Within 10 years, not only had the word processor become ubiquitous in university departments, but the expectations of scholarly productivity for tenure became built around it. In other words, it would be virtually impossible to reach those increased publication requirements for someone who refused to adopt the former "luxury" of the word processor (Figure 11.3).

continued …

Box 11.1 continued

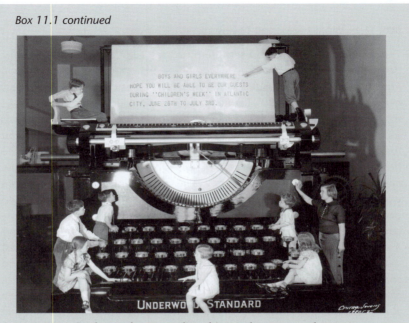

FIGURE 11.3 Students who are reading this may be unaware that typing papers for class or publication was once an extremely labor-intensive process, requiring the cooperation of many people. In this photo a school teacher is introducing her young charges to what will become lives of drudgery. © Underwood & Underwood/Corbis.

In 1990, most people lived perfectly well without cell phones, which in those days were both enormous and expensive compared with modern models. As the phone grew smaller and more convenient, however, it became a staple of business and daily life. If you are a salesperson traveling cross-country today, try telling your boss who has been anxiously dialing your cell that you left it behind because you really didn't "need" it. S/he will quickly tell you what your needs are, including possibly a new job! Within the span of a decade, most North Americans went from regarding the cell phone as a mere convenience to an absolute necessity. When I ask my students to put theirs away for the 75-minute duration of class, I feel like I'm watching a roomful of heroin addicts experiencing withdrawal.

On recent travels, I have encountered a new "luxury" that will surely pass into the category of "needs" before long. The airliners on which I fly are increasingly equipped with wifi internet access, at a fee, of course, for those who wish to use it. How long will it be before business people are expected to be using their laptops to be "productive" at 35,000 feet rather than catching up on that trashy novel they've been wanting to finish or simply catching up on much-needed sleep, much as they are now expected to have their cell phones with them at all times? In this fashion, today's "wants" are quickly converted into tomorrow's "needs," while what was once leisure time is turned into part of the work week. Apart from the fact that our workplaces and families expect us to acquire these things, how else are wants converted to needs? The average US resident is bombarded with more than 2,000 advertisements in various forms every day for goods and services. And this information is calculated to make us feel that our lives would be vastly improved by simply purchasing that new shampoo, car, beverage, or dog food. Although we are materially rich in absolute terms—Americans have more stuff than any society on earth and the average American has doubled his or her material possessions in just 25 years—has this made us feel any more satisfied? Are we as individuals or a society closer to affluence than we were, say, in 1987?

Hunter-gatherers follow a different path to affluence, what Sahlins calls a "Zen" route, after the Zen Buddhist doctrine that satisfaction derives from self-awareness and material simplicity. For hunter-gatherers, material needs are few and easily satisfied by the technical means at their disposal. Adopting the "Zen" route means that hunter-gatherers have a kind of material affluence—in that they satisfy their needs—although they have what we would consider a low standard of living. In the sense that they satisfy their needs with relatively little labor, Sahlins has called hunter-gatherers the "original affluent society." So—to return to my earlier question—what do hunter-gatherers do with their spare time? They do the things we would like to do if we had more of it: they visit, eat, play, tell jokes, invent stories, sleep, and make love.

received his first anthropological training at the New School in New York City under Alexander Goldenweiser, one of Boas' first students, before transferring to the University of Chicago to finish his PhD in 1927 under Edward Sapir and Fay Cooper-Cole. His first academic appointment took him to the University of Buffalo in upstate New York, in the midst of Iroquois country where Morgan had done most of his research. Despite having been told by his professors that Morgan was in error, White went on to read Morgan and Spencer for himself and was impressed. He then read Engels, whose *Origin of the Family, Private Property and the State* (1972, orig. 1884) had been deeply influenced by Morgan's *Ancient Society* as well, of course, by Marx (indeed, Engel's subtitle was originally *In the Light of the Researches of L.H. Morgan*).

As we have seen, a number of American anthropologists of this time were drawn to left-wing causes and were sympathetic to socialism, but White was virtually alone among such anthropologists to closely familiarize himself with the work of Marx. White's interest in Marx led him to visit the Soviet Union for eight weeks in 1929, a tour that left a lasting impression.[2] In a 1930 meeting of the American Association for the Advancement of Science, White delivered a paper entitled "An Anthropological Appraisal of the Russian Revolution." In it, he praised the

Soviet Union and predicted that the then-developing Great Depression in the West would lead to the collapse of capitalism. A firestorm resulted after his address was covered in both the *New York Times* (negatively) and *Pravda* (approvingly). *Pravda* (meaning "truth") was the Communist Party daily newspaper of the USSR. As news of the Stalinist show trials, purges, and forced collectivization of peasantry—which cost millions of lives—began to filter out of the USSR by the late 1930s, his earlier positive attitude turned toward condemnation. He remained a life-long member of the Socialist Labor Party, which was independent of and critical of the Soviet Union and its affiliate, the Communist Party USA. White regularly wrote for the SLP's newspaper, *The Weekly People*, under the pseudonym John Steel.

In 1929, White assumed an appointment at the University of Michigan, where he was soon fending off demands that he resign because of his pronouncements on politics, religion, and American culture. His lectures emphasized how cultural patterns determined individual experience, challenging both the doctrines of free will and deism—that human and natural events were directed by an omnipotent God. Political pressures from trustees, irate parents, and churches to oust him were a constant theme in his career at Michigan, where administrators tried to force him out by denying him raises for 13 years in a row (only the protection of tenure prevented his outright dismissal). Notwithstanding these pressures, he remained at Michigan for 40 years until his retirement in 1970.

White's theory of cultural evolution, first outlined in *The Science of Culture* (1949), entailed a division of all societies into three "subsystems," which he termed the "technological," "sociological," and "ideological":

> The technological system is composed of the material, mechanical, physical and chemical instruments, together with the techniques of their use, by means of which man…is articulated with his natural habitat…The sociological system is made up of interpersonal relations expressed in patterns of behavior, collective as well as individual. The ideological system is composed of ideas, beliefs, knowledge, expressed in articulate speech or other symbolic form.
>
> (1949: 362–363)

Within this scheme, White gives priority to the technological subsystem as the foundation from which the social and ideological realms of society arise: "The technological system is…both primary and basic in importance: all human life and culture rest and depend upon it" (ibid.: 366). White's hierarchical levels of society roughly conform to Marx's mode of production, juridico-political relations, and ideology, although there is not a single reference to Marx in White's *Science of Culture* (this is not surprising considering its year of publication, 1949, one year after Richard Morgan was fired from Ohio State after he was accused of being a communist). Like Marx, White argued that cultural change (evolution) originates at the level of a society's material base. However, to Marx's original formulation of historical materialism, White added the ideas of later Marxist theoreticians such as Georgi Plekhanov and Nikolai Bukharin, both of whom emphasized the role of technology in evolutionary change. (As Morris Opler noted, however, none of these influences were mentioned by White.) For White, "the primary function of culture" and the one that determines its level of advancement is its ability to "harness and control energy." White argued that the measure by which to judge the evolutionary progress of a culture was the amount of energy it could capture from the environment.

White differentiates between five stages of human technological development. In the earliest stage, people use the energy of their own muscles. In the second stage, they use the energy of domesticated animals. In the third, they employ the energy of plants (White refers here to the agricultural revolution). In the fourth, they learn to use the energy of natural resources, such as coal, oil, and gas. Finally, they harness nuclear energy. White introduced a formula, $C = ET$, where C represents the degree of cultural development, E is a measure of energy consumed per capita per year, and T is the measure of efficiency in utilizing energy harnessed. In his words: "the basic law of cultural evolution" was that "culture advances as the amount of energy harnessed per capita per year increases, or as the efficiency or economy of the means of controlling energy is increased, or both" (White 2007: 56). Therefore, "we find that progress and development are effected by the improvement of the mechanical means with which energy is harnessed and put to work as well as by increasing the amounts of energy employed" (ibid.).

White believed that there was a direct correspondence between energy capture and the elaboration of cultural practices in the "sociological" and "ideological" levels of society. Or, as he was once heard to quip, "simple technologies make simple cultures." This is the kind of thinking that Boas had condemned in his paper "The Limitations of the Comparative Method" (1996a), in which he claimed that there was no relationship between the level of a society's technological development and the complexity of its other cultural features, such as kinship and mythology. White invoked other, earlier ideas about cultural evolution as well. As scientific knowledge and technological control of the environment increased, White argued, the corresponding need for supernatural explanations would diminish. Predicting the death of religion in the face of scientific advancement, of course, had been a mainstay of evolutionary thinking since the Enlightenment. Such pronouncements were to get him in trouble more than once, as when he wrote, following the USSR's launch of Sputnik in 1957, that "a cultural system that can launch satellites into orbit can dispense with God entirely" (quoted in Peace 2004: 154). White's materialism was in this way often more outspoken (or, to his critics, dogmatic) than that of any anthropologist before or since. In his 1959 volume *The Evolution of Culture*, he even advanced the remarkable argument that aesthetic notions of feminine beauty were directly determined by technological factors: "In cultures where technological control over food supply is slight and food is frequently scarce as a consequence, a fat woman is often regarded as beautiful. In cultures where food is abundant and women work little, obesity is likely to be regarded as unsightly" (!) (2007, orig. 1959: 25). This is materialism pursued with a vengeance!

White's speculations on culture are often reminiscent of the grandiose and free-wheeling pronouncements made by his nineteenth-century predecessors, and indeed he considered himself to be working directly within their evolutionary tradition. White rejected the label of "neoevolution," contending that his theory "does not differ one whit in principle from that expressed in Tylor's *Anthropology* in 1881, although of course the development, expression and demonstration of the theory may—and does—differ at some points" (White 2007:ix). His adoption of the ideas of nineteenth-century evolutionists was in fact a bit selective, as he abandoned their savagery–barbarism–civilization stages while adopting a materialist argument. That mode of explanation of course was emphasized in Marx and Engels but absent from Morgan and Tylor. White's "law" of evolution that technological change brings about "advances" in efficiency and culture more generally does reveal another nineteenth-century attribute, however: a deep and abiding faith in progress. We will examine this question in more detail below.

Independently of White, and as a result of his more explicitly ecological approach, Julian Steward also resurrected evolutionary ideas in the 1950s. Unlike White and the nineteenth-century evolutionists, Steward proposed multiple pathways for cultural evolution (multilinear evolution), arising as a result of the distinctive combination of environmental and technological factors found in a given culture. In applying his theory, he compared the prehistoric patterns of cultural development in five centers of ancient civilization: Mesopotamia, Egypt, China, Mesoamerica, and the Andes. These centers shared "parallels of form, function and sequence" owed to their common development in semi-arid environments in which people had grown dependent on irrigation and floodwater agriculture. Such practices created large food surpluses that allowed for some craft specialization and other nonsubsistence activities as well as population growth. Population growth also fueled competition for resources, culminating in warfare. Political leadership in all five regions shifted from temple priests to warrior kings, who were often responsible for forging empires over large regions. Similar developments in these regions were not the result of uniform stages, as White, Morgan, and Tylor might have argued, but the distinctive adaptations developing in semi-arid zones dependent on irrigation agriculture. Absent these conditions, social evolution would assume different pathways.

Steward's and White's differing perspectives on evolution triggered intense debate among them, leading to that rarest of academic interventions, a third party effort at reconciliation. In 1960, Marshall Sahlins and Elman Service, who were colleagues and/or students of both White and Steward, published *Evolution and Culture*. In it, they argued that the heart of the dispute between the two was a difference between specific and general evolution. Whereas White was talking of general, long-term trends present in all cultures (the harnessing of greater amounts of energy from the environment), Steward referred to specific forms of adaptation that arose within particular environmental contexts and subsistence traditions. It remains unclear whether this intervention diminished the disputes between the two leading evolutionary thinkers of the time, but it did signal evolution's rehabilitation in anthropology after being consigned to the wilderness for many years. From being virtually banned as a topic of academic discourse in the 1930s, social evolution moved to the center of anthropological theory in the US by the 1960s.

Over the next two decades, many anthropologists framed cultural diversity within an evolutionary perspective. In *Primitive Social Organization* (1962), Service introduced a typology still employed among archaeologists; that of band–tribe–chiefdom–state. In 1967, Morton Fried published *The Evolution of Political Society*, in which he distinguished between egalitarian, ranked, and stratified societies. Fried's typology also remains widely employed among cultural anthropologists and archaeologists. The typologies of these two volumes are largely compatible, with band societies being egalitarian, tribal societies being ranked (a situation defined by Fried in which there are differences in prestige and wealth but all people retain access to the basic resources that permit survival), and chiefdoms and states exhibiting stratification (where there is structured inequality of access to the basic resources that permit survival). In other ways, the volumes represent an interesting contrast in their reliance upon different traditions of political philosophy. In explaining the evolution of stratified societies (chiefdoms and states), Service invoked an idea associated with the seventeenth-century political philosopher Thomas Hobbes, who argued that people surrender their freedom to leaders on the basis of a "social contract." While Hobbes argued that the primary service provided by leaders was that of defense, Service added other important managerial roles such as trade, redistribution, and the maintenance of irrigation systems. Fried, on the other hand, assumed a primarily Marxist position, arguing that stratified social orders exercise power on behalf of an economic elite that rules over a comparatively powerless majority. In effect, Fried, like White before him, cast anthropological evidence within an explanatory framework developed from Marx.

Pessimism, not progress

With the postmodern turn since the 1980s, evolutionary theories of culture have fallen out of favor with many cultural anthropologists, although they remain in wide use among archaeologists. For postmodernists, cultural evolution represents the kind of "totalizing discourse" that they consider part of the offensive legacy of science in anthropology. Interestingly, in their reluctance to generalize or compare cultures, postmodernists seem to be reaching back to a kind of particularism that Boas himself might recognize (even if Boas, whose writings were always notable for their clarity, would probably wince at postmodernists' often baroque jargon). Yet cultural evolutionary models are far from dead. Introductory textbooks continue to rely upon them as a meaningful way of classifying cultures and understanding culture change. Cultural materialists continue to embrace the idea that cultures change in systematic and patterned ways over time. As recently as 2002, Allen Johnson and Timothy K. Earle updated their volume *The Evolution of Human Societies*, which presents a materialist model of cultural evolution. Johnson and Earle's volume represents a synthetic approach that combines in some ways the ideas of Malthus, Service, and newer research on the "energetic efficiency" of various forms of food production. In this, they provide evidence that directly addresses one of the contentions of Leslie White: that cultural evolution is marked by a growing harnessing of energy from the environment and increased energetic efficiency. Their argument is that population growth fuels intensification of production, which increases subsistence risk and the need for new innovations (such as storage and irrigation), which in turn leads to the need for more management and control over subsistence, from which political leaders emerge as the managers of resources. Ultimately, then, this is a theory of social evolution in which the "prime mover" is population growth (a Malthusian assumption over which I argued with the authors, but to no avail!).

Where Johnson and Earle differ from White and the nineteenth-century evolutionists is in their skepticism toward the notion of "progress," which arose from their reading of the influential 1965 volume, *The Conditions of Agricultural Growth*, by Danish agricultural economist Ester Boserup. She asked under what circumstances people switch from relatively extensive horticultural production (such as shifting cultivation) to more intensive forms of farming, such as annual cropping on the same parcel of land, irrigation, use of the plow, and terracing. From White's perspective, in which "technology is the hero of our piece," the answer was obvious: these changes allowed people to support themselves with less labor and a more stable food supply. Boserup, one of the first economists to challenge this argument, showed that there was a diminishing return to labor in the shift to intensive production. That is, with each additional unit of labor added to production, a smaller increase in production resulted. Intensive agriculturalists do produce more food than shifting cultivators, but to do so, they have to work much harder. She argued that people would only resort to what in effect was a bad bargain under two circumstances: if they needed more food because of population growth, or "under the compulsions of a social hierarchy." In other words, people might be compelled to work harder because those in positions of power forced them to do so.

Boserup's book was widely read by ecological anthropologists of the 1960s, and it led many to abandon the notion that technological change in agriculture toward greater intensiveness represented "progress." Johnson gathered data on the energy exchange of various subsistence activities utilizing a CO_2 gasometer, a backpack device which calculates caloric expenditure from its wearer's exhaled breath.[3] Johnson's data compiled with a variety of societies reveal a decline in the efficiency with which people produce food as subsistence practices evolve.

What Table 11.2 reveals is that for every calorie of work performed by a hunter-gatherer, about 20 calories of food are produced; for every calorie of work performed by a farmer practicing horticulture, such as an Amazonian tribesman, only about 15 calories are produced. In an intensive agricultural society like China, where agriculture rests on wet rice cultivation, every calorie of work yields only four calories of food energy. In contrast to the framework of nineteenth-century theorists, we now recognize that agriculture has come at a steep cost in terms of labor and quality of life. Now, some of you may be wondering how our oh-so-sophisticated mechanized farming system stacks up against these systems of food procurement (above) that rely more heavily on human and animal power. At present,

TABLE 11.2   The cost of agriculture

	Work energy expended	*Caloric yield in food*
Hunter-gatherers	1 calorie	20 calories
Horticulturalists	1 calorie	15 calories
Intensive agriculturalists	1 calorie	4 calories

for a farmer growing maize in a Midwest state like Illinois or Kansas, for every calorie of energy expended in farming, only 1/10th of 1 calorie of food is actually produced. Or, to put it another way, in the United States we use 10 calories of energy to produce every single calorie of food. Unlike every other system of food procurement indicated above, North American food production operates at a huge caloric deficit—we expend far more energy than what we produce in food.

How can this be? Most of the energy expended in our food production system comes directly or indirectly from petroleum or other fossil fuels. To produce corn, a farmer tills a field with a gas-powered tractor, plants the corn seed with a mechanical planter (diesel powered), fertilizes it using nitrogen fertilizer (produced with petroleum), harvests it with a diesel combine, and finally dries it for storage with an electric drier.

Much has been made of price increases in food over the last several years, not only in developed societies but around the world. In the United States in 2001, a gallon of milk sold for a little more than a gallon of gasoline. A decade later, the same is true—except that both now cost twice what they did ten years ago! This is no coincidence. Much of these price increases have resulted from the rising price of oil on world markets; in effect, our food system transforms oil into edible calories. Does it do so with great productivity? Yes, American farmers produce about four times more corn per acre than they did in 1920, when animal power and human labor were the basis of our farming system. Does it produce food efficiently? No. Does it do so in an environmentally sustainable fashion? Obviously not.

Cross-cultural comparisons of diet also cast doubt on longstanding notions of evolutionary progress. Farming populations lack the dietary diversity of hunter-gatherers, who might make use of a hundred or more species of plants. Most shifting cultivators grow 30–50 types of plant foods and, by the time you get to intensive farming (such as rural China), people rely on a narrow range of staples (the overwhelming bulk of the diet being rice). All of the agrarian civilizations we know of from prehistory relied on the intensive agricultural production of just a few types of crops (maize for prehistoric Mexico, potatoes for Peru, wheat for Middle Eastern societies, etc.). While diet in industrialized societies is much broader than these societies (think of the range of choices in a supermarket in any upper-income neighborhood), this diversity is only made possible through the use of petroleum to transport food long distances (say, California spinach in New Hampshire), or even jet fuel to bring us winter fruits and vegetables from Chile. It turns out that our diverse diet entails an immense carbon footprint.

We see other negative consequences of food production in the health consequences of sedentism. Large, settled communities face problems of waste disposal not experienced by hunter-gatherers, who simply walk away from a camp once it becomes unsanitary. For farmers there is not only more contact with waste and disease-transmitting species like flies and rats, there is no possibility of escaping them. The result is a higher incidence of infectious disease, gastrointestinal problems, and parasites. Social tensions also increase as people are compelled to live together and come into conflict over territory. Group conflict (that is, warfare) really didn't develop until people developed agriculture. In contrast to the older view that agriculture represented "progress," today's anthropologists recognize that domestication came at a huge cost. So why did it develop? Agriculture has one and only one advantage over hunting-gathering—it can be greatly intensified to feed more people. In this sense, the newer evolutionary perspectives would concur with White that the course of evolution is one of increased harnessing of energy from the environment. In most other respects, however, they are very skeptical of claims that such changes represent unmitigated progress.

Quiz yourself

Answer True or False to each statement

1 During the 1950s and 60s, the FBI maintained surveillance records on dozens of anthropologists suspected of left-wing political leanings.
2 Boas argued that geographical regions were associated with certain types of cultures only because the boundaries of those regions (mountains, rivers, coasts) limited the ability of cultural practices to diffuse from one region to another.
3 Boas acquired the idea of culture areas from museum displays, which had always organized cultural artifacts by geographical regions.
4 A.L. Kroeber's doctrine of possibilism suggested that within a given region only a single kind of cultural adaptation was possible.
5 Julian Steward's 1936 article on Great Basin hunter-gatherers was the first application of a materialist theory to explain the characteristics of a specific culture, although it is now recognized as having reached erroneous conclusions about hunter-gatherer kinship and social organization.
6 Anthropologists now recognize that the nutritional hardship that Steward attributed to hunter-gatherers like the Shoshone was largely the result of white contact and resulting loss of territory.
7 Although hunter-gatherers work less than people in the United States, the advent of "labor-saving" technology since the 1950s has reduced the work week for Americans by nearly one full day.
8 Leslie White divided cultures into "technological," "sociological," and "ideological" levels that basically corresponded to Marx's three-part division of societies.

9 Leslie White's contention that "culture evolves as the efficiency of energy capture increases" is borne out by Johnson's data on the relationship between energy input and output in hunter–gatherer, horticultural, and intensive agricultural societies.

10 Economist Ester Boserup argued that people would only opt for intensified food production if they were forced to—either by increasing population or the demands of a dominant class of tribute-takers.

12

CONTEMPORARY MATERIALIST AND ECOLOGICAL APPROACHES

The "struggle for a science of culture"

From 1946 to 1952, Julian Steward taught at Columbia University, and then assumed a research appointment at the University of Illinois where he remained until his retirement in 1968. At Columbia, Steward taught a cohort of students who would become prominent figures in anthropology. Sidney Mintz, Elman Service, Eric Wolf, Morton Fried, Marvin Harris, Robert Murphy, and Robert Manners are among the students who incorporated aspects of Steward's theories into their research. All were involved in the late-twentieth-century introduction of materialist or Marxist perspectives into anthropology. Virginia Kerns' biography of Steward sheds some light on why so many of these scholars found a materialist approach appealing:

> Most of the students…grew up during the Depression, and many had served in combat zones during the [Second World] war. Their life experiences had inclined them toward materialist approaches to economy and political organization. They had "no trouble understanding the compelling motivations of an empty stomach," according to Murphy, and "they had seen authority emerge from the barrel of a gun."[1] While their powerful and visceral memories of hardship likely disposed them to view Steward's approach as timely and relevant, the students adapted or borrowed from his theories in noticeably distinct ways.
>
> (2003: 241)

The most influential revision of Steward's work was that of Marvin Harris (1927–2001), who fused cultural ecology with some aspects of Marxist theory. Harris grew up poor in Brooklyn during the Great Depression. He entered the US Army toward the end of World War II and, like many members of his generation of post-war American anthropologists, his college education was supported with the GI Bill. Harris loved to spend hours at the race track and he developed a complex mathematical betting system that was successful enough to support him and his wife during his years in graduate school. Harris received his PhD from Columbia in 1953 based upon research that he conducted in a former mining town in Brazil. This fieldwork experience led to subsequent research in Angola and Mozambique, then Portuguese colonies in Africa, and also inspired a longstanding interest in the contrasting systems of racial classification and race relations in the Americas. Harris taught at Columbia from 1958 until 1981, at which time he moved to the University of Florida.

The synthesis of cultural ecology and Harris' interpretation of Marxist thought is what he referred to as *cultural materialism*. This approach was first outlined in 1968 with the publication of his sweeping 800+ page work the *Rise of Anthropological Theory* (which in graduate school we affectionately referred to as *RAT*) and later, in 1979, with his volume *Cultural Materialism: The Struggle for a Science of Culture*. By the time that Harris was developing this perspective in the 1960s, it was possible to discuss Marx in the classroom without incurring as much of a political backlash as had earlier scholars. Harris, like many of his anthropological contemporaries, was heavily involved in the civil rights and anti-war movements of those years; he credited his time spent in the Portuguese colonies in Africa with raising his awareness of social and racial justice, as Angola and Mozambique then experienced their own counterparts of racial Apartheid. As a scholarly contribution to the civil rights movement, in 1964 Harris published the volume *Patterns of Race in the Americas*, which examined the fallacies of race as a biological construct. In it, he argued that racism is fundamentally economic in origin, and that different systems of plantation slavery in the United States and Brazil led to differing systems of racial classification. Four years later, Harris took part as a sympathetic faculty member in student protests of Columbia University's ties to the military during the Vietnam War and the university's plans to build what was criticized as a segregated recreation center. Other former students of Steward, Sidney Mintz and Eric Wolf, participated in the Teach-In movements at Johns Hopkins and the University of Michigan, respectively, as part of a nation-wide movement in which students and professors studied the roots of the war in Vietnam. This led to Eric Wolf's[2] 1969 volume *Peasant Wars of the Twentieth Century*. In it, Wolf argued that the economic and political dislocations fueling the anti-colonial movement in French-controlled Vietnam (which led to the introduction of US combat forces in the 1960s) were similar to those that had caused peasants to rebel earlier in the century in Mexico, Russia, Algeria, Cuba, and China. In other words, many of the twentieth century's transformative social revolutions were at their root peasant rebellions.

In *RAT*, Harris first articulated the "principle of techno-environmental and techno-economic determinism." As he expressed it:

> This principle holds that similar technologies applied to similar environments tend to produce similar arrangements of labor in production and distribution,

and that these in turn call forth similar kinds of social groupings, which justify and co-ordinate their activities by means of similar systems of values and beliefs. Translated into a research strategy, the principle of techno-environment, techno-economic determinism assigns priority to the study of the material conditions of sociocultural life, much as the principle of natural selection assigns priority to the study of differential reproductive success.

(Harris 1968: 4)

In addition to acknowledging Marx, Harris introduced a distinction in anthropological analysis that has become a key component of cultural materialist approaches. This is the *etic/emic* distinction, which Harris derived from the work of linguist Kenneth Pike. As employed in the theory of cultural materialism, an emic perspective relies on those descriptions and explanations that are meaningful to an informant, whereas etic descriptions are those used by the scientific community to generate and strengthen theories of sociocultural life. He amplified upon this distinction in his 1979 volume *Cultural Materialism*:

> The test of the adequacy of emic analyses is their ability to generate statements the native accepts as real, meaningful, or appropriate...The test of the adequacy of etic accounts is simply their ability to generate scientifically productive theories about the causes of sociocultural differences and similarities. *Rather than employ concepts that are necessarily real, meaningful and appropriate from the native point of view, the observer is free to use alien categories and rules derived from the data language of science. Frequently, etic operations involve the measurement and juxtaposition of activities and events that native informants may find inappropriate or meaningless.*
>
> (1979: 32, emphasis added)

Harris stated that both emic and etic perspectives are necessary for an understanding of human behavior and thought. Yet, his work consisted primarily of "explaining" cultural practices from an etic point of view that, as he acknowledged, may be meaningless from the perspective of those whose culture he studied. Indeed, many of his publications developed etic analyses of societies in which he did not personally conduct field research (e.g. among Middle Eastern Jews and Indian Hindus). Needless to say, some anthropologists find such disregard of the emic insider's account in favor of the etic "language of science" to be a bit arrogant. In his defense, however, it also led him to view many native practices as fundamentally logical and rational.

Much as he borrowed and redefined Pike's terminology from linguistics, Harris also utilizes Marxist terminology but does so in a way different from how Marx intended. For Harris, the material base of society (its *infrastructure*) consists of a mode of production and a mode of reproduction. Harris' appropriation and redefinition of the Marxist term "mode of production" is frustrating for students trying to discern the differences between these perspectives. Whereas Marx's mode of production includes the social relations of production in which people engage (such as patterns of work organization and property ownership) as well as the forces of production (technology and resources), Harris' mode of production consists solely of the latter. To this, Harris adds a "mode of reproduction," which consists of a society's population growth rates and its means of population regulation. Harris' argument is one of technological ecological demographic determinism, meaning that technology, ecology, and population growth/density determine other aspects of culture. The second level of culture, arising from the infrastructure is the *structure*, consisting of politics, kinship, and patterns of property ownership and labor organization (notice that Marx includes the latter two in his mode of production, or society's material base, while Harris does not). These in turn determine a society's *superstructure*, consisting of its religious, ritual, artistic, and philosophical beliefs. These terms all sound familiar from Marxism, as does the tripartite division of societal institutions and beliefs. Yet, with the exception of the cultural materialist superstructure (which is equivalent to Marx's ideology), Harris used these terms in ways substantially different from how Marx intended.

Before examining these differences in greater detail, it bears mentioning that many contemporary Marxist anthropologists such as Eric Wolf, Scott Cook, and William Roseberry largely adhere to Marx's original tripartite model of society, but others do not. Following the work of French neo-Marxist theoretician Louis Althusser in the 1960s, a school of "structural Marxist" theorists rejected the delineation of a material base and a social and ideological superstructure. Anthropologists such as Maurice Godelier and Jonathan Friedmann have argued that where kinship practices, ritual, or belief affect economic practices, these institutions should be regarded as part of a society's material foundation. They would deny that the same institution (religious ritual, for example) fulfills the same superstructural role in all places, or that kinship should always be regarded as structural in nature. Further, Godelier and Friedmann have argued that the material base of society merely establishes broad limits on society's structural and ideological practices, rather than directly determining their content. In practice, the structural Marxist argument approximates Steward's assertion that a society's "culture core" must be empirically determined in each case and does not necessarily consist of the same practices in all places. In addition, Godelier's and Friedmann's claim that a variety of structural and ideological practices may rest on the same material basis is reminiscent of Kroeber's possibilism.

Battle of the birthday cakes

I illustrate the differences in these models with the two "birthday cake" analogies shown in Figures 12.1 and 12.2.

How compatible is cultural materialism with dialectical materialism? Despite the overlapping terminology born of Harris' confusing tendency to appropriate Marxist terms and then redefine them in ways that Marx didn't intend, there are three significant areas of divergence between cultural and dialectical materialism.

Superstructure

religion, ritual,

values, philosophy, ethics, art

Structure

political organization, kinship, gender roles,

patterns of property ownership

Infrastructure

Mode of production: Mode of reproduction:

technology, resources   population size and growth rates,

                                                        methods of population regulation

FIGURE 12.1   The cultural materialist birthday cake

Ideology

religion, ritual,

values, philosophy, ethics, art

Juridico-political relations

political organization, kinship, gender roles,

Mode of production

Forces of production: Social relations of production:

technology, resources   property ownership,

                                                        organization of production,

                                                        distribution of the products of labor

FIGURE 12.2   The dialectical materialist birthday cake

The first of these concerns the relationship between technology and the social relations of production. Marx's material base consisted of a mode of production made up of two components: the forces of production and social relations of production. The social relations of production (patterns of property ownership and labor organization) are not "reducible" in Marx's scheme to technology. They are, to return to one of my favorite Latin phrases, *sui generis*! A particular system of production (whether craft production by hand or industrial production by factory assembly line) by itself does not lead to any particular form of ownership or other social relationship in the realm of production. In his magnum opus *Capital*, Marx showed that the fundamental social relation of capitalism (private property and a landless labor force that works for wages) developed independently of industrial technology, and long before the rise of a factory-based industrial system.

An anthropological example of this is the question of "Asiatic mode of production" arising in Marx's work on pre-capitalist societies, which was in turn influenced by Morgan's *Ancient Society*. This referred to certain archaic states, such as those of ancient China and Mesopotamia, that were highly centralized and bureaucratic. Marx argued that these societies underwent an evolutionary development distinct from that of western European feudalism (thus, unlike some nineteenth-century thinkers, he acknowledged a multilinear form of social evolution). Whereas European feudal societies were associated with a weak central government and powerful local lords, Asiatic despotism involved powerful and bureaucratized central governments and weak or nonexistent local landlords. To account for this pattern, the German-American historian Karl Wittfogel (1896–1988) had argued in his volume *Oriental Despotism* (1957) that centralized states came into existence because of the demands of the irrigated agriculture that supported these societies.[3] This is the famous "hydraulic hypothesis" of state formation, which was widely adopted by materialist archaeologists up to the 1980s. Their argument is that the managerial demands of complex irrigated agriculture are so great that irrigation leads to complex bureaucracy whose function is to manage water rights among farmers, control and recruit labor for construction and maintenance, and organize a system of calendrics for scheduling planting and harvesting. The cultural materialist explanation of Asiatic despotism is that the technology is prior to all other aspects of culture, and causes the growth of a distinctive set of political institutions. Does irrigation necessarily lead to a centralized, bureaucratic state because of the needs of labor management and allocation of water rights? Many cultural materialists think so, making their work technologically determinist.

Marxists argue differently. They would say that the factors causing the growth of irrigation are the social relations themselves. When a centralized state develops, it requires an expanding revenue base to operate. Ultimately, rulers of the state accomplish this by increasing the tribute that they demand from producers. One way in which they can accomplish this, in turn, is by intensifying production. Irrigation agriculture increases total agricultural output, much of which is then collected as tribute by the state. Once irrigation is established, it may indeed require greater management. But Marxists would be skeptical of any claim that technology (or more specifically, the type of agriculture practiced in a region) would by itself account for the type of state that develops.

So which perspective is correct? One of the problems with evaluating this argument archaeologically is that the time horizons in prehistory between the development of a centralized bureaucracy and evidence for irrigation are often so short that it is difficult to determine cause and effect. Timothy Earle's (1978) research on Hawaii, which combined both archaeological and ethnohistorical evidence from the paramount chiefdom of Kauai between 1600 and post-contact society of around 1800, was able to avert these chronological problems. Earle relied upon both his own archaeological data and early written accounts, such as David Malo's *Hawaiian*

Antiquities (published in 1849). Malo's work, a firsthand account of island history by a former member of a Hawaiian ruling family, suggests that Wittfogel's cause-and-effect sequence may be mistaken. That is, Malo argued that once powerful island-wide chiefs installed themselves in office they found themselves having to contend with a number of competitors for their positions. Theoretically, the paramount chief was the direct male descendant of the first chief centuries earlier, but in a society lacking written records, there were many conflicting genealogical accounts of the chiefly dynasty. These competitors were the paramount chief's own male kin, who often claimed their own right to the chieftainship by virtue of their ancestry. Chiefs were only able to stay in power by "buying off" their competitors, co-opting them by providing them with expanding amounts of revenue. Irrigation played a key role in this, and was promoted by island chiefs as a way of generating more revenue, which was then redistributed to the chief's kinsmen who otherwise might seek to overthrow him.

Malthus and "positive checks"

Another key distinction between cultural and dialectical materialism is the role that demography (population) plays in each. Marx emphasized that population growth was determined by social and economic factors, with every mode of production characterized by differing demographic trends. This is in sharp contrast to Harris, who argues that population pressure on resources is a constant in all societies. Harris' ideas about population were heavily influenced by the Reverend Thomas Malthus and his *Essay on the Principle of Population* (1798). Malthus argued that for most people and throughout all of human history the rate of population growth exceeded the rate of increase in food supplies. Malthus attributed this near-universal tendency to the "inexorable passion between the sexes," which led to a "geometric" (today we would say exponential) rate of growth. It is possible to increase the rate of food production through intensification, but this rate of increase is only "arithmetic" (linear, or additive). What prevents human populations from increasing to, say, infinity? For most people, Malthus argues that "positive checks" limit population growth through "war, disease and famine," which constantly adjust populations to a level that can be supported by available food supplies. In sum, once a given human population exceeds the amount of food available to it, starvation brings it back down to levels that can be sustained by that society's food production system. As a result, famine, disease, and poverty are an inescapable aspect of the human condition.

For a far more limited number of people, "preventative checks" (by which he meant abstinence) limited population growth. However, these measures were typically only adopted by the very wealthy, who feared a "surplus" of children and a resulting "loss of station" (i.e. downward mobility). One of the problems with Malthus' theory (there are many, as I will mention below) is that all human cultures have some knowledge of how to regulate their family size: in no human population do people reproduce up to their biological potential, unlike almost all other animal species.[4] For example, a female cat can (and often does, given the opportunity) produce up to 14,000 living descendants during her lifetime! In contrast, in no human society does population grow at this "geometric" rate, mainly because we have the knowledge and capacity to regulate the number of children we bring into the world. Malthus' claim that conscious control of fertility was limited to only members of the upper class was demonstrably incorrect even in eighteenth-century England. Men and women of all social classes regularly practiced contraception (mostly withdrawal or rhythm, although condoms were known to members of the upper classes). Indeed, the first condom to employ a spermicide apparently dates of the late 1600s! Abortion and even infanticide were widely practiced as well; up until the end of the nineteenth century, neither Protestants nor Catholics regarded abortion as sinful unless performed after "quickening," when a fetus' physical movements could be detected outside the womb. Prolonged breastfeeding, often performed until a child was 4 or 5, tended as well to suppress fertility. For most commoners, perhaps the most prevalent form of "preventative checks" was late marriage. While aristocrats were often married while quite young (usually through arranged marital alliances), most commoners put off marriage until their 20s. On the eve of the Revolution in France (1789), on average peasant women did not get married until about the age of 27, in effect cutting out the most fertile years of their lifespan. Most women only became pregnant about 4–5 times, far less than their natural fecundity.

Harris' scenario for population growth isn't quite as bleak as that of Malthus, in that he doesn't adopt the term "positive checks" and he recognizes that many human populations are able to avert such dire circumstances. Nonetheless, he accepts as a given the universality of "population pressure on resources." As human populations grow, according to Harris, they face three choices: they can starve or go to war because of food shortages, induce population regulation, or intensify production to produce more food. Of these three, starvation and war are obviously the most undesirable. Harris contends that population regulation was largely unsuccessful and/or traumatic until recent times in its reliance upon infanticide and abortion. That leaves intensification as the major response to population growth in most human societies, compelling people to either work harder or develop new technologies.

Among the volumes authored by cultural materialists over the years, population pressure is invoked as the ultimate cause of most cultural adaptations to the environment. Large-scale ritual cannibalism, Michael Harner argued (1977), was instituted by the Aztec because of population growth in the Valley of Mexico and inadequate sources of dietary protein. Yanomamo warfare arose, Ross and Ross[5] (1980) claimed, as men fought over hunting territory because of population growth and insufficient animal protein sources. The kula ring developed, Harris argued in *RAT*, to enhance trade and resource distribution among the overpopulated Trobriand Islands. Among the Kwakiutl, according to Stuart Piddocke (1968), the potlatch was instituted as a means of seasonally redistributing food among populations that had exceeded the capacity of their resources to feed them. None of these population-based explanations of cultural practices originated among the societies in question, whose members usually attributed their behavior to the compulsions of religious belief (the Aztec), the need to obtain women as wives (the Yanomamo), or the pursuit of prestige and status (the Trobrianders and Kwakiutl). Yet this fact is irrelevant to cultural materialists, who privilege their "etic" level of understanding over the more limited "emic" understanding of the members of these cultures themselves.

The curious thing about this argument is that human populations usually stabilize well below the carrying capacity of their environments; in other words, there is usually more productive capacity available in an environment than necessary to meet the demands of human populations. When we look at shifting horticultural societies, populations are usually 50 percent or less of their carrying capacity (i.e. the maximum population that can be supported in a particular place with a particular subsistence technology). The ability of the land to support much more agriculture than was traditionally practiced by indigenous populations certainly holds true in Amazonia. Harris acknowledges that groups like the Yanomamo have more than enough land to support their agricultural needs, but he argues that carrying capacity estimates fail to take into account protein supplies, as most Amazonian groups are reliant on wild, not domesticated, sources of protein. This led to the famous "protein hypothesis" of Amazonian warfare, suggesting that groups such as the Yanomamo, who say they fight over women, are in fact fighting over scarce hunting territory. This argument remains problematic, as most Amazonian populations were actually well nourished, at least before recent catastrophic changes introduced by outsiders. It turns out that while game often is relatively scarce, insect and vegetable sources of protein, such as peach palm, are not.

When faced with the inconvenient fact that in most cases populations live well below their carrying capacity, Harris redefined population pressure to mean "the bio-psychological costs" of restraining demographic growth. In other words, such procedures as abortion, abstinence, and infanticide are so disagreeable that people are willing to work harder to support the larger populations that result when such practices are not followed. People would rather have children and work harder to feed them than undergo the sacrifices required to limit their numbers. Hence, even when they are not overtaxing their resources, they are nonetheless experiencing "population pressure" in terms of the costs of regulating births. This hypothesis is nonfalsifiable in that Harris can then attribute population pressure even to populations that are stable or declining. What he neglects here is that while the ease of regulating population growth was admittedly more difficult prior to modern contraception, the hazards of giving birth in premodern times were also much greater than today. Given the range of abortifacients available to many preindustrial societies,[6] it is doubtful that abortion was more hazardous than childbirth in preindustrial societies.

There is no question that social evolution is accompanied by population growth. How is this fact to be accounted for? Unlike Malthus, Marx maintained that there is no universal law of population valid for all societies. Some social arrangements encourage people to have more children, while others discourage childbearing. We see an interesting illustration of this among West African populations, some of whom are pastoralists (herders) and others farmers. Among pastoralist Hadza, for example, average family size is only about half that of the farming Hadza neighbors.

Despite the fact that they belong to the same culture and language, the two groups have quite distinct practices with regard to bridewealth and attitudes toward marriage, which occurs much earlier among farmers. Bridewealth, the payment of wealth by a man to his prospective in-laws, is substantially higher for pastoral Hadza than for their agricultural counterparts. This, then, substantially delays marriage for both partners and effectively "cuts out" a number of a woman's prime reproductive years.

Demand for labor theories of demography (sometimes called "wealth flow" theories) emphasize such practices in terms of the costs and benefits of having additional children. Where wealth flows from children to parents (as in many agricultural societies where children provide an important source of labor or old age support), family size is almost always large. Conversely, where wealth flows from parents to children (because children produce little of value, as in industrialized societies), family size is almost always small. So, too, are families often small in pastoral societies as herding is incapable of absorbing nearly as much labor as farming. Long before the development of modern contraceptive techniques—in fact, at about the very time of Malthus' work—European population growth began to slow down as displaced peasants migrated to cities. Where there was relatively little application for child labor, people had relatively few children.

The Marxist view of population recognizes that economic factors are dominant in determining family size, which is the result of decision-making based on the costs and labor contributions of children. In addition to the economic patterns noted above (i.e. farming vs. pastoralism, outlets for child labor vs. no such outlets), another factor affecting population growth rates is the demand for taxation or labor imposed on peasants in stratified societies, where the addition of child labor is often the only means of meeting such demands. Whereas archaeologically and ethnographically documented egalitarian societies average only 0.1 percent growth per year, stratified societies average 0.9 percent. What this indicates is that as stratification occurs, peasants often consciously decide to have larger families because large families help rural households meet the demands of taxation and labor that are imposed on them by ruling classes. Ethnographic research on contemporary peasant societies, such as Java, reveal that children become net producers—contributing more than they consume—as young as the age of five (White 1975: 130). Indeed, Java serves as an excellent example of the impact of increased tributary demands on population growth. In 1830, Dutch colonial administrators imposed the "culture system," requiring peasants to either work without pay for 66 days a year on Dutch plantations or to turn over 20 percent of their land to the production of export crops which were to be paid as taxes to colonial authorities. The result was a massive increase in the peasant population, which increased at nearly 2 percent per year between 1830 and 1900 (Geertz 1963: 69). Moreover, during this time, almost nothing was introduced by the Dutch with regard to modern medicine or public health, so such increases can only be attributed to the decisions of peasant households to increase their numbers in order to better meet the demands that had been imposed on them (White 1973: 222).

BOX 12.1 Implications of Malthusian thinking

Karl Marx was well acquainted with Malthus' ideas and vehemently rejected them, dismissing him as a "bought advocate for the ruling class" and a "baboon" (!). Marx's antagonism toward Malthus arose because he saw him not as a demographer but as a propagandist who cloaked his opinions in the argument of "natural laws." Because of "inexorable" population growth, Malthus claimed that poverty and starvation were inevitable and could not be reversed through political reform or revolution, which of course was precisely what Marx advocated in the face of injustice. In England at the end of the eighteenth century, when Malthus formulated his laws of population, there appeared to be a huge "surplus" of the poor and unemployed. There was much obvious deprivation, crime, and talk of rebellion among the poor themselves. The English poor represented a hugely threatening specter in the minds of aristocrats, given that the French masses had overthrown the monarchy in 1789 in a revolution with the motto "brotherhood, liberty and equality." In the eighteenth century, the British Parliament had passed various "Acts of Enclosure," which allowed wealthy wool producers to enclose "unused" public lands for their sheep herds. These lands were in fact not fallow, but had been common lands that peasants by longstanding tradition relied on for grazing and crop production. With the enclosure of the commons, a process that was virtually complete across England and Scotland by the early nineteenth century, peasants lost much of their ability to sustain their livelihood. Enclosure created both the land base and work force necessary for England's initial industrial system, based as it was on textiles. Many displaced peasants migrated to cities to look for work and, although employment in the country's textile industry was rapidly expanding, it remained insufficient for the numbers of people forced from rural areas. Former peasants, who often found themselves unemployed and destitute as a result, said of the process that "sheep eat men."

A pressing political debate raged at the time that Malthus wrote his *Essay on the Principle of Population*. What public provision was to be made for those who had no means of subsistence? Parliament debated the renewal of "Poor Laws," which had been in effect for hundreds of years and obligated the Crown to provide welfare (in the form of food) for the destitute through rural parishes. At the same time, Parliament debated "Corn Laws," which set a minimum price for wheat ("corn" in England at the time being a term applied to any kind of grain); this law supported farmers, but did so at the expense of the poor because it raised the price of bread.

Malthus entered this policy debate with an argument against social welfare measures of any kind, not unlike his latter-day interpreter, Herbert Spencer. His argument was little different from those of conservatives today regarding welfare, and is often repeated in conjunction with the question of famine relief as well. Malthus opposed social welfare as "false charity"; if food is provided to the poor it will only allow them to survive to have more children, aggravating poverty for the next generation. The poor had become impoverished and hungry not through the "reforms" of the Corn Laws and the Acts of Enclosure, but through their own, uncontrolled fertility. Further, his notion that populations invariably exceeded the volume of food to support them was offered as a "scientific" argument against the revolutionary currents expressed in the USA and France in the late eighteenth century.

With little modification, Malthus' ideas are often the basis of "expert" analyses of famines and food scarcity in the developing world, despite the fact that few demographers adhere to them. In *The Malthus Factor* (1998), anthropologist Eric Ross notes that this is one of the most pervasive ideologies in modern society, shared by liberals and conservatives alike. Many environmental organizations, such as the Sierra Club and Audubon Society, subscribe to the thesis of "overpopulation." Authors Garrett Hardin (*The Tragedy of the Commons*) and Paul Ehrlich (*The Population Bomb*) have argued for decades that famines are Malthusian positive checks in operation. In the 1970s, Hardin and Ehrlich advocated a change in our ethical commitments to helping the hungry. To provide aid to all the hungry was unethical because, as Hardin argued, "more food means more babies." To aid everyone who lacks food would only cause catastrophe for all. Instead, he advocated "lifeboat ethics"; since the amount of food is limited, only those who will become self-sufficient from charity should receive help. Everyone else is outside the lifeboat and cannot be saved.

From this point of view, the solution to food scarcity is to withhold charity. It is also to impose strict population control programs. Hardin and Ehrlich are both advocates of involuntary sterilization based on "fitness for parenthood" (Hardin 1970: 427), an idea that goes back to the eugenics movement that developed in the US in the 1890s. These measures are even harsher than those advocated by former Klansman David Duke when he ran for US Senate from Louisiana in 1992. He advocated giving the "welfare poor" cash bonuses to be sterilized (Bridges 1994: 142). In fact, as Eric Ross demonstrated in his book, about two-thirds of all sterilizations performed in the US prior to 1980 were involuntary. Most were practiced as part of the drive of the eugenics movement to "improve" the US population by preventing the mentally ill, mentally retarded, or other "undesirables" from reproducing. The racist overtones of this movement were often explicit, with advocates believing that to improve the US population meant making it more Anglo-Saxon. Although Margaret Sanger is often recognized as a champion of women's rights to contraception, she was also an advocate of eugenics who believed that non-whites should be

continued...

Box 12.1 continued

discouraged or prevented from reproducing. Many black and Native American women were involuntarily sterilized when hospitalized for childbirth. Laws with similar intent were instituted when the Nazis came to power in Germany. They required all doctors to report to the state the names of mentally ill or mentally retarded patients, who would then be examined by a "Eugenics Court," which usually ordered them to be sterilized. By the end of the war, some 400,000 German citizens had been sterilized because of various "defects." At the Nuremburg trials after the war, when Nazi officials were confronted with their involuntary sterilization policies as a war crime, they pleaded that the inspiration of their eugenics laws were the Malthusian-inspired statutes already on the books in the USA!

Utilitarianism or hegemony?

A final, critical distinction between cultural and dialectical materialism is in the area of epistemology (remember that this is the branch of philosophy that deals with the nature of knowledge, particularly our assumptions about how the world works). Cultural materialism is positivist in that it seeks universal laws to account for behavior. As a result, it tends to make universal assumptions about human behavior. The assertion that population growth is inherent to all human groups is a case in point. So are other assumptions in cultural materialism: that people everywhere are economically rational (meaning that they select a course of action based on minimum cost and maximum benefit), utilitarian (i.e. their behavior is geared to solving practical problems), and that their actions are ecologically adaptive. Harris argues, following an analogy from Darwin, that cultural practices that fail to be rational, utilitarian, and adaptive cannot be sustained by human populations over the long term. Hence, a kind of "natural selection" operates to favor cultural practices that are sustainable while discouraging those practices that are not. The result is a kind of ecological functionalism in which cultural practices, however seemingly exotic, actually serve practical ends. While sharing a materialist view of society, Marx is anti-positivist in arguing that there are no universal laws governing behavior. Marx recognizes that people may, and in fact often do, act in totally nonfunctional or dysfunctional ways.[7] Particularly in class stratified societies, ideologies are "distorted representations" of social and economic relations that may cause people to act in ways contrary to their interests. In a famous passage from *The German Ideology* (1977b, orig. 1845), Marx writes:

> The ideas of the ruling class are in every epoch the ruling ideas, i.e. the class which is the ruling material force of society is at the same time its ruling intellectual force. The class which has the means of material production at its disposal has control at the same time over the means of mental production, so that thereby, generally speaking, the ideas of those who lack the means of

mental production are subject to it...The individuals composing the ruling class possess among other things consciousness, and therefore think. Insofar, therefore, as they rule as a class and determine the extent and compass of an epoch, it is self-evident that they do this in its whole range, hence among other things rule also as thinkers, as producers of ideas, and regulate the production and distribution of the ideas of their age: thus their ideas are the ruling ideas of the epoch.

(1977b: 178)

What would be a practical illustration of this process? As we saw earlier, Marx predicted that capitalism would generate "contradictions" leading eventually to revolution. Toward the end of his life, he came to realize the important role that ideology played in diminishing the revolutionary tendencies of workers. As we saw in Chapter 4, among these ideologies was the belief in ethnic or national superiority, leading to conflicts that prevented members of the working class from seeing their common interests. In England, this took the form of conflicts between English-born and Irish immigrant workers.

While all of the foregoing offers a critical reading of cultural materialism, in practice this theoretical perspective has produced some provocative analyses of cultural practices that had earlier been seen as simply evidence for the arbitrary and even illogical nature of culture. Indeed, for Harris, a key goal of cultural anthropology is to "unlock cultural riddles" by revealing the underlying rational bases for what have in the past been seen as irrational practices.

Unlocking cultural riddles

In a series of academic publications as well as popular books written for general audiences, Marvin Harris has attempted to show that seemingly perplexing cultural practices make sense as cultural adaptations to the environment when viewed in infrastructural and etic terms. Probably no work by Harris has inspired more commentary than his 1966 *Current Anthropology* article entitled "The Cultural Ecology of India's Sacred Cattle." The issues raised by Harris have been challenged so extensively that he returned to answer his critics in numerous subsequent publications, most extensively in his book *Good to Eat: Riddles of Food and Culture* (1985). For many observers, few things more strongly epitomize the grasp of religion on human behavior than the Hindu taboo on eating beef. To someone from a meat-eating country like the United States, the idea of cattle wandering freely and unmolested in India while people go hungry is a paradox, and a wasteful one at that. The Hindu prohibition on beef consumption would seem to be a prime illustration of how religion can compel people to act in ways that are maladaptive and contrary to common sense; in other words, that ideas can take priority over material needs in guiding human behavior.

There are numerous religious beliefs and even legal sanctions that confer sacred status on cattle in India. If you ask members of the Hindu faith to explain why they refrain from eating beef, they would do so in terms of a sacred obligation. Hindus say that a cow is sacred because of the doctrine of *ahimsa*, the principle of the unity of life. Each cow, they believe, is the vehicle for 334 million gods, making the cow the most sacred animal known to the Hindus (other sacred animals include monkeys and snakes). In Hindu sacred literature, the god Krishna is described as a cowherd and protector of cows. Cows are decorated with flowers, placed in animal shelters when they are old and sick, and urban areas employ "cowboys" to capture animals that might be harmed in a city setting for resettlement in rural areas. In short, cows are loved, venerated, and worshipped. This, obviously, would be a Hindu's emic answer to why they don't eat beef. Such beliefs are reinforced by legislation. The Indian constitution strictly regulates the slaughter of cows, and all but two states prohibit the slaughter of India's native zebu breed. The sacredness of the cow has been a recurrent political flashpoint in Indian history. A constant friction in Indian life occurs between cow-worshipping Hindus and beef-eating Muslims. Similarly, the fact that British colonialists ate beef was a rallying cry for India's independence movement; one source of Mohandas Gandhi's political support was his fervent belief in the sacredness of the cow. It should come as little surprise that India has more cows than any other country in the world—an estimated 180 million plus another 50 million water buffalo. Are all of these animals a "wasted" resource caused by an illogical religious belief?

What gave rise to the Hindu sacred cow? It is apparent from Indian history that the cow has not always enjoyed sacred status. Vedic religious texts from before 600 BC indicate that the ancestors of today's Indians consumed beef, which was a mainstay of communal religious feasts. As the human population increased, pasturage was converted to farm fields and beef became much scarcer and more expensive. Before long, beef consumption was limited to only the most privileged castes. By about 400 BC India witnessed the rise of the faiths of Buddhism and Jainism, both of which banned the killing of cattle. In subsequent centuries, milk replaced beef as ritual food, and the worship of the cow was incorporated into Hinduism, which became by far the dominant religion in India.

Harris challenges the notion that Indian cattle are a wasted or unutilized resource. The cow provides an ample range of products that are eagerly utilized by poor Hindus. These include milk and dung, which is an essential fertilizer and, when dried, is more widely used as a cooking fuel than wood. In addition, Indians make use of the leather products produced by tanneries operated by Muslims or so-called "untouchables." The most significant use for cattle, however, is as traction animals on small farms. Only the largest farms can afford tractors, while the vast majority of India's rural farmers rely on oxen (castrated male cattle) to pull their plows. The supposedly stray animals that wander through the countryside scavenge most of their food from roadsides and garbage dumps. As a source of dairy products, fuel, and traction, Harris claims that they are literally too valuable to eat: "Not only did she give milk but she was the mother of the cheapest and most efficient traction animal for India's soils and climate. In return for Hindu safeguards against the reemergence of energetically costly and socially divisive beef-eating foodways, she made it possible for the land to teem with human life" (1985: 66).

Harris' interest in the Hindu sacred cow led him to consider food prohibitions found in other religious traditions, such as the Jewish and Muslim ban on pork. The Jewish faith was formalized in the Middle East somewhere between 4,000 and 5,000 years ago. Animal skeletal remains in archeological sites throughout the region indicate that people who were the ancestors of the first Jews consumed pork until about 12,000 years ago. We also know from that evidence that major changes were occurring in the subsistence economy of the region during that time. Large areas of the Middle East were being deforested and turned into zones for intensive farming and livestock keeping, specifically, sheep, cattle and goats. All of these new land uses were incompatible with the keeping of pigs. Pigs require shade and moisture to regulate their body temperature, and both were becoming less available with the spread of agriculture. Those of you who have spent time around pigs may have observed how much they like to wallow in mud. This is not because they are naturally dirty animals, but because they need to do so to keep cool. Unlike dogs, which pant, and humans, who sweat, pigs do neither.

Unlike the other domesticated animals kept in the region, pigs also have primarily one use, that of meat. They don't provide milk, wool, or traction power for plowing. Further, they are destructive in an agricultural setting; unless they are carefully confined they destroy crops, overturn soil, and force farmers to replant. Were people to have continued to keep pigs, they would not have been able to simultaneously produce the quantities of crops and herd animals required of a growing population. Harris argues that this ecological "choice" was resolved by means of a supernatural sanction. As Judaism spread in the Middle East, a sacred commandment was also employed to keep people from consuming and therefore producing pigs. This was the "Mosaic Law" of the book of Leviticus, which declared the meat of non-ruminant animals with cloven hoofs to be unclean. The effect was the same as in Hinduism: a *source of meat was prohibited on the basis of a religious rule*. Unlike India, however, where the cow is *revered* and therefore maintained in large numbers, the pig is *despised* as spiritually polluting in Judaism (and Islam, which originated in the same environmental conditions). Unlike the sacred cow, which roams freely and in large numbers in India, the pig has been displaced from almost all of the Middle East.

Most readers may note that in the present day there are more Jews living outside the Middle East rather than in it. So why, you ask, does the pork prohibition persist outside this region? That is, why do some Jews now living in Europe and North America still observe this rule when it is no longer related to their environmental adaptation? Harris argues that once this rule came into existence, it fulfilled different functions in other settings, and so has been maintained. After their dispersal from the Middle East the Jews became a persecuted minority in Christian Europe. One of the ways minority groups under such circumstances try to protect themselves is to create a sense of solidarity within their ranks and to strengthen their sense of identity and difference with respect to those who oppress them. (The term *ghetto* originally referred to these closed, self-contained urban communities in Europe where Jews were required to live. Similar kinds of communities were created by African American migrants to US cities who faced similar residential restrictions. In such places, local identity is stressed as a way of "circling the wagons" against an outside adversary.) In the case of Jewish communities, people enhanced their solidarity by emphasizing the notion that they had a distinct identity as a people favored by a special covenant with God. Harris documents that many forgotten aspects of Jewish law as given in Leviticus were actually strengthened during this time, as Jews tried to heighten their internal solidarity in response to persecution.

In the United States, where Jews comprise a small portion of the population, there has been a great deal of cultural assimilation and a decline in the barriers that once kept Jews out of the mainstream of society. Most American Jews now intermarry with non-Jews, unlike their ancestors from Eastern Europe. Not coincidentally, relatively few American Jews these days "keep Kosher" by observing all of the dietary laws. While conservative and orthodox Jews still refrain from eating pork, they make up considerably less than half of the US Jewish population, most of whom are "reform" or entirely secular.

So why back up these essential behaviors with a sacred rule? Why, when asked, do Hindus say they act in religious terms rather than simply answering, pragmatically (and in etic terms), "we don't eat cattle because they are too important to eat"? Pragmatic rules, as Harris points out, do not carry the same weight in governing behavior as do sacred rules. Indeed, Durkheim made a similar point when referring to the power of supernatural sanctions. For example, most of us would refrain from murdering an obnoxious person because we know, however irritating they might be, that it is morally wrong to kill another person (jail, of course, is a good back-up argument for those not too influenced by moral arguments).[8] In the same sense, if a Hindu peasant has a bad harvest and is facing hunger, a pragmatic rule may not prevent him from eating his cattle. But if he gave in to temptation and had his cattle for dinner, who would plow his fields the following year, who would give milk for his children, who would fertilize his fields, who would provide fuel for his cooking fire? It is in these situations, where people are tempted to do something that would have long-term negative consequences, where sacred rules come most into play to prevent those actions. That's why, according to Harris, when asked the reasons for their action, people most often volunteer an emic reason, even when there is an etic reason lurking not far below.

For all the charged symbolic attributes of the sacred cow and the spiritually polluting pig, Harris argues that these food practices ultimately originated at the infrastructural (economic) level of society. In a later publication offering a cultural materialist analysis of the collapse of the Soviet Union, Harris delineated the relationship between the various components of society:

> Infrastructural, structural and symbolic–ideational features are equally necessary components of human social life. It is no more possible to imagine a human society without a symbolic–ideational or structural sector than it is possible to imagine one without a mode of production and reproduction. Nonetheless, these sectors do not play a symmetrical role in influencing the retention or extinction of sociocultural innovations.

(1992: 297)

What does cultural materialism tell us about the superstructural components of culture? Harris' argument is that if anthropology is to be considered a science, then research priority should be given to the infrastructural level of society because it is that level that is most likely to be governed by lawful regularities. Except to the extent that they can be explained by infrastructural causes, the structural and ideational levels of culture are largely uninteresting to Harris and his followers. What, however, if anthropology is not to be considered a science, or if we do not share the assumption that most human behavior is ultimately, fundamentally practical in intent? We will examine the answer to these questions in the next chapter.

Political ecology

Although the materialist approaches discussed in this chapter stem from differing sources (ecological perspectives vs. Marxism), there have been in recent decades some promising trends toward synthesis. Among the materialist theories developing since the 1980s has been a fusion of ecological approaches with political economy, a synthesis known as political ecology. The first use of the term in anthropology was associated with Eric Wolf (1972) who, as we have seen, pioneered in introducing Marxist political economy into the discipline. Sutton and Anderson define political ecology as "the study of the day-to-day conflicts, alliances, and negotiations that ultimately result in some sort of definitive behavior; how politics affects or structures resource use" (2004: 311). Since the 1980s, scholars in this school have examined the political and economic forces driving deforestation, environmental degradation, hunger, emigration, and social movements.

In many instances, political ecology challenges materialist and ecological perspectives that rely on Malthusianism as an explanatory device. In an early application of this approach, *Scarcity and Survival in Central America* (1979), William Durham offered an examination of the 1970 four-day "soccer war" between El Salvador and neighboring Honduras that dissented from prevailing journalistic and scholarly accounts of the time. The outbreak of the war followed a victory by El Salvador over Honduras in that year's World Cup, after which Honduras ejected Salvadoran immigrants and tried to close its national border. Many observers of the time attributed Salvadoran immigration to Malthusian population pressures, which forced migrants to flee an overcrowded landscape at home for a relatively sparsely populated Honduran frontier. Examining the land tenure and distribution of El Salvador, however, Durham found that the expulsion of the landless poor from El Salvador had occurred as a result of the expansion of commercial agriculture at their expense, and in many instances, the forcible seizure of their lands by large-scale landowners. Refuting the Malthusian claim that population grows faster than agricultural output, Durham showed that output actually kept pace with population growth rates in the years leading up to the war; the problem was that much of this output was of coffee and beef for foreign consumption as the peasantry was steadily squeezed off the land. Durham's analysis proved amazingly prescient as El Salvador itself exploded into civil uprising in the decade after its publication, a war largely attributed to a dispossessed peasant majority.

Unlike its predecessor, cultural ecology, political ecology assumes that changes in the environment do not affect all segments of society in the same way; rather, political, social, and economic differences in access to power account for the uneven distribution of costs and benefits from resource use. Recognizing that "any change in environmental conditions must affect the political and economic status quo" (Bryant and Bailey 1997: 28), political ecologists have examined how this unequal distribution inevitably affects existing social and economic inequalities. These inequalities in environmental access and use and their effect on pre-existing social and economic inequalities inevitably alter power relationships, frequently deepening prior inequalities. In recent years, as poststructuralist perspectives have entered anthropology, political ecology itself has reflected these trends. Increasingly, as we will see in the final chapter of this volume, the "political" and discursive aspects of resource use and development have tended to be foregrounded over the ecological concerns of earlier years.

Quiz yourself

Answer True or False to each statement

1 According to Harris, "etic" descriptions are those of an outside scientific observer, and are used by the scientific community to generate and strengthen theories of sociocultural life.
2 According to Julian Steward, a major factor leading postwar anthropologists to a materialist perspective was growing up in the Depression and service in World War II.
3 According to Harris, the true test of an "etic" analysis of culture is that it is not only scientific but also makes sense and is meaningful to a member of that culture.
4 While there are differences between Harris and Marx, both use the concept of a "mode of production" in an identical fashion.
5 Timothy Earle's archaeological and ethnohistorical research from Hawaii tends to support Wittfogel's idea that irrigation agriculture leads to the development of a society with centralized, managerial power.
6 Harris and Marx differ fundamentally in their attitude toward Malthus, with Marx rejecting the notion that there is a "universal law" of population growth for all societies.
7 Evidence from most societies bears out the Malthusian idea that human populations grow right up to their environment's carrying capacity, after which they decline due to war, disease and famine.
8 Abortion and other forms of population control are largely unknown outside of industrialized societies.

9 The imposition of new taxes by Dutch administrators in colonial Java led to rapid population growth, as peasants sought to increase the amount of labor available to their households.

10 Political ecology accepts the basic premise of Malthusian thinking that population growth is the ultimate cause of environmental degradation.

13

SYMBOLS, STRUCTURES, AND THE "WEB OF SIGNIFICANCE"

This chapter examines three approaches in mid- to late-twentieth-century anthropology that adopt an idealist perspective. The common feature of all materialist theories is the analytical priority they assign to the material conditions that members of a given culture confront. Idealists would not dispute the fact that culture must solve the problems of survival. What they would disagree with is that culture is merely a way of solving those problems, or that it can be explained in terms of the material conditions facing its members. In anthropology, idealism refers to any theory that suggests that behavior is governed by beliefs, meanings, and values that are to a greater or lesser degree independent of the material conditions of life. Indeed, many idealists would hold that these material conditions themselves are influenced or determined by belief.[1] Culture from these perspectives cannot be explained in terms of the biological needs of people or the manner in which they satisfy those needs.

As readers are no doubt aware, there are multiple definitions of culture employed by anthropologists. As long ago as their 1952 volume, *Culture*, Alfred Kroeber and Clyde Kluckhohn enumerated over 50 definitions of culture then in use. If we examine the differing definitions used by two influential late-twentieth-century anthropologists, Marvin Harris and Clifford Geertz, we are guided to different realms of human experience. For Harris, culture is "the total socially acquired life-style of a group of people included patterned, repetitive ways of thinking, feeling and acting" (Harris 1991: 9). Although Harris' definition doesn't betray his materialist assumptions about the origins of cultural traits, notice that it emphasizes behavior, suggesting that culture can be understood by examining the "etic behavioral acts" of people. We can contrast Harris' behavioral emphasis with the definition employed by Clifford Geertz, a major proponent of an idealist approach to anthropology: "Culture is an ordered system of meaning and of symbols, in terms of which social interaction takes place. Culture is the fabric of meaning in terms of which human beings interpret their experience and guide their action" (1973b: 145). In Geertz' definition there is an explicit recognition of what directs human action. Culture consists of the symbols by which people interpret the world. Ideas, beliefs, and meaning, then, guide human action.

Gallic structures

The first of the idealist approaches that we consider, French Structuralism, has drawn its inspiration from the field of linguistics. The founder of French Structuralism, Claude Lévi-Strauss (1908–2009; Figure 13.1), is probably as well known outside of anthropology as he is within the discipline; for decades, his work was enormously influential in continental Europe. It's important to note that the "structures" discussed by Lévi-Strauss are *not* the same as the social structure informing British structural functionalism. For Lévi-Strauss, culture arises *from the structures of the human mind, which he contends operates and is organized in a similar fashion in all places.* Although his work was much less influential in the US, to many non-anthropologists, Lévi-Strauss was the most well known representative of the discipline during the 1960s–80s. This was somewhat disconcerting for anthropologists who raised doubts about the validity of Lévi-Strauss' methods and whether any of his theories could actually be empirically verified.

Decades later, the popularity of French Structuralism among anthropologists and the educated public has diminished considerably, a fact acknowledged by

FIGURE 13.1   Claude Lévi-Strauss. On his 100th birthday, Lévi-Strauss was visited in his home by French President Nicolas Sarkozy. Lévi-Strauss passed away on November 1, 2009, a few weeks short of 101. © INTERFOTO/Alamy.

Lévi-Strauss in 1991: "The educated public in France is bulimic. For a while, it fed on structuralism. People thought it carried a message. That fashion has passed. A fashion lasts for five or ten years…That's how things go in Paris. I have neither nostalgia nor regret" (Lévi-Strauss and Eribon 1991: 91–92). Notwithstanding these changing (some would say, fickle) intellectual fashions, just before his death in 2009, the Smithsonian Institution granted Lévi-Strauss its highest award, the James Smithson Bicentennial Medal, "in recognition of his contributions to understanding the human condition through anthropological studies…Lévi-Strauss has revolutionized understanding of nonwestern cultures and has had a profound impact on other fields of human knowledge, including linguistics, art and literature" (Smithsonian 2009).

After graduating from the Sorbonne in 1932 with degrees in philosophy and law, Lévi-Strauss taught at the Lycée Jason de Sailly, one of the most prestigious French preparatory high schools, where he worked alongside Jean-Paul Sartre and Simone de Beauvoir. He returned to the university to pursue postgraduate degrees in sociology, which in France was still organized around the work of Durkheim and incorporated cultural anthropology. He became involved in the opportunity to join a French educational mission to establish the University of Sao Paulo, Brazil, and spent several years conducting research among Indian tribes of western Brazil. He returned to France to conclude his dissertation and teach at the university level, joining the French army upon the German invasion to serve as a liaison to British troops. After France was overrun, he returned to teaching, until the German racial laws imposed in France (he was born to a Jewish family) led to his dismissal from his job. In 1940, it was still possible for refugees to leave France, and he soon settled in New York, where he spent the war years in exile. There he accepted a teaching position at the New School for Social Research, which provided a home to many intellectuals exiled from occupied Europe. When Boas was struck by a fatal heart attack at a luncheon in 1942, the "father of American anthropology" expired in the arms of Claude Lévi-Strauss. It was also in New York that Lévi-Strauss first encountered the work of a fellow refugee, the Russian structural linguist Roman Jakobson.

Lévi-Strauss' structural anthropology rests on a linguistic analogy in that he argues that the human capacity for culture is similar to our capacity for language. Many of Lévi-Strauss' ideas stem ultimately from the seminal work of Ferdinand de Saussure (1857–1913), a Swiss linguist who argued for a relational view of linguistic elements. Rather than looking at language as a set of names for things, or as a set of words with meanings, Saussure's structuralism considers language as a universe of signs. Each sign entails two parts; a phonic sound (the signifier) with an idea (the signified). While the process of naming things implies a finite number of objects and concepts requiring labels, Saussure's linguistic sign acts as a two-way link between the sound (specifically, the sound image—the "psychological impression" of a sound) and the idea. It is bi-directional in the sense that just as the word "blue" may evoke notions of blue objects, a notion of something blue may elicit the sound image "blue." A sound is meaningless if it is not so linked to an idea, and likewise for an idea to be coherent one requires the capacity to articulate it.

Saussure's ideas informed the later Prague School of structural linguistics as well as American scholars such as Leonard Bloomfield and Noam Chomsky. Linguists in the Prague School, such as Jakobson, recognized that the seemingly infinite sounds in human language could be reduced to a few contrasting features. For example, we can describe the difference in which the consonant "p" is pronounced in the words PIN and SPIN. You'll notice that "p" is articulated the same way in both (linguists would call it a "bilabial stop"), but the phonetic difference between the consonants is based on "aspiration." (You can observe this if you hold your fingers in front of your lips when pronouncing both words; the aspirated consonant involves the release of a puff of air.) This is what linguists call a "contrast feature"; a single contrast which specifies a change in sound for the speaker. What structural linguistics did was to show that the infinite variety of sounds in language was based on a few categories of contrast (such as voiced or voiceless vowels, aspirated or nonaspirated consonants). The idea is that there is an elementary structure that underlies the much more elaborate combination of sounds in language. Modern transformational linguistics has extended this idea of phonetic structure to grammar. Many linguists now assume that the basic rules of grammar are inherent in the human mind. Noam Chomsky of the Massachusetts Institute of Technology argues that there is a universal grammar (a "deep structure") inherent in the human mind that allows people to then acquire specific languages. Among all of the apparent grammatical diversity among the world's languages, these grammatical structures can be reduced to a few underlying principles that, according to Chomsky, forms a mental template.

These ideas of linguistic structure were influential for Lévi-Strauss. He argued that underneath the tremendous diversity of cultural practices there are universal processes of thought. All humans have a mental structure that leads them to think in certain ways and that underlies all cultural behavior. The reason cultures differ from one another is that a society's history and environment mold people's way of seeing and understanding reality. But Lévi-Strauss' interest isn't in accounting for these differences. Instead he tries to penetrate these differing surface manifestations to get at the basic mental structure that underlies them. For Lévi-Strauss, structural anthropology tries to show how these surface phenomena reflect the underlying universal structures of thought.

The fundamental assumption of structuralism is that the human mind imposes constraints on culture. Anthropology should try to identify how these inherent mental processes are expressed in cultural practices. Cultural traits such as folklore, myths, kinship practices, and ritual have to be "decoded" to reveal their underlying structures. The primary quality of the human mind, according to Lévi-Strauss, is its tendency to create *binary oppositions*, i.e. to think in opposites. Everywhere people have a tendency to create dichotomies. Many dichotomies are culture-specific, so that many cultures recognize kinship or ritual groups that stand in opposition to each other. But Lévi-Strauss contends that underlying these culture-specific oppositions are universal contrasts that people make everywhere. Among these are:

- Sacred—Profane
- Man—Woman
- Self—Other
- Us—Them
- and most importantly for Lévi-Strauss, Nature—Culture.

Lévi-Strauss argues that all humans feel the need to distinguish between the activities in which they engage ("culture") and the activities of animals ("nature"). The realm of culture involves the attributes of cooperation, peace, safety, marriage and family, and other attributes of domesticity and home. The world of nature is one of predation, violence, danger, and promiscuity, all of which are threatening to human security. The nature—culture opposition forms the basis of Lévi-Strauss' analysis of totemic beliefs, contained in his work *Totemism* (1963). Totemism is a combined religious and kinship ideology, in which a kinship group adopts the name of an animal species. The species is believed to be a mythical ancestor of the members of that group. Lévi-Strauss argues that there are two components in totemism. The first is that a given culture consists of people who resemble each other but are also different. They resemble each other in that they all belong to the same tribe (all aligned on the side of culture vs. nature). Yet they also differ by belonging to different kin groups (there is a continuing distinction between *us* and *them*). The second component of totemism is that cultures adopt as totems animal species that resemble one another in some way, but are also different.

Totemism represents these differences by selecting similar species to symbolize the differences between kinship groups in Australian aboriginal society. One lineage may select the bat as its totem, while another selects the honeycreeper, a marsupial somewhat like a possum. How are these animals similar, but different? They certainly don't appear to be similar in terms of outward appearance. Remember, though, that we're not interested in the realm of surface appearances, but in underlying structures. According to Lévi-Strauss, the bat and the honeycreeper are similar in that both are arboreal, living in trees. They are different, in fact, opposing animals in that the bat is nocturnal (active only at night), while the honeycreeper is diurnal (active during the day). As totemic symbols, the similarities and differences between the bat and honeycreeper symbolize the similarities and differences between the members of different kinship groups.

Previous theorists put forth their own explanations for why certain animals are selected as totems. Malinowski argued that people identify with the characteristics of certain animals; these characteristics provide a source of group identity and psychological gratification, and are part of the way that myth provides a "charter" for human society. Ecological anthropologists such as Andrew Vayda or Roy Rappaport argue that certain animals are selected because totemism regulates or prohibits the hunting of game, and thus is part of a society's material adaptation to the environment. Lévi-Strauss rejects these explanations based on either the sentimental or ecological attributes of totems. He expresses this idea in an unforgettable way: certain animals are chosen as totems because they "are good to think with."

In Lévi-Strauss' first famous work, *The Elementary Structures of Kinship* (published as *Les Structures Elementaires de la Parenté* in 1949), he extended Marcel Mauss' notions of reciprocity to the analysis of marriage. This volume also reveals Lévi-Strauss' analytical roots in Durkheimian sociology. Tackling one of the oldest debates in anthropology, Lévi-Strauss argued that the purpose of nuclear family incest prohibitions is ultimately to facilitate the reciprocal exchange of women in marriage. His key assertion was that all systems of marriage were based on two major types of exchange, those involving "restricted" exchanges of women and those based on "generalized" exchange. In the former system, reciprocity was established by a direct exchange of women between two groups, the simplest of which might entail men of groups A and B exchanging sisters in marriage. An illustration of this system would be the common practice of cross-cousin marriage, in which men marry either their father's sister's daughter or mother's brother's daughter. Generalized exchange, on the other hand, is asymmetrical and delayed, in that men of group A marry their matrilateral cross-cousins (mother's brother's daughter) from group B, men of group B marry their matrilateral cross-cousins of group C, and men of group C marry their matrilateral cross-cousins from group A. In Durkheimian fashion, Lévi-Strauss argued that this system of matrilateral cross-cousin marriage promotes greater solidarity as it involves the integration of three or more separate groups in exchanges rather than simply two, as is the case for restricted exchange. Patrilateral cross-cousin marriage (to one's father's sister's daughter) results in a generational reversal of exchange cycles (that is, A–B–C reverses in alternate generations to C–B–A). This system is considerably rarer than matrilateral exchange, a fact that Lévi-Strauss attributes to its relative instability and a presumed lesser degree of solidarity.

Lévi-Strauss' *Elementary Structures* was the most ambitious effort to date to assert the so-called "alliance theory" of incest avoidance, one which comprises the dominant explanation in anthropology today of this cultural universal. Yet, it also triggered decades of debate regarding the origins of matrilateral and patrilateral exchange. In an early critique, George Homans and Harold K. Schneider (1955) disputed Lévi-Strauss' analysis, pointing out that in a statistical sense matrilateral and patrilateral marriage exchange strongly correlated with patrilineal and matrilineal descent, respectively. As such, the comparative rarity of patrilateral marriage simply reflected the relative rarity of matrilineal descent systems compared with societies with patrilineal descent, rather than any inherent superiority of matrilateral exchange in terms of solidarity. A number of Lévi-Strauss' allies, notably the British anthropologist Rodney Needham, vociferously defended Lévi-Strauss' analysis from its detractors. Needham rejected much of the evidence marshaled by Homans and Schneider, stating that they had failed to distinguish between those societies that "prescribe" (require) cross-cousin exchange and those that merely "prefer" it. Remarkably, in the second edition to Lévi-Strauss' book (published after some 15 years of raging scholarly debate over "prescription" versus "preference"), the author distanced himself from (and thereby embarrassed) his defenders, stating that Needham's semantic difference was inconsequential in his mind. Oddly resistant to

To support her argument, Ortner points out that most activities associated with women, such as housekeeping, cooking, childrearing, as well as female-dominated professions (for example, clerical work, elementary education, or nursing) are devalued relative to those activities and occupations associated with men. The logical dilemma of wedding feminist analysis (and policy prescriptions) with structuralism becomes apparent in her final paragraph, where she calls for institutional and political changes to improve women's status, together with "consciousness-raising" and a "revision of educational materials." If women's bodies lead to their universal association with the devalued realm of nature, how is it possible to bring about the change in thinking necessary to improve their status? After all, both she and Lévi-Strauss contend that the nature–culture dichotomy is fixed and universal. Ortner provides no resolution of this logical impasse.

Other logical problems beset her analysis as well. As seen below, in the work of Daniel Ingersoll, as well as Lévi-Strauss' own analysis of human diets, it is equally or even more plausible to identify the home, women's traditional realm, as the domain of culture. As Ingersoll points out, most advertising portrays the world outside the home, where men traditionally work, as a realm of competition and conflict; in other words, the domain of nature. Similarly, where Ortner attributes women's affinity with nature to their child-bearing role, one could argue at least as plausibly that they should be classed with culture because of their central importance in child socialization, the process by which an infant is converted to a cultural being. All of this points to the essentially arbitrary nature of structuralist interpretation, regardless of the amount of evidence that might be mounted to support either view equating women with nature or culture.

Finally, it should be pointed out that Ortner's analysis rested on a highly questionable ethnographic claim, that of the "universal" subordination of women. Sally Slocum's pioneering article "Woman the Gatherer: Male Bias in Anthropology" (1975) initiated a body of gender research that challenged the assumption that women everywhere were dominated by men. Slocum's own work called for a recognition of gathering as a critically important source of cultural and communicative innovation in the course of human evolution. Indeed, women's economic importance in such societies is apparent among contemporary foragers; among the !Kung, for example, approximately 70 percent of the daily diet consists of food gathered by women (Lee 1979). These economic contributions translate into a high degree of gender equality in this and other extant foraging societies, such as the Mbuti of Cameroon. As Eleanor Leacock (1983) demonstrated with her ethnohistorical reconstruction of gender roles among Native American and Australian aborigines, at the time of western contact gender relations in these societies were usually egalitarian because of the equal participation of women and men in the realm of production. If in the recent past or modern world there is gender inequality in such cultures, Leacock attributes it to their transformation by western missionization and market-oriented development, which have tended to reward or introduce patriarchy.

Is food "good to think with"?

One of the areas in which Lévi-Strauss comes into the most direct confrontation with materialist theories is his speculation on human diets. In his book *The Raw and the Cooked* (1969b) (originally published in 1964 as *Le Cru et le Cuit*), Lévi-Strauss puts forward the idea that meals as well as mythology and kinship practices express underlying thought processes. People eat certain kinds of foods on certain occasions not because they are good to eat, or because they supply a requisite amount of nutrients, but because they "are good to think with." The nature–culture distinction is expressed in the division between foods that are raw and those that are cooked. But even among cooked foods, the nature–culture opposition is reflected in the manner of preparation. Some cooked foods are closer to nature, others are closer to culture.

Lévi-Strauss' basis for this rests on an observation that in France, boiled chicken is served to the family, but roast chicken is served to guests. The reason for this was that boiled food is on the side of culture, as presumably would be the members of one's family. This is because boiling involves a cultural implement (a pot) which forms a barrier between the food and fire. Roasting, on the other hand, is on the side of nature, because roasting brings food and flame into direct contact, unmediated by any cultural product: "The boiled can most often be ascribed to what might be called an 'endocuisine,' prepared for domestic use, destined to a small closed group, while the roasted belongs to 'exo-cuisine,' that which one offers to guests. Formerly, in France, boiled chicken was for the family meal while roasted meat was for the banquet" (Lévi-Strauss 1966: 589). Lévi-Strauss proposes that close kinsmen are on the side of culture; so one would serve them food that is identified with culture. Coming from outside the home and family group, guests are associated with nature, and are therefore served roasted food. Once again, certain kinds of cultural practices exist not for practical or utilitarian reasons, but because they correspond to underlying mental structures. According to Lévi-Strauss, outsiders are to family as roasting is to boiling as nature is to culture (outsiders : family :: roasting : boiling :: nature : culture).

Following Lévi-Strauss, British anthropologist Mary Douglas (1921–2007; Figure 13.2) also employed structuralist theories to dietary practices in her 1966 volume *Purity and Danger: An Analysis of the Concepts of Pollution and Taboo*. Like Harris, Douglas set out to explain why the book of Leviticus prohibits the consumption of pork and other animals. Douglas claimed that the pig was subject to a taboo because it occupied an anomalous status in the zoological taxonomy of the ancient Hebrews. Animals with this status are considered spiritually polluting because, universally, anything that defies classification or is out of place in an ordered world brings forth feelings of defilement. Why was the pig out of place? The Israelites defined proper livestock as animals with cloven feet that chewed their cud. Because the pig has cloven feet but is not a ruminant, it is considered dirty. In other words, Douglas' explanation for the taboo on pork flesh was that:

pig : livestock :: disorder : order :: dirty : clean :: nature : culture.

FIGURE 13.2 Professor Mary Douglas, author of the influential volume *Purity and Danger*. In 2006, Queen Elizabeth II named her "Dame Commander of the Order of the British Empire." (Don't the British have wonderful honorific titles? In contrast, in my first academic job I was anointed "Temporary Assistant Professor." The plastic nameplate on my door was attached with Scotch tape.) Courtesy of Musée du quai Branly, photo Antonin Borgeaud/Scala, Florence.

This, of course, begs the question of why Leviticus defines non-ruminant cloven hoof animals as polluting, an issue that Douglas tried to resolve by expanding her discussion of the logic of biblical proscriptions on certain foods. Other components of "uncleanliness" are also considered in Leviticus: animals and birds that eat carrion (meat, as opposed to grain) are unclean because God commands Israel not to shed blood. Further, if those who belong to an endogamous group (Jews) avoid others as unclean in marriage and sex (gentiles), they will regard the animals others keep as unsuitable for eating: "On mature reflection…I can now see that the pig…carries the odium of multiple pollution. First it pollutes because it defies the classification of ungulates. Second it pollutes because it eats carrion. Third, it pollutes because it is reared…by non-Israelites" (Douglas 1972: 79).

There are logical problems with Douglas' "mature reflection" and her expanded explanation on the pork taboo. For one, pigs are no more likely to eat flesh than are dogs or goats, neither of which are regarded as polluting in Leviticus. Admittedly, dogs were not eaten by Jews, but they were kept as domesticated animals and were not regarded as polluting to the touch, as were pigs. Goats, of course, were raised and eaten. Further, the Egyptians and Sumerians tabooed the pig on the basis of entirely different religious prescriptions long before the compilation of Leviticus. Finally, if the pig pollutes because it was raised and eaten by foreigners and enemies, then why weren't cows, sheep, goats, and chickens regarded as unclean? After all, all of these animals were eaten by Israelites and gentiles alike.

BOX 13.1   Is exo-cannibalism : endo-cannibalism :: nature : culture?

Following upon his analogy of "outsiders" with "roasting" and "family" with "boiling," Lévi-Strauss offered a thought-provoking assessment of *anthropophagy* (cannibalism) in his 1965 article "Le Triangle Culinaire" (translated into English the following year as "The Culinary Triangle"). Cannibalism generally assumes two forms: endo-cannibalism, or consumption of one's own dead (generally kinsmen, as part of a mortuary ritual) and exo-cannibalism, or consumption of outsiders, who are generally enemies. This distinction led Lévi-Strauss to the following formulation, derived from his earlier work on French cooking practices: "…one could infer that cannibalism (which by definition is an endo-cuisine with respect to the human race) ordinarily employs boiling rather than roasting and where bodies are roasted…must be more frequent in exo-cannibalism (eating the body of an enemy) than in endo-cannibalism (eating of a relative)" (1966: 589).

Empirical data assembled several years later by Paul Shankman didn't bear out this imaginative hypothesis, despite his acknowledgement that Lévi-Strauss "himself is often considered a delicacy in anthropological cuisine" (1969: 54). From a sample of 60 societies known to practice ritual cannibalism, Shankman determined that 17 boiled the dead while 20 roasted. A number of societies from the sample utilized more than one method of preparing human flesh for consumption: six both boiled and roasted, an apparent anomaly given the presumed fixity of mental structures. Shankman cited, for example, the following vivid description of the many ways in which the bodies of kin are prepared for consumption among the Mayorun of Amazonia:

> When a parent, son, or other relative dies, they weep, and then, between floods of tears, they cut him into pieces; they boil the flesh or *roast* it and eat it as fresh meat; the rest they *smoke* to be eaten on other days. They usually place the entire corpse on a fire, where they remove small pieces of meat from it as it is roasting, and eat between wails and weeping, which they mix with the mouthfuls, until the deceased is entirely eaten… They save the heads until they are full of worms in the orifices and brains, and they eat these, for they like them very well mixed with chili pepper.
>
> (Figueroa in Shankman 1969: 62–63; emphasis in original)

Shankman observes that another Amazonian group, the Cubeo, who eat their enemies, also consumed humans "with equal variety":

> At a victory dance, the men wore the *smoked* genitals of the killed warriors as an ornamental trophy. After the dance the women were offered the penises to eat for fertility. Except for the intestines, deemed not fit to eat,

the enemies were consumed at a sib[2] feast and drinking party. The head, limbs, liver, and heart were spit *roasted*; the rest of the meat was *boiled*.

(Goldman in ibid.: 63; emphasis in original)

In Shankman's sample, over half of the exo-cannibals boiled their dead, while only two of the 29 endo-cannibal groups were boilers. Lévi-Strauss' predictions also ignore many different ways of preparing the dead for consumption, with *baking* being more common than *either* roasting or boiling. According to Shankman (whose article contains many tongue-in-cheek references to what many westerners might regard as a repellent practice), "the most obvious finding of this study is that Lévi-Strauss' exclusive focus on the roasted and the boiled has been spoiled by the natives who have discovered a veritable smorgasbord of ways of preparing people" (1969: 61). He concludes that Lévi-Strauss' "ideas on how to serve our fellow man will be of little use to either cannibals or anthropologists" (ibid.: 54). For his part, despite his sympathies for structuralist analysis, Edmund Leach summarized the debate begun with "Le Triangle Culinaire" with the observation that "some readers suspect that the whole argument was an elaborate joke" (1970: 28).

If structuralist analyses of food taboos remain rather unconvincing or empirically weak, the theory has offered occasionally powerful insights into other realms of cultural life. In an unpublished conference paper entitled "Stealing the Symbols," anthropologist Daniel Ingersoll (1998) argued that the purportedly universal "nature–culture" distinction is actually relevant only to western societies. Yet, he then goes on to demonstrate how corporations, which operate in the "natural" realm of Darwinian competition, appropriate the powerful language and symbols of the "cultural" realm of home, family, and love in order to stimulate consumers to buy their products. Ingersoll writes:

The house/home distinction is an important one in our culture, with "home" linguistically marked and emotionally loaded. Americans learn the difference between house and home at an early age. House: a cold space enclosed by walls. Home: a warm place animated by family and friends. Houses, as material artifacts and "real" property which may be bought and sold, appertain to the profane realm of law and market economics, natural right, and profit. Homes, as social artifacts and intangible wealth which can not be bought and sold, belong to the sacred world of fellowship, love and nurture. Paradoxically, Americans dwell simultaneously in physical houses and symbolic homes. You can steal the symbols as do advertisers from the world of business and work when they ignore "house" and hype "home."

(Ingersoll 1998: 6)

Ingersoll then proceeds to deconstruct dozens of advertisements, almost all from large multinational corporations, for their careful deployment of the language and imagery of "home" in print and broadcast advertising. In only one area of advertising (that of motor vehicles) are the realms of both nature and culture employed, albeit for different classes of vehicles. Sports cars are marketed with images of nature and competition (they are shown on a race course or, more commonly, speeding across an open expanse of highway against a pristine landscape) and even occasionally derive their names from nature (e.g. Jaguar, Impala, Mustang, and my favorite, Tiburon[3]). Minivans and family sedans are shown in proximity to scenes of domesticity, with married couples or the occasional soccer mom unloading groceries or children in suburban driveways. Since encountering Ingersoll's paper more than a decade ago, I have never viewed advertising in the same way.

Assessing French structuralism

In many respects, Lévi-Strauss' work represents a reversion to a speculative anthropology typical of its pre-fieldwork years. His first book *Tristes Tropiques*[4] begins with the remarkable admission, "I hate traveling and explorers." And indeed, many of his speculations on culture center on societies that he has never visited and for whose language he has no facility. In a 1988 interview with Didier Eribon, Lévi-Strauss stated "Why not admit it? I was fairly quick to discover that I was more a man for the study than for the field" (quoted in Rothstein 2009). Many anthropologists, then, are concerned that Lévi-Strauss' wide-ranging and often de-contextualized speculations on culture may be no more accurate than those of the nineteenth-century "armchair anthropologists." Sir Edmund Leach challenged French structuralism in a 1970 article, in which he doubted that even during his Brazilian fieldwork during the 1930s could Lévi-Strauss have spoken with "any of his native informants in their native language." Ironically, though, by the end of the 1970s, Leach became probably the most prominent English convert to French structuralism! A similar conversion occurred with the American anthropologist Marshall Sahlins, who critiqued Lévi-Strauss' thought in a 1965 article, but by the following decade was acknowledging his intellectual debt to Lévi-Strauss after working beside him at the College de France.

Insofar as they can be tested, Lévi-Strauss' specific accounts of cultural phenomena have not held up well, but the lack of empirical validation for his claims never caused him to revise his work. Instead, he argued that he constructed models of mental structures from observable reality, but that these models cannot be tested against empirical data. The reason for this is that the mental structures themselves cannot be observed and that history and the environment alter the observed outcome of these structures of thought. The underlying structures are there, Lévi-Strauss insisted, but they have to be inferred from a constantly changing and variable observed reality. In other words, Lévi-Strauss acknowledged that his theories were non-falsifiable; they can neither be demonstrated nor rejected. Nonetheless, when used well and with appropriate caveats, as in Ingersoll's "Stealing the Symbols" (1998), I think that structuralism lends itself to genuine insight.

What about Lévi-Strauss' claim that the mind operates according to universal principles? He claimed that binary thinking is innate (it is biologically based) but this is a difficult proposition to establish. He wasn't able to establish the existence of these specific binary tendencies except through circular reasoning. That is, he identified an opposition in thought, claimed that it results from a universal, biologically based tendency to think in terms of opposites, and then as proof pointed to other symbolic oppositions. People everywhere may well have a tendency to dichotomize in their thinking. There is not, however, any proof that the specific oppositions that Lévi-Strauss considered universal are in fact universal. Probably all people make a male–female distinction, but do all people make a nature–culture distinction? More likely, as Ingersoll observes, this distinction reflects a specifically western world view that conceptualizes humans as apart from nature. There is also the question of whether oppositions result from biologically-based thought patterns in the human brain. This assumption is critical to structuralism's claim that all cultures express universal processes of thought. At least one author (C.K. Ogden, *Opposition*, 1967, orig. 1932) provided an alternative theory of the human tendency to dichotomize. Ogden argued that oppositions in myths and other cultural practices based on language derive from the perception of two-sided spatial relationships. These are spatial relationships that all people experience from their own bodies: the dichotomy between right and left limbs, and the front and back of their body. These are universal spatial relationships that lead people to dichotomize. The difference with structuralism is that while people everywhere have a tendency to create oppositions, there is no reason to believe that those oppositions are universal in all cultures.

Geertz and Turner

To a large extent, the work of Clifford Geertz (1926–2006) developed in response to the decontextualized analyses of culture arising from French structuralism. Together with Victor Turner (1920–1983), Geertz was the most prominent scholar in the field of symbolic or interpretive anthropology. During the 1960s, Geertz was considered an important but marginal figure in anthropology, but since the 1980s he has been regarded as a leading source of inspiration for postmodern perspectives. Although he never identified himself as a postmodernist, he was among the first to assail the kind of explanatory and ecological-materialist consensus that dominated the field in the 1960s–80s. His rejection of a scientific model of anthropology had the same polarizing effect as Marvin Harris' ardent promotion of it. Just a week after Geertz' death, Lionel Tiger of Rutgers University wrote (in what must be considered an entirely tactless obituary) that his "influence and impact were real but fundamentally unfortunate in the social sciences" in that he inspired other anthropologists to engage in "a lame and confused form of literary scholarship" (Tiger 2006:A12). Needless to say, Geertz' many followers would vigorously dispute this assessment!

Like the materialists we have just considered, Geertz was a product of military service during World War II and the GI Bill. His undergraduate education centered on English and philosophy and, in fact, he did not enroll in any anthropology courses until becoming a graduate student. After entering the graduate program in Harvard's Department of Social Relations, he worked between 1952 and 1954 as part of a research project in Indonesia funded by the Ford Foundation with the goal of promoting economic growth. Geertz' early work from this time is quite different from the interpretive approaches he developed in the latter half of the 1960s. His 1963 book *Agricultural Involution* is a study of ecological change in indigenous agricultural systems following the introduction of Dutch colonial rule in Java. This is the book by which he is most well known to cultural ecologists, but it is his most atypical work. After a faculty appointment at Berkeley, Geertz moved to the University of Chicago in 1960. Ten years later he left Chicago to establish the School of Social Science at the Institute for Advanced Study in Princeton, New Jersey, the same research center whose faculty had once included such luminaries as Albert Einstein. There he remained for the rest of his career.

Victor Turner came to symbolic anthropology via a different route. Born in Glasgow, Scotland, he spent the war years in England as a conscientious objector assigned to dig up unexploded bombs (which, as you can imagine, is a good deal more hazardous than most active combat duty). Coming across books by Mead and Radcliffe-Brown in a local library, he was inspired to become an anthropologist, and in the postwar years studied with Max Gluckman at Manchester University. During his fieldwork among the Ndembu of Zambia in 1950–54, Turner's anthropological views were almost certainly shaped by African movements for decolonization of the time as well as the nature of Ndembu society. A society of about 17,000 people with the rare and paradoxical mix of matrilineal descent and patrilocal postmarital residence, the Ndembu experience high levels of mobility due to marriage, divorce, and remarriage. The transience and underlying conflict of Ndembu society seemed ill-suited to the assumptions of social equilibrium emphasized in the functionalist theory that still prevailed in British anthropology. As we'll see, Turner came to recognize the essential role of symbols in motivating Ndembu behavior, but unlike Geertz he retained certain structural functionalist premises.

Geertz' turn toward a more interpretive anthropology was first outlined in his 1966 article, "The Impact of Concept of Culture on the Concept of Man." At the beginning of the article, Geertz asks a simple question, "What is a man?" This question has of course occupied social philosophers for centuries and lies at the heart of anthropology. The older view, Geertz observes, was one of *consensus gentium*: there are some things that all people everywhere will agree on. This was originally part of the classical Greeks' efforts to identify universal human values, true in all times and places, such as individual freedom, charity, or honor. In anthropology, this view led to the search for *cultural universals* or institutions and practices found in all cultures. All people everywhere have supernatural beliefs, they have some kind of family organization, some way to produce and distribute goods and some system of political authority. Indeed, it is this notion that informs the layout of introductory cultural anthropology texts, which are organized with separate chapters on economics, politics, belief systems, kinship, and so on. But, Geertz asks, do these universals really tell us anything of importance about any actual, living humans? No; in fact he regards these categories of behavior as "fake universals." To know that all people have some belief in the supernatural tells us nothing about religious experience in any of its particular manifestations. There are no meaningful generalizations that can be made about humans that tell us anything worthwhile about any specific group of people. The reason for this is that "man unmodified by the customs of particular places does not exist." If we were to understand humans simply in terms of the generalizations of cultural anthropologists, however, the resulting person would be a blank caricature of a person, a sort of formless monstrosity. Geertz argues instead that it is our nature to be cultural beings, and because symbols so powerfully guide our behavior in ways that are incomprehensible outside of our cultural setting, a North American is fundamentally a different person from the Balinese whose rituals figure so prominently in Geertz' work.

As an illustration of this, Geertz describes the trance state that the Balinese enter during ritual. Bali is one of the islands making up Indonesia and is home to most members of that country's Hindu minority. During these episodes of trance the Balinese perform all sorts of amazing actions, including biting the heads off chickens, stabbing themselves, speaking in tongues, and writhing in ecstasy. How should the cultural anthropologist understand this behavior? Will the generalization that "all humans have supernatural practices" help the anthropologist appreciate why the normally composed Balinese give way to these utterly unrestrained behaviors? Geertz argues that ecological or materialist models that regard religion as "just" superstructure cannot *"get at"* what this behavior means for those who participate in it. They can't explain why some symbols affect people so powerfully that they slip into trance or uncontrolled hysteria. They cannot help us understand why a Christian whose forehead is daubed with a smudge of a cross on Ash Wednesday might dissolve in tears from the experience. The act, and the ashes, symbolize in concise form the most important elements of the Christian experience: sin, redemption, death, resurrection. How can a mere description of this "etic behavioral act" render comprehensible the meaning of such a simple yet emotion-laden gesture?

In his 1973 book *The Interpretation of Cultures*, Geertz called for a radical reworking of anthropology and a break with its scientific pretensions. The introductory chapter, "Thick Description: Toward an Interpretive Theory of Culture," laid out the approach that he was to follow for the rest of his professional life. Geertz argued that the study of culture cannot and should not emulate the natural sciences. Anthropology has much more in common with the humanities. The reason for this is that to understand cultures, we need to study meaning rather than behavior. Anthropologists have to seek understanding rather than causal laws:

> The concept of culture I espouse…is essentially a semiotic [symbolic] one. Believing, with Max Weber, that man is an animal suspended in webs of significance that he himself has spun, I take culture to be those webs, and the analysis of it (i.e. anthropology) to be therefore not an experimental science in search of law but an interpretive one in search of meaning.
>
> (Geertz 1973b: 5)

The signposts of action

For Geertz and other symbolic anthropologists like Turner, culture is an assemblage of symbols that are "signposts" for action. By definition, symbols may have no meaning for people outside that culture, but are often tremendously powerful for people within it. Indeed, within a culture most gestures or sounds have multiple meanings (in the words of Victor Turner, symbols are "multivocal," or "speak" with many voices). Geertz draws on an example offered by Gilbert Ryle of the human "wink" to show why anthropology must study meaning rather than simply behavior, as cultural materialists might advocate. A twitching eyelid involves exactly the same behavior as a wink, but these outwardly similar actions differ in their entirety because the wink communicates meaning while a twitch does not. Further, the wink itself may mean different things to different observers and to the person doing the winking. It can signal a shared understanding, a common conspiracy, recognition of an acquaintance, romantic interest, a nervous tic, or simply a displaced eyelash. As a far more dramatic example, consider the swastika. A hated symbol of racism and totalitarianism in Europe and the US, the swastika has been illegal to display in Germany since the end of World War II. Yet the same image is the symbol for good fortune among the Hopi of the American Southwest and signifies rebirth among Hindus; hence, it is regarded as a sacred symbol in both cultures. The swastika is often encountered on Southwestern Indian textiles and baskets, while Hindus decorate walls, the roofs of houses and temples with the image, and often use it as a wedding decoration (Figure 13.3). This image thus provokes very different but equally powerful reactions depending upon who encounters it. Indeed, in recent

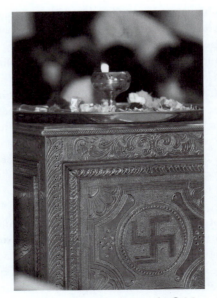

FIGURE 13.3   Candle and offerings in a Hindu temple. © Marco Secchi/Alamy.

years Europe's Hindus have protested a proposed European Union continent-wide ban on the use of the symbol.

From his work among the Ndembu, Turner similarly pointed out that symbols are powerful distillations of meaning. Turner analyzed the meanings associated with the *chising'a*, an Ndembu hunting shrine consisting of little more than a forked stick placed in the ground and a grass braid. The meanings associated with the shrine encompass the relationships between hunters and nonhunters, the hunter's family and extended kin, fertility, ancestor worship, hunting skill, and fairness in the distribution of meat. In total, Turner identifies fifteen different meanings associated with this simple shrine. "It can almost be said that the greater the symbol, the simpler its form" (Turner 1967: 296). If we reflect upon an even simpler symbol—two perpendicular pieces of wood that are unequal in length—we have the Christian cross, an evocative symbol for Christians and non-Christians alike, although often for very different reasons. In 1998, Polish Catholics erected a cross outside "Auschwitz I" as a memorial to those who died there.[5] Many Jews were outraged when the cross was erected, regarding it as an affront to the memory of the 1.5 million Jews murdered at "Auschwitz II," also known as Birkenau. Though speaking a common language and sharing a common nationality, Polish Catholics and Jews remain divided over the symbol and its placement. This conflict was especially fraught with complex emotions when the site was visited in 2008 by a German-born Pope who had been forced into the Hitler Youth as a teen. During his visit, Pope Benedict judiciously chose to speak in Italian rather than his native German.

Notice, then, that if symbols are multivocal, there arises the likelihood of misunderstanding, differences of opinion about their meanings, and conflicts between individuals and groups in their use of symbols. What did it mean when that student winked at me in class? Was she acknowledging something that I had just said? Was she sharing an inside joke at the expense of another class member? Culture, thus, is not a homogeneous or evenly shared set of understandings, as might be implied by the materialist's notion of an "ideological superstructure." Nor is it possible for an ethnographer to write, as did earlier anthropologists, that "the Samoans believe x, y and z," because it is likely that individual Samoans will differ in how these beliefs and associated symbols are understood. Rather, to interpret a culture requires that we examine an event in terms of particular actors' motives, intentions, values, and the particular meanings that they attribute to the associated action, speech, and gestures.

Culture as drama and culture as text

Reflecting a family background in theater (Turner's mother founded the Scottish National Players), Turner pioneered the development of an approach that he called the "social drama." By this, he meant the description of social processes that involved as much conflict as continuity of social structure. As he wrote of this approach, "When the interests and attitudes of groups and individuals stood in obvious opposition, social dramas did seem to me to constitute isolable and minutely describable units of social process" (Turner 1975: 33). The social drama, for Turner, is an optimal unit of analysis because it has a beginning, a middle, and an end. In his writings on the Ndembu, Turner related how conflict began with the breach of a cultural norm, usually on the part of an individual or family. It would then escalate into a dispute between social groups. There followed some form of redress or adjustment, "ranging from informal arbitration to elaborate rituals, that result either in healing the breach or public recognition of its irremediable character" (Turner 1985: 74). This "dramatalurgical" view of social life was not unique to Turner—recall as well that Erving Goffman drew parallels between social behavior and theater—but it finds a direct counterpart in Geertz' approach to ethnographic writing. Yet, Turner's analysis of the role of symbols in Ndembu ritual also points to a significant difference with Geertz. It is through ritual, and its attendant symbols, that social breaches are healed and the social order is renewed. Hence, while acknowledging that conflict is intrinsic in any social order, Turner retained—like his major professor Max Gluckman—something of a functionalist emphasis on social equilibrium and reproduction. In writing of the Ndembu *mudyi* (milk) tree, Turner invokes the Durkheimian notion that in symbolizing the relationships between kin groups, the tree "stand[s] for the unity and continuity in the widest Ndembu society, embracing its contradictions" (1967: 21). Periodic rituals that invert the social structure, such as carnival or Gluckman's "rituals of rebellion," result in a temporary state of "anti-structure" in which customary identities and roles are turned upside down. Yet, in the end, through the resumption of their earlier status, society's members attain an enhanced state of *communitas*, or social cohesion. Geertz makes no such functionalist assumptions, but considers how symbols render social life meaningful for its members.

For Geertz, culture is *textual*; it is an elaborate assemblage of symbols that the anthropologist must strive to interpret. Events such as the Balinese cockfight are as complex as novels: they have characters with their own motivations, they have plots, and they are loaded with symbolic attributes. The result is that his "reading" of an ethnographic scene such as the Balinese cockfight reveals this to be much more than just a blood sport, but it is a symbolic representation of how Javanese men view themselves and the nature of their own lives, their relations to one another, and their adversaries in the world beyond their village. Balinese cockfighting, Geertz argues, is itself interpretive: "it is a Balinese reading of Balinese experience, a story they tell themselves about themselves...[it is] a kind of sentimental education. What [a Balinese person] learns there is what his culture's ethos and his private sensibility look like when spelled out externally in a collective text" (1973a: 45). Indeed, Geertz' description of the event reads much more like a short story than the dry treatises then dominating scientific anthropology, and as a result it is one of the most famous, evocative, and enjoyable pieces of anthropological writing. In writing himself and his wife into the account as both participants and observers, Geertz anticipates the later reflexive turn in some postmodern anthropology. For Geertz, the interpretation of culture is like the interpretation of a text. To understand Javanese culture, one must do exactly the same things one would do if trying to understand any highly symbolic text. That is, the ethnographer seeks to interpret the meanings of symbols for the actors involved, and to see how their behavior is affected accordingly: "Doing ethnography is like trying to read (in the sense of 'construct a reading of') a manuscript—foreign, faded, full of ellipses, incoherencies, and tendentious commentaries, but written not in conventionalized graphs of sound but in transient examples of shaped behavior" (Geertz 1973b: 10).

The Balinese cockfight

The objective of anthropological writing should be "thick description," which Geertz contrasted with the decontextualized, ahistorical analyses of French structuralism. By this he means a highly detailed, almost novelistic description of individual scenes of action. Anthropological description should make readers feel like they are part of that setting, able to understand the motivations of those who make up the scene. His account of the Balinese cockfight breaks with prior anthropological conventions by beginning in the first person, foregrounding his role as an observer and participant in the action that he describes. After weeks of being ignored by the residents of the Balinese village in which he and his wife are attempting to conduct research, an unanticipated event brings about his sudden acceptance. The article describes a frantic and confused chase in which Geertz and his wife find themselves fleeing from the authorities with the other spectators and participants in the cockfight. Despite their popularity with Balinese men, cockfights are illegal. The unexpected appearance of the police during one of these fights sent everyone, including the anthropologists, scurrying to safety. Geertz writes:

> On the established anthropological principle, "When in Rome," my wife and I decided, only slightly less instantaneously than everyone else, that the thing to do was to run too. We ran down the main village street, northward, away from where we were living, for we were on that side of the ring. About half-way down another fugitive ducked suddenly into a compound—his own, it turned out—and we, seeing nothing ahead of us but rice fields, open country, and a very high volcano, followed him. As the three of us came tumbling into the courtyard, his wife, who had apparently been through this sort of thing before, whipped out a table, a tablecloth, three chairs, and three cups of tea, and we all, without any explicit communication whatsoever, sat down, commenced to sip tea, and sought to compose ourselves.
>
> (1973a: 415)

When the police barged into the compound moments later, the "host" indignantly explained to them that he and his American guests had been drinking tea that afternoon and knew nothing of the cockfight. To their amazement, Geertz and his wife listened as their host accurately described their work in the community as social scientists, despite the almost nonexistent interactions they had earlier been granted by community members. This story serves two purposes. First, it draws the reader (or, to continue the theatrical metaphor, the audience) into the society along with the anthropologist. Just as this event led to Geertz making the transition from "outsider" to "participant," so too it makes the audience feel as if they are active participants in the drama that ensued from the police raid. The other purpose is to establish the subjective authority of Geertz' account. Geertz can tell us what this ritual "*really means*" because he was there. Not only was he there, but he was embraced by members of the society who respected him for fleeing from the police, instead of simply flashing his credentials "as an important foreigner" to avoid arrest. In this work, he makes a conscious break with the "objective" third-person perspective of scientific anthropology. This makes for some very stimulating and creative ethnographic writing. But it also poses obvious problems for anthropologists who retain a scientific model of the discipline. How do you know whether a particular interpretation of culture is the correct one?

Geertz acknowledges that his interpretations are not objectively verifiable; indeed, he states that his interpretation of Balinese culture is an interpretation of his informants' interpretations of what they are up to. In other words, anthropological writings themselves are already second or third order interpretations. It is entirely probable that another anthropologist, working with different informants and observing different realms of action, will produce a different portrait of that culture. That's why Geertz and his followers explicitly reject the natural science model for anthropology. Here you encounter anthropology with a very different goal from that of materialist or functionalist theories, which attempt to account for the causes of cultural practices (remember our early distinction between "explanation" and "interpretation?"). Explanation is not the goal of symbolic anthropology; what Geertz and others are out to demonstrate are the meanings of behaviors, not their causes. Of course, a behavior can present as many meanings to observers as there are observers (remember our example of the wink). This is a major reason why Geertz' work helped to inspire the newer postmodern orientations in anthropology that reject the possibility of a single authoritative understanding of culture.

Literary seductions: whose text do we interpret?

Some have argued that Geertz' powerful and evocative prose "seduces" the reader into accepting an incomplete and apolitical view of Balinese culture, one which omits much of the historical, gender, and political economic context in which the cockfight takes place. That is the argument of William Roseberry (1950–2000), one of the best known anthropological interpreters of Marx. In his 1982 article, "Balinese Cockfights and the Seduction of Anthropology," Roseberry draws from Geertz' own footnotes to suggest that his account of the cockfight fails to pose critical questions about Indonesian society and history. Depicting the cockfight as exclusively the domain of men, Geertz entirely neglects the gender hierarchy of such events. While noting that "traditional markets [where the fights were held] were staffed almost entirely by women," Geertz mentions parenthetically that women were consigned to trivial bets on the sidelines of the cockfighting ring. Elsewhere, Geertz states that "the sport has been one of the main agencies of the island's monetization," yet he pays no attention to how a subsistence economy has been transformed into a monetary economy, with a resulting growth in village stratification. Finally, and perhaps most critically, Geertz ignored the developing political conflicts within Indonesian society of the time (the late 1950s), which would explode in just a few years. Not long after Geertz' sojourn in the field, the Indonesian government embarked on a massacre of hundreds of thousands of so-called "communists," but there is no hint in "Deep Play" of these simmering class and political tensions. And yet the cockfight itself is mentioned in Geertz' text as an expression of Balinese nationalism: "Balinese regard the island as taking the shape of a small, proud cock, poised, neck extended, back taut, tail raised, in eternal challenge to large, feckless, Java" (1973a: 418). Nor do we ever really learn the social origins of status in Balinese society—crucial information if these fights are, as Geertz tells us, symbolic battles over status. Patterson's critique of later postmodern approaches could apply as well to Geertz' interpretive approach: "By viewing identities as texts that were created by intersubjective communication, the postmodernists decanted concerns about class politics and struggle from anthropology at a time when states around the world were becoming increasingly repressive and their neoliberal policies allowed transnational corporations to suck the life out of workers, peasants, and tribal peoples" (2001: 156).

Roseberry is not simply saying that Geertz' thick description isn't "thick" enough, but that there is a limitation to the whole culture-as-text approach advocated by interpretive anthropologists, notably their frank acknowledgement that their interpretations are not empirically verifiable. If you are a literary critic or a novelist, it doesn't matter that your interpretation of a work of fiction or poetry is completely at odds with someone else's. But as Patterson argues, there is much more at stake when we study human society: we're not seeking knowledge about *texts*, but about people's *lives*. Anthropologists work in places where there is acute racial injustice, class oppression, genocide, hunger, and economic exploitation. As the more politically-engaged postmodernists such as Scheper-Hughes note, it is vitally important that anthropologists document these things. At the very least, if we are going to represent culture as a text, then we should at a minimum ask whose text we are talking about. What other voices are not being included in that text? And why are some voices (such as those of Geertz' male, relatively elite informants) elevated over others, such as the women consigned to the margins of this important ritual event? More seriously, Roseberry, like most materialists, is troubled by the notion that our view of a society is simply an interpretation of it, one that cannot be verified. If we consider all knowledge claims equally valid in the sense that none can be verified, then we must automatically accept claims that refute or challenge those that we ourselves are advancing. This, Roseberry argues, is a degree of ethnographic detachment that abdicates the researcher's responsibilities to the communities s/he studies given the real injustices that their members experience in their daily lives.

Ethnoscience

A third variety of idealism developed among American anthropologists Ward Goodenough, Charles Frake, Stephen Tyler, and James Spradley in the 1950s and

1960s. This is known as ethnoscience or cognitive anthropology. These approaches developed out of a frustration with the way in which earlier anthropologists gathered most of their data. Although anthropologists as far back as Malinowski had described their task as one of trying "to grasp the native's point of view...to realize *his* vision of the world" (1984: 25), in practice ethnographers usually imposed the conceptual categories of Western society on their ethnographic descriptions. In contrast, ethnoscientists sought to render descriptions that employed the mental categories of native participants themselves for a given domain of perception. In a procedure known as *componential analysis*, ethnoscience analyzes vocabulary terms to determine the characteristics by which the objects in that domain are sorted. This approach is heavily influenced by the theories of Benjamin Lee Whorf and Edward Sapir (the Sapir–Whorf hypothesis) on the relationship between language and perception. They argued that perceptions of reality are shaped by the language we speak, so that the world does not appear the same to speakers of distinct languages. As Whorf wrote, "We cut nature up, organize it into concepts, and ascribe significances as we do, largely because we are parties to an agreement to organize it in this way" (1956: 213). Similarly, the underlying assumption of ethnoscience is that our knowledge and perceptions of the world are organized taxonomically, and that the elicitation of these taxonomies through language can reveal how people view the world. This is, obviously, a highly systematic effort to identify an emic view of the world through language (in contrast to French structuralism, which might be considered an etic approach to understanding mental processes). Indeed, ethnoscientists claimed that because the same methodology could be employed in any cultural context to describe a semantic domain, theirs was an approach inherently more scientific than earlier, less systematic data gathering.

At various times, ethnoscientists have collected the terms used in native languages for kinship terms, plants, animals, colors, parts of the body, diseases; in other words, virtually anything for which people have a working vocabulary. The collection of these terms and taxonomies is intended to reveal how people perceive a particular aspect of the natural and social worlds. The method of ethnoscience begins by identifying a *contrast set*, or words that refer to mutually exclusive categories belonging to a semantic domain. Here, as in French Structuralism, the influence of structural linguistics is fairly evident. The argument of ethnoscientists is that contrast sets represent significant conceptual distinctions in native thought, and that knowledge of any given domain is organized taxonomically. In theory, the taxonomy provides us with a guide as to how the speakers of a certain language view the world and act in it. Ethnoscientific analysis begins at the most specific level of inquiry possible. For example, in developing the domain of "vehicles," a Martian anthropologist visiting the United States would begin by eliciting classifications at the level of individual types and ask questions that yield the informant's taxonomic knowledge. For example:

Anthropologist: "What is that?"
Informant: "It's a car."

Anthropologist: "Is that a car, too?"

Informant: "No, that's a pickup truck."

Anthropologist: "Is a pickup truck a kind of car?"

Informant: "No, a pickup truck is a kind of vehicle."

Anthropologist: "Is a car a kind of vehicle?"

Informant: "Yes."

Anthropologist: "What kind of vehicles are there?"

Informant: "There are cars, pickup trucks, motorcycles, semi-trailers, and bicycles. You, I observe, arrived here in a flying saucer."

This procedure would be repeated for each of the contrast sets within the semantic domain until a complete taxonomy is created. When applied to other languages and cultural settings, ethnoscience is intended to produce an explicitly *emic* view of cultural concepts—one that presumably reflects how people within those languages perceive the world around them. It has been used extensively in the field of ethnobotany to generate models of local knowledge of plants. Such analyses have been undertaken in part to identify the medicinal properties of plants that are known only to the members of those cultures.

Charles Frake, David McCurdy, and James Spradley have conducted some innovative ethnoscientific research in the United States. Much of this has taken place among subcultures such as occupational groups (waitresses, for example, often have an elaborate vocabulary for types of customers and the food they order), street people, ethnic groups, and so on. Janet Davis, a student of ethnoscientist David McCurdy, conducted ethnographic research with junior high school students in Minneapolis. Part of the research involved compiling a taxonomy of students' perceptions of things that teachers do at school and things that kids do. The result illustrates how students' perceptions of their social world differ from that of teachers and parents, and also provides us with a guide to why students behave the way they do (Figure 13.4).

Problems of rules and cultural consensus

For ethnoscientists, the analytical implications of this strategy reflect their idealist assumptions about culture. Ward Goodenough conceives of culture in cognitive terms, as the knowledge and rules employed by people in determining how to act:

> a society's culture consists of whatever it is that one has to know or believe in order to operate in a manner acceptable to its members…culture is not a material phenomenon; it does not consist of things, people, behavior or emotions. It is rather an organization of those things. It is the forms of things that people have in mind, their models for perceiving, relating and otherwise interpreting the world.

(1964: 36)

FIGURE 13.4 "Tie kids to desk?"!! It sounds like a detention facility. Could this be why online learning is so popular? Notice that "teaching," the activity that teachers themselves probably consider most important, is condensed to a single contrast set, "Talk a whole lot" (taken from Spradley and McCurdy 1988). Used by permission of Waveland Press Inc.

It is implicit in Goodenough's definition that if we have elicited a perfect knowledge of the rules that people have within their heads, we should have a perfect knowledge of how people actually behave. At that time ethnoscientists were claiming to usher in a new, highly systematic method of data collection. Underlying this claim is the assumption that what people think about their behavior is an accurate reflection of how they behave. Yet, if our emic understandings of culture accurately predicted our behavior, we would live in a world in which cars never ran red lights, marriage was a life-long institution, theft and murder never occurred, and many other emic-level understandings of contemporary society permeated everyday social life. We can readily see from these few instances that knowing the rules for behavior does not predict what people really do.

Another, equally vexing problem that critics have pointed out is the assumption that ethnoscientists make of cultural consensus. Most anthropologists today would regard this as a quaint if not entirely naïve notion, instead viewing cultural understanding as partial, contested, and socially constructed by one's class, ethnic and gender identity. In contrast, ethnoscientists assumed that all members of a given culture operate with the same framework of knowledge. Some years ago I conducted a classroom experiment to assess this claim. As a result, I found that

American college students and college faculty define the domain "types of college professors and staff" in very different ways. In an anthropological methods class, I wrote down all the names of the faculty and staff in our department on 3 × 5 note cards and asked a student to sort them by piles in terms of similarities and differences. I expected she would sort them by "sociologists," "anthropologists," "secretaries," and "work study students." But her piles seemed completely random assortments to three categories that were entirely different from mine. I asked her the basis of her decision-making, and she said she sorted them into the categories, "people I like and respect," "people I don't like," and "people I don't know"! Notice, too, that the way our hypothetical earthling informant above classified vehicles may not be the way all people would respond to the anthropologist's question. Some, for example, might respond by excluding bicycles as human-powered or confining their definition to four-wheeled vehicles. Ethnoscientists are probably correct in asserting that language shapes our perceptions; they no doubt overstated the case that all speakers of a particular language view the world in the same fashion. Finally, it bears mentioning that while ethnoscience might be considered a rigorous methodology, it engenders simply a description of a given cultural reality rather than a theory that is either explanatory or interpretive. As later postmodernists have often observed, our knowledge and perceptions are highly determined by our position in society, a fact that casts considerable doubt on the claim that ethnoscience yields an authoritative map of native culture. Indeed, this may well be one reason that ethnoscientific approaches largely waned with the rise of postmodern viewpoints in the 1980s.

Quiz yourself

Answer True or False to each statement

1 Like Marvin Harris, Clifford Geertz defines culture as human behavior and the shared traditions that guide it.
2 Geertz argues that generalizations about human thought and behavior (for example, that "all people have supernatural beliefs") are basically meaningless in that they fail to help us understand the belief systems of specific cultures.
3 According to Victor Turner, all symbols are multivocal in that they present multiple meanings to the members of society.
4 The task of anthropology, according to Geertz, is to produce a single, authoritative interpretation of culture that all readers would agree with.
5 Anthropologist William Roseberry criticizes Geertz' article on the Balinese cockfight for ignoring the broader gender, historical, and political context of Balinese (Indonesian) society.
6 According to Claude Lévi-Strauss, the "structure" that underlies all cultural behavior is a mental process involving binary oppositions.
7 According to anthropologist Sherry Ortner, "men" are on the side of "nature" because of their work outside the home, while women are on the side of "culture" because of their role in raising (enculturating) children.

14

POSTMODERN POLITICAL ECONOMY AND SENSIBILITIES

The demise of the "Enlightenment–modernist project"

Postmodernism (or what is often called poststructuralism[1] in anthropology) is not a unitary phenomenon or point of view, and for that reason is not easily discussed in a succinct fashion. It is an altered way of viewing the world that has permeated the arts, philosophy, architecture, the social sciences, and even theology, medicine, and advertising, all of which have manifested postmodern assumptions in different ways. As a starting point for examining postmodernism, we need to understand its relationship to modernity; in other words, to that which preceded it. Despite all the differences and disputes that have occurred within western science and philosophy over the last several centuries, philosopher Jürgen Habermas contends that a unified set of underlying assumptions about knowledge characterized western thought from about 1600 (Habermas 1987). This set of assumptions is what he calls "the Project of Modernity." This "project" developed during the Enlightenment, with the birth of the sciences at the beginning of the seventeenth century, and informed virtually all scientific and philosophical inquiry from then until the mid-1970s:

> The project of modernity formulated in the eighteenth century by the philosophers of the Enlightenment consisted in their efforts to develop objective science, universal morality and law, and autonomous art according to their inner logic…The Enlightenment philosophers wanted to utilize this accumulation of specialized culture for the enrichment of everyday life—that is to say, for the rational organization of everyday social life.
>
> (Habermas 1987: 149)

Hence, the Project of Modernity embraced the following aspects of knowledge, many of which we examined in the first chapter of this volume:

a) Generalization—The natural and social (human) worlds operate according to a set of underlying universal principles or laws. This claim is reflected in the notion of *positivist* science, which seeks to discover such laws through the application of observation and reason.

b) Science—scientific knowledge is indispensable for understanding the world and is superior (*privileged*) to all other forms of understanding because it is based on observation and reason. Science is capable of producing a singular truthful account of the world.

c) Objectivity—an objective reality exists independent of any observer, and all scientists are capable of producing comparable knowledge of that reality, regardless of their individual characteristics or position in society.

d) Progress—the application of scientific knowledge to human problems will result in human progress, a betterment of the human condition. Social problems, ignorance, and conflict can all be alleviated through the application of science. A belief in progress, as we have seen, originated in the Enlightenment and became a tenet of all political persuasions during the eighteenth and nineteenth centuries. From Comte, who believed that science would yield "order and progress," to Marx, who grudgingly praised capitalism for freeing society from "the isolation of rural life," modernist thinkers agreed that scientific progress would improve the conditions of people's lives.

Regardless of the discipline in which they worked or the theory that informed their scholarship, these underlying assumptions were shared by most western scholars between 1600 and the early 1970s. If one thing unites all of the theoretical perspectives that we have examined so far in cultural anthropology, from early evolution to structural functionalism, Marxism, psychological anthropology, French structuralism, and cultural materialism, it is that the social world can be explained by the application of scientific observation, which would in turn produce truthful generalizations. Since the beginning of the Enlightenment, "progress" has been reflected in the drive for mastery of the natural and social worlds through engineering and large-scale social planning. Governments of varying political ideologies have all sought progress through the application of social policy in realms as diverse as urban design, transportation, agricultural and industrial development and, of course, education. In the fields of planning and architecture, high modernism was best represented in the work of Le Corbusier (pseudonym of the Swiss-born Charles-Édouard Jeanneret-Gris, 1887–1965), who viewed the modern (planned) city as a "machine for living." His vision of the future was one in which planners and architects rationally allocated space for living, traffic, shopping, and work according to a universal set of criteria ("master plans"). Such plans were virtually identical regardless of the culture or geographical features of the region for which they were proposed—whether France, North America, Poland, Russia, or Brazil, all of which adopted variants of Le Corbusier's planning.

The effect of standardized master plans was to obliterate previously existing traditions and "irrational" uses of space and materials and to replace them with modern, more "efficient" designs. By eradicating slums and erecting housing projects, policymakers believed they could also eliminate social problems such as poverty and crime. It was Le Corbusier (and others, including the Euro-American architects of the Bauhaus school, such as Mies van der Rohe) who gave us the unadorned steel and glass "boxes" associated with modernist architecture. Le Corbusier once declared that "all ornamentation is a crime"; buildings, in other words, should be strictly functional. In 1925, he developed his *Plan Voisin* for "renovating" much of Paris, by which he favored leveling the city's older neighborhoods with their narrow, crooked streets and replacing them with freeways and high-rise housing units. Parisian authorities resisted such plans, but if he did not find a receptive audience at home, there were plenty of governments elsewhere that succumbed to his doctrines. Le Corbusier's principles became the basis for virtually all urban planning from the late 1940s onward in both the communist east and the capitalist west. In fact, upon Le Corbusier's death in 1965, US President Johnson said: "His influence was universal and his works are invested with a permanent quality possessed by those of very few artists in our history." In its obituary, *Pravda*, the official newspaper of the Soviet Union added, "Modern architecture has lost its greatest master."[2] It is interesting that during the height of the Cold War, both communists and capitalists could agree about the virtues of "scientific" urban planning.

Such doctrines have lost most of their appeal since the 1970s. Author and social critic James Howard Kunstler, who advocates a "new urbanism" that seeks to enhance, rather than diminish, the distinctive character of urban neighborhoods, has derided Le Corbusier's doctrines as destructive and ugly:

> Le Corbusier [was]…the leading architectural hoodoo-meister of Early High Modernism, whose 1925 *Plan Voisin* for Paris proposed to knock down the entire Marais district on the Right Bank and replace it with rows of identical towers set between freeways. Luckily for Paris, the city officials laughed at him every time he came back with the scheme over the next forty years—and Corb was nothing if not a relentless self-promoter. Ironically and tragically, though, the Plan Voisin model was later adopted gleefully by post-World War Two American planners, and resulted in such urban monstrosities as the infamous Cabrini Green housing projects of Chicago and scores of things similar to it around the country.
>
> (Kunstler 2010)

David Harvey and *The Condition of Postmodernity*

In his sweeping and exhaustive 1989 volume, *The Condition of Postmodernity* (humbly subtitled "An Inquiry into the Origins of Cultural Change"), CUNY geographer and anthropologist David Harvey attempts to chart the differences between the "Enlightenment–modernist" project and postmodernity. He does so through a materialist lens, examining how global economic changes since the 1970s have revolutionized our view of the world and rendered many Enlightenment

FIGURE 14.1 The Pruitt–Igoe public housing complex of St. Louis in 1956. Pruitt–Igoe was closely patterned after Le Corbusier's *Plan Voisin* for the urban renewal of Paris. © Bettmann/CORBIS.

assumptions seemingly obsolete. Symbolically, Harvey dates the emergence of postmodernity to 3:32 pm on July 15, 1972, when the federal government dynamited the Pruitt-Igoe public housing complex in St. Louis, Missouri (1989: 39). The high rise complex (Figure 14.1) had been designed by prize-winning planners in the Le Corbusier school and had been constructed to house the residents of a low income neighborhood that had been demolished to make room for a freeway. But the people who were torn from their neighborhood—once a cohesive if impoverished community—and placed in high rise apartments found the housing project alienating, dehumanizing, and unlivable. Interestingly enough, the original community from which they were relocated was racially integrated, but the public housing authority that ran the Pruitt-Igoe complex insisted that the buildings be racially segregated by bloc, with whites living in separate buildings from their former black neighbors! Designed to eradicate social problems through rational planning, Pruitt-Igoe only created new ones of vandalism, drug dealing, and other criminality. Ultimately the government was left with no alternative but to once again relocate its residents and demolish the complex.

Pruitt-Igoe came to stand for the arrogance of architects who claimed the right to impose their planning criteria on a passive and disempowered "target" population. Planners believed that local priorities and desires could effectively be disregarded because they were not based on privileged (that is, *scientific*) forms of knowledge. For Harvey, the abandonment of Pruitt-Igoe and other modernist policy schemes based on scientific principles symbolized the hubris and ultimate failure of the Project of Modernity.

BOX 14.1 James Scott: an appreciation

In his 1998 book *Seeing Like a State: How Certain Schemes to Improve the Human Condition Have Failed*, political scientist James Scott notes that modernist planning schemes have almost always been justified to an often skeptical public by invoking Enlightenment notions of progress (i.e. "This project will make your lives better! Trust us, we're engineers!") In truth, he argues, such schemes are usually motivated by the state's attempt to extend its power over its citizens by deepening their dependence on it and undermining earlier bonds of community, kinship, and belief. If state planning represented science and reason, then "primordial" bonds of kinship and community were "prescientific," "irrational," and "anti-modern."

Among the failed modernist policies that Scott identifies were the Soviet Union's collectivization of agriculture during the 1930s, when independent peasants were brutally uprooted and turned into wage laborers on huge, inefficiently run state farms. He also mentions "utopian" planned cities in which no one wanted to live, such as Brasilia—the unpopular and unpopulated inland capital of Brazil—and the communist-era Czech city of Zlin, both of which were designed by members of Le Corbusier's architectural studio (Figure 14.2). Among other grandiose state-run schemes, Scott also mentions educational curricula that are standardized across entire nations and that

FIGURE 14.2 The Three Powers Plaza and Presidential Palace in Brasilia, a capital city designed from scratch by modernist architects beginning in 1956. The city is noted for its huge expanses between buildings and the fact that it is almost impossible to reach any destination on foot (notice the absence of any people in this photo). Despite its status as the country's capital, it empties out during the weekends, as government workers head home to the more lively (livable?) cities of Rio de Janeiro or São Paulo. © Robert Harding Picture Library Ltd/Alamy.

continued...

Box 14.1 continued

measure results in standard test scores rather than critical thinking (his book was published before "No Child Left Behind," but clearly that would fall under this category).

Although he is a political scientist, most of Scott's publications are based on ethnographic field research conducted in Southeast Asia. Indeed, I count him among my favorite ethnographers, mainly because (unlike some of my fellow anthropologists) his incisive thinking is wedded to such clear writing. Scott is well known for his 1985 book *Weapons of the Weak: Everyday Forms of Peasant Resistance*. In it, he addressed the question of peasant rebellion, a topic that interested many anthropologists (such as Eric Wolf) during the 1960s and 70s. Why, he asked, do peasants appear to put up with unspeakable misery and oppression instead of rising up to challenge their overlords? After all, overt rebellions are fairly rare given the number of peasants in the world and the conditions under which they live. Some, such as anthropologist George Dalton (1974), argued that the absence of open rebellion demonstrates that many anthropologists have simply exaggerated the degree of oppression that peasants experience. Similarly, Gramsci would argue that peasants are the victims of hegemonic ideas that lead them to accept the social order in which they live. Scott challenged these notions by pointing out the overwhelming retaliation of states and overlords, who usually crush open rebellions with exceptionally violent methods. For example, a peasant protest in El Salvador in January, 1932, in which several hundred Pipil Indians stormed a garrison and demanded agrarian reform, ended with the Salvadoran government's massacre of 40,000 people in retaliation over a period of months. So why don't peasants rebel? Simply put, they know what the stakes are when they overtly challenge authority, and they prefer to remain alive, thank you very much.

Beneath that veneer of apparent acceptance, however, Scott showed that peasants deploy an extensive repertoire of strategies to express their discontent. These include a host of individualistic and often much harder-to-detect tactics, such as sabotage, theft, foot-dragging, dissembling, arson, "feigned ignorance," and other actions that employers and the state find infuriatingly difficult to eradicate. Soldiers who weary of war simply desert, or may self-inflict an injury that will get them sent home.

Think of all the things you've done on your own low-wage, humiliating jobs to either get out of work or get back at the boss. How many of us goof off on the job or surf the internet until a co-worker whispers, "hey, the boss is coming! Look busy" (Figure 14.3). These strategies are what Scott calls "weapons of the weak" and "everyday forms of peasant resistance." On a large-enough scale, such individual actions of non-compliance constitute an "avalanche" of social discontent that can change the course of history.

FIGURE 14.3   "Jesus is coming. Look busy." Of course, unlike your boss, Jesus *always* knows when you're goofing off! Courtesy of the artist, April Hopkins.

After noting how conscripted French peasants became difficult to retain in Bonaparte's ranks as the Napoleonic wars dragged on year after year, Scott extends his analysis to US history. He argues that a key factor leading to the defeat of the Confederacy during the Civil War was not military superiority by Federal forces, but mass desertions by poor Southern whites who simply left their army ranks and went home. Such men were not slave owners themselves and were subject to conscription, while the owners of 20 or more slaves were automatically exempted from military service by law! This double standard, as you can imagine, was not exactly a morale builder for your average footsoldier told to charge into a wall of musket fire at Gettysburg. Scott writes:

> The collapse of the Confederate army and economy in the course of the Civil War in the United States is a further example of the decisive role of silent and undeclared defections. Nearly 250,000 eligible whites were estimated to have deserted or to have avoided conscription altogether… Poor whites, especially those from the non-slaveholding hill country, were deeply resentful of fighting for an institution whose principal beneficiaries were excluded from service by law…On the plantations themselves, the shortage of white overseers and the slaves' natural affinity with the North's objective, gave rise to shirking and flight on a massive scale. As in France, one could claim that the Confederacy was undone by a social avalanche of petty acts of insubordination carried out by an unlikely coalition of slaves and yeomen…
>
> (1985: 30)

Postmodernism, Harvey says, is a broad cultural shift in the assumptions by which we seek to understand the world, comparable to the cultural shift that took place in the Enlightenment after 1600. It is expressed in all fields, ranging from art to architecture to music, philosophy, and the social sciences. Aesthetically, postmodernism seeks to break with the aesthetic styles of the past that emphasized uniformity and consistency. Modernist architecture of the twentieth century created spare functional styles devoid of ornament: buildings were steel, glass, and concrete structures that corresponded to Le Corbusier's "machine for living." A high rise built anywhere in the United States during the 1950s–60s looked much like a high rise built anywhere else in the United States, or in the western world, for that matter. On the other hand, postmodern architecture stresses distinctiveness, embracing a variety of styles taken from different historical and local contexts. Ornament and often whimsical features replace spare function (Figure 14.4). Postmodern art breaks with the notion that a work should reflect a single style of representation (whether realist, impressionist, cubist, etc.). Instead, a postmodern painting may be a collage of different styles representing different historical periods.

Most importantly *for the purposes of anthropology*, postmodern philosophy rejects the assumptions of the Enlightenment–modernist project involving rationality,

FIGURE 14.4 Completed in 1991, the Harold Washington Public Library in Chicago evidences the postmodern urge for ornamentation and historical "quotation." Notice the "acroteria" ornaments on the roof and cornices of the building. From a distance the acroteria resemble medieval gargoyles in their placement, but closer up you can see that they represent owls—a symbol of knowledge—and corn stalks, representing the Midwest. The windows feature Romanesque arches of classical antiquity. Other features of the building intentionally mimic aspects of famous nineteenth-century buildings throughout Chicago. I admit that I love this building, but others find it grotesque. Postmodern architecture and art tend to inspire such contrasting reactions in people. © B.O'Kane/Alamy.

objectivity, and progress. Postmodernists argue that humans cannot know about the world in ways that are not tinged by their particular perspective or bias. Knowledge is socially constructed, in that it is the product of the individual's position in society, with regard to their race, gender, social class, other identity, and experience. Postmodern critics claim that the sciences have simply taken the knowledge claims of dominant groups (usually white European males) and privileged them above all other groups. Science "delicenses" the claims to knowledge of all other groups, notably women, minorities, colonized people, and others lacking access to power. The signature philosophical stance of postmodernism is thus a profound distrust about the claims of science to produce reliable knowledge and to bring about a betterment of the human condition. Indeed, one of the most prominent achievements of twentieth-century science, some postmodernists argue, has simply been more effective and efficient ways of killing, controlling, or impoverishing greater numbers of people.

What is the cause of this shift in knowledge? Postmodernists themselves reject any explanatory account of culture, claiming that all such efforts (whether Marxist, Freudian, structural-functional, cultural ecological, etc.) comprise a western scientific "metanarrative" that privileges the white, western, usually male scientist over the Other whose culture is being "explained." However, David Harvey (Figure 14.5) has tried to explain *why* postmodern ideas have flourished in the late twentieth century. He has done so from a Marxist perspective, examining the rise of postmodern sentiments and philosophies (i.e. ideology) in terms of changes in the underlying material basis of society. In other words, he identifies the rise of postmodern aesthetics and assumptions as a result of changes in late-twentieth-century capitalism, specifically arising since the 1970s. These trends include:

a) The perception that the pace of social change is steadily increasing while geographical distances are shrinking, a condition that he refers to as "*time–space" compression* (Harvey 1989: 147). We all know that we seem to have less and less time available to us, and that the pace of change has increased. In fact, these changes outpace our ability to make sense of them. Consider changes in computing and telecommunications hardware, so that today's "state of the art" computer or cell phone is "obsolete" in six months. Harvey's point is that the pace of social change has accelerated to the point that by the time we analyze and understand conditions in the world around us that understanding is often no longer applicable. The world, in a sense, has become a moving target where knowledge is concerned.

b) A perception that national boundaries are increasingly fluid and even meaningless. We see this in many ways: our ability to communicate instantaneously with any part of the world, our near-instantaneous awareness of developments in other regions, and the fact that a homogenized global consumer culture is emerging based on McDonalds, Coca Cola, and Levis.

c) The increased ethnic diversity of most states. Postmodernists refer to this as increased awareness of the "Other," meaning anyone different from us in culture, language, appearance, and experience. But we're not just more

FIGURE 14.5 Trained in geography at Cambridge, David Harvey (born in Kent, England, in 1935) is currently Distinguished Professor of Anthropology at the City University of New York. He is among the top 20 most cited authors in the Humanities, and his book *The Condition of Postmodernity* was identified by *The Independent* as one of the 50 most important scholarly works published since 1945. Bear in mind that Harvey does not subscribe to postmodernism himself; in fact, he feels that it obscures our understanding of the world more than it clarifies it. Nonetheless, he is fascinated with the pervasiveness of postmodern viewpoints in so many realms of knowledge and has strived to account for why this kind of thinking is now so dominant. Photo courtesy of David Harvey.

aware of cultural diversity than we were 20 years ago; the fact is that most developed nations are much more diverse places than they formerly were. Between 1969 and 2010, an estimated 25 million immigrants legally entered the United States, most of them from Latin America and Asia. During that time, the number of immigrants living in the US more than quadrupled. Without these trends, the US population would be declining slightly rather than growing, while in western Europe, child-bearing among native-born white Europeans is well below replacement level. Were it not for an influx of migrants from Africa, the Middle East, and Eastern Europe, Europe would be a dying continent. It is no coincidence that the election of the United States' first African-American president has been attributed, in part, to an increasingly multi-cultural electorate.

d) Various economic trends associated with postmodernism, which point to growing stratification and a disappearing middle class. These include downward mobility, in which the economic prospects of those entering the job market are worse than those of their parents. We have also witnessed sharply declining real incomes and benefits for most wage earners; instability of employment due to layoffs and downsizing; and widening disparities between rich and poor. For many sectors of society, even before the severe recession that began in 2008, there was a level of economic anxiety unknown since the Great Depression.

Harvey argues that all of these trends associated with postmodernism are rooted in the contemporary configuration of capitalism, one that has emerged since the 1970s. Remember that from a Marxist perspective, to understand a society's prevailing ideas (its ideological aspects, including the distinctive world view associated with postmodern society) requires us to examine the economic and social context in which they occurred. Harvey argues that since the early 1970s, metropolitan capitalism (that is, capitalism as practiced in the developed countries of North America and Europe) has undergone a shift in its "mode of regulation." Marxists refer to this as the rules and processes by which investment and capital accumulation take place at a given point in history; it is basically the "rules of the game" under which capitalism is organized. Ultimately, Harvey argues, postmodernity originates in a change in the mode of regulation by which capitalism has operated since the early 1970s.

Recall from our earlier discussion that Marx identified an inherent tendency toward crisis in capitalism. During the nineteenth century, when workers enjoyed few rights and governments abstained from any regulation of capitalist economies, Marx argued that these crises would result in deepening misery among working people, culminating in a social revolution. And indeed, the history of unregulated capitalism was one of periodic economic crises. By 1932, with western economies in the midst of the deepest crisis they had ever experienced, many believed that Marx's predictions were about to come true. But the following year also marked the end of the first capitalist mode of regulation, one of laissez faire, which entailed a minimum of government regulation of the economy.

As we saw earlier, both government and business acted to reform capitalism during the 1930s. Among these changes were greater federal protection of the right of workers to organize unions, leading to increased wages, benefits, and shorter hours, all of which reduced the appeal of more radical solutions to economic crisis. The federal government also introduced Social Security retirement and disability benefits, unemployment insurance, and long-term home financing, turning a nation of renters into a nation of homeowners. And, as we also saw, some employers, such as Henry Ford, recognized their own long-term self-interest in policies that supported higher wages for their workers. "Fordist mass consumption" involved steadily rising wages, allowing workers to purchase goods that could previously only be owned by a wealthy few—such as the automobile! By the end of the Great Depression, Harvey notes, a Fordist mode of regulation came to prevail in the industrialized economies of the west. This mode of regulation not only limited class conflict, but helped overcome the periodic crises of under-consumption in capitalism, which earlier had arisen from companies' efforts to hold down wages. In other words, according to Harvey, the Fordist mode of regulation that was in place by the end of the 1930s sought to resolve the contradictions of capitalism that Marx had identified in the nineteenth century. This mode of regulation persisted for decades, and was accompanied by rising wages and living standards for most working class Americans.

One attribute of Fordist mass consumption was the cultivation of corporate brand loyalty, something that you see vividly portrayed on the current television series "Mad Men," set in a New York advertising agency in the early 1960s. When I was growing up in suburban Chicago during that decade, you identified yourself by the products you consumed, largely because of the images and emotions cultivated by mass advertising. But this trend to self-identify in terms of consumption really all began in the 1940s with Fordist mass consumption and its attendant advertising to promote the products of American industry.

Sure, in my suburban home town of Palatine, Illinois, we were Lutheran or Catholic, Irish or German (how's that for ethnic diversity?). But besides that, you were a Ford family or a GM family, although we did allow a few Chryslers in the neighborhood. Nobody, and I mean *nobody*, in my town drove a foreign car, except for one eccentric woman who owned a VW beetle. We were pretty sure she was a communist. You drank Old Style, Miller, or Schlitz. You smoked Luckys, Camels, or Kools (the latter was the choice of our family physician, who often smoked when seeing patients in his examining room!). Marlboros in those days were originally pitched as a "women's cigarette"; the rugged "Marlboro man" had not yet come into existence, much less developed lung cancer. My colleague David Gartman points out in his book *Auto Opium* (1994) that General Motors cleverly arranged the pricing and features of its brands in terms of the upward mobility that Americans had come to expect by the late 1940s. The idea was that when you were starting out in your career, you would buy a Chevy, then as you moved up professionally, you would graduate to a Pontiac, then an Oldsmobile, then a Buick, and finally—as you were closing in on retirement—you would acquire that ultimate symbol of status, a Cadillac. But my dad stuck with Buicks. He thought it appeared vulgar to strive beyond your means.

What about my family? We might have started out as Swedish and Czech immigrant working class people in my great-grandparent's day, but thanks to Fordist mass consumption by the time I was growing up we were Buick-driving, martini-drinking, middle class suburbanites (gin and vermouth please. We knew all about those subversive people who drank vodka martinis). Oh, and my dad smoked unfiltered Camels until the Surgeon General's 1964 report on lung cancer. After that, he switched to a "more soothing" menthol filtered brand on the advice of our good family doctor. Literally my earliest memory was of the night that my dad brought home his first new car. It was December, 1962, and as he came home from work one night he stopped at the dealership to pick up the 1963 Buick LeSabre that he had specially ordered from the factory months before. I still remember sitting in my astronaut pajamas in the picture window of our home waiting for the headlights to appear. Once he pulled in the driveway, my mother bundled us up and we all trooped out into the cold night to admire the car's special custom-ordered interior. Dad had even splurged on such "optional extras" as rear seat belts! The federal government did not require rear seat belts as standard equipment on cars until 1965.

If you had a sudden stop and bashed your head against the dashboard, you just hosed it off (the dashboard, that is) and went on your way. If you were to visit our family doctor to treat your concussion, he would probably just prescribe an extra martini for that night.

But 1969 was the personal high point of Fordist mass consumption. It was the year dad traded in the LeSabre and brought home a new Buick Electra 225, named after its enormous 225 inch length and fondly known by GM aficionados as a "Deuce and a Quarter." It was the biggest car Buick made, and it employed the same body frame as a Cadillac Fleetwood. Clearly, we had "arrived." Six years later, as a high school junior, that was the car that I learned to drive in. Thirteen years later I cruised across the country in it from Chicago to Los Angeles when I began graduate school. Sadly, as cars tend to do in the upper Midwest, it rusted away by the late 1980s even while the drive train just kept chugging. I think it had about 3½ billion miles on it by then.

Forty years to the month after my dad drove home our new Electra, I purchased a 1969 Deuce and a Quarter on eBay from an owner in California. It is my own piece of the pinnacle of Fordist mass consumption (Figure 14.6).

Beneath the hood she has the original 430 cubic inch V–8 engine paired with a four-barrel carburetor to deliver 360 horsepower. What a hypocritical thing for a liberal environmentalist to be driving, right? Be assured that I can only afford to drive her down hill, and only then when there is a stiff tailwind. This is more along the lines of what anthropologists would call a sacred object than a mode of transportation.

FIGURE 14.6   "Luna," a fitting name, I think, given the original 1969 Buick "trumpet gold" paint code, and the fact that year's signature event was the Apollo landing. The name was suggested to me by a student in my Anthropological Theory class. Photo courtesy of the author.

Time–space compression

Even as proud UAW members were putting together my 69 Deuce and a Quarter on the Buick assembly line in Flint, Michigan, Fordism was under siege by some unanticipated developments. Increasingly, much of the formerly colonized world—particularly Latin America and Asia—was becoming industrialized, and entering into competition with US and European industry. Third World industries were often successful in this competition for markets because the local wage structure (i.e. one based on extensive poverty and political repression, which kept workers from organizing and kept wages low) allowed them to turn out products for a fraction of the cost of comparable items manufactured in the developed countries. The oil crisis of 1973, induced by an embargo of western countries by OPEC because of the West's support for Israel in that year's "Yom Kippur" war, resulted in dramatic rises in the cost of petroleum for industries and consumers.

In 1973, gas prices went in a few weeks from 39 cents a gallon to $1.80—when you could find it! (That would be equivalent in real terms to about $8.00 a gallon today.) The US automobile industry, in particular, was caught off-guard as Americans stopped buying Detroit's gas-guzzlers, finding that the Japanese already offered a more economical product. Industries in the developed countries were forced to restructure in ways that reduced production costs and/or increased profits. It's no coincidence that American cars of the 1970s suffered a huge decline in quality, as competition with the Japanese led to cost-cutting in raw materials among the US manufacturers. Some of the US "economy" cars of the time were absolutely perverse, such as the American Motors aptly-named "Gremlin." Readers who are familiar with the term know that it originated during World War II to refer to some undiagnosed but persistent problem with mechanical equipment (an engine that would mysteriously stall or electrical system that would fail on a bomber). They might as well have named it the AMC Lemon or "Kick Me!"

But in general, during the early to mid-1970s, US firms found it necessary to reduce inventories, reduce workforces through automation and sub-contracting, and employ resources and labor more flexibly. Fordism, which had guaranteed much of the working class full-time employment and continuously rising wages, was one of the first victims of this restructuring. One response to the economic crisis of the early 1970s was to abandon it for a new mode of regulation, which Harvey refers to as "flexible accumulation." Flexible accumulation sought to bolster capitalist profits in two ways: a) by lowering the production costs associated with manufacturing, and b) by expanding markets for goods. The most obvious way to reduce costs meant moving production abroad to take advantage of lower wages in the Third World. This became possible by the 1970s due to transportation and shipping innovations; notably, the development of containerized shipping and cargo jet transport. It is hard to believe now, but until the advent of jetliners at the end of the 1950s only one piston engine aircraft, the Lockheed Constellation (introduced just before the jet age in 1957), was able to complete a coast-to-coast nonstop flight. Before then, flying times in piston engine aircraft from New York to Los Angeles on the fastest routes were about 12 hours and required a refueling stop.

The first US commercial jet airliner to enter service in the United States was the Boeing 707, followed soon after by a similar aircraft, the Douglas DC–8. American Airlines introduced the 707 to domestic service in early 1959 with a coast-to-coast flight time of four hours. Pan Am introduced the 707 a few months earlier on its New York to Paris run, completing the transatlantic flight in a miraculous seven hours. Despite these developments, the US did not pioneer in the development of jetliners. The revolutionary British de Havilland Comet commercial jet entered service over Europe in 1952, but within two years it was withdrawn after a series of disastrous crashes. Can you tell that I'm a bit of an aviation buff?

With the advent of the new jets, no place on earth was more than 24 hours distant from any other place, making possible an unprecedented movement of goods and people. It now became possible for North American consumers to purchase fresh winter fruits, vegetables, fresh fish, and even cut flowers grown or harvested in South and Central America. All of these are transported daily from South to North via numerous 747 cargo jets. Before the advent of such large-capacity cargo jets in the late 1960s, we simply didn't have access in supermarkets to lettuce, strawberries, grapes, broccoli, or really any fresh vegetables or fruits between about November and April.

Containerized shipping dramatically lowered transport costs by eliminating any need to load and unload tens of thousands of individual goods of varying sizes and weights from the holds of ships and then reload them on trucks and trains. Instead, containers are loaded directly at a factory in China, stacked by crane onto a ship in Shanghai, shipped across the Pacific, transferred by crane onto a rail car in the US and sent directly to a retailer's warehouse. From there the container is trucked directly to a retail store. The container is not opened until it actually reaches the retailer, an innovation that cut the shipping costs of goods to a small fraction of their former level. This in turn meant that companies were no longer tied to particular locales, but could move manufacturing worldwide to take advantage of lower wage rates. For the first time, it became profitable for US-based companies to manufacture and ship durable consumer goods—ranging from portable electronics to televisions and automobiles—from other countries with a vastly lower wage structure.

But this process of economic globalization was not simply the result of technological changes in shipping, manufacturing, and communication (Figure 14.7). It involved a dismantling of an international economic consensus dating from 1944, established at the Bretton Woods (New Hampshire) economic conference. It was at this meeting, held toward the end of World War II, at which the outlines of the postwar economic order were negotiated among representatives of 45 allied nations. The conference's priorities were guided by the Fordist doctrines of economic planning then dominant in the United States and Great Britain. So that national governments could achieve their social and political objectives, including the creation of social welfare systems and postwar rebuilding, Bretton Woods established exchange controls and a system of tariffs and other forms of trade "protection" that limited the capacity of corporations and individuals to move investment capital across borders. As the Bretton Woods conferees recognized, if corporations were able to

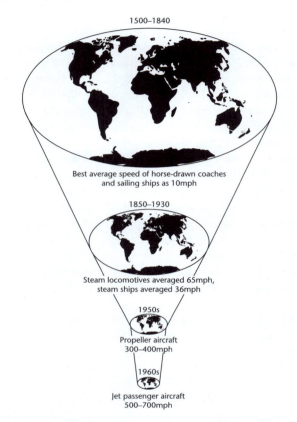

1500–1840

Best average speed of horse-drawn coaches
and sailing ships as 10mph

1850–1930

Steam locomotives averaged 65mph,
steam ships averaged 36mph

1950s
Propeller aircraft
300–400mph

1960s
Jet passenger aircraft
500–700mph

FIGURE 14.7   David Harvey's representation of how changes in transportation technology
have, in effect, "shrunk" the world since the early nineteenth century (1989: 241). Here's
a great example of this process in terms of transportation and communication. The Treaty
of Ghent, which ended the War of 1812 between Britain and the United States, was
signed in Belgium on December 24, 1814. Long before news of the treaty could reach
the United States by sail ship, British forces attacked New Orleans. The assault led to
the famous Battle at Chalmette Plantation on January 8, 1815, with heavily entrenched
American forces under the command of Andrew Jackson. The British suffered more
than 2,000 casualties, including almost all of their officer staff. (Most fallen soldiers were
buried near the site, but the body of General Packenham, the British commander, was
embalmed in a barrel of rum and sent home for burial.) More than another month of
fighting in North America was to continue before the combatants learned that they had
actually been "at peace" since the previous December! Today, of course, news travels so
quickly via the internet that Michael Jackson's death in 2009 was noted on his Wikipedia
entry even before the media reported it. Courtesy of Wiley-Blackwell.

easily shift their financial resources from one country to another, governments would be hamstrung in their ability to impose the tax policies critical to economic planning. In addition, tariffs on goods produced more cheaply elsewhere allowed national governments to protect their own industries and jobs within their borders. But by the early 1970s, the advent of jet transport and containerized shipping had created *a politically powerful constituency*, mostly of major corporations in the USA and Western Europe, that favored dismantling such regulations as a way to expand their investments abroad. These forces secured a critical victory in 1973, when the US government abandoned fixed exchange rates and allowed its currency to freely "float" against others. With the world's largest economy opting out of the Bretton Woods framework, all other industrial capitalist nations eventually followed suit. The year 1973 then marked the emergence of a truly global economy, in which investment capital was free for the first time to seek out areas of the world that offered the highest possible profits.

In addition, corporations strongly favored the negotiation of "free trade" policies eliminating tariff barriers and trade restrictions between countries. These policies have been introduced through trade pacts such as the North American Free Trade Agreement (NAFTA) and are reinforced by bodies such as the World Trade Organization. Organized in 1994, the WTO has binding arbitration authority over the world's governments. If one government feels that another has imposed an "unfair" barrier to trade through, for example, tariffs designed to keep out foreign goods in order to protect domestic manufacturers, the WTO can adjudicate that dispute. Should it find in favor of the plaintiff it can order the removal of the "unfair" tariffs or allow the plaintiff to impose its own retaliatory trade measures. In effect, the WTO has removed most countries' sovereignty over their own economies.

All of these policies ruptured the so-called "labor–capital" social pact that had been in place since the 1930s, in which manufacturers had conceded wage increases to organized labor in exchange for rising productivity. In those manufacturing industries that remained in the developed countries, unions soon came under attack. In August, 1981, the Reagan administration fired over 11,000 striking air traffic controllers, after which their union was decertified. After the President essentially signaled to employers that it was acceptable to break unions by firing strikers, it became commonplace during the 1980s and 90s for companies to compel workers to go on strike—usually by demanding steep wage and benefit concessions that unions were unwilling to accept—and then replace them with strikebreakers. In other cases, companies resorted to lay-offs of full-time workers, replacing them with temporaries, or shifting production to sub-contractors in the Third World. Today, record numbers of workers in the developed countries are temporary, part-time, and minimum wage.[3] Right after Walmart, the largest employer in the United States is now Manpower International, a temporary labor service. The consequences of this shift are seen in the demise of older industrial centers, steeply declining real wages and rates of unionization, and huge, growing disparities between rich and poor. Since 1973, private sector wages have deteriorated more than 40 percent in real (inflation-adjusted) terms. This is the "brutal" part of flexible accumulation, the part whose consequences are apparent to virtually everyone who remembers the heyday of Fordist mass consumption, permanent life-long employment, and steadily rising wages in the 1950s and 60s.

What have been the effects of this restructuring of the work force in cultural terms? Harvey points out that our awareness of the "Other" has grown with the widening socioeconomic disparities since the 1970s. Immigration into the United States has sharply accelerated in recent years. Many of these new immigrants have been displaced by free trade policies such as NAFTA and CAFTA (the Central American Free Trade Agreement), which have destroyed subsistence agriculture in Mexico, Central America, and the Caribbean. In large part this is because as a condition of NAFTA, Mexico was forced to abandon its tariffs on US maize, by which it had protected the livelihoods of subsistence farmers that make up much of the rural population. Forced off the land by cheap US-grown corn, many former peasants see no alternative but to go "al Norte." Indeed, while NAFTA was partly sold to skeptical members of Congress as a measure that would shore up the Mexican economy and stem immigration, immigration from Mexico has actually soared in the wake of the trade law. Immigrants have been consciously recruited by employers who find that their insecurity allows companies to lower wages even more. In the Midwest, for example, meatpacking was once the preserve of well-paid unionized jobs, invariably held by white working class men. It is now the domain of minimum-wage (and sometimes sub-minimum wage) immigrant labor from Latin America and Asia. Other, more privileged immigrants are well-educated English-speaking software designers and other white-collar workers—mainly recruited from South Asia—insatiably demanded by the information and service sectors that have replaced heavy manufacturing.

Finally, within the US population, substantial sectors of the working and middle classes (*especially* minorities) have found themselves sliding into marginal jobs or long-term unemployment. African-American men, who traditionally made up much of the manufacturing and low-skill labor sectors, have been displaced by the export of manufacturing jobs and influx of immigrants into low wage employment. After expanding in size during the 1970s and early 80s, the black middle class has actually shrunk both in numbers and as a percentage of the black population. The result of all of these trends has been downward mobility for many formerly middle-class people into low-wage labor, and in many cases, into unemployment and homelessness. Readers may find this *impossible* to believe, but I never met an involuntarily homeless person until my first visit to Mexico City in 1978, and not because I led a sheltered existence. As a teen, I spent nearly every weekend in various parts of Chicago, including some very low income neighborhoods. Yes, there were some Americans—mostly drug addicts and hard-core alcoholics—who lived on the streets, but no one who was otherwise functional and capable of work. The "homeless" as a social category comprised of millions of people who could not afford housing *simply did not exist* in the United States until the 1980s. There is probably no category of people in our society considered more alien and threateningly different than the homeless: indeed, the homeless are *cognitively* threatening because they remind us of how insecure all of us are before prevailing economic changes. It is perhaps no surprise that as individuals they are often targeted for random violence by other, more comfortable members of society. In all these ways, the creation of "Others" in our midst occurs continuously under flexible accumulation.

The other way in which corporations have responded to growing competition for markets depends on generating ever-new demand for products. This has had much more subtle effects than union busting and the export of manufacturing. Here the goal of industry is to accelerate the turnover time of production and consumption: in other words, to produce things more rapidly than before, to change product lines and styles more quickly, and thereby encourage consumers to buy and abandon goods increasingly often. These changes usually involve superficial alterations to existing products, or even just changes in packaging ("Same great taste, brand new look!"). Increasing the turnover time of production has led to major changes in the organization of work. As already noted, employers rely more heavily on temporary workers, so that the workforce can be expanded or reduced on short notice. Workers are also trained flexibly so they can be reassigned from one task to another. This strategy has involved changes in the types of goods produced. Increasingly, investment capital has shifted from durable consumer goods to the production of short-term services (for example, the entertainment industry), disposable items, and fashions subject to rapid planned obsolescence. Meanwhile, retailers have stimulated consumption through a constant turnover of inventory. In the mid–1950s, less than 5 percent of all items in retail stores were sold at a discount from the sticker price; currently, the figure is closer to 40 percent.

Who provides the demand for such things? Certainly not the increasing numbers of minimum wage and temporary workers. The 1980s and 90s were marked by a massive upward redistribution of wealth: in the US, almost 90 percent of the new wealth created during the 1980s alone went to the wealthiest 7 percent of the population. The percentage of wealth controlled by the top 1 percent of the population more than doubled between 1970 and 2000 (from 6 percent of the total to 14 percent). This trend has accelerated since 2002 because of an increasingly regressive tax code and falling real wages for most workers. The *nouveau riche* and "yuppies" that have emerged following the demise of Fordism are the primary market for these items. In the shift from durable goods to rapidly obsolescent fashion has emerged, according to Harvey, the "instability and fleeting qualities of a post modernist aesthetic that celebrates difference, ephemerality, [and] spectacle" (1989: 156).

A second factor that augments these trends has been quantum advances in telecommunications. Television and the internet have become the primary mediums by which desires are generated for the flood of goods turned out under flexible accumulation. But television, computers, and satellite communications have not only barraged us with seductive images of new goods; they have also changed our perception of the world. Satellite communication has compressed our perception of the world into near-simultaneous images that subvert established barriers of time and space, cause and effect, and reality and advertisement. We find ourselves, for example, in the unprecedented situation of watching events, such as the terror attacks of 9/11 and the Iraq and Afghan Wars, in real time. During the initial invasion of Iraq in 2003, we watched people dying on the battlefield and bombs falling at the very instant they were happening. We view such events of life and death on a medium that is otherwise primarily for entertainment. As a result, the world takes on a kind of intense unreality. Indeed, postmodernity has given us a new term for the blending of genres that result from modern telecommunications: "infotainment." The increased turnover time of contemporary capitalism, together with an increasing penetration of our daily lives by electronic media, have altered both our desires and perception of the world. Postmodern philosopher Jean Baudrillard (1994) has argued that the proliferation of media images of glossy, opulent settings populated by physically perfect individuals has created a world of meanings, behaviors, and objects that have no real counterpart in the lives of most people. Advertising and an increasingly entertainment-oriented media hold up such objects as universally desirable and even necessary, although for the vast majority of humanity they are unattainable.

As a result of advances in telecommunications, transportation, and the rapid change of product styling, flexible accumulation has contributed to a sense of heightened "time–space compression," what Harvey terms "processes that so revolutionize the objective qualities of space and time that we are forced to alter… how we represent the world to ourselves" (1989: 240). His point is that "the history of capitalism has been characterized by speed-up in the pace of life, while so overcoming spatial barriers that the world sometimes seems to collapse inwards upon us" (ibid.). Harvey's observations here mirror those of the science fiction writer Alvin Toffler, who was already referring to the US as a "throwaway society" by 1970. Toffler argued then that people now experience more events within a given interval than at any time in the past. What effects does this have on individual psychology? One is a growing "temporariness in …both public and private value systems…and the diversification of values within a fragmenting society" (Harvey 1989: 286). Another is a kind of sensory overload, in which the present changes so quickly that the individual ceases to be able to understand it clearly. The nature of the media (television and the internet) by which we view the world leads us to conflate entertainment, fact, and advertisement. Another observer, Charles Panati, warns that increasing turnover time has drastic effects on the individual's psychology, perceptions, and relationships:

> At no previous time in history has humankind experienced such rapidfire and costly turnover. Rapid obsolescence may have other consequences. Psychologists believe that the fast turnover of products can breed a mentality of short-term reasoning, philosophy, and expectations that infiltrates all aspects of life. In our relationships, will we replace each other long before our actual usefulness and lifetime are up?

> (1989: 176)

Another aspect of postmodern aesthetics—their constant allusion to the past— also makes sense under these conditions. Nostalgia, Harvey observes, is represented in everything from a proliferation of museums as a form of entertainment to the incorporation of "retro" styles in a wide range of consumer goods. Nostalgia stems from the fact that the past seems much simpler, more stable, and easier to understand than the present. I think this is why middle-aged guys who sense that somehow things were better in earlier decades (and for many of them, it was) come over to talk about my new old car when I stop to fill its tank, every dozen miles or so.

This, Harvey notes, is precisely the kind of environment of uncertainty and flux in which postmodern epistemologies can flourish. By the time books are published, for example, they are already often out of date. As he observes, "it is impossible to say anything of solidity and permanence in the midst of this ephemeral and fragmented world...Everything, from novel writing and philosophizing to the experience of laboring or making a home has to face the challenge of accelerating turnover time and the rapid write-off of traditional and historically acquired values. The temporary contract in everything...then becomes the hallmark of postmodern living" (Harvey 1989: 291).

Finally, I would point out that the sense of transience and ephemerality associated with postmodern aesthetics is also accelerated by the impact of flexible accumulation on our daily lives. A major consequence of declining real wages has been the nearly universal two-income household, or households in which members hold multiple jobs. During a stop on his re-election campaign in 2004, President Bush encountered a woman who told him that she had three jobs and her husband had two. The President commented that "this is a truly American story," seemingly out of admiration for the woman's work ethic. But the impact of these trends on domestic life has been nothing less than shattering in many cases. The inability of many American married couples to spend significant amounts of time communicating or engaged in leisure together must certainly contribute to the soaring divorce rates in our society. With our domestic arrangements constantly in flux through separation, divorce, remarriage, and "blended" and "unblended" families, the sense of permanence that was once associated with high modernist Fordism has vanished from the fabric of our daily lives as well.

Quiz yourself

Answer True or False to each statement

1 The "Enlightenment–modernist" project entailed a commitment to science, and a belief that its application would result in social progress.
2 Although modernist social planning and architecture were prevalent in the capitalist countries of the twentieth century, they were rejected as "bourgeois" by communist governments.
3 In *Seeing Like a State*, James Scott argues that governments often adopt large-scale projects in order to render their citizens more dependent on the state and to better control them.

4   In *Weapons of the Weak*, Scott contends that peasants usually do not openly rebel because in most circumstances they are satisfied with social and economic conditions.

5   Postmodern architecture, as in Chicago's Public Library, shuns adornment and stresses strict functional utility.

6   According to David Harvey, the response of western governments to the Great Depression fundamentally changed the "mode of regulation" by which capitalism was organized.

7   Although Fordism gradually came to an end during the 1970s and 80s, the incomes of most working people in the United States have continued to rise since then.

8   By creating hundreds of thousands of new jobs in Mexico, free trade pacts such as NAFTA have had the effect of slowing Mexican immigration to the United States.

9   Jet transport and containerized shipping created strong incentives for US manufacturers to move their operations to areas of lower wages in Latin America and Asia.

10   According to Harvey, one effect of "flexible accumulation" has been increased reliance on the "turnover time of production and consumption," which creates the impression of an accelerating rate of social change.

15

THE CONTEMPORARY
ANTHROPOLOGICAL MOMENT

Foucault's skepticism: the signature stance of postmodernity

If the "Enlightenment–modernist" project was characterized by an abiding commitment to rationality, science, and progress, many anthropologists since the advent of postmodernity have expressed a profound skepticism toward claims of objectivity in the understanding of culture. The roots of this approach in anthropology are associated with European (mostly French) philosophers and social theorists, although, as we've seen, they were also anticipated to some extent by the interpretive anthropology of Clifford Geertz and even earlier linguistic anthropologists. *Hermeneutics* is the basis of many of the recent critiques of scientific anthropology as it has been traditionally practiced. It is the branch of philosophy that studies the interpretation of meaning; in this sense, hermeneutics is a philosophical counterpart to literary theory, which involves the interpretation of texts for their symbolic and substantive content. Following the claims of German philosopher Martin Heidegger (1889–1976), the hermeneutic perspective holds that an individual's knowledge of the world is always conditioned by his or her culture, identity, and social position. Heidegger explicitly rejected the western cultural tradition that emphasizes reason and objectivity as means of understanding the world. Above all, for Heidegger, language and the culture in which it is rooted are the key elements guiding our interpretation of the world. We have already encountered a variant of this argument independently in the linguistic relativity hypothesis of American linguists Edward Sapir and Benjamin Lee Whorf. In a sense, European postmodern philosophers carried the Sapir–Whorf argument to its logical conclusion.

French philosopher Jacques Derrida (1930–2004), a follower of Heidegger, argued that all cultures construct their own worlds of meaning that are self-contained and to a large extent impenetrable to outsiders. When anthropologists compile ethnographic descriptions within a scientific tradition they force native meanings into the conceptual categories of the ethnographer, which by their very nature cannot adequately capture the original meanings (we also saw how antecedents of these ideas were advanced by ethnoscientists in the 1960s, although they also coupled these claims with a rigorous scientific methodology). Derrida is considered the most prominent advocate of *deconstruction*, an approach to critically reading a text in order to *uncover* its implicit meanings rather than overt message. Richard Rorty, one of the most prominent American interpreters of Derrida, states that "'deconstruction' refers in the first instance to the way in which the 'accidental' features of a text can be seen as betraying, subverting, its purportedly 'essential' message" (1995: 171). How, for example, does the language, metaphor, or imagery employed in a text reveal an author's unstated assumptions or meanings, even those that contradict (i.e. "subvert") the text's overt message? Shortly, we'll examine how this approach has been employed in anthropology, particularly with regard to the representation of cultural "Others" in popular media.

Another guiding influence in postmodern anthropology has been the work of the French social historian Michel Foucault (1926–1984), whose influence in contemporary cultural anthropology cannot be overstated. He is best known in anthropology for reformulating the way in which we conceptualize power, viewing it as a dimension of individual or institutional claims to knowledge. The earlier prevailing notion of power in anthropology was one associated with Marx, who saw it as emanating from two sources. The first of these was differential control over resources ("the means of production"), so that those who owned vital resources, such as factories, farms, and mines, exercised control over those who were without property of their own and therefore had to labor for wages. This, in other words, is the power that an employer (the bourgeoisie) exerts over his/her employee (the proletariat). The second component of power mentioned by Marx is the coercive (political) power of the state, which claims a monopoly over the sanctioned use of force. In capitalist societies, the state has the exclusive power to fine, jail, or execute those who refuse to follow its dictates. For Marx, these two dimensions were conjoined in that those economic elites who controlled the means of production also had a disproportionate control of the state through their influence with legislators, regulatory agencies, and presidents and prime ministers. During Marx's time, for example, when workers challenged employers by going out on strike or organizing unions, they were often arrested or even fired upon by the police or military, both of which, of course, are components of the state.

While not denying these components of power, Foucault argued that the traditional Marxist conception is far too restrictive. His work builds upon the ideas of French structural Marxist Louis Althusser, who observed that states govern both through force and an "ideological state apparatus," or the institutions (such as education, law, and politics) by which the state promotes its version of "truth." Similarly, for Foucault, power does not simply involve physical or economic coercion, but is exercised through discourse and knowledge and, as such, power relations pervade all of society's institutions. Claims to knowledge and the truth are the means by which institutions, bureaucracies, and even individuals dominate others. In modern society, this takes the form of a command of the language of science, which is employed by powerful corporations, institutions, and the state to control those who lack this command. When the state undertakes a policy that is likely to threaten the well-being of some segment of its citizenry, it deploys the language of science in order to justify that policy and to overcome citizen resistance to its decision. Similarly, asylums, hospitals, prisons, and other total institutions control and subjugate their residents through their "expert" ability to diagnose, "treat," and "rehabilitate" those under their control, as well as to punish those who resist that bureaucratic control.[1] Who is considered to be mentally ill? Who gets to determine this diagnosis? What does it mean to be identified as mentally ill for those who are so designated? Posing these questions in *Madness and Civilization* (1965), Foucault shows the answers to these questions have changed over time as the power arrangements in society changed. In an age dominated by the Church, it might be priests who do the defining; in another, it is doctors or psychologists who have this power. Hence, power suffuses all institutions and is exercised through a command of expert knowledge, which effectively disenfranchises all who lack that command or the requisite credentials. The values that we think of as constant, timeless, and absolute (e.g. what constitutes deviance or mental illness) are really in constant flux relative to who has power and how it gets used. Because western society's institutions and the state have typically been controlled by white males, however, their ability to deploy the language of science has tended in practice to disempower minorities, women, and colonized people. In short, it is power, wealth, and privileged status, rather than "evidence," that determines what is "true."

Approaches from hermeneutics and deconstruction and the notion of knowledge as power have joined to critically assess the way in which past anthropologists have represented other cultures. In the modernist tradition, anthropologists claimed a complete and authoritative knowledge of the societies in which they conducted their research. Yet, traditional ethnographies contained little information about the circumstances of the anthropologists' field research, which, after all, is the basis of their claims to knowledge. Fieldworkers have to be in particular places at particular times; it is physically impossible for them to observe everything within the community or region that they study. Similarly, the circumstances of their fieldwork, where they reside, the people with whom they associate, as well as their own emotional state and personal beliefs all influence the observations they gather. This is what has contributed to the "crisis" of replicability that we discussed early on in this volume, where we saw that some anthropologists studying the same culture arrived at completely different conclusions, something that should not occur in scientific research. As an illustration of how serendipitous circumstances can affect one's findings, an undergraduate professor of mine once related how he, as a young and naïve graduate student, arrived at his field site and moved into the only house in the village with a room to rent. Unfortunately, his landlord/roommate turned out to be the local policeman in a village in which numerous illegal and illicit acts took place. You can imagine how the anthropologist's limited choice of residence colored his interactions with other villagers. They were, needless to say, *very* polite but also very *unforthcoming* with information! This "crisis," however, may be something of an overstatement, as we rarely hear about the much more common (if less provocative) cases in which ethnographic accounts of the same locales agree. My own PhD research took place in a Belizean community studied 20 years earlier by economic anthropologist Michael Chibnik, and I encountered nothing that would contradict Chibnik's account, other than changes attributable to the passage of time.

Dispersion

Contemporary critics of scientific anthropology note that ethnographies have traditionally been written as if the anthropologist were an all-seeing (omniscient) and objective observer. In his 1989 volume *Works and Lives: The Anthropologist as Author*, Clifford Geertz argued that anthropologists construct their texts using literary devices that seek to establish their credentials for objective observation and ethnographic competence. These are designed to enhance the scientific authority of the author, while disguising the author's subjective biases, emotional state, and field experiences. The all-knowing, dispassionate third-person narrative style is coupled with a smattering of native terms to convey the impression that the anthropologist really "was there" and knows what he or she is talking about. In his introduction to the volume, Geertz writes: "The ability of anthropologists to get us to take what they say seriously has less to do with either a factual look or an air of conceptual elegance than it has with their capacity to convince us that what they say is a result of their having actually penetrated (or, if you prefer, been penetrated by) another form of life, of having, one way or another, truly 'been there.' And that, persuading us that this offstage miracle has occurred, is where the writing comes in" (1989: 4).

For the reason that ethnographic texts are constructed, as well as the problems of replicability, objectivity, and interpretation posed earlier in this volume, postmodernists reject the claims of scientific anthropology as "deeply mendacious," in the words of Stephen Tyler (1984: 328). Elsewhere, Tyler writes that "Reason is simply the means by which we justify the lies we tell...No one has ever demonstrated the independence of reason, of logic and mathematics from the discourses that constitute them" (1986: 135). Science, following Foucault and Lyotard, is held to be a cultural construct of western society that has historically oppressed powerless groups. Hence, those who claim to be scientific and objective in their approach to knowledge (including anthropologists) are complicit in this oppression. Postmodernists view science as but one of many competing claims to knowledge whose "truthfulness" is not necessarily any greater than any other claim. So what do postmodernists recommend in place of the Enlightenment assumptions that have characterized scientific anthropology? It is important to recognize that there is no single "postmodern" school, and indeed, some of the alternatives advocated by those who reject scientific anthropology also conflict with one another. However, three distinct trends seemed to have emerged from the postmodern critique of scientific

BOX 15.1   "The Wizard of Oz meets the Wicked Witch"

Inspired by Geertz' approach in *Works and Lives*, University of Iowa anthropologist Mac Marshall undertook a textual analysis of two famously conflicting ethnographic accounts. In his 1993 article, "The Wizard of Oz Meets the Wicked Witch of the East: Freeman, Mead, and Ethnographic Authority," Marshall closely analyzes the language chosen by the avowedly scientific anthropologist Derek Freeman in his 1983 volume *Margaret Mead and Samoa: The Making and Unmaking of an Anthropological Myth*. As you recall, Freeman disputed Mead's conclusions on Samoan society as heavily skewed by her alleged ethnographic ineptitude, naiveté, and personal bias. But this argument is advanced at least as much by Freeman's use of rhetoric as by his command of ethnographic "facts." Through a simple enumeration of the nouns, verbs, and adjectives Freeman uses to describe his research versus that of Mead, Marshall shows how Freeman deploys language in a way to brutally undermine his rival's ethnographic authority on Samoa while enhancing his own. Marshall writes:

> In building what he calls his "refutation of Mead's conclusions," Freeman combines a number of devices to undermine the reader's confidence in her. One technique is to describe her as *young*, *sparsely experienced*, and physically *small* and *slight*. Freeman also works to impress the reader with the brevity of Mead's time in Samoa by repeatedly referring to what he calls her *brief sojourn* of seven months there. He contrasts this with his "own research in the 1940s, the years 1965 to 1968, and 1981." Another of Freeman's techniques might be called the invocation of objectivity. For example, he casts suspicion on Mead by describing her as a person of *deeply held and felt beliefs* who was a *fervent devotee* of the *cherished doctrine of extreme cultural determinism*. Freeman uses *fervent* or *fervency* five different times in reference to Mead's, Ruth Benedict's, and Franz Boas' *beliefs*. The words Freeman chooses are those of religion rather than science—*belief, devotee, doctrine, extreme, fervency, vision, zealous*—thus reinforcing the separation he wishes to make between Mead and himself as a social scientist. In reference to his own researches in Samoa, Freeman draws on the language of science: *calculate, cases, detailed analysis, observations, samples, recorded, experiment*, and *tabulated*.
>
> (1993: 605; emphasis in original)

Marshall's approach to Freeman's book is a powerful examination of how avowedly scientific ethnographers employ rhetorical devices *no less* than the authors of novels, short stories, or newspaper editorials who want to persuade readers of their point of view. Marshall concludes, however, that Freeman employs such tactics so conspicuously and in such a heavy-handed manner that he ends up undermining his own credibility.

anthropology since the 1980s and have moved to the forefront of anthropology as it is practiced in the contemporary moment.

For one, most postmodernists would agree that ethnographic accounts should be heavily concerned with how they "represent the Other" (people traditionally studied by anthropologists, usually held to be colonized and indigenous people, women, and ethnic and sexual minorities). These concerns rose to prominence in anthropology after American literary critic Edward Said published his influential book, *Orientalism*, in 1978. Said used the term to designate a Western academic and artistic tradition of prejudiced interpretations of the East. Originating in Christian–Moslem conflict during the Crusades, such prejudices were more fully shaped by the attitudes of European imperialist interventions in the eighteenth and nineteenth centuries. In western popular culture of the last several decades, "orientalist" prejudices assumed the form of a rich Arab sheik in robes, a common media stereotype during the oil crisis of the 1970s. In the 1990s that figure was replaced by a swarthy and sinister Arab terrorist as a villain figure in western movies. Reflecting such concerns about representation, many anthropologists argue that they should be guided by an imperative to "privilege" the "voice of the Other" over that of the ethnographic observer. Describing traditional accounts in which the fieldworker spoke of the society that he or she studied as "repugnant," Marilyn Strathern writes that "the object [of postmodern ethnography] is a joint production. Many voices, multiple texts, plural authorship" (1987: 264–265). Presumably an ethnographic account that fully privileges local knowledge over ethnographers' concepts and categories would consist of completely unedited statements of native informants. Even before the rise of such critiques in anthropology, Andrew Strathern compiled such a book in the volume *Ongka: The Life and Times of a Melanesian Big Man* (1979). This is essentially an autobiographical account dictated by Ongka, a leader of the Kawelka tribe, in which he told Strathern to simply translate his account verbatim into English and not to edit it in any fashion. While this might be seen as an effort toward greater sensitivity to native perceptions and knowledge, it still doesn't address the critique of hermeneutic philosophers who argue that a faithful translation between languages and cultures is impossible.

As a start toward rendering more sensitive representations of the Other, postmodern ethnographers emphatically reject the imposition of an etic mode of analysis as materialist, functionalist, or structuralist anthropologists define it; similarly, they reject any "totalizing discourse" or "metanarrative" that frames or sets out to explain cultural practices in terms unfamiliar to the members of that culture.[2] What this means is that every theoretical perspective examined so far in this volume, whether functionalism, cultural ecology, Marxism, French structuralism, or Freudian psychological anthropology, are seen as manifestations of privileged, western, scientific claims to knowledge. Perhaps the most economical characterization of what he called *The Postmodern Condition* was offered by French philosopher Jean-Francois Lyotard (1924–1998) as a complete "incredulity toward metanarratives" (1984: xxiv). Science is simply one discourse, according to Lyotard, in a sea of competing discourses, and its elevation above other claims to truth is simply the result of its support by powerful states, corporations, and institutions. An early study that might be seen to embody some of these assumptions of postmodern ethnography was James Fernandez' *Bwiti: An Ethnography of the Religious Imagination in Africa* (1982). Rather than organizing his chapters in the fashion of conventional ethnographies, Fernandez selected chapter headings that correspond to conceptual categories unique to the Fang, the African society that is the subject of his study (e.g. "Compositions of the Past" rather than "Historical Background"). Fernandez' work, emphasizing parallel truths, multiple meanings, and the relationship between power and knowledge, represents one model of how postmodern ethnography might engage with recent criticisms of scientific approaches.

Secondly, many contemporary anthropologists reject the rhetorical strategies of past ethnographic observers, who fashioned their writing to make them appear to be objective observers. This requires greater attention to how anthropologists construct their texts (Figure 15.1). Hence, past anthropologists "wrote themselves out of the story" by utilizing generalizations, the third-person voice, and passive constructions

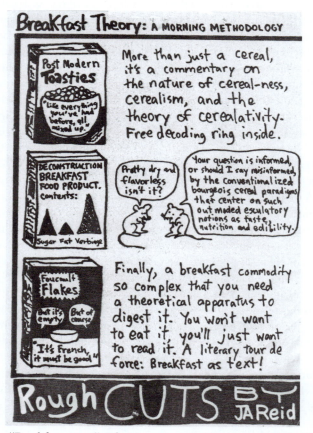

FIGURE 15.1   "Breakfast as text": I first encountered this cartoon back in 1989, but I'm still looking for that decoding ring. Courtesy of *In These Times*.

(e.g."various parts of manatee are regularly consumed by Belizean Garifuna" instead of "My Garifuna host served me various parts of manatee"). The problem with the former construction is that it begs the question of how the anthropologist claims to know this "fact" about a particular culture. Indeed, the passive construction obscures this issue entirely. Obviously, if we're just talking about a single meal, this is a minor point. But traditional ethnographic accounts have described *entire cultures in this third-person manner*, in effect blurring the relationship between what the anthropologist writes about a society and how he or she acquired such knowledge. Since anthropologists cannot possibly be everywhere and cannot possibly interact with everyone when they are in the field, critics contend that they should avoid the tendency to generalize in this manner. Instead, some, such as Lila Abu-Lughod, an anthropologist at Columbia University, assert that ethnography should be about *"telling stories,"* relating only events and anecdotes that the anthropologist has personally seen or heard without claiming to generalize to an entire society. Similarly, postmodernists say that anthropology should be *"reflexive,"* foregrounding the experience and perspectives of the fieldworker, so that the reader at least knows which biases he or she is subjected to when reading the ethnographic account, as well as the personal and political circumstances that led to its creation. Hence, Abu-Lughod's writings often foreground her identity as a Palestinian-American woman, one who experienced a difficult pregnancy during part of her fieldwork. Reflexive writing of this sort is supposed to reveal the social positioning of the knowledge claimed by the anthropologist, implicitly rejecting the idea of privileged and objective knowledge. Some science-oriented skeptics have ridiculed this as "anthropology about the anthropologist," and as little better than travel writing or journalism. Note that it would be difficult to accomplish both the first and second goals that I mention above simultaneously (of privileging the voice of Others, while engaging in reflexive story telling). Yet again, this doesn't highlight a contradiction in postmodern thought, because *there is no single variant of postmodernism.*

Finally, many contemporary anthropologists feel the need to take seriously and confront the relationship between their discipline and colonial hierarchies of power. And, of course, in many instances, anthropologists were directly or indirectly complicit with systems of colonial administration or counter-insurgency, as we saw in the case of the British functionalists and the US government's Project Camelot. Different anthropologists, it seems, have reacted to this concern in different ways; indeed, how to deal with this relationship between colonialism and anthropology appears to be among the greatest source of contention among postmodernists themselves. If the anthropologist originates from a traditionally colonizing society (e.g. Great Britain or the United States) and makes a formerly colonized group of people (e.g. Africans or Latin Americans) the "subject" of their study, are they recreating a colonial hierarchy when they conduct fieldwork? While some anthropologists dismiss this as a kind of nihilistic rejection of the traditional ethnographic model, the question is a serious one when we consider that white Euro-American anthropologists are indeed seen by their "subjects" as representatives of their societies. Anthropologists working in formerly colonized countries are almost always put in the same cognitive category by our informants with development experts, Drug Enforcement Agency and CIA agents, foreign embassy staff, Peace Corps volunteers, and missionaries, all of whom set out to change native societies. For some anthropologists, traditional ethnography in "Third World" contexts is so closely related to colonialism in its implications that they reject it altogether.

For some who adopt this view, the solution to this dilemma is to embark upon deconstruction of media and institutional representations of cultural Others. Drawing inspiration from both political ecology and Foucauldian notions of knowledge as power, poststructuralists such as James Ferguson (1994) and Arturo Escobar (1995) have characterized the "development encounter" as a form of hegemonic discourse originating in powerful institutions (e.g. the US Agency for International Development or the World Bank) whose policies seek to reshape the cultures, ecologies, and economies of the postcolonial world. Designed to recreate formerly colonized societies in the image of the now-industrialized countries, development is seen as an imposition of western assumptions that privilege scientific rationality over local knowledge and cultural traditions, not to mention the desires of development "recipients" themselves. Discursive approaches seek to elucidate the means by which powerful institutions legitimate their actions to state sponsors and the broader public, although anthropologists whose ethnographic research has centered on the "development encounter" itself point out limitations when this view is applied to the outcome of such projects (Rossi 2006). "While [development knowledge] may function hegemonically," Gardner observes from her study of one such project, "it is also created and recreated by multiple agents, who often have very different understandings of their work" (1997: 134). Finally, discursive approaches do little to illuminate how the intended beneficiaries of development practices in the Global South interpret, accommodate, or resist these policies; nor do they explain why development programs yield results so often at variance with the discourse on which they are based (Little and Painter 1995: 605). In a sense, such criticisms reiterate those already raised about theories such as structural functionalism and ethnoscience that presume that agents' behavior is isomorphic with their knowledge and claims about the social world.

Deconstruction of cultural representations is also featured in the volume *Reading National Geographic* (1993) by anthropologist Catherine Lutz and sociologist Jane Collins. Their work analyzes about 600 photographic images featured in issues of that magazine over much of the twentieth century. Their rationale for doing so is that *National Geographic* is the basis on which many Americans form their impressions and knowledge of nonwestern cultures. By deconstructing these images and texts, we gain some insight, the authors claim, into Americans' view of cultural Others. The authors argue that the placement and editing of photographs in *National Geographic* tends to elide cultural difference (except at the most superficial level) and to side-step difficult questions of strife, inequality, discrimination, and poverty. As the authors state, "Clearly, photographic practice at *National Geographic* is geared to a classic form of humanism, drawing readers' attention through its portrayals of difference, and then showing that under the colorful dress and the skin, as it

FIGURE 15.2 Advertisement from 1955, showing an African-American man in a "traditional" portrayal as a porter. Notice that he is even speaking in a kind of servile black dialect. Another ad from about the same time shows a black bellman bringing white hotel clients a tray with Pabst Blue Ribbon beer and a couple of glasses. He says to himself, "Those sho am quality folks!"

were, we are all more or less the same" (Lutz and Collins 1993: 61). The author's interpretations, persuasive as they might seem, are then ultimately undermined by interviews they conducted with regular readers of *National Geographic*, who revealed differing, and often conflicting, "readings" of the text and images.

Another, similar volume, William O'Barr's *Culture and the Ad: Exploring the World of Otherness in Advertising* (1994), deconstructs American print advertising images over the twentieth century in terms of their portrayal of African Americans, American Indians, Asians, and other non-whites. Unlike Lutz and Collins, who emphasize the relatively static (and respectful) portrayals of Others over decades of issues of *National Geographic*, O'Barr shows how these portrayals have changed, often dramatically, with the change in society's attitudes toward various ethnic groups. Until the 1960s, for example, African-American males in print advertising were almost always depicted as bellmen, train porters, elevator operators, or shoe-shine men, while women were almost always domestics and cooks (Figure 15.2). Such images were used as props to sell products and services to white consumers and thereby engaged white stereotypes of blacks; the notion that African-American communities had their own "black bourgeoisie" with disposable income apparently did not occur to advertising executives prior to the 1970s. Many of these portrayals were gratuitously racist, linking blacks to watermelon or fried chicken, for example, items which were completely unrelated to the service or product featured in the ad. Within the space of about a decade, African Americans were no longer featured

FIGURE 15.3   Bell Telephone (AT&T) ad from 1970, selling not a product, but its image as an equal opportunity employer of blacks in managerial positions.

to sell products, but to promote corporate images as progressive "color-blind" employers. By the early 1970s, almost all advertising was by companies featuring African Americans not in servile occupations as domestics and bellmen, but in roles as managers and decision-makers (Figure 15.3). The emphasis had changed from product and service to corporate image. Only as the decade progressed were African Americans increasingly seen as consumers in their own right.

For still other anthropologists concerned about the relationship between anthropology and colonialism, one strategy has been to conduct more domestic fieldwork. Indeed, in a discipline once defining itself as the study of small-scale, nonwestern societies, significant numbers of dissertations and research projects now involve domestic fieldwork. One of the most powerful of such ethnographies, Philippe Bourgois' *In Search of Respect: Selling Crack in El Barrio* (1996), is based on fieldwork performed in Spanish Harlem among crack dealers and prostitutes, a project conducted while Bourgois was writing up his dissertation on banana workers in Costa Rica. Bourgois' book was met by immediate critical acclaim, yet even here there emerge the questions of cultural translation and representation that so preoccupy many postmodernists. How well can a white graduate student "penetrate" the world of Puerto Rican drug dealers and prostitutes, and how do the differences in their identities affect the kind of information Bourgois was able to gather? He himself reports that most of his informants believed, at least initially, that he was an undercover narcotics cop, while the police thought he was a suburban kid visiting Harlem to score drugs. Bourgois' portrayal of inner city violence, drug addiction, and misogyny is brutally frank, and has been widely heralded as perhaps the most important and powerful ethnography to have been produced in urban America. Yet it has also had its critics. David Nugent wondered why Bourgois paid scant attention to the larger population of East Harlem that does not participate in the street culture of drugs and prostitution: "They condemn it, shield themselves and their children from it and…develop alternative forms of practice and association that contest street culture" (Nugent 1997: 687). Failing to at least acknowledge this alternative way of life leads Bourgois, Nugent continues, "to run the risk of negatively stereotyping life in El Barrio" (ibid.). Many of Bourgois' subsequent writings dealt with the personal and ethical dilemmas of fieldwork under these circumstances, while his account has been criticized on more than one occasion for resurrecting in a new guise Oscar Lewis' controversial argument for the "culture of poverty." Some have claimed that not only has Bourgois recreated a colonial hierarchy of observer and culturally Other subjects, but that his work could be read as attributing the poverty of inner city residents to their own behaviors, rather than structural economic factors beyond their control.[3] One otherwise sympathetic reviewer worried that just as Lewis' works had been misused by US policymakers in the 1960s to blame the poor for their poverty, "conservatives bent on blaming poor people of color will find plenty of grist for their ideological mill" (Foley 1997: 378).

Other anthropologists plead for the continued relevance of fieldwork in formerly colonized societies as a way of challenging traditional colonial hierarchies, and reject the retreat from ethnography in such places to textual analysis and domestic research. UC Berkeley anthropologist Nancy Scheper-Hughes views textual approaches as "cop-outs," a way of simply avoiding tough questions and the examination of injustice. Her work in Brazilian shantytowns and South African slums has engaged, in often excruciating detail, the notion of "structural violence," of how social and economic inequality affects the health and psychological well-being of the poor and marginalized. Much like Bourgois' portrayal of crack dealers, Scheper-Hughes' massive ethnography *Death Without Weeping* (1993) paints a tragic portrait of impoverished women in a Brazilian *favela*. Her informants lived in such desperate impoverished circumstances that they literally expected most of their infant children to die, and faced their losses with stoic indifference. In her 1995 article, "The Primacy of the Ethical," she writes critically of other postmodernists who avoid fieldwork in favor of textual analysis, which she considers a retreat from engaging with the poor in solidarity:

> Many younger anthropologists today, sensitized by the writings of Michel Foucault on power/knowledge, have come to think of anthropological fieldwork…as similar to the medieval inquisitional confession through which church examiners extracted "truth" from their native and "heretical" peasant parishioners. One hears of anthropological observation as a hostile act that reduces our "subjects" to mere "objects" of our discriminating, incriminating, scientific gaze. Consequently, some postmodern anthropologists have given up the practice of descriptive ethnography altogether. I am weary of these postmodernist critiques, and, given the perilous times in which we and

our subjects live, I am inclined toward compromise, the practice of a "good enough" ethnography. While the anthropologist is always necessarily a flawed and biased instrument of cultural translation, like every other craftsperson we do the best we can with the limited resources at hand…Seeing, listening, touching, recording can be, if done with care and sensitivity, acts of solidarity. Above all, they are the work of recognition. Not to look, not to touch, not to record can be the hostile act, an act of indifference and of turning away.

(Scheper-Hughes 1995: 417–418)

While chiding postmodernists who reject the process of fieldwork, Scheper-Hughes also breaks with Enlightenment notions of objectivity that preclude a "politically committed and morally engaged anthropology" (ibid.: 409). From this point of view, a "moral model" of anthropology should express solidarity with those who have historically been oppressed by colonialism, racism, and injustice. Scheper-Hughes and Bourgois represent a new wave of "critical medical anthropologists" who probe the structural causes of health disparities, drug abuse, and other forms of "social suffering." In so doing, they break with an older tradition in medical anthropology that employs biomedical concepts and theories but neglects structural factors in health disparities. In one such work, *Righteous Dopefiend* (2009), Bourgois and Schonberg construct an experimental ethnography that crosses several genres. Drawing upon a decade of ethnographic observations, informant narratives, and stark black-and-white photographs, Bourgois and Schonberg create a deeply personal and often disturbing portrayal of homeless heroin addicts in San Francisco, one rooted in a political economic analysis of homelessness. Among critical medical anthropologists, Paul Farmer (2003) has gained international recognition for combining ethnographic work in the slums of Haiti with human rights advocacy on behalf of their impoverished residents. In one much-cited work, he situates individual biographies of poor Haitians within the oppressive circumstances in which they live: "Case studies of individuals reveal suffering, they tell us what happens to one or many people; but to explain suffering, one must embed individual biography in the larger matrix of culture, history, and political economy" (Farmer 1996: 267).

Revisiting old conflicts

While the sociocultural and political economic circumstances that David Harvey associates with postmodernity are qualitatively new and unprecedented, the conflicts within anthropology that postmodern approaches have generated are not entirely new. There has always been a tension within anthropology between those who view it as a scientific endeavor and those who regard it as a branch of the humanities. Recall that Boas himself, while avowedly "scientific" in his systematic collection of anthropological data, also rejected the generalizing "law giving" tendencies of the natural sciences as inappropriate for understanding human culture. Ruth Benedict, who had a successful secondary career as a poet, viewed the mission of anthropology through the lens of her strongly held cultural relativism; indeed, her bestselling *Patterns of Culture* (1934) was acclaimed much more for its literary rather than explanatory qualities. Alfred Kroeber, who in addition to earning his PhD in anthropology under Boas also held a Master's degree in literature, perhaps summed up these tensions within the discipline best. He once famously described anthropology "as the most scientific of the humanities, and the most humanistic of the sciences" (quoted in Kroeber 2003: 144).

Yet, postmodernism represents a break with these earlier humanistic tendencies. The influence of hermeneutics and deconstruction in anthropology calls into question the very existence of an objective reality on which all observers—whether scientists or humanists—can agree. If, as Heidegger and Derrida would argue, all writing is nothing more than interpretations of interpretations, then ethnographic accounts become little more than fiction, ultimately to be judged according to their persuasiveness. This is a position that Boas, Kroeber, and Benedict, for all their humanistic impulses, would absolutely reject. Postmodernists assert that abandoning the language of science allows "voices" other than those of white Euro-American males to be finally heard. These are the perspectives of women, minorities, the poor and oppressed, who were traditionally absent from literature and the sciences. It is no surprise, then, that the rise of postmodernism in the humanities and social sciences has also coincided with the "culture wars" taking place on university campuses regarding what should be taught, and from what perspective. University English departments, in particular, are ferocious battlegrounds of this sort, with contentious arguments between older white male faculty who typically promote a "traditional" canon of classic literature and younger faculty, often women and people of color, who favor teaching the works of women and minorities. Such battles center on what is to be taught and what an educated university student should know about literature. Should they be steeped in Shakespeare, Donne, Hawthorne, and Melville? Or should they be equally familiar with Alice Walker, Maya Angelou, Nikki Giovanni, and Langston Hughes? These are not simply matters of intellectual disagreement among academics, because they have significant political and professional consequences for the make-up of higher education. Younger faculty who favor a non-traditional canon find themselves evaluated for tenure and promotion by their more senior and more traditionally-oriented colleagues (often derided as "silverbacks," after the senior alpha males of gorilla hierarchies). On occasion senior faculty have been known to retaliate with negative tenure decisions against junior colleagues who don't conform to their preferred canon.

Within anthropology, those who challenge the discipline's postmodern tendencies have directed three major criticisms against its assumptions. The first of these is that while postmodernists have pointed out the difficulties of conducting empirically objective ethnographic research, these difficulties do not in principle make such research impossible. In a 1989 article in *American Anthropologist*, Tim O'Meara argues that most postmodern critiques of scientific anthropology disingenuously misrepresent the goals and methods of such approaches, describing a model of inquiry that even scientific anthropologists themselves would not recognize. Recall from Chapter 1 our distinction between "nomological/deductive" theories that are highly predictive of future events and "statistical/probabilistic" theories that describe causal relationships. Some postmodern critics conflate the two, arguing that because anthropology is not predictive in the sense of chemistry or physics, it cannot claim to produce causal explanations or adopt the mantle of scientific credibility. Yet no anthropologist has ever presumed to be able to predict future events. Meanwhile, as they reject causal explanation in favor of "interpretation," postmodern anthropologists often in practice fall back on explanation as much as their scientific counterparts, while carefully avoiding the use of the words "explanation" or "cause." O'Meara singles out Clifford Geertz in particular for this practice:

> These explanations are usually disguised in interpretive euphemisms, but they are there nonetheless. Geertz is the most prolific euphemizer, circumventing the standard English word "explain" with such terms as "render accessible," "dissolve the opacity of," "grasp," "clarify," "reduce the puzzlement of," "render intelligible," "interpret," and of course "thickly describe." In spite of these circumlocutions and his programmatic statements to the contrary, however, Geertz gives believable explanations of much Balinese behavior. For example, in the first few pages of "Deep Play: Notes on a Balinese Cockfight," Geertz explains why the Indonesian government tries to stop cockfighting, opium smoking, begging, and the uncovering of breasts (it sees them "as primitive, backward, unprogressive, and generally unbecoming an ambitious nation"); why illegal cockfights can be held in the village (the officials are bribed), why he and his wife were accepted by the villagers (they showed their solidarity by fleeing with the villagers from a police raid); why Balinese men are obsessed with their fighting cocks (fighting cocks are masculine symbols par excellence); why babies are not allowed to crawl and children's teeth are filed (to distinguish them from beasts, which are abhorred); and so on.
>
> (1989: 364–365)

As we saw earlier, contemporary anthropologists like Lila Abu-Lughod reject scientific generalization for a host of reasons, claiming that "as part of a professional discourse of 'objectivity' and expertise, it is inevitably a language of power...even if we withhold judgment on how closely the social sciences can be associated with the apparatuses of management, we have to recognize how all professional discourses by nature assert hierarchy" (1991: 150–151). The alternative, non-hierarchical ethnographic form Abu-Lughod favors is "telling stories" of the particular incidents that arise during the process of fieldwork. In this fashion, she suggests, one averts the privileged claims of scientific generalization and objectivity in favor of the anthropologist's partial and subjective knowledge. But what is the purpose of such "stories," and why does she decide to relate one anecdote over another? In his discussion of "moral models" in anthropology, Roy D'Andrade offers a withering criticism of the underlying assumptions of this method. "Telling stories," he says, deceptively serves to advance an argument and a generalization about a culture, even while denying that that is its purpose:

[Abu-Lughod contends that] by telling a story about someone, the ethnographer does not have to make any generalizations and thereby appears to avoid the danger of hegemonic discourse. However, the appearance is deceptive; quite the reverse happens in fact. It is a natural assumption of the reader that any narrative is, in some important sense, typical of what happens in that place, unless told otherwise. Kenneth Burke calls this rhetorical strategy that of the "reductive anecdote"—the world is "summarized by" and "reduces to" the story one tells about it. *Presenting an anecdote is just as essentializing and totalizing as stating a generalization.* Consider, for example, the well-known anecdote about George Washington and the cherry tree: it acts just like the generalization "Washington was honest" but hides the claim. Hence Burke's comment on the rhetorical use of anecdotes: beware of people just telling stories.

(1995: 405; emphasis in original)

Secondly, critics argue that postmodern assertions about the subjectivity of all knowledge are self-refuting and therefore cannot be logically sustained. If all claims to knowledge are "culturally constructed," and science as a way of knowing about the world is no more valid than any other claim, then why should we accept as valid the assertions of postmodernists? After all, such assertions would simply be another unverifiable claim to knowledge. James Lett expressed it this way: "If the cultural origins of science undermine the authority of scientific analyses, why do not the cultural origins of interpretive anthropology undermine the authority of postmodern analysis?" (1991: 315). Even Marvin Harris acknowledged that scientific anthropology can generate only "partial truths," as postmodernists would argue, in that no anthropologist can have a complete knowledge of another culture (this, indeed, is why he devoted ethnographic priority to "etic behavioral infrastructures"). Similarly, he accepted that science occurs within an institutional and social context that structures the particular interests and theoretical orientations of the scientist. Harris' argument was that the notion of science that postmodernists criticize is a "straw-man" simplification of Baconian empiricism, with which no modern scientist actually operates. The critical difference between scientific and postmodern ways of knowing, he claims, is that "science is less skeptical than postmodernism only in its refusal to concede that one partial truth is as good as any other. Science, unlike postmodernism, refuses to accept all partial truths as equally truthful…The question for the science-oriented anthropologist is not whether objective social science is possible, but how to judge whether one partial constructed truth is better than another" (Harris 1995: 67).

The final criticism derives from the second argument above. Many postmodernists celebrate the rejection of science as a way of liberating the voices of Others who have been silenced by hegemonic, patriarchal Euro-American scientists, many of whom work in the service of oppressive bureaucracies and states. To further this argument, postmodernists claim that scientific knowledge has not produced the human progress that it promised, but has given us a military-industrial complex founded on mass annihilation, an increasingly toxic and unlivable planet, and dehumanizing forms of social planning that strengthen states while destroying communities. From the Holocaust to Hiroshima to Pruitt-Igoe to global warming, science has only consolidated control over society in fewer and fewer (white, male) hands, while inflicting often unspeakable horrors on its "subjects." This notion of attending to previously neglected perspectives has a very tolerant sound to it. But in practice, its implications are troubling. David Harvey lauds the postmodern sensitivity to the neglected voices of the Other as in one sense the most liberating aspect of postmodern thought. Yet he also notes that our relations to the Other are mediated by colonial and capitalist forms of labor control, requiring the kind of analysis promoted by political economists. Harvey views other trends in postmodernism more darkly as undermining any possibility of reasoned action against repressive institutions. In viewing culture as a text for deconstruction rather than as relationships and meanings with structural-historical determinants, postmodernists

> celebrat[e] the activity of masking and covering-up all the fetishisms of locality, place or social grouping, while denying that kind of meta-theory which can grasp the political economic processes…that are becoming ever more universalizing in their depth, intensity, reach and power over daily life.
>
> (Harvey 1989: 116–117)

Another Marxist-oriented anthropologist, Thomas Patterson, expressed similar concerns. He faults the critical trends in postmodern thought for an increasing divisiveness within the discipline, as postmodernists turned their critical gaze inward toward their colleagues and disciplinary politics rather than the momentous changes taking place in the global political economy over recent decades:

> …the fields of reference for critique and politics mentioned in the titles of the postmodernists' books were not imperialism, colonialism, or capitalism but rather what was happening in university departments and in the profession…By viewing identities as texts that were created by intersubjective communication, the postmodernists decanted concerns about class politics and struggle from anthropology at a time when states around the world were becoming increasingly repressive and their neoliberal policies allowed transnational corporations to suck the life out of workers, peasants, and tribal peoples.
>
> (Patterson 2001: 155–156)

To be fair, however, there are many influenced by postmodernism, such as Scheper-Hughes, who have similarly lamented the discipline's self-absorption at the expense of engagement with class oppression.

Many critics of postmodernism warn that if a rejection of science allows all "voices" to be heard, then logically that should include not only the voices of minorities and colonized people. Rather, we should also attend to other voices that many of us would prefer not to hear, or at least that we would not want to accord as much validity as other viewpoints. Should we tend to the "voices" of those who believe in alien abduction on UFOs, or that the lunar landings were staged in a Hollywood studio? Much more gravely, as anthropologists Jon McGee and Richard Warms put it, "If all voices should be heard...does that mean fascist voices and the voices of white supremacists or neo-Nazis are no less worthy of respect than others?" (2008: 536). Indeed, there is a troubling relationship between hermeneutics and fascism that is perhaps not coincidental. Benito Mussolini, whose fascist government came to power in Italy in 1922, explicitly embraced hermeneutic assumptions about the relativity and subjectivity of all knowledge: "From the fact that all ideologies are of equal value, the modern relativist deduces that everybody is free to create for himself his own ideology and to attempt to carry it out with all possible energy" (quoted in Ross 1980: xxvii). Mussolini as a relativist. Who would have thought?

While much of the discourse of postmodernism adopts an overtly moral tone, identifying science with oppression, its founders have themselves been associated with troubling amoral positions and affiliations. Paul De Man (1919–1983), the founder of *deconstructionism*, immigrated to the United States after World War II and held a professorship in philosophy at Yale University for many years. He was probably the most important intellectual influence on Derrida. After his death, it emerged that while living in Nazi-occupied Belgium during the early 1940s, De Man had broadcast anti-Semitic propaganda on Belgian radio and authored more than 200 articles for pro-Nazi newspapers. Throughout his career, De Man had successfully concealed his history as a Nazi collaborator both from US immigration authorities and his colleagues at Yale. The most influential hermeneutic philosopher of the twentieth century, Martin Heidegger, enthusiastically joined the German Nazi Party upon Hitler's rise to power in 1933. Subsequently, as Rector of Freiburg University, he oversaw the firing of all Jewish professors from that institution. Recall that Heidegger had rejected reason as a source of truth; instead, he said it was the innate and unique superiority of German culture and language that led him to recognize, in his words, "the inner truth and greatness of Nazism." Heidegger was so closely associated with the propagation of Nazi views that after World War II, French occupation authorities in Germany forbade him from teaching until 1951. Are such associations between elements of postmodern thought and fascism coincidental? I would argue that it is precisely when one rejects reason and rules of evidence in favor of subjective knowledge based on intuition, identity, or politics that we get such aberrations as Nazi "racial science" that gave us the Holocaust, or Stalin's "proletarian science" that gave us Lysenkoism.

Clearly, the Enlightenment's assumptions of infinite progress through the application of scientific knowledge have not come to pass, at least not in all realms of experience. Science has been harnessed to warfare, oppressive forms of planning, and the rejection of local knowledge in favor of hierarchal institutions and corporations. But postmodern critics of science conveniently overlook those many areas where it has improved people's lives, whether through medicine or the improved dissemination of knowledge and goods. Scientific knowledge by itself is neither good nor bad, but it does reflect the institutional and political context in which it occurs and to which it is applied. For all its limitations, if we do hope to make a positive difference in this world—to make a moral impact on it as Nancy Scheper-Hughes advocates—we first have to have knowledge about the world that is accurate and evidence-based and not merely a reflection of our subjective views and desires. Indeed, this is one area that concerns D'Andrade about "moral models" of anthropology; specifically whether politically-engaged anthropologists will report evidence that conflicts with their political agendas.

You may infer from all of this that I take a largely negative view of postmodernism's impact on anthropology. If so, prepare yourself for a surprise. I remember these issues first arising in the discipline as I was finishing my PhD dissertation in the late 1980s, under the direction of a strongly materialist and quantitative anthropologist, Allen Johnson. At first, my reaction to some of the postmodern claims about knowledge was "you've got to be kidding!" For the first half of the 1990s I remained convinced that this was just a nihilistic trend that would soon exhaust itself, and that anthropology would recover its proper "scientific" credentials. But the debates go on, and meanwhile I find that my appreciation for at least some of the questions posed by postmodernists has grown over the years. Postmodernism has raised some exceptionally important issues that anthropologists simply ignored in the past: how we claim to know what we know, how we represent the people who we study, how we construct our written work to advance our arguments, and above all, how our subjective states and field circumstances affect the way we gather information. I also find myself fundamentally in agreement with Foucault's argument that the command of knowledge constitutes an important source of power in contemporary society, even as I completely reject the more relativistic notions that regard all knowledge claims as simply competing, and therefore equivalent, discourses.

I recall having lunch with a science-oriented quantitative medical anthropologist who was visiting my campus, and I mentioned that I had just finished a manuscript for Duke University Press (my 2003 co-edited book, *Banana Wars*). He raised a suspicious eyebrow and asked, "Don't they mostly publish postmodern stuff?" Partly in jest, I replied, "But we're all postmodernists now!" He literally choked and acted as if I had gone over to the *Dark Side*, but he shouldn't have been so surprised. In the end, postmodernism, whether we like it or not, has profoundly shaped all cultural anthropology in recent years, and it has even (perhaps unconsciously) entered into my own work. After finishing my most recent monograph (2008, *Slipping Away: Banana Politics and Fair Trade in the Eastern Caribbean*), I realized that I had done something that I had never done before in a publication. I began the book by writing in the first person and relating a troubling personal anecdote, of being robbed at machete point while in the field in St. Lucia. I found myself "telling a story" that I hoped would stand as a generalization, representing the broader theme of what the book is about: the structural violence associated with an imploding rural economy, brought on by a trade war that destroyed much of the Caribbean's export agriculture. Without being aware of it, I had become, to some extent, the kind of "reflexive" anthropologist that some postmodernists advocate albeit, and most critically, one who still accepts the overwhelming importance of evidence and honesty in making an argument. This is how I have chosen to respond to the postmodern critique, while cherishing the values of careful scholarship imparted by all the anthropologists who have come before me. Ultimately, it is up to you to decide how to make use of the ideas and debates presented over the preceding chapters. And so I close this volume with the same quote by which Marx introduced *Capital*, his sweeping study of an earlier revolutionary era:

"Go your own way, and let the people talk"—Dante

Quiz yourself

Answer True or False to each statement

1 The hermeneutic perspective holds that an individual's knowledge of the world is always conditioned by his or her culture, identity, and social position.

2 Deconstruction is an interpretive approach that examines how the language, metaphor, or imagery employed in a text reveal an author's unstated assumptions or meanings.

3 Michel Foucault argues that the claim to command scientific knowledge on the part of bureaucracies, the state, and corporations allows them to exercise power over other groups in society.

4 Clifford Geertz used the approach of deconstruction to show how past anthropologists employed rhetorical devices in their writing to enhance their ethnographic authority.

5 Mac Marshall employed the approach of deconstruction to show how Derek Freeman's rhetorical techniques served to undermine his rival Margaret Mead's ethnographic authority on Samoa while enhancing his own.

6 Anthropologist Lila Abu-Lughod rejects ethnographic generalizations because, in her view, they "privilege" the anthropologist's claims to knowledge over those of the people they study.

7 Some postmodern anthropologists reject ethnographic research entirely in Third World settings because they believe such endeavors recreate colonial hierarchies of power and privilege.

8 Anthropologist Roy D'Andrade is critical of those who would "just tell stories" in place of scientific generalization, noting that such anecdotes serve as disguised generalizations anyway.

9 Scientific anthropologists claim that postmodern assertions about the subjectivity of all knowledge are self-refuting and therefore cannot be logically sustained.

10 Hermeneutic philosophers such as Paul De Man and Martin Heidegger are known to have had strongly pro-Nazi sympathies prior to and during World War II.

NOTES

1 Of politics and paradigms

1 As we will see, this argument is similar to that of A.L. Kroeber, who argued that culture has a "superorganic" existence that transcended the seemingly idiosyncratic contributions and beliefs of any one individual.

2 Alfred Kroeber once referred to himself as "one-half humanist," while as president of the American Anthropological Society in 1948, Ruth Benedict asserted that "today the scientific and humanist traditions are not opposites nor mutually-exclusive" (quoted in Wolf 1964: 1–2).

3 On *Car Talk*, one of my favorite National Public Radio programs, Tom and Ray Magliozzi, a couple of wise-cracking mechanics from Boston spend about equal time talking about their relationship woes as automobile repairmen. Tom, who has been around the marital block a few times, offered this variation on the riddle: "If a married man says something in a forest and his wife isn't there to hear it, is he still wrong?"

4 From my Midwestern origins, I bet that Lake Wobegon has NYC beat hands-down on this one. Growing up in Illinois in the 1960s and 70s, we probably ate lime jello three times a week, often with chunks or fruit or tiny marshmallows embedded in it (kind of like bugs in prehistoric amber). My mother continues to believe that it can substitute for green salad or a vegetable.

5 In this case and several that follow, I am indebted to Daniel Cathcart and Thomas Klein for their wonderfully insightful and humorous volume, *Plato and a Platypus Walk Into a Bar: Illustrating Philosophical Concepts through Jokes* (2006).

6 Most of Feyerabend's writings are from the 1960s and 70s, before the term "postmodernism" was coined, so you might consider Feyerabend a "pre-postmodernist"!

2 Claims and critiques of anthropological knowledge

1 Lewis' stated purpose was not to challenge or reassess Redfield's work, but to examine the impact of Mexico's post-revolutionary policies on a peasant community. Hence, he hoped to use Redfield's findings as a baseline for his own study.

2 As Margaret Mead later recalled, "Oscar was very upset that Redfield hadn't been interested in murder and other problems. He went to work and read the newspapers to

discover how many murders had been committed that Redfield hadn't noticed while he was there…Redfield was interested in harmony. He wanted to know what made things go well. Oscar, *as everybody knows,* was interested in what made things go badly" (in Murra 1974: 144; emphasis in original). In her biography of Lewis, Rigdon observed, "It is tempting to speculate that because Lewis was born into a family that had lived for years in (to greatly understate the situation) conflictive environment… he came by way of reality, to a negative and hostile view of the world" (1988: 42).

3 Freeman, *of course*, doesn't disclose *his* own sexual history, pointing to an interesting double standard in his evaluation of Mead's work. While Mead's behavior was an open book and source of scandal at the time, her male counterparts seemed to have escaped comparable scrutiny.

4 This term appears repeatedly in the published version of the *Diary*, although Hortense Powdermaker, one of Malinowski's famous students, argued forcefully that it is mistranslated from the Polish, which contains no exact equivalent for this racial epithet.

5 I am using the convention most widely used by contributors to the Clifford and Marcus volume, but in practice I would submit that evocation means interpretation as described earlier.

6 Scheper-Hughes' work reflects the error of characterizing postmodern approaches in singular or monolithic terms. While decrying the putative claims to objectivity advanced by traditional anthropologists, she is also highly critical of postmodern approaches that celebrate interpretation and retreat into textual analysis over engagement with the world. Indeed, the bulk of her work since the 1980s has addressed gender oppression, poverty, infant mortality, and institutional racism.

3 The prehistory of anthropology

1 No single or authoritative version exists of Polo's manuscript, originally known as *Il Milione*. Because the manuscript was hand-copied for the first two centuries of its existence, some 150 different versions of the account exist, many of them riddled with copyists' errors.

2 Jefferson, like Locke, was also famously a man of contradictions where the principle of human equality was concerned. Locke had invested heavily in a company involved in the African slave trade, while of course Jefferson was a large slaveholder himself.

3 Sachs notes that in 1820, the shy and innocuous composer Franz Schubert was arrested by Viennese police merely for associating with the dissident poet Johann Senn, who himself was imprisoned and exiled (2010: 76).

4 The senior Darwin's evolutionary theory was expressed, rather imaginatively, not in the dry scientific prose of his grandson, but in rhyming verse!

4 Marx

1 Among the few members to oppose the bill in the House of Lords was the radical Lord Byron, who described the unemployed workers as "a much injured body of men sacrificed to [the] views of…individuals who have enriched themselves by those practices which have deprived the frame workers of employment…I have seen the state of these miserable men, and it is a disgrace to a civilized country" (Sachs 2010: 81).

2 Much as new social media (Facebook and Twitter) have received credit for the spontaneous uprisings of the "Arab Spring" in 2011, historians have attributed the rapid succession of rebellions in Europe during 1848 to new technologies (in addition, of course, to the social conditions that gave rise to them). Intimately linked for the first time by railroad and telegraph, workers throughout Europe learned of insurrections in other capitals within hours of one another.

3 Fukuyama's expression "the end of history" was first coined by Hegel to refer to the Prussian state in the early 1800s, which he believed had reconciled all previous historical

contradictions. This was the same state, however, whose censorship made it almost impossible for Marx to publish his work. Hegel had earlier praised Napoleon as a "world historical" leader, but shrewdly shifted his support to Napoleon's enemy, Prussia, after Napoleon's fall from power in 1815. Such ideological twists and turns are suggestive of the difficult political circumstances in which intellectuals operated in the post-Enlightenment.

4 The use of the term Depression to refer to severe economic contraction was first coined by President Herbert Hoover, who felt that the prevailing term for such conditions ("Panic") was too…panicky.

5 In today's severe recession, it has become an article of faith on the political right that the New Deal did not end the depression, but only wartime manufacturing of World War II brought it to an end. This argument seems to be made mainly in opposition to current efforts by the federal government to stimulate the economy. This claim is demonstrably false: historian Eric Rauchway (2008) demonstrated that in its first six years—even before the US entered World War II—the New Deal had slashed the jobless rate by two thirds, from 30 percent to 10.5 percent. By 1936 the economy had completely recovered the 35 percent loss in GDP that it had suffered between 1929 and 1933.

6 Although widely if erroneously attributed to medieval theologians, the notion of the divine right does not actually appear until the sixteenth century, in the writing of French philosopher Jean Bodin.

7 Similarly, one might observe that such popular modern metaphors as "life is a jungle" or "it's a dog-eat-dog world" symbolically represent social and economic relationships in a competitive, market-based economy.

8 In Poland during the communist era, workers used to cynically joke that "under capitalism, man exploits man. Under socialism, it's the other way around."

9 Further, most such societies justified their employment of police state tactics against internal dissidents as "defending socialism."

5 Durkeim and Weber

1 Robert Merton, a later American functionalist sociologist, distinguished between "manifest" and "latent" functions, with the former being the practical and socially-recognized role of a practice, and the latter being the social function of a practice as understood from a Durkheimian perspective.

2 Altruism poses an explanatory challenge to modern-day sociobiologists (who also call themselves behavioral ecologists). This school of thought assumes that individuals are driven to maximize the transmission of their genes to the next generation, something that is obviously incompatible with surrendering your life so that someone else may live. They have "resolved" this dilemma by claiming that altruism typically occurs between closely related persons, who share a large number of similar genes. Hence, in helping my siblings survive even at the cost of my own life, there is a good probability that they would pass on genes identical to mine to their offspring. As the British geneticist J.B.S. Haldane (1892–1964) memorably expressed it, "I will lay down my life for two brothers or eight cousins" (quoted in McElreath and Boyd 2007: 86). Because an individual would share, on average, half of his alleles with a brother and one-eighth with a cousin, this would be the number of relatives he would have to save in order to genetically "break even." Needless to say, this theory doesn't take us very far in understanding the motives of, for example, a firefighter who enters a life-threatening situation in order to save a child (or even a pet) to whom he or she is not related!

3 The longstanding English version of this work represented this expression as "the idiocy of rural life," but there is now consensus among most Marxist scholars that this is a mistranslation. Newer translations suggest a less pejorative reference to peasants, but there are indications in Marx's other work, especially *The Eighteenth Brumaire of Louis Bonaparte* (1977a, orig. 1852) that he did not hold the peasantry in especially high

regard. In that work, he drew an imaginative analogy between peasants scattered on their isolated plots across the countryside and potatoes in a sack.

4　Such categories are considerably more slippery in modern capitalism, where it might be possible to be both a wage earner and an operator of a small business that employs other workers. Indeed, to the extent that workers have pension plans made up of a stock investment portfolio, they could be considered to have a foothold in both social classes.

5　There are in fact significant differences between the positions of Andre Gunder Frank and Alain De Janvry with regard to persisting underdevelopment in many regions of the world, but both would dispute the claim of modernization theory that underdevelopment is the result of a *lack* of integration of the postcolonial world into world markets. Indeed, Frank argued that formerly colonized societies were impoverished and underdeveloped *to the extent* that they were integrated into the world capitalist system.

6　Spencer, Darwin, and an evolutionary parable for our time

1　I would only hasten to point out that Carnegie's advocacy of a competitive marketplace is somewhat paradoxical. Like most industrialists of his time, he championed the beneficial effects of competition while trying to eliminate as many competitors as possible from the industry in which he participated (in this case, steel). Indeed, Carnegie famously resisted US government efforts to break up "trusts" (monopolies) in order to restore a more competitive capitalist economy.

2　Largely from direction by the Kremlin, there were some interesting experiments introduced in child-rearing in the USSR during the 1920s and 30s, such as giving children in pre-school or kindergarten toys that were too large for a single child to play with, necessitating group play. It was thought that this re-shaped social environment would bring about a collectivist spirit as these children grew up. If my experience with children is any guide, they probably just thought the adults who sponsored these "games" were incredibly lame.

3　The fate of Darwinian scientists in the Soviet Union was shared by many scholars, including the economists who aligned themselves with A. V. Chayanov, whose models of peasant economic behavior ran afoul of Leninist doctrines. Lenin regarded landholding peasants as a source of "spontaneous capitalism" in agriculture and therefore potential enemies of the Soviet state. Ultimately, such beliefs were key to the decision to collectivize agriculture and convert Russian peasants into wage workers on state-run farms. For opposing collectivization Chayanov was repeatedly arrested during the 1930s and finally shot in 1940. After his imprisonment his work was banned in the USSR, but when it was finally translated into English long after Chayanov's death, his ideas influenced a generation of economic anthropologists (Chayanov 1966; Sahlins 1972; Cancian 1989).

4　For a chilling portrait of Russian life during this time, you might look at Alexander Solzhenitsyn's massive three-volume memoir (*The Gulag Archipelago* 2007) detailing his fall from grace as a Red Army officer and imprisonment in the gulags, or Sheila Fitzpatrick's absorbing volume *Everyday Stalinism: Ordinary Life in Extraordinary Times* (2000), which is based on material accessed from recently opened Russian archives.

5　There is the famous story of Sir James Frazer, author of *The Golden Bough*, a still widely read theory of magic and religion. Once when asked if he had ever met any of the savages whose beliefs he documented, Frazer responded "God forbid!"

6　One of Morgan's later critics, Robert Lowie, identified this as *promiscuous sexual communism*. The term has become associated with Morgan's position, although he did not himself employ it. Nonetheless, he seemed to feel that people at the stage of savagery were pretty randy.

7　The only known exceptions are in extremely stratified societies such as Pharaonic Egypt, in which rulers might marry their sisters in order to consolidate power within a single family. This exemption from the incest taboo only applied to ruling families and not to commoners of those societies, however, and in fact was ideologically justified by the claim that Pharaohs and their families were regarded as deities.

8   On the other hand, Morgan did advocate on behalf of American Indians in the face of pressure from white settlers to deprive them of their traditional lands, calling repeatedly but unsuccessfully upon the federal government to protect their land rights. After Custer's defeat at Little Big Horn, he took the unpopular stance of defending the Dakota tribes in print: "Who shall blame the Sioux for defending themselves, their wives and their children, when attacked in their own encampment and threatened with destruction... The group name of the country cannot bear many wars of this description" (quoted in Patterson 2001: 32).

7 Boas and the demise of cultural evolution

1   As Robert Austill, a US Army soldier in the Philippines, described his mission in 1902, "The people of the United States want us to kill all the men, f*ck all the women, and raise up a new race in these Islands" (Bradley 2009: 97).
2   My hometown of Palatine, Illinois, was settled by German farmers in the early nineteenth century. In a cemetery dating to the 1870s most of the pre-1917 grave markers were in German, while *all* burials after 1917 had English language tombstones.
3   Lowie alludes here to the song "A Wandering Minstrel I," from Gilbert and Sullivan's *Mikado*.

8 Culture and psychology

1   Whereas more than 90 percent of all American PhD degrees in economics are still awarded to men (the corresponding figures for political science are about 78 percent and for sociology 58 percent), currently a slight majority (about 52 percent) of all PhD degrees in anthropology are actually awarded to women.
2   Mead divorced Fortune and married Bateson, her third husband, in 1936.
3   Indeed, this was the impetus for Mead's investigation of adolescence in Samoa, the subject of her first best-selling volume, *Coming of Age in Samoa* (1953, orig. 1928).
4   By the way, you would think that someone who directed *Psycho* and *The Birds*, not to mention years of weekly TV shows on the Alfred Hitchcock Hour during the 1960s that gave my generation the willies, would be pretty much fearless himself. Yet Hitchcock was possessed of a terrific fear of eggs (yes, eggs).
5   Even more controversial than the work on wartime intelligence discussed in this section was the employment of about 20 US anthropologists with the War Relocation Authority (WRA), which administered the ten relocation camps to which about 140,000 Japanese Americans had been forcibly removed. Anthropologists were recruited by the WRA to gather information needed to run the camps effectively and to quell unrest among their residents (Patterson 2001: 93).
6   Accusations of sadism and treachery are, however, inevitably directed at foes in wartime, as Dower (1986) pointed out in his assessment of wartime characterizations of the Japanese. Indeed, he offers examples of US wartime popular culture that would have been interpreted in a similar light by the Japanese. Among them is a *Life* magazine cover of an American woman contemplating a Japanese soldier's skull sent her as a souvenir by her husband in the Pacific war.

9 Structure and function

1   The US Defense Department has recently recruited social scientists to gather information on the ground in Iraq and Afghanistan for similar purposes, an initiative

known as the "Human Terrain Project." In 2009, one anthropologist was murdered by one of her erstwhile "informants," who doused her with gasoline and then set her on fire. The employment of anthropologists to further US military goals has been accompanied by a great deal of controversy in the discipline, as well as rationales by Human Terrain personnel that are not unlike those of the earlier functionalists. That is, a common justification is that the military might as well have good information, as they're going to occupy these countries regardless of what they know about them. The problem, of course, is that when anthropologists take sides in a war, they make it impossible for future researchers to conduct their research in that area without danger or suspicion of their motives. I amplify upon this consideration in the next chapter.

2 In an older publication (Moberg 1992), I examined how the British tried to impose the system of indirect rule among the Garifuna in Belize, a people who proved, in the words of administrators, to be frustratingly *ungrateful* for the benefits of colonialism and resistant to administration. Apparently out of the belief that one native culture is much like another, a nineteenth-century Colonial Governor compelled the Garifuna in the colony to elect local mayors, known in Spanish as *alcaldes*, after the pattern observed in Maya communities. While Mayan *alcaldes* did have some power and were soon enough co-opted as local colonial functionaries, the *alcalde* system just didn't "take" among the Garifuna. Although they dutifully elected *alcaldes,* in practice most Garifuna largely ignored them as representatives of the colonial state.

3 Indeed, *the* place to study colonial history for any former part of the British Empire is at the Public Records Office in Kew, just outside London, whose more than 90 miles of shelf space accommodate all those records amassed throughout the Imperial period.

4 She did report that western beliefs linking sex and pregnancy had largely, if not completely, supplanted the beliefs documented by Malinowski, notably, that pregnancy could be caused by an ancestral spirit (*baloma*) entering a woman's body (Weiner 1976: 121).

5 Economics is often regarded as the dismal science because of its assumptions that want and scarcity are universal conditions, largely because of the assumed tendency of human populations to outgrow economic output. We will "critically examine" (i.e. demolish) this assumption in a later chapter dealing with Malthus.

6 Women are curiously lacking from this analysis, except as the providers of sexual services.

7 Davis' political bias may be suggested by the fact that he was a founding member of the Hoover Institution, a prominent US right wing "think tank."

10 Decolonization and anti-structure

1 His legacy is celebrated each year by the Society for Applied Anthropology, which issues an annual award to an outstanding practitioner of applied anthropology.

2 At approximately the same time, several anthropologists at UCLA were providing information to US-supported counterinsurgency efforts in Southeast Asia, especially Thailand. The AAA had adopted a resolution opposing the war in Vietnam in 1966. Yet when Eric Wolf, Joseph Jorgenson, and Gerald Berreman revealed the UCLA anthropologists' involvement in counterinsurgency, an AAA committee headed by Margaret Mead condemned Wolf and his co-authors for their statements while claiming that the counterinsurgency research was "well within the traditional canons of acceptable behavior for the applied anthropologist" (quoted in Patterson 2001: 126).

3 Some relevant quotes, familiar to many Latin Americans, but not to most citizens of the United States:

I don't see why we need to stand by and watch a country go communist due to the irresponsibility of its own people. The issues are much too important for the Chilean voters to be left to decide for themselves.

US Secretary of State Henry Kissinger, 1970

> Not a nut or bolt shall reach Chile under Allende. Once Allende comes to power we shall do all within our power to condemn Chile and all Chileans to utmost deprivation and poverty.
>
> Edward M. Korry, US Ambassador to Chile, 1970

4 The coup and its aftermath are responsible for the fact that September 11 is regarded as a day of infamy throughout Latin America for reasons entirely different from its commemoration in the United States.

5 While Pinochet was consolidating his power in Chile, in neighboring Argentina, a military government launched a reign of terror against suspected leftists that resulted in an estimated 30,000–50,000 deaths and disappearances. Among the most insidious practices of the time was requiring abducted pregnant women to give birth in captivity, after which they were murdered and their babies adopted by military officers and police (Robben 2005: 292–295).

6 Why it is invariably grandmothers and not other relatives whose death occurs at the time of exams would itself make an interesting line of inquiry. I feel tremendous remorse at the hundreds of grandmothers whose deaths have been caused by my exams over the course of my career.

7 Tacking the word "short" onto this phrase describing a lifetime of human misery always reminded me of a great line from a Woody Allen movie, in which he complained about a restaurant that *"the food was terrible. And the portions were so small!"*

8 This reminds me of a nationally-reported incident in 2004, when a worker in Alabama was fired from her job because her car displayed the bumper sticker of a presidential candidate opposed by her boss.

9 Like the British anthropologists of the same period, Bourdieu's work also grappled with decolonization. He conducted fieldwork with the Kabyle Berbers of Algeria during the late 1950s as the French army sought to crush the Algerian independence movement. The experience left a searing impression on Bourdieu, who remained a vocal opponent of colonialism and neoliberal globalization to the end of his life.

11 Ecological and neo-evolutionary approaches

1 We now know that Steward's model was mistaken in his tendency to overstate hunter-gatherer reliance on hunting; in fact, most hunter-gatherers are neolocal and bilateral instead of patrilocal and patrilineal. The reason is that groups maintain access to a wide range of territories and rely at least as much on female gathering as they do male hunting. Hence, contrary to Steward's assertion, there is no need in most hunter-gatherer societies to keep men together for defense and hunting. In effect, what many considered a pioneering paper in cultural anthropology for its first application of a materialist approach to culture was based upon erroneous data!

2 Many American leftists toured the early Soviet Union as a sort of pilgrimage "to see the socialist future," even though such visits were heavily scripted and controlled by Soviet authorities.

3 This originated as a rather ingenious if nefarious Nazi wartime technology, in which German factory managers were required to calculate the energy expenditure of various types of labor so that scarce food rations could be allocated to their workers accordingly.

12 Contemporary materialist and ecological approaches

1 Murphy's statement references a famous comment by Chinese Communist leader Mao Zedong that "power comes from the barrel of a gun." This might be considered a summary—albeit a bit crude—of the Marxist position that the power of the state ultimately rests on its ability to direct the actions of its citizens through coercion.

2 Forced to flee his native Austria by the Nazis, Wolf (1923–1999) fought in a US Army alpine battalion in Italy. Like most male anthropologists of his generation, he attended college on the GI bill. During the 1970s, Wolf led the infusion of Marxist theory into anthropology, with most of his work focusing on Latin American peasantry. His 1982 volume *Europe and the People without History* is considered a modern anthropological classic.

3 Wittfogel, interestingly, had been an ardent Communist before World War II, leading him to be briefly imprisoned by the Nazis before escaping to England. He turned against the Soviet Union when it signed its non-aggression pact with Hitler in 1939, and migrated steadily rightward in his politics. He became a fiercely anti-communist Cold Warrior by the late 1940s.

4 Readers may wonder how this fact is compatible with Malinowski's assertion that the Trobrianders, at least at the time of his fieldwork, denied the relationship between sex and pregnancy. What is curious about the Trobriand case is that, despite considerable sexual activity, women did not exhibit high levels of fertility, a fact that some have attributed to possible contraceptive effects in some ingredients of the Trobriand diet. Similar patterns have been identified in some societies of the Amazon, where the consumption of foods containing high levels of plant estrogens seems to reduce female fertility.

5 Some years later (1998), Eric Ross broke with Malthusian theory, authoring an incisive volume criticizing the Malthusian assumptions underlying both economic development theory and the 20th-century eugenics movement.

6 French anthropologist George Devereux (1976) documented in considerable detail techniques of inducing abortion in 400 pre-industrial cultures.

7 Indeed, Marx's claim that all social orders contain "the seeds of their destruction," is an acknowledgment that no social or economic arrangement will exist over the long term.

8 My wife, who lived for many years in Biloxi, tells of a trial in Mississippi in which a defendant was acquitted of murdering a man who had acquired a notorious local reputation. Interviewed after the trial, one of the jurors was asked why he voted to acquit. The juror said, "Well, I'm not sure whether he killed him, but that s.o.b. sure needed killin'."

13 Symbols, structures, and the "web of significance"

1 In *Stone Age Economics*, Marshall Sahlins made the memorable point about hunter-gatherer societies that work "is intermittent and susceptible to all manner of interruption by cultural alternatives and impediments ranging from heavy ritual to light rainfall" (1972: 86).

2 A sib is a kind of unilineal descent group whose members cannot establish a precise genealogical relationship. It is a common unit of social activity and feasting among Amazonian peoples.

3 Meaning "shark" in Spanish.

4 The title means "Sad Tropics"; although the book has long been available in translation, the French title is still employed in English editions.

5 Outside of Poland, it is not known that most of those who died at the camp known as "Auschwitz I" were non-Jewish Poles who were considered political prisoners. Two of them, Fr. Maximilian Kolbe and Sr. Edith Stein, have been canonized by the Catholic Church.

14 Postmodern political economy and sensibilities

1 This term arose initially among French scholars of the 1970s and 80s who broke with Lévi-Strauss' structuralism, but it also refers to approaches that stress meaning and the fragmented nature of culture over theories, such as Marxism, that emphasize the economic and political structures of society.

2   Soviet architecture under Stalin reflected his preference for neo-classical designs. Upon his death in 1953, however, the USSR's new leadership under Nikita Khruschev immediately embraced Le Corbusier's high modernism.

3   I entered the labor force as a junior in high school, when I worked part-time at a fast food restaurant. I earned the prevailing federal minimum wage of $2.20 an hour. Students laugh in disbelief when I tell them that, but if the minimum wage had kept up with inflation, it would today be about $13 per hour rather than $7.25.

15 The contemporary anthropological moment

1   Ken Kesey's 1962 novel set in a mental hospital, *One Flew over the Cuckoo's Nest*, offers a powerful (if fictional) illustration of this process. Nurse Mildred Ratched exercises tyrannical and humiliating control over the patients in her ward, but does so through the legitimizing discourses of "therapy" and "treatment," which patients are powerless to counter. In the end, she crushes the resistance of a particularly defiant patient, Randall Patrick McMurphy, through the once-common surgical procedure of lobotomy.

2   I apologize to readers for employing such baroque language, but it hints at the opaque way in which some of these guys talk. Don't dare go to a AAA meeting without your decoding ring, or you'll be lost! Quite a few anthropologists speak like the mouse in Figure 15.1.

3   This criticism, I think, neglects the many passages in Bourgois' book, as well as related articles, in which he addresses the long-term structural economic changes underlying inner city unemployment. Interestingly, many of Bourgois' own informants rejected such explanations, instead faulting themselves and other participants in the crack economy for their poverty or addictions. As one of Bourgois' informants in a later study describes himself, "There's nothing righteous about dopefiends. They're assholes; they'll screw you" (Borgois and Schonberg 2009: 1).

REFERENCES

Abu-Lughod, Lila. 1991. "Writing Against Culture" in Richard G. Fox, ed. *Recapturing Anthropology*. Santa Fe, NM: School of American Research.

Abu-Lughod, Lila. 1995. "A Tale of Two Pregnancies" in Ruth Behar and Deborah A. Gordon, eds. *Women Writing Culture*, pp. 339–349. Berkeley, CA: University of California Press.

Asad, Talal. 1972. "Market Model, Class Structure and Consent: A Reconsideration of Swat Political Organisation." *Man* 7 (1): 74–95.

Barnouw, Victor. 1963. *Culture and Personality*. Homewood, IL: Dorsey Press.

Barth, Fredrik. 1959. *Political Leadership Among Swat Pathans*. Monographs in Social Anthropology. London: London School of Economics.

Barth, Fredrik. 1966. *Models of Social Organization*. Occasional Paper No. 23. London: Royal Anthropological Institute of Great Britain and Ireland.

Baudrillard, Jean. 1994. *Simulacra and Simulation*. Trans. Shelia Faria Glaser. Ann Arbor: University of Michigan Press.

Benedict, Ruth. 1934. *Patterns of Culture*. New York: Mentor.

Benedict, Ruth. 1946. *The Chrysanthemum and the Sword*. Boston, MA: Houghton Mifflin.

Benedict, Ruth. 1973. *An Anthropologist at Work: Writings of Ruth Benedict*. Margaret Mead, ed. New York: Equinox.

Black, George. 1988. *The Good Neighbor: How the United States Wrote the History of Central America and the Caribbean*. New York: Pantheon.

Boas, Franz. 1963 (orig. 1911). *The Mind of Primitive Man*. New York: The Free Press.

Boas, Franz. 1966a (orig. 1896). "The Limitations of the Comparative Method of Anthropology" in *Franz Boas: Race, Language, and Culture*, pp. 270–280. New York: The Free Press.

Boas, Franz. 1966b (orig. 1936). "*Methods of Cultural Anthropology*." *Race, Language and Culture*. New York: The Free Press.

Boas, Franz. 1974a (orig. 1894). "Human Faculty as Determined by Race" in George W. Stocking, Jr., ed. *A Franz Boas Reader: The Shaping of American Anthropology, 1883–1911*. Chicago, IL: University of Chicago Press.

Boas, Franz. 1974b (orig. 1919). "Scientists as Spies" in George W. Stocking, Jr., ed. *A Franz Boas Reader: The Shaping of American Anthropology, 1883–1911.* Chicago, IL: University of Chicago Press.

Boserup, Ester. 2005 (orig. 1965). *The Conditions of Agricultural Growth.* New Brunswick, NJ: Transaction Publishers.

Bourdieu, Pierre. 1977. *Outline of a Theory of Practice.* Trans. Richard Nice. Cambridge: Cambridge University Press.

Bourdieu, Pierre. 1984. *Distinction: A Social Critique of the Judgement of Taste.* Trans. Richard Nice. Cambridge, MA: Harvard University Press.

Bourgois, Philippe. 1989. *Ethnicity at Work: Divided Labor on a Central American Banana Plantation.* Baltimore, MD: Johns Hopkins University Press.

Bourgois, Philippe. 1996. *In Search of Respect: Selling Crack in El Barrio.* New York: Cambridge University Press.

Bourgois, Philippe and Jeffrey Schonberg. 2009. *Righteous Dopefiend.* Berkeley, CA: University of California Press.

Bradley, James. 2009. *The Imperial Cruise: A Secret History of Empire and War.* New York: Little, Brown and Company.

Bridges, Tyler. 1994. *The Rise of David Duke.* Oxford, MS: University Press of Mississippi.

Bryant, Raymond L. and Sinead Bailey. 1997. *Third World Political Ecology.* London: Routledge.

Bullard, Robert. 2000. *Dumping in Dixie: Race, Class, and Environmental Quality.* Boulder, CO: Westview.

Butler, Rohan d'Olier. 1985. *The Roots of National Socialism, 1783–1933.* New York: AMS Press.

Caffrey, Margaret. 1989. *Ruth Benedict: Stranger in the Land.* Austin, TX: University of Texas Press.

Cancian, Frank. 1989. "Economic Behavior in Peasant Communities" in Stuart Plattner, ed. *Economic Anthropology.* Stanford, CA: Stanford University Press.

Carnegie, Andrew. 1901. *The Gospel of Wealth and Other Timely Essays.* New York: Century.

Casas, Bartolomé de las. 1992 (orig. 1542). *The Devastation of the Indies: A Brief Account.* Trans. Herma Briffault. Baltimore, MD: Johns Hopkins University Press.

Cathcart, Thomas and Daniel Klein. 2006. *Plato and Platypus Walk into a Bar: Understanding Philosophy Through Jokes.* New York: Abrams Image.

Chayanov, A.V. 1966. "Peasant Farm Organization" in D. Thorner, B. Kerblay and R.E.F. Smith, eds. *A. V. Chayanov on the Theory of Peasant Economy.* Homewood, IL: Richard D. Irwin for the American Economic Association.

Chomsky, Noam. 1965. *Aspects of the Theory of Syntax.* Cambridge, MA: MIT Press.

Cole, Sally. 2002. "'Mrs. Landes Meet Mrs. Benedict': Culture Patterns and Individual Agency in the 1930s." *American Anthropologist.* 104 (2): 533–543.

Curran, Vivian Grosswald. 2000. "Herder and the Holocaust" in F.C. DeCoste and Bernard Schwartz, eds. *The Holocaust's Ghost: Writings on Art, Politics, Law, and Education.* pp. 399–410. Edmonton: University of Alberta Press.

Dalton, George. 1974. "How Exactly are Peasants 'Exploited'?" *American Anthropologist.* 76 (3): 553–561.

D'Andrade, Roy. 1995. "Moral Models in Anthropology." *Current Anthropology.* 36 (3): 399–408.

Davis, Kingsley. 1937. "The Sociology of Prostitution." *American Sociological Review.* 2 (5): 744–755.

De Beauvoir, Simone. 1953. *The Second Sex.* New York: Knopf.

De Janvry, Alain. 1981. *The Agrarian Question and Reformism in Latin America.* Baltimore, MD: Johns Hopkins University.

Delaney, Sarah. 2009. "Vatican Economist Says Christians Must Put Ethics Back into Business." Catholic News Service. August 24. http://www.catholicnews.com/data/stories/cns/0903797.htm (accessed August 12, 2011).

Devereux, George. 1976 (orig. 1955). *A Study of Abortion in Primitive Societies*. New York: International Universities Press.

Douglas, Mary. 1966. *Purity and Danger: An Analysis of the Concepts of Pollution and Taboo*. New York: Praeger.

Douglas, Mary. 1972. "Deciphering a Meal." *Daedalus*. 101: 61–82.

Dower, John. 1986. *War Without Mercy: Race and Power in the Pacific War*. New York: Pantheon.

Du Bois, Cora Alice, Abram Kardiner, and Emil Oberholzer. 1944. *The People of Alor: A Social-Psychological Study of an East Indian Island*. Minneapolis, MN: University of Minnesota Press.

Durham, William C. 1979. *Scarcity and Survival in Central America: Ecological Origins of the "Soccer War."* Stanford, CA: Stanford University.

Durkheim, Emile. 1933 (orig. 1893). *Division of Labor in Society*. Trans. G. Simpson. New York: Macmillan.

Durkheim, Emile. 1951 (orig. 1897). *Suicide*. Trans. J. Spaulding and G. Simpson. New York: Free Press.

Durkheim, Emile. 1974 (orig. 1906). "The Determination of Moral Facts," in *Emile Durkheim: Sociology and Philosophy*. pp. 35–62. New York: Simon and Schuster.

Durkheim, Emile. 2002 (orig. 1912) "The Elementary Forms of the Religious Life," in Michael Lambek, ed. *A Reader in the Anthropology of Religion*. pp. 34–59. Malden, MA: Blackwell.

Earle, Timothy K. 1978. *The Economic and Social Organization of a Complex Chiefdom: The Halelea District, Kauai, Hawaii*. Ann Arbor:, MI Museum of Anthropology, University of Michigan.

Edwards, David B. 1998. "Learning from the Swat Pathans: Political Leadership in Afghanistan, 1978–1997." *American Ethnologist*. 25 (4): 712–728.

Ehrlich, Paul. 1971. *The Population Bomb*. New York: Ballatine Books.

Engels, Frederick. 1972 (orig. 1884). *The Origin of the Family, Private Property, and the State*. New York: International Publishers.

Escobar, Arturo. 1995. *Encountering Development: The Making and Unmaking of the Third World*. Princeton, NJ: Princeton University Press.

Evans-Pritchard, E.E. 1937. *Witchcraft, Oracles and Magic Among the Azande*. London: Oxford University Press.

Everett, Daniel L. 2008. *Don't Sleep, There are Snakes: Life and Language in the Amazonian Jungle*. New York: Vintage.

Farmer, Paul. 1996. "On Suffering and Structural Violence: A View from Below." *Daedalus*. 125 (1): 261–283.

Farmer, Paul. 2003. *Pathologies of Power: Health, Human Rights and the New War on the Poor*. Berkeley, CA: University of California Press.

Farmer, Paul. 2008. "Mother Courage and the Future of War." *Social Analysis*. 52 (2): 165–184.

Ferguson, James. 1994. *The Anti-politics Machine: Development, Depoliticization and Bureaucratic Power in Lesotho*. Minneapolis, MN: University of Minnesota Press.

Fernandez, James. 1982. *Bwiti: An Ethnography of the Religious Imagination in Africa*. Princeton, NJ: Princeton University Press.

Feyerabend, Paul. 1978. *Science in a Free Society*. London: Verso.

Firth, Raymond. 1964. *Essays on Social Organisation and Values*. London: Athlone.

Fitzpatrick, Sheila. 2000. *Everyday Stalinism: Ordinary Life in Extraordinary Times*. New York: Oxford University Press.

Foley, Douglas. 1997. "Reviewed work(s): *In Search of Respect: Selling Crack in El Barrio,* by Philippe Bourgois." *Journal of the Royal Anthropological Institute.* 3 (2): 377–378.

Fortes, Meyer and E.E. Evans-Pritchard. 1940. "Introduction" in M. Fortes and E. E. Evans-Pritchard, eds. *African Political Systems.* London: Oxford University Press.

Foucault, Michel. 1965. *Madness and Civilization.* New York: Pantheon.

Foucault, Michel. 1984. *The Foucault Reader.* New York: Pantheon.

Frank, Andre Gunder. 1969. *Capitalism and Under-Development in Latin America.* New York: Monthly Review Press.

Frank, Justin. 2007. *Bush on the Couch: Inside the Mind of the President.* New York: Harper Collins.

Freeman, Derek. 1983. *Margaret Mead: The Making and Unmaking of an Anthropological Myth.* Cambridge, MA: Harvard University Press.

Freud, Sigmund. 1989 (orig. 1927). *The Future of an Illusion.* New York: Norton.

Freud, Sigmund. 2001 (orig. 1913). *Totem and Taboo: Some Points of Agreement Between the Mental Lives of Savages and Neurotics.* London: Routledge Classics.

Fried, Morton. 1967. *The Evolution of Political Society.* New York: Random House.

Fukuyama, Francis. 1992. *The End of History and the Last Man.* New York: Free Press.

Galtung, Johan. 1967. "Scientific Colonialism: The Lessons of Project Camelot." *Transition.* 30 (April–May): 10–15.

Gardner, Katy. 1997. "Mixed Messages: Contested 'Development' and the 'Plantation Rehabilitation Project,'" in R.D. Grillo and R.T. Stirrat, eds. *Discourses of Development: Anthropological Perspectives.* Oxford: Berg.

Gartman, David. 1994. *Auto Opium: A Social History of American Automobile Design.* New York: Routledge.

Geertz, Clifford. 1963. *Agricultural Involution: The Process of Agricultural Change in Indonesia.* Berkeley, CA: University of California Press.

Geertz, Clifford. 1966. "The Impact of the Concept of Culture on the Concept of Man" in J. Platt, ed. *New Views of the Nature of Man.* pp. 93–118. Chicago, IL: University of Chicago Press.

Geertz, Clifford. 1967. "Under the Mosquito Net: Review of Bronislaw Malinowski, *A Diary in the Strict Sense of the Term, and Coral Gardens and their Magic.*" *New York Review of Books,* September 14. http://www.anthrofoology.com/post/3070979163/clifford-geertz-under-the-mosquito-net (accessed August 26, 2011).

Geertz, Clifford. 1973a. "Deep Play: Notes on the Balinese Cockfight" in *The Interpretation of Cultures.* pp. 412–454. New York: Basic Books.

Geertz, Clifford. 1973b. "Thick Description: Toward an Interpretive Theory of Culture" in *The Interpretation of Cultures.* pp. 3–33. New York: Basic Books.

Geertz, Clifford. 1989. *Works and Lives: The Anthropologist as Author.* Stanford, CA: Stanford University Press.

Genesis. 1992. *The Catholic Rainbow Study Bible,* 2nd edn. El Reno, OK: Rainbow Studies International.

Giddens, Anthony. 1979. *Central Problems in Social Theory: Action, Structure and Contradiction in Social Analysis.* Berkeley, CA: University of California Press.

Gluckman, Max. 1963. *Order and Rebellion in Tribal Africa.* Glencoe, IL: Free Press.

Gmelch, George. 2009. "Baseball Magic" in Pamela A. Moro and James E. Myers, eds. *Magic, Witchcraft and Religion: A Reader in the Anthropology of Religion.* Boston: McGraw-Hill.

Goffman, Erving. 1990 (orig. 1960). *The Presentation of Self in Everyday Life.* New York: Penguin.

Goodenough, Ward. 1964. "Cultural Anthropology and Linguistics" in Dell Hymes, ed. *Language in Culture and Society: A Reader in Linguistics and Anthropology.* New York: Harper and Row.

Gordon, David, Richard Edwards, and Michael Reich. 1982. *Segmented Work, Divided Workers.* Cambridge: Cambridge University Press.

Gough, Kathleen. 1968. "Anthropology: Child of Imperialism." *Monthly Review.* 19 (11): 12–27.

Gramsci, Antonio. 1971. *Selections from the Prison Notebooks.* Ed. Quintin Hoare and Geoffrey Nowell-Smith. New York: International Publishers.

Greenwald, Glenn. 2010. "The Two Faces of Winston Churchill." http://www.salon.com/news/opinion/glenn_greenwald/2010/08/16/churchill (accessed October 19, 2010).

Gregg, Dorothy and Elgin Williams. 1948. "The Dismal Science of Functionalism." *American Anthropologist.* 50 (4): 594–611.

Habermas, Jürgen. 1987. "Modernity vs. Postmodernity" in Paul Rabinow and William M. Sullivan, eds. *Interpretive Social Science: A Second Look.* Berkeley, CA: University of California Press.

Hanes, Richard C. 1982. "Cultural Persistence in Nevada: Current Native American Issues." *Journal of California and Great Basin Anthropology.* 4 (3): 203–221.

Hanes, Richard C. and Laurie Collier Hillstrom. n.d. *Paiutes.* http://www.everyculture.com/multi/Le-Pa/Paiutes.html (accessed October 25, 2010).

Haraway, Donna J. 1989. *Primate Visions: Gender, Race and Nature in the World of Modern Science.* New York: Routledge.

Haraway, Donna J. 2004. "Morphing in the Order: Flexible Strategies, Feminist Science Studies, and Primate Revisions" in Donna Haraway, ed. *The Haraway Reader.* New York: Routledge.

Hardin, Garrett. 1968. "The Tragedy of the Commons." *Science.* New Series 162 (3859): 1243–1248.

Hardin, Garrett. 1970. "Parenthood: Right or Privilege?" *Science.* New Series 169: 427.

Harner, Michael. 1977. "The Ecological Basis for Aztec Sacrifice." *American Ethnologist.* 4 (1): 117–135.

Harris, Marvin. 1964. *Patterns of Race in the Americas.* New York: W. W. Norton.

Harris, Marvin. 1966. "The Cultural Ecology of India's Sacred Cattle." *Current Anthropology.* 7: 51–66.

Harris, Marvin. 1968. *The Rise of Anthropological Theory.* New York: Harper & Row.

Harris, Marvin. 1980. *Cultural Materialism: The Struggle for a Science of Culture.* New York: Random House.

Harris, Marvin. 1985. *Good to Eat: Riddles of Food and Culture.* New York: Simon and Schuster.

Harris, Marvin. 1991. *Cultural Anthropology,* 3rd edn. New York: Harper Collins.

Harris, Marvin. 1992. "Distinguished Lecture: Anthropology and the Theoretical and Paradigmatic Significance of the Collapse of Soviet and East European Communism." *American Anthropologist.* 94: 295–305.

Harris, Marvin. 1995. "Anthropology and Postmodernism" in Martin F. Murphy and Maxine L. Margolis, eds. *Science, Materialism and the Study of Culture.* pp. 62–80. Gainesville, FL: University Press of Florida.

Harvey, David. 1989. *The Condition of Postmodernity: An Enquiry into the Origins of Cultural Change.* Oxford: Blackwell.

Herder, Johann Gottfried von. 1968. *Reflections on the Philosophy of the History of Mankind.* Ed. Frank E. Manuel. Chicago, IL: University of Chicago Press.

Herrnstein, Richard J. and Charles A. Murray. 1996. *The Bell Curve: Intelligence and Class Structure in American Life.* New York: the Free Press.

Herskovits, Melville J. 1952. *Economic Anthropology.* New York: Alfred A. Knopf.

Higham, Carol L. 2000. *Noble, Wretched and Redeemable: Protestant Missionaries to the Indians in Canada and the United States, 1820–1900.* Albuquerque:, NM University of New Mexico Press.

Homans, George and David M. Schneider. 1955. *Marriage, Authority and Final Causes.* New York: Free Press.

Ingersoll, Daniel W. 1998. "Stealing the Symbols." Paper presented at the annual meeting of the Southern Anthropological Society, Wilmington, NC. March 28.

Johnson, Allen W. and Timothy K. Earle. 2002. *The Evolution of Human Society,* 2nd edn. Stanford, CA: Stanford University Press.

Johnson, Allen W. and Douglass Price-Williams. 1996. *Oedipus Ubiquitous: The Family Complex in World Folk Literature.* Stanford: CA Stanford University Press.

Kardiner, Abram. 1955. *The Individual and His Society: The Psychodynamics of Primitive Social Organization.* New York: Columbia University Press.

Kerns, Virginia. 2003. *Scenes from the High Desert: Julian Steward's Life and Theory.* Urbana, IL: University of Illinois Press.

Kesey, Ken. 1962. *One Flew Over the Cuckoo's Nest.* New York: New American Library.

Kipling, Rudyard. 1919. *Rudyard Kipling's Verse,* vol. 2. Garden City, NJ: Doubleday.

Koppelman, Alex. 2009. "Barack Obama's Lucky Tie." http://www.salon.com/news/politics/war_room/2009/09/10/lucky_tie (accessed October 21, 2010).

Kreisman, Jerald J. and Hal Straus. 1989. *I Hate You. Don't Leave Me: Understanding the Borderline Personality.* New York: Avon.

Kroeber, Alfred. 1939. *Cultural and Natural Areas of Native North America.* Publications in American Archaeology and Ethnology, vol. 38. Berkeley, CA: University of California.

Kroeber, Alfred and Clyde Kluckhohn. 1952. "Culture: A Critical Review of Concepts and Definitions." *Papers of the Peabody Museum of American Archaeology and Ethnology,* vol. 47. Cambridge, MA: Harvard University.

Kroeber, Karl. 2003. "Curious Profession: Alfred Kroeber and Anthropological History." *Boundary 2.* 30 (3): 141–155.

Kunstler, James Howard. 2010. "A Reflection on Cities of the Future." http://www.kunstler.com/mags_cities_of_the_future.html (accessed November 5, 2010).

Landes, David S. 2000. *Revolution in Time: Clocks and the Making of the Modern World.* Cambridge, MA: Harvard University Press.

Langness, L.L. 2005. *The Study of Culture,* 3rd. edn. Novato, CA: Chandler & Sharp.

Latour, Bruno and Stephen Woolgar. 1979. *Laboratory Life: The Social Construction of Scientific Facts.* London: Sage.

Laufer, Berthold. 1918. "Review: *Culture and Ethnology,* by Robert H. Lowie." *American Anthropologist.* 20 (1): 87–91.

Leach, Edmund. 1970. *Lévi-Strauss.* London: Harper Collins.

Leach, Edmund. 1981 (originally 1954). *Political Systems of Highland Burma: A Study of Kachin Social Structure.* London: Athlone.

Leacock, Eleanor. 1983. "Interpreting the Origins of Gender Inequality: Conceptual and Historical Problems." *Dialectical Anthropology.* 7: 265–284.

Leake, Jonathan. 2010. "Don't Talk to Aliens, Warns Stephen Hawking." *The Sunday Times* (London). April 25. http://www.timesonline.co.uk/tol/news/science/space/article7107207.ece (accessed August 23, 2011).

Lee, Richard B. 1969. "!Kung Bushman Subsistence: An Input-Output Analysis" in Andrew Vayda, ed. *Environment and Cultural Behavior.* Garden City, NY: Natural History Press.

Lee, Richard B. 1979. *The !Kung San: Men, Women, and Work in a Foraging Society.* New York: Cambridge University Press.

Lett, James. 1987. *The Human Enterprise: A Critical Introduction to Anthropological Theory.* Boulder, CO: Westview.

Lett, James. 1991. "Interpretive Anthropology: Metaphysics and the Paranormal." *Journal of Anthropological Research.* 47: 305–309.

Lévi-Strauss, Claude. 1961. *Tristes Tropiques*. New York: Criterion Books.

Lévi-Strauss, Claude. 1963. *Totemism*. Trans. R. Needham. Boston, MA: Beacon Press.

Lévi-Strauss, Claude. 1966. "The Culinary Triangle." *Partisan Review.* 33: 586–595.

Lévi-Strauss, Claude. 1969a (orig. 1949). *The Elementary Structures of Kinship.* Trans. R. Needham. Boston, MA: Beacon Press.

Lévi-Strauss, Claude. 1969b. *The Raw and the Cooked.* New York: Harper and Row.

Lévi-Strauss, Claude and Didier Eribon. 1991. *Conversations with Claude Lévi-Strauss.* Chicago, IL: University of Chicago Press.

Lewis, Oscar. 1951. *Life in a Mexican Village: Tepoztlan Restudied.* Urbana, IL: University of Illinois Press.

Lewis, Oscar. 1959. *Five Families: Mexican Case Studies in the Culture of Poverty.* New York: Mentor.

Lewis, Oscar. 1960. *Tepoztlán: Village in Mexico.* New York: Holt, Rinehart, Winston.

Lewis, Oscar. 1963. *The Children of Sánchez: Autobiography of a Mexican Family.* New York: Vintage.

Little, Peter D. and Michael Painter. 1995. "Discourse, Politics, and the Development Process: Reflections on Escobar's 'Anthropology and the Development Encounter.'" *American Ethnologist.* 22 (3): 602–616.

Lowie, Robert. 1920. *Primitive Society.* New York: Boni & Liveright.

Lutz, Catherine A. and Jane L. Collins. 1993. *Reading National Geographic.* Chicago, IL: University of Chicago Press.

Lyotard, Jean-François. 1984. *The Postmodern Condition: A Report on Knowledge.* Minneapolis, MN: University of Minnesota Press.

Malinowski, Bronislaw. 1927. "The Life of Culture" in G.E. Smith, B. Malinowski, H.J. Spinden and A. Goldenwieser, eds. *The Diffusion Controversy.* New York: Norton.

Malinowski, Bronislaw. 1939. "The Group and the Individual in Functional Analysis." *American Journal of Sociology.* 44 (4): 938–964.

Malinowski, Bronislaw. 1945. *The Dynamics of Culture Change: An Inquiry into Race Relations in Africa.* Ed. P. Kaberry. New Haven, CT: Yale University Press.

Malinowski, Bronislaw. 1984 (orig. 1922). *Argonauts of the Western Pacific.* Long Grove, IL: Waveland Press.

Malinowski, Bronislaw. 1989 (orig. 1967). *A Diary in the Strict Sense of the Term.* Trans. Norbert Guterman. Stanford, CA: Stanford University Press.

Malinowski, Bronislaw. 2001 (orig. 1944). *A Scientific Theory of Culture and Other Essays.* New York: Routledge.

Malinowski, Bronislaw. 2010 (orig. 1929). *The Sexual Lives of Savages in Northwest Melanesia.* New York: Taylor and Francis.

Malthus, Thomas Robert. 1985 (orig. 1798). *An Essay on the Principle of Population.* New York: Penguin Books.

Marshall, Mac. 1993. "The Wizard of Oz Meets the Wicked Witch of the East: Freeman, Mead, and Ethnographic Authority." *American Ethnologist.* 20 (3): 604–617.

Martin, Emily. 1992. "The End of the Body?" *American Ethnologist.* 19 (1): 121–140.

Marx, Karl. 1977a (orig. 1852). "The Eighteenth Brumaire of Louis Bonaparte" in David McLellan, ed. *Karl Marx: Selected Writings.* Oxford: Oxford University Press.

Marx, Karl. 1977b (orig. 1845). "The German Ideology" in David McLellan, ed. *Karl Marx: Selected Writings.* Oxford: Oxford University Press.

Marx, Karl. 1977c (orig. 1845). "Theses on Feuerbach" in David McLellan, ed. *Karl Marx: Selected Writings.* Oxford: Oxford University Press.

Marx, Karl. 1977d (orig. 1870). "To Meyer and Vogt, 9 Apr. 1870" in David McLellan, ed. *Karl Marx: Selected Writings.* Oxford: Oxford University Press.

Marx, Karl. 1977e (orig. 1843). "Towards a Critique of Hegel's *Philosophy of Right:* An Introduction" in David McLellan, ed. *Karl Marx: Selected Writings.* Oxford University Press.

Marx, Karl. 1993 (orig. 1858). *Grundrisse.* New York: Penguin.

Marx, Karl and Frederick Engels. 1957. *Marx and Engels on Religion.* Moscow: Foreign Language Publishing House.

Marx, Karl and Frederick Engels. 1979 (orig. 1848). "Manifesto of the Communist Party" in *Karl Marx, Frederick Engels: Collected Works*, vol. 6. New York: International Publishers.

Mauss, Marcel. 2002 (orig. 1950). *The Gift.* Oxford: Routledge.

McArthur, Margaret. 1960. "Food Consumption and Dietary Levels of Groups of Aborigines Living on Naturally Occurring Foods" in C.P. Mountford, ed. *Records of the Australian-American Scientific Expedition to Arnhem Land, vol. 2: Anthropology and Nutrition.* Melbourne: Melbourne University Press.

McElreath, Richard and Robert Boyd. 2007. *Mathematical Models of Social Evolution: A Guide for the Perplexed.* Chicago, IL: University of Chicago Press.

McGee, R. Jon and Richard L. Warms. 2008. *Anthropological Theory,* 3rd edn. New York: McGraw Hill.

McGee, William. 1901. "Man's Place in Nature." *American Anthropologist.* 3 (1): 1–13.

Mead, Margaret. 1934. "Preface" to Ruth Benedict's *Patterns of Culture.* New York: Mentor.

Mead, Margaret. 1950 (orig. 1935). *Sex and Temperament in Three Primitive Societies.* New York: Mentor.

Mead, Margaret. 1953 (orig. 1928). *Coming of Age in Samoa.* New York: Modern Library.

Medvedev, Zhores. 1969. *The Rise and Fall of T.D. Lysenko.* New York: Columbia University Press.

Mendonsa, Eugene L. 1982. *The Politics of Divination: A Processual View of Reactions to Illness and Deviance among the Sisala of Northern Ghana.* Berkeley, CA: University of California Press.

Millikan, Marx F. and Walt W. Rostow. 1954. "Notes on Foreign Economic Policy" in Christopher Simpson, ed. *Universities and Empire: Money and Politics in the Social Sciences during the Cold War.* New York: New Press.

Moberg, Mark. 1992. "Continuity under Colonial Rule: The Alcalde System and the Garifuna in Belize, 1858–1969." *Ethnohistory.* 39: 1–19.

Moberg, Mark. 1996. *Myths of Ethnicity and Nation: Immigration, Work and Identity in the Belize Banana Industry.* Knoxville, TN: University of Tennessee Press.

Moberg, Mark. 2008. *Slipping Away: Banana Politics and Fair Trade in the Eastern Caribbean.* New York: Berghahn.

Moore, Jerry D. 2009. *Visions of Culture,* 3rd edn. Lanham, MD: Altamira.

Morgan, Lewis Henry. 1909 (orig. 1877). *Ancient Society.* Chicago, IL: Charles H. Kerr.

Morgan, Lewis Henry. 1997 (orig. 1870). *Systems of Consanguinity and Affinity of the Human Family.* Lincoln, NE: University of Nebraska Press.

Murra, John, ed. 1974. *American Anthropology, the Early Years.* St. Paul, MN: West Publishing.

Nietzsche, Friedrich. 1976 (orig. 1885). "Thus Spoke Zarathustra" in *The Portable Nietzsche.* Ed. and trans. Walter Kaufman. New York: Penguin.

Nugent, David. 1997. "Reviewed work(s): *In Search of Respect: Selling Crack in El Barrio* by Philippe Bourgois." *American Ethnologist.* (24) 3: 685–687.

O'Barr, William. 1994. *Culture and the Ad: Exploring the World of Otherness in Advertising.* Boulder, CO: Westview.

Ogden, C.K. 1967 (orig. 1932). *Opposition: A Linguistic and Psychological Analysis.* Bloomington, IN: Indiana University Press.

O'Meara, J. Tim. 1989. "Anthropology as Empirical Science." *American Anthropologist.* 91 (2): 354–369.

Opler, Morris E. 1961. "Cultural Evolution, Southern Athapaskans, and Chronology in Theory." *Southwestern Journal of Anthropology.* 17 (1): 1–20.

Ortner, Sherry B. 1974. "Is Female to Male as Nature Is to Culture?" in Michelle Rosaldo and Louise Lamphere, eds. *Woman, Culture and Society.* pp. 67–87. Palo Alto, CA: Stanford University Press.

Panati, Charles. 1989. *Extraordinary Endings of Practically Everything and Everybody.* New York: HarperCollins.

Patterson, Thomas. 2001. *A Social History of Anthropology in the United States.* New York: Berg.

Peace, William J. 2004. *Leslie A. White: Evolution and Revolution in Anthropology.* Lincoln, NE: University of Nebraska Press.

Piddocke, Stuart. 1968. "The Potlatch System of the Southern Kwakiutl: A New Perspective" in Edward E. LeClair, Harold K. Schneider and Melville Herskovits, eds. *Economic Anthropology: Readings in Theory and Analysis.* New York: Holt, Rinehart, Winston.

Potter, Elizabeth. 2001. *Gender and Boyle's Law of Gases.* Bloomington, IN: Indiana University Press.

Poulantzas, Nicos. 1978. *State, Power, Socialism.* London: New Left Books.

Price, David. 2004. *Threatening Anthropology: McCarthyism and the FBI's Surveillance of Activist Anthropologists.* Durham, NC: Duke University Press.

Putnam, Robert D. 2000. *Bowling Alone: The Collapse and Revival of American Community.* New York: Simon and Schuster.

Radcliffe-Brown, A.R. 1952. *Structure and Function in Primitive Society.* London: Oxford University Press.

Radcliffe-Brown, A.R. 1957. *A Natural Science of Society.* Glencoe, IL: The Free Press.

Radcliffe-Brown, A.R. 1977. "Religion and Society" in Adam Kuper, ed. *The Social Anthropology of Radcliffe-Brown.* London: Routledge & Kegan Paul.

Radin, Paul. 1926. *Crashing Thunder: The Autobiography of an American Indian.* New York: D. Appleton.

Rand, Ayn. 1962. "Introducing Objectivism." *Los Angeles Times.* July 8: 35.

Rauchway, Eric. 2008. *The Great Depression and the New Deal: A Very Short Introduction.* New York: Oxford University Press.

Redfield, Robert. 1930. *Tepotzlan, A Mexican Village: A Study in Folk Life.* University of Chicago Press.

Rich, Frank. 2006. *The Greatest Story Ever Sold: The Decline and Fall of Truth, From 9/11 to Katrina.* New York: Penguin Press.

Richards, Audrey. 1957. "The Concept of Culture in Malinowski's Work" in Raymond Firth, ed. *Man and Culture: An Evaluation of the Work of Bronislaw Malinowski.* London: Routledge.

Rigdon, Susan M. 1988. *The Culture Façade: Art, Science, and Politics in the Work of Oscar Lewis.* Urbana, IL: University of Illinois Press.

Robben, Antonius C.G.M. 2005. *Political Violence and Trauma in Argentina.* Philadelphia, PA: University of Pennsylvania Press.

Roheim, Geza. 1945. *The Eternal Ones of the Dream: Psychoanalytic Interpretation of Australian Myth.* New York: International Universities Press.

Roheim, Geza. 1950. *Psychoanalysis and Anthropology: Culture, Personality and the Unconscious.* New York: International University Press.

Rorty, Richard. 1995. "Deconstruction" in Raman Seldon, ed. *The Cambridge History of Literary Criticism, Volume VIII: From Formalism to Poststructuralism,* pp. 166–196. Cambridge: Cambridge University Press.

Rosaldo, Renato. 1989. *Culture and Truth: The Remaking of Social Analysis.* Boston, MA: Beacon Press.

Roseberry, William. 1982. "Balinese Cockfights and the Seduction of Anthropology." *Social Research.* 49: 1013–1028.

Ross, Eric B. 1980. "Introduction" in Eric Ross, ed. *Beyond the Myths of Culture: Essays in Cultural Materialism,* pp. xix–xxix. New York: Academic Press.

Ross, Eric B. 1998. *The Malthus Factor: Poverty, Politics and Population in Capitalist Development.* London: Zed.

Ross, Eric B. and Jane Ross. 1980. "Amazon Warfare." *Science.* 207: 510–513.

Rossi, Benedetta. 2006. "Aid Policies and Recipient Strategies in Niger: Why Donors and Recipients Should Not Be Compartmentalized into Separate 'Worlds of Knowledge'" in David Lewis and David Mosse, eds. *Development Brokers and Translators: The Ethnography of Aid and Agencies.* Bloomfield, CT: Kumarian.

Rostow, Walt Whitman. 1960. *The Stages of Economic Growth: A Non-Communist Manifesto.* New York: Cambridge University Press.

Rothstein, Edward. 2009. "Claude Lévi-Strauss, 100, Dies; Altered Western Views of the 'Primitive.'" *New York Times.* November 4. http://www.nytimes.com/2009/11/04/world/europe/04levistrauss.html (accessed November 2, 2010).

Sachs, Harvey. 2010. *The Ninth: Beethoven and the World in 1824.* New York: Random House.

Sahlins, Marshall. 1972. *Stone Age Economics.* Chicago, IL: Aldine.

Sahlins, Marshall and Elman Service. 1960. *Evolution and Culture.* Ann Arbor, MI: University of Michigan Press.

Said, Edward W. 1978. *Orientalism.* New York: Pantheon Books.

Sanjek, Roger. 1990. "Fire, Loss, and the Sorcerer's Apprentice" in Roger Sanjek, ed. *Fieldnotes: The Makings of Anthropology.* Ithaca, NY: Cornell University Press.

Sapir, Edward. 1949. *Culture, Language, and Personality.* Berkeley, CA: University of California Press.

Scheper-Hughes, Nancy. 1993. *Death Without Weeping: The Violence of Everyday Life in Brazil.* Berkeley, CA: University of California Press.

Scheper-Hughes, Nancy. 1995. "The Primacy of the Ethical: Propositions for a Militant Anthropology." *Current Anthropology.* 36 (3): 409–440.

Schorr, Juliet B. 1992. *The Overworked American: The Unexpected Decline of Leisure.* New York: Basic Books.

Scott, James. 1985. *Weapons of the Weak: Everyday Forms of Peasant Resistance.* New Haven, CT: Yale University Press.

Scott, James. 1998. *Seeing Like a State: How Certain Schemes to Improve the Human Condition Have Failed.* New Haven, CT: Yale University Press.

Service, Elman. 1962. *Primitive Social Organization.* New York: Random House.

Shankman, Paul. 1969. "Le Rôti et le Bouilli: Lévi-Strauss' Theory of Cannibalism." *American Anthropologist.* 71: 54–69.

Shostak, Marjorie. *Nisa: the Life and Words of a !Kung Woman.* London: Earthscan.

Slocum, Sally. 1975. "Woman the Gatherer: Male Bias in Anthropology" in Rayna R. Reiter, ed. *Toward an Anthropology of Women.* New York: Monthly Review Press.

Smith, Adam. 2005 (orig. 1776). *An Inquiry into the Nature and Causes of the Wealth of Nations.* Penn State Electronic Classics Series. Hazleton, PA: Penn State University. http://www2.hn.psu.edu/faculty/jmanis/adam-smith/Wealth-Nations.pdf (accessed September 27, 2010).

Smith, Marian W. 1959. "Boas' 'Natural History' Approach to Field Method" in Walter Goldschmidt, ed. *The Anthropology of Franz Boas.* San Francisco, CA: H. Chandler and the American Anthropological Association.

Smithsonian Institution. 2009. "James Smithson Bicentennial Medal Presented to Claude Lévi-Strauss." Smithsonian National Museum of Natural History. June 12. http://www.mnh.si.edu/press_office/releases/2009/Smithson%20Bicentennial%20Award%20release__final%20draft%20(2).pdf (accessed November 3, 2010).

Solzhenitsyn, Alexander. 2007. *The Gulag Archipelago, Volumes 1 and 2: An Experiment in Literary Investigation*. New York: Harper Perennial Modern Classics.

Spradley, J. and D. McCurdy. 1988. *The Cultural Experience*. Long Grove, IL: Waveland Press.

Stephens, John Lloyd. 1841. *Incidents of Travel in Central America, Chiapas, and Yucatan*. New York: Harper and Brothers.

Sterk, Claire. 1999. *Fast Lives: Women Who Use Crack Cocaine*. Philadelphia, PA: Temple University Press.

Steward, Julian. 1936. "The Economic and Social Basis of Primitive Bands" in R. Lowie, ed. *Essays in Anthropology Presented to A. L. Kroeber*, pp. 331–345. Berkeley, CA: University of California Press.

Steward, Julian H. 1968. "Cultural Ecology" in D. Sills, ed. *International Encyclopedia of the Social Sciences*, vol. 4. pp. 337–344. New York: Macmillan.

Steward, Julian H. 2002 (orig. 1938). *Basin Plateau Aboriginal Sociopolitical Groups*. Salt Lake City, UT: University of Utah Press.

Steward, Julian H. and Louis C. Faron. 1959. *Native Peoples of South America*. New York: McGraw-Hill.

Stocking, George W. 1982. *Race, Culture, and Evolution: Essays in the History of Anthropology*. Chicago, IL: University of Chicago Press.

Strathern, Andrew. 1979. *Ongka: A Self-Account by a New Guinea Big Man*. New York: Palgrave Macmillan.

Strathern, Marilyn. 1987. "Out of Context: The Persuasive Fiction of Anthropology." *Current Anthropology*. 8: 251–281.

Striffler, Steve and Mark Moberg, eds. 2003. *Banana Wars: Power, Production and History in the Americas*. Durham, NC: Duke University Press.

Sutton, Mark Q. and E.N. Anderson. 2004. *Introduction to Cultural Ecology*. Lanham, MD: Altamira.

Sweet, Matthew. 2001. *Inventing the Victorians*. New York: St. Martin's Press.

Tiger, Lionel. 2006. "Clifford Geertz Obituary: Fuzz, Fuzz, It was Covered in Fuzz." *Wall Street Journal*. November 7. A12.

Turner, Victor. 1967. *The Forest of Symbols: Aspects of Ndembu Ritual*. Ithaca, NY: Cornell University Press.

Turner, Victor. 1975. *Revelation and Divination in Ndembu Ritual*. Ithaca, NY: Cornell University Press.

Turner, Victor. 1985. "The Anthropology of Performance" in Edith Turner, ed. *On the Edge of the Bush: Anthropology as Experience*. Tucson, AZ: University of Arizona Press.

Tyler, Stephen A. 1984. "The Poetic Turn in Postmodern Anthropology: The Poetry of Paul Friedrich." *American Anthropologist*. 86 (2): 328–336.

Tyler, Stephen A. 1986. "Post-Modern Ethnography: From Documentary of the Occult to Occult Document" in James Clifford and George E. Marcus, eds. *Writing Culture: The Politics and Poetics of Ethnography*. Berkeley: University of California Press.

Tylor, Sir Edward Burnett. 1865. *Researches into the Early History of Mankind and the Development of Civilization*. London: John Murray.

Tylor, Sir Edward Burnett. 1871. *Primitive Culture: Researches into the Development of Mythology, Philosophy, Religion, Art and Custom*. London: John Murray.

Voltaire. 1918 (orig. 1759). *Candide*. New York: The Modern Library.

Vorhees, Josh. 2011. "Study Shows Fox News Viewers Less Informed on Major Stories." Slate. com. November 21. http://slatest.slate.com/posts/2011/11/21/fairleigh_dickinson_publicmind_poll_shows_fox_news_viewers_less_informed_on_major_news_stories. html (accessed February 16, 2012).

Wallace, Anthony F.C. 1952. *The Modal Personality of the Tuscarora Indians as Revealed by the Rorschach Test*. Washington, DC: Bureau of American Ethnology.

Wallace, Anthony F.C. 2003. *Revitalizations and Mazeways: Essays on Culture Change*. Lincoln, NE: University of Nebraska Press.

Weber, Max. 1970. *From Max Weber: Essays in Sociology*. Ed. H.H. Gerth and C. Wright Mills. New York: Oxford.

Weber, Max. 2005 (orig. 1930). *The Protestant Ethic and the Spirit of Capitalism*. Trans. T. Parsons. New York: Routledge.

Weiner, Annette B. 1976. *Women of Value, Men of Renown: New Perspectives on Trobriand Exchange*. Austin, TX: University of Texas Press.

White, Benjamin. 1973. "Demand for Labor and Population Growth in Colonial Java." *Human Ecology*. 1: 217–236.

White, Benjamin. 1975. "The Economic Importance of Children in Colonial Java" in Moni Nag, ed. *Population and Social Organization*. The Hague: Mouton.

White, Leslie. 1930. "An Anthropological Appraisal of the Russian Revolution." Paper delivered at the annual meeting of the American Association for the Advancement of Science. Cleveland, Ohio.

White, Leslie. 1947. "Evolutionism in Cultural Anthropology: A Rejoinder." *American Anthropologist*. 49: 400–411.

White, Leslie. 1949. *The Science of Culture: A Study of Man and Civilization*. New York: Grove Press.

White, Leslie. 1966. *The Social Organization of Ethnological Theory*. Rice University Studies, vol. 52. Houston, TX: Rice University Press.

White, Leslie. 2007 (orig. 1959). *The Evolution of Culture: The Development of Civilization to the Fall of Rome*. Walnut Creek, CA: Left Coast Press.

Whorf, Benjamin Lee. 1956. *Language, Thought and Reality*. Cambridge, MA: MIT Press.

Wissler, Clark. 1938 (orig. 1917). *The American Indian*. New York: Oxford University Press.

Wittfogel, Karl. 1957. *Oriental Despotism*. New Haven, CT: Yale University Press.

Wolf, Eric R. 1959. *Sons of the Shaking Earth*. Chicago, IL: University of Chicago Press.

Wolf, Eric R. 1964. *Anthropology*. Englewood Cliffs, NJ: Prentice-Hall.

Wolf, Eric R. 1972. "Ownership and Political Ecology." *Anthropological Quarterly*. 45(3): 201–205.

Wolf, Eric R. 1982. *Europe and the People Without History*. Berkeley, CA: University of California Press.

Wolf, Eric R. 1999 (orig. 1969). *Peasant Wars of the Twentieth Century*. Norman, OK: University of Oklahoma Press.

Worsley, Peter. 1968. *The Trumpet Shall Sound: A Study of "Cargo" Cults in Melanesia,* 2nd edn. New York: Schocken.

Zenko, D. 2006. "A Field Guide to Monsters of the World." http://monsterguide.blogspot.com/ (accessed October 13, 2010).

INDEX